DARK GENIUS
OF WALL STREET

ALSO BY EDWARD J. RENEHAN, JR.

The Kennedys at War

*The Lion's Pride:
Theodore Roosevelt and
His Family in Peace and War*

The Secret Six

John Burroughs: An American Naturalist

DARK GENIUS
OF WALL STREET

*The Misunderstood
Life of Jay Gould,
King of the Robber Barons*

EDWARD J. RENEHAN, JR.

BASIC
BOOKS

A Member of the Perseus Books Group
New York

Copyright © 2005 by Edward J. Renehan, Jr.

Published by Basic Books,
A Member of the Perseus Books Group

Books published by Basic Books are available at special discounts for bulk purchases in the United States by corporations, institutions, and other organizations. For more information, please contact the Special Markets Department at the Perseus Books Group, 11 Cambridge Center, Cambridge, MA 02142, or special.markets@perseusbooks.com.

Designed by Jeff Williams

Cataloging-in-Publication data for this book is available from the Library of Congress.

ISBN 0-465-06885-5

05 06 07 08 / 10 9 8 7 6 5 4 3 2 1

Dedicated to the memory of
Alf Evers
Catskills historian extraordinaire
1905–2004

CONTENTS

Preface   IX

1   The Mysterious Bearded Gould   I

2   Ancestors   7

3   Twelve Lines by Night   13

4   A Deliberate Student   21

5   Rat Traps and Maps   29

6   Hidden Mysteries of Life and Death   37

7   Gouldsboro   45

8   Our Best Friends Tell Us Our Faults   53

9   Cunning Lunacy   61

10 The Gouldsboro War   69

11 A Particular Future   75

12 Much to Get Done   89

13 The Erie in Chains   95

14   Blue Fire   105

15   The Abused Machinery of the Law   115

16   An Almighty Robbery   127

17   Scoundrels   139

18   The Smartest Man in America   149

19   Where the Woodbine Twineth   163

20   Mephistopheles   179

21   A Special Stinkpot   185

22   A Damned Villain   203

23   Transcontinental   215

24   Consolidation   229

25   Everything but a Good Name   247

26   Wires and Els   259

27   Ambition Satisfied   275

        Epilogue: The Goulds after Jay   297

        Acknowledgments   313

        Notes   315

        Index   335

In mid-December 1892, the banker Jesse Seligman gave an interview to a reporter from the *New York Tribune*. Seligman's friend Jay Gould had been buried a week earlier. He described the dead mogul—whose empire had included the Western Union Telegraph Company, the Missouri Pacific, the Union Pacific, and the Manhattan Elevated Railroad—as "the most misunderstood, most important, and most complex entrepreneur of this century." Seligman said he found it "ironic" that Gould was always cast as the arch demon in any telling of the nation's recent financial history. If Gould was a sinner, asked Seligman, exactly who were the saints?

Seligman ran down the list of contenders, starting with Cornelius Vanderbilt. The foulmouthed and brutal old Commodore never claimed to have any agenda other than his own aggrandizement. Was he really to be revered? (On one famous occasion, when asked to contribute to the poor, Vanderbilt cited his modest beginnings, pointed to a line of people waiting for bread, and said, without a hint of irony, "Let them do what I have done.") Next Seligman called up the memory of Daniel Drew, the pious founder of the Drew Theological Seminary, with whom Gould and Jim Fisk had joined forces to defeat Vanderbilt and gain control of the Erie Railroad. The Bible-thumping Drew had started his career herding cattle across the Alleghenies in the late 1820s and then brought his habits as a drover to Wall Street, watering stocks just as he'd always watered his beef. "Was Mr. Drew really any better than Mr. Gould?" Seligman asked. And what of John D. Rockefeller, the avid, competition-crushing monopolist whose exclusive freight contracts (spurred by Gould's clever involvement of Rockefeller in a secret partnership controlling a lucrative Erie Railroad subsidiary) had played such a key role in the Gould-controlled Erie?[1] "Why," asked Seligman, "is Rockefeller held in so much higher esteem than Gould in the public mind?"

Certainly Gould was shady at times, said Seligman, mentioning in particular that lengthy experiment in stock manipulation dubbed the Erie Wars. Seligman also acknowledged Gould's infamous 1869 campaign to corner the gold market in collaboration with Fisk: an escapade that triggered the Black Friday panic and ruined many investors. The same event cemented Jay's reputation as a financial vampire. This was an image that an energetic press continued to burnish thereafter, once it was realized that the crimes of Jay Gould, whether true or not, sold well on street corners. But Seligman did not see Gould as any more or less a criminal than most operators of his era: "I can't say that Mr. Gould was, in his moral nature, much better, much worse, or much different than any other shrewd and sharp player of his generation," said Seligman. "I've known them all. I've known Jay Gould better than most. And I can tell you he deserves no more notoriety than those against which, and with which, he played. If he was exceptional, it was as a strategist. He had a certain genius. Time and time again, Wall Street never saw him coming."[2]

Ignoring Seligman's plea, three generations of biographers, taking their cues from the nearly uniform bad press Gould received in life, built him into an evil genius of almost Wagnerian proportions: dark, soulless, and unstoppable. In his *History of the Great American Fortunes* (1909), Gustavus Myers copied the tone of the first potboiler bios from the 1890s when he described Gould as "a human carnivore, glutting on the blood of his numberless victims; a gambler destitute of the usual gambler's code of fairness in abiding by the rules; an incarnate fiend of a Machiavelli in his calculations, his schemes and ambushes, his plots and counterplots."[3] Matthew Josephson, a socialist at the time he put together his Depression-era book, *The Robber Barons* (1934), created an entirely damning portrait of Gould as a heartless thief and confidence man. "No human instinct of justice or patriotism or pity caused [Gould] to deceive himself," said Josephson, "or to waver in any perceptible degree from the steadfast pursuit of strategic power and liquid assets."[4] Then, twenty-eight years later, Richard O'Connor did little more than parrot Josephson in his *New York Times* best-seller, *Gould's Millions* (1962). In fact, in all the years since Jay's death in 1892, only two obscure academic biographies for business historians, Julius Grodinsky's *Jay Gould: His Business Career* (1957) and Maury Klein's *The Life and Legend of Jay Gould* (1986), have provided balanced, substantial, and reasonable accounts of Gould's brilliant professional history.[5] Thus, through the years, Gould has been cobbled down in the popular mind to the ultimate one-dimensional villain of American financial life: a talented and highly opportunistic Wall Street leech benefiting from commerce created by others. ("The whole interest of Gould," wrote Robert Riegel in *The Story of the Western Railroads* [1926], "lay in manipulation of the securities of his various companies. The development of the roads was an entirely minor concern. In all cases the property was used to aid his financial transactions."[6])

But the case for Gould as an exemplary, successful, long-term CEO is there to be made. The highly imaginative, ruthless, and easy-to-vilify Gilded Age manipulator of securities markets was also a detail-oriented owner of companies: a workaholic who painstakingly consolidated dying railroads, transformed them into highly profitable megalines, and then did the same in maximizing the profitability of the Western Union, skillfully steering all his concerns through choppy economic seas in the 1880s.

Other aspects of Gould's dark legend collapse just as easily under scrutiny. For example, much has always been made of Gould's will, in which he left not one dime to any charity. But few have noted Gould's significant philanthropies in life: efforts at good works that he transacted anonymously once he realized the press would allow no noble deed of his to go unpunished. Gould's few publicized attempts at good works were all greeted with derision by the *New York Times*, the *New York Herald*, and other papers bent on castigating him. Every one of Gould's philanthropic endeavors of which reporters got wind were portrayed as inadequate, feeble gestures at face-saving that paled beside the weight of the man's presumed grave sins. Thus, after several such experiences, Gould no longer publicized his giving. Nevertheless, he continued to give, usually with the explicit requirement that his name not be brought up in connection with whatever charity was at hand. In turn, the press criticized him for his lack of generosity. "The good deeds of this man must have been more than usually unobtrusive to have so completely escaped notice," commented the *New York World* in October 1891. "It is incredible that his life should have been devoid of them, but neither in number nor in kind have they been sufficient to extort admiration or create imitators."[7]

Then we also have Gould the human being whom one encountered face to face across a table or on a street corner. Here he is as painted by Josephson and company: brusque, intolerant, curt and cruel, dismissive of underlings, blisteringly critical, always self-satisfied, and never loyal to anyone not of his blood. As Robert I. Warshow put it in *Jay Gould: The Story of a Fortune* (1928), Gould's "allies were many, but none his friends; at one time or another in his life he broke almost every man who worked with him."[8] But in fact, Gould's long-term colleagues over the course of decades included Russell Sage, the Ames family of Boston, Sydney Dillon, and numerous others who linked their fortunes with his and were never betrayed. On a personal level, his household domestic servants, including several to whom he awarded college scholarships, remembered him fondly decades after he was dead. As well, the reportedly unapproachable Jay Gould maintained close relationships to the very last year of his life with the majority of the friends he'd made during his impoverished Catskills boyhood, most of them humble farmers and merchants.

Falsely and cruelly caricatured by the press in life, Gould has been sentenced to the same fate in death. Although he was guilty of every crime transacted by his generation of American capitalists, Gould's operations were nevertheless no more sinister than those of the financiers and industrialists against whom he competed: men whose personal reputations have soared above his over the past century. In the end, Gould's chief public relations error seems to have been his over-arching success. His antagonists in business, after having been burned by him, provided grist for the mills of a hungry press when they dubbed him the "Mephistopheles of Wall Street." It was easier, and more nurturing to the pride of the wounded, to suggest a pact with Satan than to admit that Jay was in fact the Michelangelo of Wall Street: a genius who crafted financial devices and strategies, and who leveraged existing laws, in stunningly original ways.

Gould's story is too important to get wrong, for his impact on his country and his era was monumentally large. A recent inflation-adjusted listing of the all-time richest Americans, which compared fortunes as percentages of GNP, placed Gould in eighth place. Although he ranked behind such luminaries as John D. Rockefeller (1), Cornelius Vanderbilt (2), and John Jacob Astor (3), Gould came out ahead of Henry Ford (11), Andrew Mellon (12), Sam Walton (14), J. P. Morgan (23), and Bill Gates (31). His success was profound, his productivity was astonishing, and his motivations and tactics were fascinating.[9]

In essaying a new, full biography of Jay Gould, my aim is to create a true, unbiased picture of Gould as both financier *and man*. With regard to Gould's business life, I intend to serve as neither his prosecutor nor his defense attorney, but to lay out the facts as we have them. With regard to Gould's personal life, my purpose is to fill the vast gap left by previous biographers. In sum, I seek to present, for what will be the first time, an informed, objective, and integrated depiction of Gould in all his complex (and sometimes conflicting) guises: unpredictable Wall Street pirate, level-headed manager of corporations, and dynastic paterfamilias.

EDWARD J. RENEHAN, JR.

DARK GENIUS
OF WALL STREET

Chapter 1

THE MYSTERIOUS BEARDED GOULD

5–6 DECEMBER 1892

OUTSIDE THE TOWNHOUSE at the northeast corner of Forty-seventh Street and Fifth Avenue a stray adventurer did a good business selling freshly printed calling cards with the chiseled name of one of the sons: Edwin Gould. "This will get you in, dead certain," he assured those who forked over their two-dollar notes. Then he vanished with his profits just as his first customers were brusquely shown the door and the balance refused admittance.[1] Old Jay Gould—who lay stiff and cold in the living room of 579 Fifth Avenue—would have applauded both the huckster's boldness and his wile. Jay had always believed that shrewd aptitude should be rewarded and its absence punished. He despised fools.

This fact was well known to the men who jostled through the crowd to present their more genuine credentials: Russell Sage, J. P. Morgan, and William Rockefeller among them. Inside, standing by the casket, Ogden Mills was heard to compliment the "naturalness" of the corpse. A butler told Mills that Jay's body had spent the previous three days propped in a chest full of ice. This accounted for the healthy red flush of his cheeks. Railway tycoon Henry Villard studied the many flowers, including an orchid spray for the coffin arranged to spell out "Grandpa," and commented how Jay would have enjoyed them. Jay's love of flowers, said Villard to no one in particular, was one of the few things that signaled his humanity. As he spoke, Villard pulled a keepsake blossom from an ornate pastiche of blooms sitting near the head of the casket. It was arranged in the form of a ship, fully rigged, inscribed with the words VOYAGE ENDED, SAFE IN PORT.[2]

Voyage ended indeed. The nation's newspapers breathlessly competed to summarize Jay's strenuous circumnavigation of life and business. Editors from Boston to San Francisco vied to see who could come up with the most pejorative turns of phrase, and those in his hometown were scarcely moved to defend him. "He exercised a large influence over the careers of many who had commercial aspirations," wrote Gould's longtime nemesis James Gordon Bennett, Jr., publisher of the *New York Herald*. "That influence tended to lower the moral tone of business transactions. The example he set is a dangerous one to follow. The methods he adopted are to be avoided. His financial success, judged by the means by which it was attained, is not to be envied. His great wealth was purchased at too high a price. He played the game of life for keeps, and he regarded the possible ruin of thousands as a matter in which he had no concern."[3]

Bennett's competitors at the *New York Times* used the occasion of Gould's death to extol Astor and A. T. Stewart, who "in serving their own ends were serving the public ends, while Gould was a negative quantity in the development of the country."[4] Over at the *New York World*—a paper Gould owned briefly before selling it to Joseph Pulitzer—editorialists opined that "ten thousand ruined men will curse the dead man's memory. Convicts . . . will wonder what mental defect robbed them of such a career as Gould's. The public has no great interest in the death of Jay Gould because Jay Gould in his life never showed any interest in the public, . . . This is not a death that will cause any public sorrow."[5]

More than one minister that Sunday insisted that Gould—who had passed on 2 December, a Friday—was already burning to a terrible crispness in the eternal fires of hell. "He was the human incarnation of avarice, a thief in the night stalking his fellow man," declared the rector of St. Paul's Episcopal Church on Madison Avenue.[6] The minister's flock, nearly all of them moneyed aristocrats, had hated Gould as much for his audacious rise from poverty as for his dark cunning in business transactions. They believed that they were all, to a man, better than him, despite his $72 million. "The bane of the social, intellectual and spiritual life of America today is the idolatrous homage to the golden calf," shouted an editorial in the *World*. "Nothing else has contributed so much to promote this evil condition as the worldly success of Jay Gould. We must refuse to practice and disseminate the vices of which he was the most conspicuous model in modern times."[7] To this at least one minister is known to have added that little better could have been expected from someone of Gould's race. It was, they said, an age-old story.

Gould would have been amused. An unenthusiastic Presbyterian by birth and a perfunctory Episcopalian by marriage, the financier had long encouraged an entirely different view of himself. In an age of fashionable anti-Semitism, Jay (Jason) Gould routinely remained quiet when characterized in the press as a self-aggrandizing Jew, a Shylock. Joseph Pulitzer—who long before had sought to shed his own Jewish pedigree—complained that "the mysterious, bearded Gould" was "one of the most sinister figures to have ever flitted batlike across the vision of the American people."[8] At the same time, Henry Adams described his brother Charles Francis Adams's archrival in railroading as a "complex Jew . . . small and slight in person, dark, sallow, reticent, and stealthy."[9] Gould himself sardonically welcomed such descriptions, telling associates that his "presumed Hebraic origin" could only enhance his reputation as a force against which resistance would prove fatal.[10]

◇   ◇   ◇

There is no record of what Gould's only close Jewish friend, Jesse Seligman, had to say about this coldly rational analysis of how common bigotries, however reprehensible, could be used to one's advantage. Seligman was among those who sat about the crepe-bedecked parlor, silently contemplating that most rare of sights: *Jay Gould at rest, Jay Gould without an agenda*. Here Gould lay, still and silent in his black walnut casket, surrounded by the small circle of family and associates who understood him far better than all the scribbling journalists of the world put together.

Nevertheless, the reporters continued to scribble. "Those who assembled . . . never loved the dead man, and the dead man never loved them," a writer for the *New York World* declared, as if he had cause to know. "He had never loved any of his kind, save those of his blood; so it is the cold truth that there was no sorrow by his bier. There was decent respect—nothing more."[11] To those present, however, the grief of the moguls seemed genuine enough. Seligman was seen to cry. Whitelaw Reid—publisher of the *New York Tribune,* the one newspaper that had been conspicuously and consistently friendly to Gould in life—held Jay's eldest daughter, twenty-three-year-old Helen (Nellie to all who knew her well), in a long, weeping embrace for more than thirty minutes. Rockefeller, Sage, and Villard joined loudly in the hymns.

Through much of the afternoon, the twenty-eight-year-old George Gould, who lacked not only his father's slimness but also his rapid mind and personal discipline, knelt and prayed beside the corpse. Whether he prayed for his father's immortal soul or for the wit necessary to run the complex empire to which he now fell heir, no one knew. Most hoped, however, that George was at least smart enough to pray for wit. Sitting near the sobbing Nellie, the other children—Edwin (twenty-five), Howard (twenty-one), Anna (sixteen), and Frank (who'd just turned fifteen two days after his father's death)—all seemed quite taken over by grief. They loved the man who was a sphinx to most others. Money aside, none of them knew where they would go from here.

On the morning of the sixth, at ten precisely—for Gould was always punctual—a somber procession of eight black coaches departed for Woodlawn Cemetery in the Bronx. One hour later the cortege pulled up before a lush, Ionic mausoleum of granite and marble set on a large tract of land overlooking an ornamental lake. Gould had last been to this decorous place of defeat, built at a cost of $125,000, in January 1889. That morning had been similar to this one: stern winds, biting cold, and ice underfoot as pallbearers carried the small, broken body of the first Helen, Jay's wife of twenty-six years, to the sterile emptiness of the new crypt. As all who knew him realized, Jay's grief at that time had been profound. In fact, it had been total. "The ordeal has changed him very much," wrote a reporter for the *World.* "It has added to the slight stoop in his shoulders and increased the careworn look in his face. Mr. Gould himself is not a well man. . . . His wife's death is a great blow to him."[12] Now, nearly four years later, Jay returned to his Helen, whom he'd always called Ellie, never again to leave her.

Once within the immense edifice of the tomb, Chancellor Henry Mitchell MacCracken of the University of the City of New York (destined to be renamed New York University four years later) read a commitment prayer while behind him two workmen prepared for a grim task. Wearing thick insulated gloves, the workers held small pails of smoldering lead. Upon MacCracken's signal they moved forward and, spoonful by spoonful, applied the liquid to the cracks on all sides of Gould's coffin before screwing down the lid. "There was something indescribably awful about that act," Gould's niece Alice Northrop remembered many years later. "And it was so slow! So unmercifully slow!"[13] Then, at last, the men laid the coffin of Jay Gould in place beside that of his wife and set the marble cover on the crypt.

Gould's ornate tomb represented something more than just a Gilded Age grasp at pharaohlike immortality. It also represented the final iteration—and logical end—for the luxurious garrison lifestyle to which Gould had become accustomed over the long years. The *Times's* coverage of his interment did not fail to note the presence, on the outskirts of the cemetery, of a number of "unwashed, long-haired" men wearing red neckerchiefs.[14] These malcontents (anarchists) muttered and cursed and seemed to send forth the promise of violence. Still, as they had always done before, they remained at bay, furtively eyeing the burly Pinkerton detectives who arrived with the Gould party and remained on guard once the family departed. The Pinkertons—a presence at the ummarked Woodlawn tomb for the next decade—and the sealing of the coffin were precautions not just against malcontents but also against grave robbers like those who had stolen and ransomed the body of A. T. Stewart some years before. But of course, a few jaded types down in New York's financial district offered a different interpretation. Writing in the *Herald,* Bennett speculated that the guards and the sealed casket were meant to keep Gould from finding his way out and returning to raid Wall Street one last time.

◇   ◇   ◇

There was considerably less cynicism in the Catskill Mountains town of Roxbury, some 130 miles northwest of Woodlawn. Here, upon receiving word of Gould's passing, a ragtag collection of rustics gathered at a small church on a hillside to hymn-sing and say prayers. Many of those assembled were of the More family—kin to Gould's mother, who had died when Jay was just four years old. Others were old associates who had long ago engaged in friendly wrestling competitions with the boy Gould and who later, in 1856, had congratulated the ambitious twenty-year-old on the appearance of his self-published *History of Delaware County and the Border Wars of New York*.

None of these fine Christian people amounted to anything. They were little folks leading unimportant lives. They had not seen much of Jay after he finally, as a young man, decided to seek his fortune beyond the limits of their isolated province. (Unlike most other self-made men, Gould never traded on his humble background. "The fact of my father's poverty," he once told a persistent reporter, "is not worth one dime to me.")[15] Only in his last years did Gould—hungry to recapture something of his youth—return to Roxbury for any length of time. He'd been back for short visits during the summers of 1887 and 1888. Though he did not say so, at the time of the latter trip he was already suffering from the tuberculosis that would kill him. Accompanied by several of his children and a niece during the 1888 excursion, Gould roamed Roxbury's unpaved streets, dropped in on old friends, and strolled the grounds of the local cemetery. He also fished for trout at Furlow Lake in nearby Arkville. Recent gossip had it that George Jay Gould—the much-talked-about eldest son and heir—was buying land and planned to build a house on Furlow's shores. Now, at the memorial service, Jay's friends and cousins shook their heads and said it was a pity what had happened. They'd looked forward to having their bright boy home again.

Still, not all of Gould's old Catskills associates felt nostalgic. "Jay Gould will be dead a week tomorrow . . . , " diarized Julia Ingersoll, daughter of Gould's first great benefactor in business, Zadock Pratt. "He leaves 72 millions, he still owes my father a few thousands. Will he be sorry now that he owed anything in this world to anyone? Why did my darling Father say once, when someone called Gould such fearful names, 'hush! do not say it loud.' Because he suffered ingratitude at the man's hands uncomplainingly, is that the reason why I feel strangely as if I could never speak unkindly of him? What has he put in the upper treasury to draw on, where he has gone?"[16]

Chapter 2

ANCESTORS

D OWN WEST SETTLEMENT ROAD about two miles out from the small village of Roxbury, New York—a rural Catskills hamlet more anciently known as Beaverdam and later West Settlement—one comes upon a rough slice of rocky land upon which stands a substantial frame house. The house rests beneath a ridge and looks out over a long, thin valley. Given over to dairying for more than two hundred years, this place, unmarked and anonymous, provided the stage for the early childhood of Jay Gould, who was born here on 27 May 1836. In 1880, a reporter for the *New York Sun* charged with investigating Gould's roots described these 150 acres as running "far up a hill back of the house and far down a hill in front . . . on the other side of the highway. The nearest neighbor is a quarter of a mile away. Stone fences run hither and thither, losing themselves in clumps of beech and maple trees. There is an apple orchard, and down at the bottom of the hill the Creek, as it is called, winds its way through the thick dingle."[1]

By the time of Jay's birth, the Gould family had been on this piece of ground for two generations, but the line of Goulds in North America went back much further. Jay's great-grandfather, Abraham Gold (born in 1732 in Fairfield, Connecticut, a coastal town on Long Island Sound), served as a lieutenant colonel in the Fifth Regiment of the Fairfield County Militia and died a hero at the Battle of Ridgefield on 27 April 1777.[2] This Abraham was in turn the great-grandson of the progenitor of the Gold/Gould line in the United States, one Major Nathan Gold.[3] A Puritan and a dynamic, voracious entrepreneur, Nathan emigrated from St. Edmundsbury, England, in 1647. He subsequently amassed enough wealth to be described in contemporary records of the 1670s as Fairfield's richest resident. During 1674, Gold joined eighteen other colonists in petitioning King Charles II to grant Connecticut its charter. Gold's fortune, based in land and merchant ships, gave him the leisure to pursue public service as a major in the county militia, a magistrate, and a judge in the colony's General Court.[4]

His only son, Nathan Gold, Jr.—born in 1663—continued the tradition of public service when he spent twenty-two years as Fairfield's town clerk. Nathan also put in two terms as chief justice of Connecticut's highest court and subsequently took on the job of lieutenant governor, the office he held at the time of his death in 1723.[5] Married first to Hannah Talcott, one of Fairfield's many Talcotts, Nathan, Jr., later wed Sarah Burr, one of the town's equally ubiquitous Burrs. (Sarah was an aunt of Aaron Burr, Sr., who would go on to found Princeton University and sire the Aaron Burr destined for infamy.) Throughout his days, Nathan, Jr., remained a steadfast Puritan of the Congregational/Presbyterian stripe, expressing always a fierce intolerance of Episcopalians. At one point Lieutenant Governor Gold asked the General Court to pass a law to restrict the Episcopal clergyman of Stratford to that community and thus keep him out of Fairfield. Nathan, Jr., had several children by his first wife, Hannah, one of whom—Samuel—was born on 27 December 1692, in Fairfield.[6] An affluent local businessman, Samuel married Esther Bradley on 7 December 1716.[7] The couple had six children, the youngest of whom was Abraham, Jay Gould's great-grandfather, the man destined to die in the Battle of Ridgefield.[8]

Abraham married another of the Fairfield Burrs, Elizabeth, daughter of John Burr, in 1754.[9] When Abraham died fighting the British in 1777, he left Elizabeth a widow with nine children. Two years later, Elizabeth and her family wound up homeless after the British systematically torched the town of Fairfield. Undaunted, Elizabeth rebuilt and went on to raise her brood, which consisted of four girls (Abigail, Elizabeth, Deborah, and Anna) and five boys (Hezekiah, John Burr, Abraham, Jr., Jason, and Daniel).[10] It was the children of Abraham and Elizabeth who began spelling the family name *Gould* instead of *Gold*. According to Anna's descendants, the reason for the change was simplification. Although written *Gold*, the name had always been pronounced *Gould*.

Three of the sons—Hezekiah, John Burr, and Daniel—took up maritime careers and died at sea.[11] As for Jason, he married and spent his life as a man of affairs in Fairfield.[12] But it was Jay Gould's grandfather—Abraham Gould, Jr.—who took the most original and unprecedented path. He was twenty-two when he married Anna Osborne in 1788. Shortly thereafter, when Abraham told his bride he had thoughts of going to sea, she perhaps thought for a moment about his dead brothers and then suggested another plan: a career in farming and a move to a newly opened region in New York's Catskill Mountains.[13] Thus Abraham and Anna joined in migration with a small group of Connecticut families, among them the family of Abraham's cousin Talcott Gold.

According to W. H. Munsell's *History of Delaware County, 1757–1880*, a party of "land lookers" consisting of some twenty families came into Delaware County from Fairfield in 1789. The group ferried across the Hudson River from Oakhill Landing, below the town of Hudson, to the village of Catskill, in Greene County. Then they traveled over rough trails and unbridged streams, with just a blaze upon a tree here and there to guide them. The pilgrims arrived at the town of Stamford early in the spring, making camp some distance below the mouth of Rose's Brook—a tributary to the East Branch of the Delaware—from which point a few of their horses wandered off into the woods. Abraham Gould and two others—George Squires and Josiah Patchin—went after the beasts. The trio wound their way up Rose's Brook, where they discovered that their horses had been taken in hand by Israel Inman, a hunter and one of the earliest settlers in the area. Inman led Gould and his compatriots to his rude house in a nearby valley "and with all the well known hospitality of a pioneer, treated them to a repast of venison steak." Later on, when Inman learned the men's intentions, he helped them choose a nearby location for settlement.[14]

"They examined the lands in the valley of Fall Brook," young Jay Gould wrote in his *History of Delaware County and the Border Wars of New York*. "Having decided upon making a permanent location there, they returned again to the party with the missing horses. They could prevail on but two other persons of the party to join them, Nehemiah Hayes and David

Squires, making in all five persons."[15] Thus five families took up leases—
pledging rents to a lordly patroon, heir to the Hardenbergh Patent—in what
became West Settlement and would later be called Roxbury. The balance of
the Connecticut party made homes in adjacent hamlets, most in the areas of
Hobart and Stamford, all of them tenants of the Hardenbergh proprietors.[16]

A hundred years later, visiting the scenes of his childhood, Jay Gould
would wonder out loud what possessed his forebears to settle such "barren
and unpromising" terrain.[17] The prominent literary naturalist John Burroughs—who grew up side by side with Jay Gould—would eventually ro-
manticize this landscape. In an essay of the 1870s, Burroughs described how
the East Branch of the Delaware drained "a high pastoral country lifted into
long, round-backed hills and rugged, wooded ranges by the subsiding im-
pulse of the Catskill range." But the terrain Burroughs hailed as "ideal for
pasture" was in fact no good for anything else.[18] A thin layer of red clay top-
soil covered an uncompromising foundation of Devonian rock and shale.
The slopes of the mountains were taken over by substantial stands of oak,
maple, hickory, cherry, pine, beech, elm, spruce, and chestnut, together with
vast clusters of hemlock. Unbreakable by the plow, the few open fields were
largely useless for growing anything but grass. For this reason "Captain
Abraham Gould"—as grandson Jay called him in his *History*—and his
neighbors embarked upon careers in dairying, producing milk for their own
consumption and cheese and butter for shipment to Albany and Manhattan.

The life here was tough, bearing no resemblance to the relatively affluent
Fairfield society in which Abraham had been raised. Patiently and steadfastly over the years, Abraham labored hard to build his herd (which never
numbered more than about twenty cows) and master his 150 acres. Prosperity proved elusive; poverty seemed always just a bad season away. Abraham
and Anna welcomed a son, John Burr Gould (the first white male child born
at West Settlement, and the future father of Jay Gould) on 16 October 1792.
A daughter, Elizabeth, had been born two years earlier. Eight more children
followed.[19] When Captain Abraham died in 1823, John inherited the lease
on the unproductive homestead, which he seems for the moment to have
viewed as an opportunity rather than a trap. It was in this hopeful mood that
he began to shop for a wife.[20]

◇   ◇   ◇

The More family of Moresville (now Grand Gorge, just over the mountain from Roxbury) was the closest thing to an aristocracy the Catskills wilderness had to offer. A native of Strathspey, Scotland, John More had emigrated with his wife, Betty Taylor More, and two small children in 1772. Soon after his arrival in New York, More built a house at Hobart, thus becoming the first white man to settle Delaware County. He later moved near the town of Catskill on the Hudson and eventually built his last cabin in 1786 at what became "the Square" in the town of Moresville. Having located himself at the junction of several well-traveled trails, More opened a tavern-inn and became moderately wealthy. While fathering six more children, he also, over time, took on employment as a millwright, magistrate, postmaster, and Presbyterian lay leader. By the 1820s, Moresville had transformed from a lonely outpost to a prosperous and busy village. Betty died in 1823 at the age of eighty-five. The hearty John lived on until 1840. When he died, at age ninety-five, he left no fewer than eighty-eight grandchildren and numerous great-grandchildren to mourn him.

Although most of More's descendants settled outside of Moresville in West Settlement, one son, Alexander Taylor More, remained in town. He and his wife, Nancy Harley, produced fourteen offspring. Their second eldest, Mary, came into the world on 20 June 1798.[21] And it was Mary, in the mid-1820s, who caught John Burr Gould's eye. We know little about her save that she was supposedly comely and nurtured a deep piety that complemented John Gould's ancestral Puritanism. Their courtship was very likely Testament-based; hence it was also slow. When they wed in 1827, he was thirty-five, she twenty-nine. Mary moved her loom into one of the five large bedrooms in John's house and also brought a few stray pieces of furniture—tokens and keepsakes of the home in which she'd been raised—which she installed in the large sitting room to the left of the entrance hall, this room being dominated by a huge fireplace. During her first spring at the Gould homestead, Mary spent days upon days digging gardens around the house, eventually surrounding the place with immense beds of roses and hyacinths.

John Gould needed several stout sons to help him run the barely profitable farm. There was not only the herd and the cheese and butter making to tend to, but also—in season—the picking of apples from a small orchard, the running of a cider press, and the tapping of sugar maples. A few sturdy lads would come in very handy. Nevertheless, Mary presented him with five girls in a row: Sarah (1828), Anna (1829), Nancy (1831), Mary (1832), and Elizabeth (1834). Not until 1836 was the couple blessed with a male child, and then just barely: a tiny premature infant. Jason "Jay" Gould was to stay small compared to his peers physically, if not in other ways, for every one of his few fifty-six years.

Chapter 3

TWELVE LINES BY NIGHT

J AY GOULD'S FATHER was a complicated and tragic figure. John Burr Gould's tribal memory, passed on by his parents, told him that he came from substantial people: all those prosperous Golds, Burrs, and Talcotts who for generations had loomed so large in Connecticut history. Yet John's own precarious position in life, like that of his father, fell considerably short of the heights scaled by his formidable ancestors.

Granted, by the standards of his own humble neighborhood, John Gould was a success. In other words, he was a bit less badly off than most. In addition to his herd, pastures, sugar maples, and orchard, he also owned the only cider press in town. Nevertheless, his lot in life was not substantial and he knew it. Having been educated more than thoroughly by his well-lettered parents, John Gould was versed enough in the world to fully comprehend his poverty. Early on he developed a bitterness that manifested itself as snobbery. Part of the problem was that Gould had few people among his rural neighbors on whom to exercise his considerable intelligence. In any event, Gould seems to have been the classic provincial intellectual, convinced he was worthy of better things than his confined corner of the country could offer and always looking out at the larger world with envious scorn. John Burroughs would recall "Mr. Gould" as a rather "stiff necked" fellow who sought to live "in a little better style than the other farmers."[1]

Still, despite John Burr Gould's pretensions, the Goulds—like most everyone else in Roxbury—led a modest existence. Mary made all the family's clothes. The lion's share of their food came right off the homestead; the furniture was handmade.[2] One of the few store-bought items in the house was an imported—but nevertheless inexpensive—tea set, for which Mary had her husband build an elaborate cupboard with glass doors. There the set remained for years, permanently on display but rarely used lest its precious pieces suffer a chip or crack. Jay Gould's sister Anna would remember the tea set—quite a rare sight in that rural district at that time—serving as wordless validation of the family's position, marking them as people of a certain quality despite other appearances to the contrary.

Virtually everything we know about the Gould household during the first years of Jay's life comes from reminiscences penned by Gould's surviving sisters not long after Jay went to his tomb, these written at the request of his eldest daughter. "When your father came into our home," Anna wrote, "there were five of us little girls, and when one morning our grandmother told us we had a little brother and we saw him with our own eyes, our joy knew no bounds. It was but a little time before we could hold him and make him smile, and reach out his tiny hands to come to us."[3] Jay's eldest sister, Sarah, remembered him in his earliest years as the "pet and idol of the household," pampered and admired by all the girls, part brother and part baby doll.

The recollections of Jay's sisters also give us the few glimpses we have of Jay's mother, Mary, who died in January 1841, when Jay was just a few months short of five. "The only memory he had of her," wrote Sarah, "as he told me during the latter years of his life, was the messenger summoning us from school in order that she might give us her dying blessing. He said he had never forgotten how cold her lips were when she gave him her last kiss of love." Sarah—who, as we shall see, had reasons to prefer the memory of her mother over that of her father—believed that Jay inherited from Mary all "his ambition [and] that evenness of temper which enabled him to control himself even when a boy, and still more when he became a man. He also inherited from her his ability to turn everything to his financial profit."[4]

John buried Mary in the Old School Baptist Church Cemetery between Roxbury and Kelly Corner near Stratton Falls, close by the neighborhood's "Yellow Meeting House," where Mary had always worshipped. (Here, thirty-nine years later, Jay Gould would erect an obelisk commemorating his parents and two of his sisters.) Anna Gould, eleven years old when her mother died, remembered snow on the ground as John Gould and several other men carried Mary to her grave. She also recalled the sound of dirt thumping down on the handcrafted casket, and the solemn hymns sung in the windy desolation of the graveyard. Little Jay walked beside her, holding her hand, curious but seeming not to comprehend much of what went on.[5]

In the next few years, death would be a frequent visitor to the Goulds. Needing a mother for his large family, John Gould married again that summer of 1841 only to see his new wife, a woman named Eliza, die on 19 December.[6] John laid Eliza beside Mary in the cemetery of the Yellow Meeting House. Five months later the fifty-year-old Gould—a study in perseverance—was married once more, this time to Mary Ann Corbin, a neighbor more than a decade his junior. After this happy event, the family seemed poised for a period of stability; but fate had other plans. Late in 1842, eleven-year-old Nancy succumbed to a sudden illness. Writing decades after, Sarah Gould described yet another snowy visit to the cemetery, her stepmother Mary Ann large with child as she trudged up the hill. On 3 March 1843, Mary Ann presented John with a son, Abraham, to be called variously Abram and Abie by his sisters and brother. Joy reigned again, for a time. But two years later Mary Ann was dead. Perhaps thinking himself cursed, John did not take any more wives. Instead he left the care of his two boys, now aged nine and two, to his four surviving daughters.

◇　◇　◇

As an old woman, Sarah Gould would observe that Jay had seen a great deal of "trouble" before he reached the age of ten.[7] This trouble, Sarah made clear, was not limited to family deaths but extended to other episodes as well, including at least one dramatic, character-defining experience caused by John Gould's strict adherence to unorthodox and stoutly independent political beliefs.

Unlike the majority of his neighbors, Gould, a Democrat in politics, refused to take part in the general insurrection that dominated the Catskills and the adjacent Hudson River Valley in the 1840s. At the time, the farmers of the region were in arms against the proprietors of various land grantees, among them the holders of the immense Hardenbergh land grant—just under 2 million acres in Ulster, Orange, Green, Sullivan, and Delaware Counties—given in 1708 by Queen Anne to Johannes Hardenbergh and his associates. ("The vast compass of the Hardenbergh patent," wrote the future monopolist Jay Gould in his *History of Delaware County and the Border Wars of New York*, "when its limits had been surveyed and located—a grant of something less than two millions of acres to a single individual—was a species of monopoly, which, even the British government, with her aristocratic notions, failed to relish, and an order was [later] issued preventing grants of more than a thousand acres to single individuals, or when associated together, of a number of thousand equal to the number of associates."[8]) In the midst of this antirent excitement, armed bands of "down-renters," wearing calico outfits and painted up as "Indians," intimidated rent collectors with tarring and feathering while using the same tactic to pressure fellow tenants to join their rebellion. The local Roxbury antirent Indians usually summoned each other using traditional dinner horns. At one point they even passed legislation prohibiting the blowing of such horns for their customary purpose, lest some farmer's announcement of supper be confused with a warning of rent collectors on the horizon. As Jay would write:

> During the summer of this year [1844] parties were frequently seen in disguise, and several peaceable citizens who had chanced to think differently from themselves, belonging to what was termed the up-rent, or law and order party, had been molested and severely threatened. . . . The first open act of hostility was perpetrated on the sixth of July, upon the premises of Mr. John B. Gould, who, regardless of the threats and the timely warning of the association to desist from blowing his horn, had continued to use it as a signal. . . . Upon the day in question, he had as usual blown his horn at noon, when five Indians, equipped and armed for fight, presented themselves at his door, and demanded redress for the insult he had given to the authority of the association. A spirited and angry discussion ensued, when they were compelled to retreat from the premises. . . .

The following Tuesday, another company of Indians set out for the Gould homestead with instructions to seize the horn, and if necessary mete out to Mr. Gould a salutary coat of tar and feathers. The sun had just arrived at the meridian, when a favorable opportunity presenting itself, the signal whoop was given, and the savage horde sprung from their hiding places, and with demon-like yells rushed up and surrounded Mr. Gould, who was standing with his little son in the open air in front of the house. We were that son, and how bright a picture is still retained upon the memory, of the frightful appearance they presented as they surrounded that parent with fifteen guns poised within a few feet of his head, while the chief stood over him with fierce gesticulations, and sword drawn. Oh, the agony of my youthful mind, as I expected every moment to behold him prostrated a lifeless corpse upon the ground. . . . But he stood his ground firmly; he never yielded an inch.

John Gould yelled for his hired man to bring muskets from the house. "Conscious of right, he shrank from no sense of fear—and finally, when a few neighbors had gathered together, a second time [the Calico Indians] were driven from the premises without the accomplishment of their object."[9] The down-renters never again visited the Gould homestead. In 1845 John Gould rode with the local militia to restore order after the governor of New York declared Delaware County to be in a state of insurrection.

The tension of the rent wars entered nearly every phase of life. At one point during the troubles, a larger boy, the son of a down-renter, threatened Jay with drowning at "Stone Jug," the little schoolhouse by Meeker's Hollow. Thereafter, John Gould announced that none of his children would ever again attend the school. He and two of his up-renter brothers-in-law, Philtus and Timothy Corbin, built a schoolhouse of their own on lands between their adjacent farms. They named the place Beechwood Seminary.

John Burroughs and Jay Gould—each destined for his own kind of notoriety—attended school together for ten years, first at Stone Jug and later at Beechwood Seminary. More than four decades after the fact, Jay's sister Elizabeth (known as Bettie) would tell her daughter, "There was always a bond of sympathy between your uncle and [John Burroughs]."[10] Writing when he was well into his eighties, Burroughs recalled of his old friend, "You might have seen in Jay Gould's Jewish look, bright scholarship, and pride of manners some promise of an unusual career."[11] The two trouted together in Rose's Brook, Furlow Lake, and Meeker's Hollow, and Burroughs frequently slept overnight at the Gould family home.[12] As regards the most popular schoolyard sport, wrestling, Burroughs recalled that in a match the small and seemingly unathletic Jay was surprisingly "plucky and hard to beat. . . . He seemed made of steel and rubber."[13]

Like other boyhood friends, Gould and Burroughs helped each other out of jams when they could. A particularly telling instance occurred one day in 1848, when Gould was twelve and Burroughs eleven. Burroughs, having forgotten an essay assignment until the last minute, copied something from an almanac and tried to pass it off as original. Detecting Burroughs's subterfuge, the teacher stiffly informed him that he must, as punishment, either hand in twelve lines of verse before the end of the day or stay after class. Shortly, with the teacher not looking, Jay scrawled some doggerel on his slate and, nudging John, passed it under the desk for him to copy. Burroughs promptly (and shamelessly) did so, in this way avoiding detention.

Jay's verse survives:

> *Time is flying past,*
> *Night is coming fast,*
> *I, minus two, as you all know,*
> *But what is more*
> *I must hand o'er*
> *Twelve lines by night*
> *Or stay and write.*
> *Just eight I've got,*
> *But you know that's not*
> *Enough lacking four;*
> *But to have twelve*
> *It wants no more.*

In supplying Burroughs's need, Jay demonstrated the stark yet elegant economy that would characterize so many of his later solutions to problems.

His efficient collection of words was designed to accomplish a specific job in the most direct manner possible. Jay completed John's assignment to the letter of what was required, supplying twelve very short lines: just the amount to meet their teacher's demand, but not one syllable beyond what was necessary.

Chapter 4

A DELIBERATE STUDENT

J AY GOULD WAS a fastidious and serious child, seemingly delicate until challenged, and possessed of a somber maturity that belied his youth. He was remarkably focused. "I knew him once to work at times for three weeks on a difficult problem in logarithms," Sarah recalled. "He would never accept assistance in working out hard problems."[1]

No small part of Jay's tenacity derived from the early realization that he hated farming. It usually fell to him, as the elder of only two sons, to perform many of the toughest chores about the Gould homestead. Daily he brought the cows in for milking and then drove them back to pasture. Routinely he worked at the butter churn, did the heavier tasks associated with the making of cheese, and in varying seasons pressed apples and collected and boiled sap into maple syrup. His father relied on him as well to ride the horse pulling the hay rake while the father did the cutting. It all added up to a round of simpleminded drudgery that Jay described to a friend as "torture."[2] Often when his father came hunting him to do some work about the place, Jay would hide himself in some secluded corner to pursue his sums and vocabulary and Latin. "It is too bad," he told Sarah, "but I must study, you know."[3]

During the spring of 1849, after deciding that he'd learned everything Beechwood could teach him, thirteen-year-old Jay petitioned his father to send him to the private academy run by a Mr. Hanford at Hobart, a full nine miles from the Gould farm and its labors. Initially refusing this request, John Gould eventually changed his mind when it became clear Jay was not to be denied. "All right," the father said after several weeks of constant badgering and argument, "I do not know but you might as well go, for it is certain you will never make a farmer."[4] At Hobart, Jay boarded with a blacksmith, for whom he kept the books, attending the academy by day. This continued for just five months, however, with Jay making the long walk home each weekend to visit with his sisters and brother and check that all was well. He moved back home the following autumn, the Beechwood having taken on an energetic new teacher just recently graduated from the state normal school at Albany.

John Burroughs would recall that it was under James Oliver (whom he described as "a superior man") that he and several other Roxbury boys got their "real start."[5] Gould, in turn, would write admiringly of Oliver's high-mindedness and "elevated character."[6] In 1893, as an old retiree, the gentleman whose prominent former students still called him "Mr. Oliver" recalled the fourteen-year-old Jay as a "deliberate" student. "He was not a boy given to play much. He was never rude and boisterous, shouting, jumping and all that sort of thing." But neither was he, as some biographers had already begun to suggest, a snitch or a brownnose. "His mental and moral fibre were such that it would have been impossible for him to appeal to a teacher against a school-fellow. His self-reliance and self-respect would have revolted against such a proceeding." Like Sarah, Oliver noted Jay's stark independence and penchant for refusing help. "If he was sent to the blackboard to work a sum he would stay there the entire recitation rather than ask for a solution."[7]

On 9 April 1850, Oliver instructed his older students to write a composition on the theme "Honesty Is the Best Policy." Gould did as he was told, creating a document that more than one newspaper editorialist would throw in his face later on.

HONESTY IS THE BEST POLICY

By this proposition we mean that to be honest; to think honest; and to have all our actions honestly performed, is the best way, and most accords with precepts of reason. Honesty is of a self-denying nature; to become honest it requires self-denial; it requires that we should not acquaint ourselves too much with the wicked; that we should not associate with those of vulgar habits; also, that we should obey the warnings of conscience.

If we are about to perform a dishonest act, the warnings of conscience exert their utmost influence to persuade us that it is wrong, and we should not do it, and after we have performed the act this faithful agent upbraids us for it. This voice of conscience is not the voice of thunder, but a voice gentle and impressive; it does not force us to comply with its requests, while at the same time it reasons with us and brings forth arguments in favor of right.

Since no theory of reasoning can be sustained without illustration, it will not be unbecoming for us to cite one of the many instances that have occurred, whose names stand high upon the scroll of fame, and whose names are recorded in the pages of history,—George Washington, the man who never told a lie in all his life. In youth he subdued his idle passions, cherished truth, obeyed the teaching of conscience, and "never told a lie." An anecdote which is much related and which occurred when he was a boy, goes to show his sincerity. Alexander Pope, in his "Essay on Man," says "An honest man is the noblest work of God."

And again, we find numerous passages in the Scripture which have an immediate connection to this, and summing up the whole, we cannot but say, "Honesty is the best policy."

—JASON GOULD[8]

While Jay spent time on such exercises as these, his father was busy confronting harsh realities. The autumn of 1850 found twenty-two-year-old Sarah and sixteen-year-old Bettie employed as schoolteachers. Only twenty-one-year-old Anna and eighteen-year-old Mary (known as Polly) remained to keep house, but each had a sweetheart and looked likely to be leaving the parental hearth before long. (Polly was by now practically engaged to James Oliver.) Jay—the eldest son and heir—had already made clear that he wanted no part of the farm, which exacted so much in labor and delivered so little in return. As for Abram, at seven years he could not contribute much. In the short term, these facts led John Gould to take on a young hired man, Peter Van Amburgh, who proved diligent and reliable. But nearing sixty, and rapidly approaching the point where the homestead on which he'd been born might prove too much for him, the elder Gould soon reached for a far more radical solution.

During July 1851 John Burr Gould signed papers with Roxbury resident Hamilton Burhans wherein he agreed to trade the Gould farm for Burhans's business on the village's Main Street and Burhans's house around the corner on Elm Street (today's Vega Mountain Road). Burhans—whose brother Edward was the most prosperous merchant in town—had recently been a dealer in tin, sheet iron, and stoves. This was a business of which John Gould had no knowledge; nevertheless he hoped to make a go of it with the help of his clever son Jay. "There is no use my trying to make a farmer out of Jay," he told Sarah. "I cannot do it [but] I think, if I make this change, that probably he will be satisfied."[9] In other words, John Gould hoped the headstrong boy who refused to apprentice on the farm would consent to apprentice in the tin business. Gould's agreement called for the actual swap to take place in April 1852. Seven months before this date—in September 1851—Jay, now fifteen, was sent to board with the Burhans family, work in the tin shop, and learn the business.[10]

Jay's days at Beechwood were now finished, but in his spare time he continued to pursue applied mathematics—specifically the sciences of engineering and surveying. At some point in the autumn he borrowed surveying tools from Edward Burhans and began to tutor himself in their use. Evidently not thrilled with the idea of a career in the Roxbury tin business, Jay told Sarah that surveying represented his "ticket out" of town. "Jason does not intend to stay in B[eaverdam], . . ." she wrote a cousin in February. "I don't know where he will go."[11] But Jay did. A Beechwood friend, Abel Crosby, had recently introduced him to a surveyor by the name of Snyder.[12] About to embark upon a mapmaking tour of neighboring Ulster County, Snyder offered Jay twenty dollars a month to assist in the project.

That March, with Snyder's offer in hand, Jay explained his opportunity to his sisters as a prelude to having a hard conversation with his father. "We begged and pleaded with him not to go," Sarah recalled. "We thought he was too young. I never expected to see him again."[13] In the end, though greatly disappointed, John Gould gave his permission for Jay to take the job. Early in April—barely a month before his sixteenth birthday, and in the same week his family made the move from the farm into town—Jay took off for Ulster with a mere five dollars in his pocket.

◇ ◇ ◇

Jay Gould was never one to make a Horatio Alger myth out of his early struggles. Indeed, he recounted them only once, in the 1880s, when summoned to appear before a U.S. Senate committee and there deliver a sworn account of his history. Thus the story of young Jay's first venture into the business world comes straight out of the *Congressional Record*.

Snyder the mapmaker provided Jay with surveying tools and assigned him to work a precisely defined corner of Ulster County. He also handed Jay a small account book. "As you go along," he said, "you will get trusted for your little bills, what you will eat, and so on, and I will come round afterwards and pay the bills." Thus armed, Jay set off—sketching, measuring, and plotting the raw data that would eventually become part of Snyder's master map. He was three days out when, after stopping overnight with a farmer, he started to enter the fee for room and board in his little book. The farmer stopped him: "Why, you don't know this man! He has failed three times. He owes everybody in the country, and you have got money and I know it, and I want the bill paid." Upon hearing this, Jay turned his pockets out and said, "You can see that *I* tell the truth; I have no money." The farmer nodded. "I'll trust *you*," he said, "but I won't trust that man."

According to Jay's testimony, he subsequently went through most of the day without food for fear of creating another scene with his account book. Late that afternoon, alone in the woods, he collapsed in tears. "It seemed to me as though the world had come to an end. I debated . . . whether I should give up and go home, or whether I should go ahead." Gathering himself together and settling on the latter course, he boldly asked for food at the next house he came to and was made welcome by a farmer's wife. When Jay explained that he would enter the money owed in his book, the woman agreed. A few minutes later, however, as Jay hiked down the road with his gear, he heard the farmer calling behind him. Turning around, Jay braced himself for the worst but was relieved to learn that the farmer merely wanted him to come back to the house and make a noon mark (a north-south line run through a window in such a way that the sun strikes the line at noon precisely, thus allowing one to set a clock). After Jay performed the task, the farmer offered him a dollar, out of which Jay had the man deduct "a shilling" for his dinner. "That was the first money I made in business," Jay remembered, "and it opened up a new field to me, so that I went on from that time and completed the surveys and paid my expenses all that summer by making noon-marks at different places."[14]

It was September before Snyder finally admitted to Jay and Peter Brink, another young surveyor working on the Ulster map, that he was yet again bankrupt and could not pay the money due them both. In lieu of their salaries, Gould and Brink took Snyder's rights to the map and then brought in another youthful surveyor by the name of Oliver J. Tillson as a third partner. Unlike his compatriots, Jay did not have much ready cash; so he hired himself out to his partners at a rate of thirty dollars per month plus board, at the same time agreeing to a reduced share of the proceeds from the map. (Brink and Tillson would split 80 percent of the profits between them, leaving the balance of 20 percent for Jay.) Jay Gould "was all business in those days, as he is now," Tillson remembered four decades after the episode. "Why, even at mealtimes he was always talking map. He was a worker, and my father used to say: 'Look at Gould; isn't he a driver?'"[15] Three months later, when the map was done and the partners settled up, Jay walked away with five hundred dollars as his share of the proceeds.

After spending the Christmas holidays of 1852 with the family at their new home in downtown Roxbury, Jay set off for Albany, where he had arranged a small commission to help survey a planned plank road between Albany and Shakersville. At Albany he roomed in a house owned by one of his More uncles and—with a cousin, Iram More—enrolled at the Albany Academy, a college preparatory school. "School commences at 9 in the morning and closes at two in the afternoon," Jay wrote his sisters. "One recess of five minutes. Eat twice a day."[16] When they were not in school, Iram helped Jay do his work for the plank road survey. (In this job Jay taught himself to use a theodolite, a complex instrument for measuring horizontal angles with great accuracy.) The two young cousins took their meals together, studied together, and also worked together for a time as lobbyists knocking on doors at the New York State Capitol. The object of their support was a bill funding a complete survey of the Empire State. The bill—introduced by a representative from Manhattan and destined to fail—called for separate maps documenting each county, these to be assigned by a process of independent bidding. "If this bill passes," Jay wrote James Oliver, "I think I will realize enough to see me through Yale College and that is the extent of my hopes."[17]

Jay sounded serious and sober in all of his letters home. Nevertheless, his sisters frankly worried about his association with cousin Iram, who had recently been dismissed for drunkenness from a school in the Catskills town of Richmondville. Liquor was a subject on which the Gould girls were unusually sensitive. They well remembered their own mother, Mary, calling her father—Alexander Taylor More—to her deathbed, where she begged him to give up liquor. ("Poor old man," Polly Gould wrote, ". . . how quick the tears would roll down [my mother's] face when she saw him coming intoxicated.") Now—confronted with the slow but steady failure of his dairying business, his relegation to the grim tin shop, and the increasingly obvious unreality of all his aristocratic pretensions—John Gould had taken to the bottle as well. "Father has one fault—you know what it is as well as I," Polly commented in a note to James Oliver. Elsewhere she wrote, "Trials and afflictions of the severest kind have made him such a man as he once was not but he has taken a poor way to drown his trouble. I can but hope he will yet reform, although I know a man of his age seldom changes his habits, they seem so fixed that they cannot be altered. . . . I do hope it may be a good lesson for Jason and I believe it will."[18] Polly had nothing to worry about. Not long after she penned her complaints about John Gould, Jay stated to a friend his outright belief that happiness consisted not so much in indulgence as in self-denial.

Although the mature Jay would, out of politeness, sometimes take an occasional glass of claret or champagne, he would much more routinely shun drink just as he did tobacco, games of chance, and the habit of swearing. Whether he considered these things evil or simply unproductive, we cannot know—but one is inclined to think the latter. Unlike his father, who eschewed church entirely, Jay went through the motions of attending services—first to humor his sisters, later to humor his pious wife and daughters. But he would never—unlike his mother, sisters, wife, and daughters—express his faith outright by announcing himself "born again" in Jesus. Passionate feeling for dogma was never Gould's style. He seems to have nurtured only the most elementary religious belief: a nominal and socially acceptable devotion to that abstract thing called the Lord, but nothing more. What mattered was the here and now. "As regards the future world," he told a friend at about this time, "except what the Bible reveals, I am unable to fathom its mysteries; but as to the present, I am determined to use all my best energies to accomplish this life's highest possibilities."[19]

Chapter 5

RAT TRAPS AND MAPS

W**ITH HIS SURVEY WORK** on the plank road accomplished, Jay resigned from the Albany Academy in early March of 1853 and set out to tour four colleges in which he thought himself interested: Yale, Rutgers, Brown, and Harvard. As well, he planned to see the sights in Manhattan—his ticket that far having been purchased by his Grandfather More in exchange for a favor. Accompanied on this leg of the trip by cousin Iram, Jay carried with him an elaborate, beautifully detailed mahogany box in which his and Iram's drunken, senile grandfather had packed what the old man believed to be a most miraculous innovation: a brightly painted mousetrap of his own contrivance. Jay's charge was to take the gadget around and show it to manufacturers then attending the World's Exhibition at New York's Crystal Palace.

The mousetrap led to the first coverage Jay would ever get from the New York papers: an unheroic tale of petty theft. Jay and Iram were walking toward the Palace at Fortieth Street and Fifth Avenue when a man suddenly rushed up to Jay, grabbed the box, and started to run. After a block-long chase, the cousins eventually collared the mugger, whom Jay subsequently described as "a great strong fellow." The thief proved so large and tough, Jay later recalled, that he eventually "regretted" he had caught him and "and tried to let him go, but the fact is one of my fingers caught in a button hole

of his coat and before I could get off there was a crowd around us and a po-
liceman." When the thief protested that the box was actually his and that Jay
and Iram were the ones trying to steal it, the officer brought all three down
to the police station to sort things out. Once inside the precinct house, Jay
loudly challenged the mugger to say what was in the box and thus prove his
ownership, which of course he could not do. Then Jay himself announced
the contents and asked the police to lift the lid. Gould later enjoyed telling
the story of how, upon seeing the absurd thing he had gotten arrested over,
the thief's face "assumed such an expression of disgust that I could not help
laughing at him." (Later on, the wry judge hearing the case had it put in the
court record that the suspect was most certainly the largest rat ever caught
by a mousetrap.) The *New York Herald* devoted half a column to the adventure of the two "plucky visitors" to New York's mean streets—one of the few
times the paper would ever mention Jay Gould favorably.[1] The *Herald* publicity even generated enough interest in the mousetrap so that Jay was able
to negotiate a small licensing deal for Grandfather More.

That business done, Iram More returned to the mountains and Jay continued, over the next two weeks, to visit the four schools in which he would
never enroll. There is no record of his stopping at Fairfield on his way to or
from nearby New Haven. There is no indication of his pausing in that town
to contemplate ancestral sites or to visit his father's first cousin, Captain
John Gould, the son of old Captain Abraham's brother Jason, and the rich
owner of a fleet of schooners plying the China trade. Captain John Gould
had recently replaced Elizabeth Burr Gold's Revolutionary-era house with a
large mansion. But it seems none of this was even known to Jay, as the two
sides of the family had lost touch years before. As well, the fact of his humble background and means may have stopped Jay from presuming to present himself.

Back in Roxbury by early April, Jay found a grim scene. Polly was temporarily under the weather with recurrent fevers and an ominous cough. In
addition, Jay's friend Orrin Rice Bouton—a fellow seven years Jay's senior
known to associates by his middle name, Rice—had recently put his divin-
ity studies at Schenectady's Union College on hold.[2] Rice lay abed in his
parents' Roxbury home fighting a bad case of typhoid that threatened his
life. This same fever also afflicted Mary More Burhans, wife of Edward and
a cousin of Jay's mother.[3] Jay and his sister Bettie braved the threat of infec-

tion to visit and help tend both Rice and Mary. In fact, Jay spent so much time at the Burhans's home that rumors of a romance between he and the Burhans's daughter Maria circulated through town. Then on Sundays, Jay escorted his sister Anna to the Windham church of the young Reverend Asahel Hough, a divine whom Anna would eventually marry. (Years later Anna would remember her brother driving her to Windham in a three-seat wagon pulled by "a nice team of large high-spirited gray horses."[4]) In the evenings, Jay did his father's books, these revealing the ever dismal finances of the senior Gould. Adding to Jay's worries was news from Albany that the Empire State survey bill had died, along with its sponsor.

Despite all this, Jay remained optimistic for himself in the long run. He said as much to Abel Crosby one night while sitting by the fire in the tin shop. After long hours of banter on other subjects, Jay suddenly announced, "Crosby, I'm going to be rich. I've seen enough to realize what can be accomplished by means of riches, and I tell you I'm going to be rich." When Crosby asked by what method Gould proposed to achieve this feat, Jay answered, "I have no immediate plan. I only see the goal. Plans must be formed along the way."[5]

As his dreams of wealth grew, his dream of a college education ironically faded. "I have long indulged that fortune will throw me in the way of a better education," he wrote a cousin, Taylor More, "but as the period seems to be getting farther and farther distant unless I sacrifice a great deal, I am fearful I shall never realize it. I intended as soon as my finances would permit to take a course through college, but as my father requires a share of my time here it seems wrong to do otherwise than remain for the present."[6] Shortly, when it became obvious that a college education would always elude him, he began to disparage the item as unnecessary, and as no substitute for the practical learning accomplished in the trenches of the real world. "I might," he told a friend, "have a stock of Geometries, Chemistries, Algebrays, Philosophies and the whole catalogue of studies that make up the routine of a finished education piled shoulder high on either side—all, I am fearful, could not hinder me from dreamy delusive visits into the world of rat traps and maps."[7]

Jay's immediate plan was to undertake his own survey and map of Albany County. Just as he turned seventeen, he sent out letters to prominent men of that county soliciting their subscriptions and offering to include views of various towns and residences "whose proprietors offer a proper remuneration."[8] He then hired two assistants—Cousin Iram and another young man—whom he instructed in the rudiments of surveying. Over the coming weeks, in between supervising his assistants and doing some of the survey work himself, Jay, operating out of his uncle's Albany home, personally went door to door in every township selling advance orders for the finished map. He also advertised in local newspapers to sell even more.

While all this went on, Jay began to plan a similar endeavor for Delaware County. He mailed out a prospectus to likely underwriters in August, just as fieldwork on the Albany map wrapped up. Once again, he proved himself an indefatigable publicist. After recruiting his Roxbury schoolmate John Champlin to help with the Delaware project, he solicited another contemporary—Simon D. Champion, publisher and editor of the local *Bloomville Mirror*—to help promote the map. A few months earlier, when Champion was seeking to broaden his subscriber base, Jay had sent him five dollars by way of contribution to the cause. "It is small indeed," he admitted, "but I promise to do better in the future. By the way, I think the friends of our paper ought to do something to sustain the enlargement without an increase in price; you may put me down for five dollars annually and during the political campaign. I will send you a list of some of the poorer families to have the *Mirror* sent to."[9] Now Jay looked for his quid pro quo. "In Delaware County," he wrote to Champion, "the Supervisors ought to encourage [the use of maps in schools] by buying maps for each of the School Districts. I want you to give me an editorial to this effect. . . . You must model the editorial over to suit yourself but it must be as strong as it can be made and come direct from you."[10]

Jay's move back to Roxbury in late summer, to more closely supervise the Delaware map, coincided with a fall taken by the drunken John Burr Gould that put him on crutches for several months. "Father grows old fast," Polly wrote, "and I can see that both mind and body are failing."[11] Thus Jay found himself, as a sideline, running the family's unprofitable tin shop. At the same time, other complications rose up one after another and were dealt with, the one constant annoyance being staff. In the end, Iram had to be fired from the Albany and Delaware County map projects over sloppy work and drunkenness. Other surveyors came and went. And Champlin, who wished to become a lawyer, eventually departed to return to school. Just as Champlin left the scene, Jay added to his own considerable workload when he secured part interest in a contract to help build the previously surveyed plank road between Albany and Shakersville.

Albany attorney and politico Hamilton Harris wrote years later about his first meeting with Jay Gould, whom he would represent in numerous court battles and lobbying efforts over the next forty years. Early in August 1853, Harris received a visit in his office from the directors of the Shakersville Road Corporation, these worthies being accompanied by "what appeared to me a small boy, dark eyed and dark haired." Harris thought the lad was one of the directors' sons. The question at hand involved opponents to a particular section of the road who were seeking to gain an injunction enjoining construction. Harris had barely started laying out his vision for an elaborate legal defense when the small boy piped up with a question. Was there anything, Jay asked, to stop the company from going ahead with construction before the enemies of the road obtained their injunction? When Harris answered there was not, the "little fellow" sat down and "commenced to figure at a table." After calculating a bit, Gould looked up and asked Harris if, in the absence of an injunction, he could protect them from prosecution while they proceeded with the road. "I told him yes. I would protect them until an injunction was served."[12]

As he would so many times later in life, Jay now used the letter of the law to his complete and utter advantage. That same day he hired every laborer and rented every dray he could find. The following morning he purchased and hauled vast supplies of lumber using the good credit of the Shakersville Road Corporation as his collateral. Then he put three teams to work on eight-hour shifts, day and night, the work of the night crew being lit by torches. By the morning of the day the road's opponents obtained their injunction, the disputed section of highway stood finished.

◇ ◇ ◇

Gould's work increased through the winter and into the spring of 1854. While the Delaware map project still labored toward publication, the proprietors of the Newburgh and Syracuse Railroad commissioned Jay to survey the line's course through Delaware County. Then Jay's own Delaware

County project led to something else altogether, when the New York State Agricultural Society—a group formed in 1832 to foster, promote, and improve New York's food and agriculture industry—offered him a small commission to write a full-length history of his home county based on primary source documents and interviews with the area's older inhabitants.

These combined projects added up to an enormous burden for someone just turning eighteen. "He worked himself too close," Champion remembered decades later. "The load he was carrying was too heavy for him." Finally, in June, after finishing several weeks of grueling fieldwork for the railroad map, Jay collapsed with typhoid fever in Roxbury, where he lay sick for nearly three weeks. Given the way Polly described his symptoms, one wonders whether Jay didn't suffer a nervous breakdown at the same time. "His mind has been as weak as his body and he seems now more like a child than like *Jay*," Polly wrote to James Oliver. "He has been very nervous, so much so that we have been very careful about doing anything or saying anything that would in the least excite him. It would make him tremble sometimes just having the Doctor come in unexpectedly."[13]

Jay's sickness delayed his sister Sarah's wedding to George W. Northrop, a widower with five children who lived in Lackawack, Ulster County. Originally scheduled for 28 June, the nuptials did not finally occur until two weeks later, 13 July. During his sickness Jay partook only of buttermilk, trout soup, and barley coffee. Years later, relatives recalled the gaunt and pale Jay standing like a stick at Sarah's wedding, an emaciated ghost of himself in a suit two sizes too large. His depleted stamina matched his depleted resources. In order to raise cash he shortly sold his rights in the Delaware map, which still remained his responsibility to finish. "He has sold his Delaware map," wrote Polly at the time, "to Smith, his engraver, so as to clear about one thousand dollars free of all expenses. That we consider better than to trust to selling the map himself. . . . If he has only learned how to spend it aright! It is as much to know how to spend money as how to make it."[14]

The prompt resumption of work after Sarah's wedding—probably too much too fast, albeit with the help of two assistants—exhausted Jay once more. He came down with a major infection of the bowels on 31 July. The excruciating pain was relieved only slightly by large doses of morphine. Anna

and Polly, the only sisters at home now that Sarah lived in Lackawack and
Bettie was away teaching school in Margaretville, tended to him day and
night. While Jay lay abed, Peter Van Amburgh—the hired man from the old
farm—ran the store. For three days it appeared that the already skeletal Jay,
now completely unable to take or retain food, might die. "You know this disease terminates one way or the other, *soon*," Polly wrote Sarah, preparing her
for the worst.[15] But the worst was not to be. Jay's crisis passed, and in ten days'
time he was walking tentatively about the shop, speaking of all the chores he
had before him. "I shall be glad when [the map] is done," Sarah wrote, "so
that the child will have less to think about or I don't know as he ever will get
entirely well."[16] Jay's doctors advised that he should lay down the burden of
his projects temporarily. But as Polly reported to Sarah, "the idea of giving up
all employment seemed to make him worse than ever."[17]

Though still weak, Jay was recovered enough by September to attend the
Delaware County Democratic Convention as a Roxbury delegate. Simon
Champion showed up in the same capacity, and both made the most of their
opportunity to meet some of the region's movers and shakers. Despite Jay's
successful navigation at the convention, his sisters remained fearful about his
health. He had yet to gain back the weight he'd lost. The girls were also concerned about his incessant cough. "If his days on earth are to be short," Polly
wrote Sarah, putting off a trip to Lackawack, "I must spend those few with
him, for than him I have on earth but *one* dearer friend."[18]

Through October and November Jay remained close to home, dealing
with the tin shop and working on his history of the county. Early in December, ignoring pleas from Anna and Polly that he not brave the winter
weather, he left on a business trip meant to last just a few days: an errand to
see to some last details of the Delaware map. Jay rode a horse over the
mountain on a frigid day, stopped at the home of one of his doctors in
Moresville, and there fell ill with pneumonia. Two weeks would pass before
he was well enough to make the journey home; thus Anna traveled to
Moresville, where she nursed Jay in the empty house of old Grandfather
More, who'd passed away the previous March. Even after Jay finally made it
back to Roxbury—just in time for Christmas—he remained confined to
bed. Nevertheless he was cheerful enough to send a hearty note to Simon
Champion:

Roxbury, Dec. 28, 1854
S.B. Champion Esq.

Friend Champ:

How shall I commence a letter to you? Would you believe me were I to say
I was puzzled whether to commence with a broad business letter caption
"Mr," etc., "Dear Sir," etc. or whether to sit down and imagine an actual
mouth to mouth chat proceeding? Well, you see that at the top of my letter
is that cold, formal commencement, but just then the recollection of the
pleasant times we have had together, and the time for which I hope is not
altogether past, put every shadow aside, and I almost imagine myself in the
Mirror office at this moment. It is a long time since I have heard from you,
except by Mr. Peters a week since. But through the weekly invitation of the
Mirror I commenced to write last week, but my hand shook so that I had
to give it up. Now, Champ, you are a man of newspapers and advertise-
ments and proprietor of the *Mirror* office. I want to study up something for
me to do. The doctor stands over my shoulder and criticizes every movement as an alarming symptom. His orders are for the present "Live on
soups made of shadows." To say the word *map* requires a portion of castor
oil, and the thought of transacting any kind of business is equal to jumping
into a mill pond in winter time. But I have dismissed their sympathies and
regulate my own diet. I find health and strength to improve in conse-
quence. I have cutter and harness, and if you will only furnish sleighing I
am at your service. Now, Champ, if you have time to answer this, tell me a
good funny story. I have hardly raised a smile for five weeks.

Yours respectfully,
Jay Gould.[19]

Chapter 6

HIDDEN MYSTERIES OF
LIFE AND DEATH

AFTER HIS PNEUMONIA, Jay spent a full eighteen months in and around Roxbury. By February he was recovered enough to take a part-time job working behind the counter in Edward Burhans's general store, leaving what little work there was at the tin shop to Peter Van Amburgh. In his spare moments he focused on his growing history, a strenuous effort. He was barely on his feet again in March 1855 when he and the rest of the Goulds received yet another blow. Polly died suddenly from consumption (tuberculosis), a disease that, according to what John Burr Gould told his children, had stalked the Gould clan for generations. Polly's tragic end left her betrothed, James Oliver, completely disconsolate. Jay as well felt as though "a dark pall" had been pulled over "everything, even the sunniest day."[1] Nothing, not even the April birth of Sarah's son Howard Gould Northrop, could bring up Jay's spirits.

Given his mood and his weakened state, it is no wonder that Jay now settled down, bided his time, and considered his options. He had some $2,000 in the bank, profits from his various map and contracting projects. But his plans were large and he felt the need for even more capital. Thus his employment with Burhans. Thus, as well, other employments together with the occasional speculation. Whatever he didn't need he sought to turn into cash. John Burroughs, now a young schoolmaster in a distant village, bought two old books: a German grammar and a work on geology. Burroughs paid Gould eighty cents that, as he recalled years later, "Jay was very happy to get."[2]

It was while working at the Burhans store that Jay encountered the Dartmouth-educated John William McLaury, destined to become the last of Gould's great Roxbury friends.[3] About Gould's age, McLaury had recently come to town to take on duties as principal of the new Roxbury Academy, a boarding school financed by Edward Burhans. Not long after his arrival, McLaury stopped at the Burhans store to order textbooks. "I was pleasantly greeted by a handsome young gentleman who kindly offered to assist me in selecting the text books to be used," McLaury remembered. "Taking a pen he began writing at my dictation, occasionally suggesting the books he considered best for particular studies." Jay's remarks and criticisms impressed McLaury. "I soon learned that his knowledge of books was not limited to mathematics and the physical sciences. . . . He was fond of literary and scientific studies and he must have spent much time with books for he had acquired an extensive knowledge of a wide range of subjects." The two got on famously. Shortly, realizing Jay's skill as a surveyor, McLaury offered him a small stipend to teach the subject at the academy.

Gould also became active in the Roxbury Academy's literary club. Though composed mainly of students, the close-knit organization included several professional men of the community. At McLaury's invitation, Jay began to show up for the weekly debates, at which he exhibited "not only extended knowledge but superior powers of reasoning and ability as an orator rarely attained by one so young." McLaury recalled that Jay "had a happy faculty of expressing his ideas in clear and vigorous language that made his arguments very forcible." He remembered Jay becoming especially passionate one night when the conversation of the club turned toward contemplation of the afterlife. There must, Gould insisted, be some "sublime point" to human existence; but that point would become clear only after one advanced "to the next plane, the second level, the higher consciousness otherwise known as Heaven." A few days after that debate, Jay and McLaury "happened to meet at the home of a lady who was in trouble. She was mourning the recent loss of a child. Someone . . . talking to her concerning the condition of infants in the future world . . . had cruelly emphasized the possibility of their being forever lost. She asked our opinion." This caused Jay, in his effort to comfort the woman, to consider out loud a host of creeds and faiths—not all of them Christian or even Judeo-Christian—with which McLaury was surprised to find him familiar. "Subsequently, when together, we enjoyed discussing theological themes."

McLaury's and Gould's consideration of death continued in May when they undertook a starkly macabre bit of research. The two visited a small cabin on the outskirts of town and watched with clinical detachment as a young man of the village, Amos Gray, lay dying. Gray, as McLaury recalled, "was nearly all night long breathing out his soul, his poor old mother wringing her hands in great distress. While deeply sympathizing with her in her sorrow, yet we did not permit ourselves to yield to emotions of sentiment. Possibly we may have arrived at that age when young manhood thinks it unmanly to weep or be sentimental. However that may have been, I remember we viewed the dying process from a physical and psychic standpoint; we longed to fathom what we knew to be impossible—the hidden mysteries of life and death."

Given that Gray suffered from the same sickness that had taken Polly, it seems astonishing that Jay could subject himself to such a scene or would want to. Yet he did. Still, the enlightenment he sought eluded him. Walking away from the house of death, after poor Gray had gone on to whatever awaited him, Jay commented sadly to McLaury that he guessed all their philosophical speculations were valuable only as "intellectual food," thoughts for the brain to chew on, and "not of much importance in the material world."[4]

Given his early losses as a child, his own close brushes with death, and Polly's demise, Jay would always remain acutely aware of the brevity of one's time on earth. "Time is flying fast, " he'd written as a twelve-year-old helping out his classmate John Burroughs. But Gould's whimsical poem was not, perhaps, entirely nonsense. As a niece who knew him well would one day suggest, those four words were "indicative of a feeling that seems to have been always in the mind of Jay Gould from his childhood on, a feeling which apparently, though perhaps unconsciously, spurred and drove him . . . seldom permitting him pleasure in leisure or relaxation. Again and again he came to speak of the shortness of life and the necessity of doing while there was yet time to do."[5]

◇ ◇ ◇

Through the balance of 1855 and into the first months of 1856, Jay continued to teach the art and science of the survey at Roxbury Academy, and to work on his history. While Gould labored away, local gossip, later recycled by more than one biographer, kept alive the rumor of his romantic involvement with Maria Burhans. This legend lingered for so long in Roxbury that some forty years later Hamilton Burhans still felt compelled to debunk it. "As gossip had it, he was to marry her," Burhans wrote in 1896, "but it was never so; Jay Gould was too bashful; he never talked matrimony to anybody at that time; he never conceived any such idea."[6]

Shy, perhaps, but also curious. After Peter Van Amburgh married, Jay asked in a letter that Van Amburgh provide him with "a chapter or two on matrimonial felicity, that strange uneven sea of human existence upon which I never expect to embark myself. So tell us the secrets, Peter, and much joy to my old and true friend; indeed, you have my best wishes for a long and prosperous life and a ripe old age, which your industry and prudence so well deserve, and if you ever get in trouble I will divide my last shirt with you."[7] For the moment, marriage seemed not even a distant possibility. Simon Champion remembered that Jay "was not given to running with girls much or at all when he was with me. . . . I was a single man too then, and we never talked over the question of marriage."[8]

Still, Jay got at least some rhetorical practice in the romantic arts. As his sister Bettie would recall, Edward Burhans "had an Irishman as a sort of man of all work around the store, and this man had a sweetheart somewhere at a distance. He could not write and Jay used to write his love letters for him—whole sheets of foolscap full of the most endearing terms." Bettie remembered that Jay "exhausted the list of adjectives and adverbs to tell her how sweet she was . . . and the man would be so delighted that he would show [the letters] all around before he sent them. He would ask Jay to use lots of such words, and the more superlative they were the more he was pleased."[9]

As for Jay and Maria Burhans, if there was ever anything between them, a business disagreement between Edward Burhans and Jay Gould—this featuring the classic hint of betrayal for which Gould would later become notorious—undoubtedly put an end to it. Early in 1856, heirs to several small local land parcels came to the store seeking Ed Burhans, a dabbler in real estate to whom they wished to sell their properties. But Burhans was not about, and Jay, recognizing a bargain in the price being asked, moved swiftly to preempt him. Combining his savings with a few hundred dollars supplied by his father, Jay bought the properties himself.

According to Hamilton Burhans—both a devoted friend of Jay's and an envious business rival of older brother Edward—not long after Gould purchased the lots he sold them again to adjoining farmers at what Burhans described as "a handsome profit."[10] In fact, after Jay repaid his father, some $5,000 remained, a lordly sum for one not yet twenty. The profit probably made the true cost of the transaction—Edward Burhans fired him—seem more than worthwhile. Although quite legal, Jay's move to edge out the man who paid his salary was hardly ethical. In time, as Gould's notoriety grew on other fronts, an unfriendly press would cite this land deal as the point at which young Gould became a financial predator.

In between these speculations, Jay at last finished his book. The volume, a dense one, sat complete by April 1856. Although the project had been underwritten in part by the New York State Agricultural Society, Jay himself was responsible for its publication. The young man sold subscriptions for several hundred copies. Then he commissioned a Philadelphia printer-binder to bring the volume to press. All was in place, and Jay's manuscript had arrived at the Philadelphia publisher, when word came of tragedy: a catastrophic fire at the printer's offices in which all had been lost. "I am under the unpleasant necessity," he wrote James Oliver, "of informing you of the total destruction by fire of my *History of Delaware County*." Not only was the manuscript incinerated, but so were the printer's plates. "I shall leave for Philadelphia in the morning to ascertain the exact state of my affairs. If nothing less can be done, I shall set myself hard to work to rewrite it, as you know I am not in the habit of backing out what I undertake, and shall write night and day until it is completed."[11]

Sifting through the wreck of the Philadelphia plant, Jay and his printer were able to salvage only a few proof sheets, which Jay carried back to Roxbury. Through May and June, Gould, now twenty, devoted long hours to reconstituting his opus. In this work he relied heavily on the pitifully small pile of salvaged proofs, his notes for the original draft, and a few fragmentary extracts published previously by Champion in the *Bloomville Mirror*. The book finally appeared in September 1856 under Jay's homegrown Roxbury imprint.

But he was not there to see it. He had by that time departed the town—a place he would never again call home—intent on making his fortune.

◇   ◇   ◇

Of Jay's old friends only John Burroughs and John Champlin—the latter ending his days as chief justice of the Michigan State Supreme Court—wound up so cowed by Gould's bad press that they failed to maintain communication. (When in his dotage, Burroughs became chummy with Gould's eldest daughter and only at that point learned of Jay's vigorous, oft-stated fondness for his books.) "I never saw Jay after the Roxbury days—not to speak with him," Burroughs commented in 1919. "Our paths lay far apart. I never followed his career very closely." Once during the late 1860s, at the Treasury Department in Washington, D.C., the Deputy Comptroller brought in some officers from a bank in New York and asked the would-be writer Burroughs—then supporting himself as a department clerk—to show the gentlemen the vault. Gould was one of the party. "He did not recognize me, though I knew him instantly. I showed them the vault, but did not make myself known to Jay."[12]

Twenty years later, Burroughs—by now a well-known author—encountered Gould one last time. "I was walking up Fifth Avenue, when I saw a man on the other side of the street, more than a block away, coming toward me, whose gait arrested my attention as something I had known long before. Who could it be? I thought, and began to ransack my memory for a clue. I had seen that gait before. As the man came opposite me I saw he was Jay Gould. That walk in some subtle way differed from the walk of any other man I had known. It is a curious psychological fact that the two men outside my own family of whom I have oftenest dreamed in my sleep are Emerson and Jay Gould; one to whom I owe so much, the other to whom I owe nothing; one whose name I revere, the other whose name I associate, as does the world, with the dark way of speculative finance."[13]

Others of the Roxbury crowd remained in touch, each of them receiving brief surprise visits from Gould every few years. Accompanied by a small army of lieutenants and usually in a friendly rush, the financier would arrive like a welcome storm out of the blue, most often while passing near one or another of his old associates' homes on the way to some more significant destination. James Oliver, who had migrated to Kansas, received numerous visits from Gould during the latter's inspection trips of his western railroad properties. As well, whenever Gould found himself within striking distance of Roxbury, he called on Hamilton Burhans (who owned and operated a number of retail establishments after selling the Gould farm to one of Rice Bouton's cousins) and Peter Van Amburgh, who farmed. Gould also called on Simon Champion, who spent his life as the editor of various obscure Catskills newspapers, and Abel Crosby, who found success as a jobber of hardware, iron, steel, and mill supplies just south of the Catskills at Rond-out, New York.

Similarly, Jay kept tabs on Rice Bouton. Following a two-year stint (1858–1860) as president of Missouri's Chapel Hill College, Rice commenced a three-year tenure (1860–1863) in the president's post at Macon College in the same state. After that he returned to Roxbury, where he took McLaury's place as principal at the Roxbury Academy, remaining until the school's closure in 1869. Thereafter, for the next fifteen years, Rice oversaw Methodist congregations in the Catskills towns of Bovina, Windham, Stamford, Franklin, and Coeyman's Hollow. Gould and Bouton saw each other sporadically during this time but were destined to reconnect more solidly in 1884, at which point Rice moved to Manhattan after having been called to take over the famous Five Points Mission in what was then the worst of New York's slums. After 1884 and until Rice's death in September 1891, Jay favored him with occasional unsolicited checks for the mission and equally occasional invitations to dinner at his Fifth Avenue home.

In mid-1875, John McLaury, who had lost contact with Gould after they both left Roxbury, dropped in at Jay's Manhattan townhouse. The two had not seen each other in at least fifteen years. (During the intervening time McLaury married a girl from Harpersfield in the Catskills and relocated to North Carolina, where he chaired the department of mathematics at Charlotte College, now the University of North Carolina, Charlotte.) "[Jay] received me very cordially," McLaury recalled. "He had changed in his appearance but the change was not as much as I expected." The mogul insisted his old friend stay to dinner and meet the family. Afterward, as McLaury prepared to depart, Gould in a hushed voice inquired to know whether everything was "all right" with him. "Which indeed it was," McLaury remembered. "I'm pleased to say I required nothing more of Jay than a hearty handshake and a fond remembrance."[14]

Chapter 7

GOULDSBORO

S EVEN YEARS BEFORE he married Sarah Gould, George Northrop had embarked upon a partnership in a Pennsylvania tannery with two other Catskills businessmen. Gilbert and Edward Palen—Northrop's brothers-in-law by his first wife, Caroline Palen—hailed from Palenville, a village in the Catskills where their forebear Jonathan Palen had set up a large tanning enterprise in 1817.[1] By mid-1856, after nine years of earnest effort, the Northrop-Palen speculation in the Pocono Mountains, 160 miles southwest of Roxbury, had begun to look a success, and the three partners announced plans to move their households closer to their investment.

The neighborhood of the Northrop-Palen enterprise, on the east side of Brodhead Creek in Pennsylvania's Monroe County, had originally been known as Frogtown. But now Gilbert Palen christened the place with a classier moniker: Canadensis, the name being taken from the hemlock tree *Tsuga canadensis*, whose bark contained a variety of tannic acid particularly suited for the conversion of raw pelts into sole leather.[2] Given the great hope and anticipation with which Northrop and the Palens were preparing to uproot their lives and embrace their futures, Jay Gould must have heard and seen a great deal about the money to be made in leather manufacturing.

This was a promise that shone no more in the Catskill Mountains. During the late eighteenth and early nineteenth centuries, the Catskills had been known as the blue mountains. This name derived from the dense "blue" stands of hemlocks that dominated the region's northern and eastern slopes. Indeed, at the turn of the nineteenth century, the Catskills boasted numerous ancient forests sheltering hemlocks that were not uncommonly one hundred feet tall, four feet wide, and two hundred years old. These forests came down over the course of just five decades, as the leather markets of New York and Boston grew, and the single-minded "bark peelers" destroyed more and more of the ancient stands. In 1835, approximately 40 percent of New York State's tanneries operated in the Catskills counties of Delaware, Greene, Orange, Schoharie, Sullivan, and Ulster. By the time Northrop and the Palens launched their operation in Canadensis, the hemlock forests of the Catskills and the tanneries that had fed on them were just memories. (Henry David Thoreau, on a visit to the Catskills in 1844, looked at one of the denuded mountainsides and, borrowing a phrase from his friend Ralph Waldo Emerson, compared it to a "sucked orange."[3]) Thus men like Northrop and the Palens—although settling for inferior alder or oak bark when they had to—did not hesitate to move like locusts, following the increasingly distant chain of untouched hemlocks north into the Adirondacks and southwest into the Alleghenies and Poconos.

One who participated in this economic migration was Zadock Pratt, famous in his day as the "Greene County Tanner." Pratt's hometown, Prattsville (the former Schoharie Kill) lay some twelve miles from Roxbury. Sixty-six years old in 1856, Pratt possessed a massive tanning-based fortune.[4] His father, Zadock Pratt, Sr.—one of the earliest Catskills tanners— had set up shop in the town of Jewett, Greene County, in 1802. Ten years later, in 1812, Zadock, Jr., made his first great killing in business when he sold the U.S. Navy 100,000 ash-wood oars hewn from the otherwise useless forests that dominated his home region's southern and westward slopes. Twelve years after that, in 1824—having sold his interest in the family business to his two brothers for $14,000—the thirty-four-year-old Zadock started his own tanning establishment on the banks of the Schoharie Creek.

Pratt's tannery eventually grew to become one of the largest operations of its kind. In peak years, it produced as many as 60,000 sides of sole leather, these processed by nearly one hundred Pratt employees. (According to

Pratt's precise record-keeping, his tannery turned out a total of more than 1.5 million sides over twenty years. Writing in the early 1850s, a few years before his association with Jay Gould, Pratt calculated that—up to that point, at Prattsville and other tanning centers in which he had an interest— he had cleared 10,000 forest acres, used 250,000 cords of hemlock bark, employed 40,000 men, and formed more than thirty partnerships, all of which he "closed . . . in peace." [5]) The operation at Prattsville thrived until 1845, at which point the master finally closed his shop, with the ten square miles surrounding the town thoroughly stripped of hemlock, and similar forests within forty to fifty miles having also been plundered.

Like all tanners, Pratt continually sought new hemlock-rich areas in which to invest. But unlike his peers—who routinely abandoned their settlements as ghost towns once the hemlocks ran out—Pratt sought to restore and reuse exploited lands. (Reportedly, when he first made his investment in the region of the Schoharie, Pratt assured those who already lived there that he intended to "live with them, not on them," thus making a long-term commitment to the place as a citizen.[6]) As Pratt brought down the forests of the Schoharie Valley, he converted the fertile ground into prime agricultural space and, in anticipation of closing his tannery, took care to finance farms for his workers. Pratt also encouraged and financed other businesses (such as a blacksmith shop, a chair- and cabinet-making workshop, a hat-making workshop, machine shops, foundries, and small factories) to support and serve the posttanning community he envisioned for the future.

As well, Pratt built more than one hundred homes (each ornamented with pilasters and sunburst gable windows), endowed the Prattsville Academy, saw to the construction of three churches (Dutch Reformed, Methodist, and Episcopal), planted 1,000 shade trees (hickory, maple, and elm), installed ornamental ponds in the village's downtown, and put down bluestone sidewalks. He himself wound up owning a 365-acre dairy farm on the banks of the Schoharie. A social visionary who sincerely cared for the welfare of those he employed, Pratt created one of New York State's first great planned communities: a picturesque, idyllic garden of a place that in his own time was praised by the press as "the gem of the Catskills."[7]

Once he closed his tannery, where he had been an active on-site manager six days a week for two decades, Pratt devoted some of his newly found free time to politics. After stints as justice of the peace and town supervisor, he served two terms in Congress and was offered the Democratic nomination for New York governor in 1848, an honor he declined. While he dabbled in public office, Pratt also continued his long association with the local militia, in which he eventually rose to the rank of colonel. (In 1825 he had commanded the brigade that escorted LaFayette into the town of Catskill during the French general's triumphant tour of the United States.) Possessed by a great love of military history, Pratt was known to spend long Sunday afternoons reenacting famous battles with his men: Pratt always in command, playing Napoleon or some other likely general.

Though Pratt enjoyed great fortune in his professional life, his private life was laced with tragedy. He buried three wives—the sisters Beda and Esther Dickerman, followed by Abigail Watson—in just eighteen years. Abigail lasted long enough to give the colonel three children, one of whom died in infancy. Abigail's sister Mary, whom the colonel married in 1838, raised Pratt's surviving son and daughter, apparently moving deftly from the role of aunt to that of mother. After Mary also died in 1868, the elderly Pratt would marry yet again. In 1869, two years before his death, the seventy-nine-year-old took as his wife Suzi Grimm, a twenty-eight-year-old secretary from the offices of the Manhattan trade journal *Shoe and Leather Reporter*.

Like many people of great accomplishment, Pratt was somewhat eccentric and also possessed of a powerful ego. When he invested $50,000 and opened his own bank in 1843, all of the notes bore his likeness. That same year, when an itinerant stonecutter passed through town, Pratt employed the man to carve his profile on a massive rock outcropping five hundred feet above the rich valley of the Schoharie. Once this was done, the artist went on to chisel various emblems from Pratt's life: his favorite horse, a hemlock tree, the tannery, the Pratt coat-of-arms, and so forth. Pratt even set him to carving a regal tomb that went unfinished once water started to leach into the chamber. (Many years after the initial work, Pratt funded more carving at the site to memorialize his son, George Watson Pratt, a Union Army officer who died one week after being wounded at the second battle of Manassas, also known as Bull Run.) "Pratt's Rocks" remain to this day, perched high above Route 23 on the eastern approach to the village Pratt loved so much.

◇ ◇ ◇

Jay Gould first encountered Pratt—forty-six years his senior—during the summer of 1852 while Gould was working on the map of Ulster County, where Pratt and one of his many partners controlled the tanning outpost of Samsonville. In January 1853, once the Ulster project was done, Gould wrote Pratt—whom he was obviously eager to cultivate—with a proposal that the colonel commission a similar map of Greene County. Pratt declined to fund that project but pronounced himself impressed by Gould and promised he would keep him in mind for future tasks.

Writing in the 1890s, J. W. McLaury recalled the chilly, rain-soaked spring morning in 1856 when "an old gray haired man, tall, erect, booted and spurred, his boot tops extending above his knees, mud bespattered over his clothing from head to feet," arrived in Roxbury and loudly asked for Gould. "He introduced himself as Col. Pratt [and said he] wanted Mr. Gould to make a survey of his farm."[8] In the coming weeks Gould not only surveyed Pratt's acres at Prattsville but also attempted to make himself useful in other ways, at one point proposing to write the tanner's biography. What Pratt thought of this idea is not on record, but the book never emerged.

However, Pratt does seem to have employed Gould in writing some other things, such as speeches and important letters. As Gould's sister Bettie would tell her daughter not long after Jay's death: "The famous speech that Col. Pratt delivered before an Agricultural Society—if I remember rightly—in Kingston, was written by your Uncle Jay. The Col. paid him something for it. Everyone wondered at the time that he [Pratt] was equal to such a speech. All the papers quoted from it at the time and commented on the wisdom of the author." Bettie remembered Jay reading the draft speech—on the topic of the horse as a beast of labor—aloud to herself and their father at the tin shop, and John Burr Gould making a few suggestions for additions "which [Jay] made in the way of interlining, and then afterwards rewrote it. . . . Your uncle wrote other things for [Col. Pratt]—a number of them."[9] According to Jay's friend Peter Van Amburgh, Pratt paid Gould a hundred dollars for the Kingston speech alone, this at a time when the average wage for an eight-hour day stood at one dollar.[10]

But Jay's goal was not to be Pratt's high-priced ghostwriter or secretary. He had been energized by George Northrop's tales of tanning. He also knew that Pratt himself had invested in the Aldenville area of Pennsylvania as early as 1849. Working from this foundation, Gould sought to interest Pratt in starting yet another tannery operation. Jay said he believed there was promise in the as-yet untouched tracts of hemlock rumored to lurk between the Lehigh and Delaware Rivers in Pennsylvania's Luzerne County. Not only did the content of those forests sound ideal, he told Pratt, but the recently constructed Delaware & Lackawanna Railroad also offered an advantageous and heretofore unavailable avenue for shipping raw pelts and finished sole leather in and out of the Pocono wilderness. (The importance of the Delaware & Lackawanna was not lost on Pratt, who in 1847 had personally subscribed $10,000 to subsidize the building of the Hudson River Railroad, by which he subsequently speeded his tanned leather to Manhattan.)

Commissioned by Pratt to investigate the possibilities, Gould traveled to the Poconos in early August. There he hiked through the woods for several days, carrying a compass and some surveying gear, until—jubilantly—he found what he was looking for. Gould took Pratt to the site a week later and showed the old man vast vistas dominated by hemlock and alder as far as the eye could see. Convinced, Pratt on the spot formed a 50-50 partnership with the enterprising young man who dreamed of great things.

They were an odd couple. Pratt was tall, old, and prosperous. Jay was short, young, and hungry. The contract between them no longer survives; its precise terms are unknown. But one can make reasonable assumptions. Pratt's main contributions to the enterprise were to be his expertise and his capital, while Gould's was to invest his youthful energy. In letters, Pratt made it clear that day-to-day responsibility for the operation—into which he would eventually sink as much as $120,000—was to be Jay's and Jay's alone. Pratt would be available for consultation and advice. He would answer all questions as to how to set up and manage the plant, acquire raw pelts, and market the finished leather. But Jay was the man who would have to make things happen on the ground.

Later that month, Gould bought property for the tannery on the banks of the Lehigh. He also struck deals with local landowners to take the bark from their trees. At the start of September he brought in some fifty workers and commenced clearing land. According to Gould's own account, prepared for his senior partner, he personally chopped down the first tree and then supervised its slicing into boards for the tannery's first structure: a blacksmith shop. Gould spent his initial night in the woods sleeping on a bed of hemlock boughs under the shelter of the blacksmith shop's newly raised roof. Four days later, Jay and the crew finished constructing a dormitory—rude but large, and capable of accommodating everyone comfortably. By way of dedication, the rough band of laborers gave a round of cheers for their diminutive but popular boss, passing by acclamation a motion that the place thereafter be named Gouldsboro. Reporting this to Pratt, Jay hastily added, "Three hearty cheers were then proposed for the Hon. Zadock Pratt, the *world renowned Great American Farmer*, and a more hearty response I am certain this valley never before witnessed."[11]

Privately, Jay, not yet twenty-one, must have been more than pleased. Great-grandfather More had settled Moresville. The Palens had their Palenville, and Pratt his Prattsville. How could the notion of Gouldsboro not have been satisfying to the boy who had always worked so hard, the boy—now a man—who was finally making some headway in the world?

Chapter 8

OUR BEST FRIENDS
TELL US OUR FAULTS

A T THE START OF THEIR ENTERPRISE, the relationship between Pratt and Gould was that of accomplished sage instructing and nurturing a grateful, even doting, student. Jay seems at first to have sincerely welcomed the steady stream of advice, instructions, and prompts that flowed from Prattsville. "I am much obliged to you for all your suggestions," Jay gushed to Pratt on Christmas Eve. "I find them a *good dictionary*."[1]

Gould was completely submissive when Pratt informed him that the pelts for tanning, and all of Pratt & Gould's finished leather, were to be acquired and disposed of through the Manhattan brokerage of Corse & Pratt, a firm half owned by Pratt's son George. And he acquiesced immediately when Pratt, a compulsive tinkerer always exploring new tools and approaches, decided the Gouldsboro plant should be the first in the nation to perfect a new tan-ning technique of which he'd recently read in a trade journal. The wet-spent tan-bark process called for the large chunks of wet refuse bark, normally discarded in traditional tanning, to be burned as fuel. Given this resource, the Gouldsboro tannery could, in theory, run on steam rather than waterpower, thus avoiding the seasonal annoyance and delay of an iced river. But first, an efficient method for burning had to be devised.

Jay and his men remained industrious throughout the winter. A second dormitory went up along with a barn, a wagon house, a post office, and four family homes. The last were built in anticipation of experienced senior tanners—men possessing arcane skills of which Jay was entirely ignorant—whom Pratt would recruit and send in time for the spring start-up. Most of the actual tanning facilities stood ready by February 1857, at which time the first hides arrived from Corse & Pratt. By March, several tanners were busy overseeing the laborers. At first called upon to be carpenters, now the men of Gouldsboro transformed into cogs of the tanning machine, each learning to harvest hemlock bark, prepare hides in sweat pits, and perform other skilled tasks.

Gould was little interested in these details. He preferred to occupy himself with logistics. In his detailed letters to Pratt, he itemized and explained his organization of the tannery's inventory system and cash accounts. Interestingly, Jay also made certain to report several exercises outside the direct realm of business that mimicked Pratt's numerous paternalistic ventures in Prattsville. As Gouldsboro grew over the months, and more and more wives and children arrived, Jay led a drive to raise money for a church and cemetery. He also built a school, hired a teacher at his own expense, and made it a requirement that all school-aged children enroll. "Pride in community," he wrote Pratt, "will inspire and encourage our men to pride and excellence in work."[2]

Problems, however, were on the horizon. The start-up phase of the operation, with all its construction, had of course consumed large amounts of capital. Jay regularly had to draw on Pratt for funds. No income whatsoever—let alone profit—could be anticipated until the tannery was operating at capacity. And capacity was to prove elusive for many months as the master tanners of Gouldsboro experimented and labored to refine the wet-spent tan-bark process. (In addition to delays associated with design implementation, the steam engine purchased for the Gouldsboro tannery failed shortly after delivery, as did its manufacturer before a replacement engine could be obtained.) "Although you know far more than any man in the country about these matters," Gould wrote a bit testily to Pratt in October, his honorifics now tinged with just a hint of sarcasm, "I am inclined to think that my original suggestion—building a water-wheel as a backup to the more modern plan—may have saved us time, expense and frustration."[3]

While his staff dealt with the problems at Gouldsboro, Jay made frequent visits to the leather district of Manhattan, called the Swamp. This part of town—which ran down Spruce and Ferry Streets on the east side, just south of today's City Hall—had once literally been a swamp: a mosquito-ridden quagmire to which early-seventeenth-century tanners retreated when citizens complained about the foul smells emanating from their shops. During the eighteenth and early nineteenth centuries, as New York became more of a city and tanning moved into the northern woodlands, the Swamp evolved into a row of storefronts and warehouses where buyers, sellers, and speculators dealt in raw pelts and tanned hides. "The Swamp," Zadock Pratt wrote in 1853, "is to tanners what Wall Street is to financiers."[4] Here leather merchants such as Corse & Pratt kept their offices, as did importers of hides and exporters of leather. Brokers like George Pratt routinely visited the shipping firms, bargaining to get the best-quality hides for their clients at the most competitive prices. The same broker would in turn sell the tanner's finished leather, negotiating the highest prices possible, all on a commission basis. Often the brokers would as well supply short-term financing to tanners, providing raw pelts on credit and then deducting the cost of those pelts plus interest, together with commissions for buying and selling, from the proceeds of leather sales.

"I've come to realize that it is the merchants," an observant Gould wrote his father during the summer of 1857, "who command the true power in this industry. The tanner appears to take the greatest share of capital, but merely processes that capital, his expenses being extensive, his risk real, and his labor heavy. The shippers deal with the next largest sums, but again have extensive expenses and much work to do. The brokers, meanwhile, take what seems the smallest share but is in fact the largest. Theirs is nearly pure profit made on the backs of the shippers and the tanner, never their hands dirtied."[5] Writing to Hamilton Burhans in September, Jay confided that he went "with George Pratt on his rounds, interested to learn the ways of the leather district. I'm not sure Mr. Pratt enjoys my shadow, but I feel the need to understand these processes. I want to gain a grasp of the bartering, and to meet the men of the trade. I have learned much of buying hides—too much—and look forward hopefully to one day having some leather to *sell*, should the beasts of steam permit."[6]

It was a rough year for the young man to start in the trade. During the summer and autumn of 1857, a financial panic swept the country, ending ten years of boom times in the wake of the Mexican-American War. The immediate event that touched off the Panic was the August failure of the New York branch of the Ohio Life Insurance and Trust Company, a major financial force that collapsed following massive embezzlement. On the heels of this disaster, numerous British investors removed large sums from American banks (this withdrawal raising questions about the banks' overall soundness). At the same time, a fall in grain prices hurt rural economies, and a pileup of manufactured goods in warehouses led to massive layoffs. With the fall of shipping revenues, several railroads failed, as did a score of western land speculations associated with the rail infrastructure. Thousands of investors faced ruin. General confidence received another shake in September when 30,000 pounds of gold being transported from the San Francisco mint to eastern banks went down with the SS *Central America*, causing some speculators to call into question the government's ability to back paper currency with specie. The situation had grown so bad by October that authorities called a bank holiday throughout New England and New York State. Nearly a thousand Manhattan merchants declared themselves bankrupt before the end of December, reporting losses totaling $120 million for that city alone.

Recovery would not come for a year and a half, and the full impact of the Panic would not dissipate until the start of the Civil War. In the meantime, a few shrewd customers found profits amid the ruin. Moses Taylor, president of City Bank, devoured railroad stocks frantically and also used depressed prices as an opportunity to grab control of New York City's largest gas company. Leonard Jerome, future grandfather of Winston Churchill, became a millionaire almost overnight simply by shorting dozens of stocks in the midst of the disaster. And "Commodore" Cornelius Vanderbilt moved in on several financially troubled rail lines (among them the New York & Harlem) with ferocious swiftness, beginning the process by which he would, within ten years, become a dominant force in American railroading.

While vultures on Wall Street feasted, the Panic reached out in October to take a direct swipe at Gould. During the second week of that month a rumor circulated that Pratt & Gould had suspended operations. Writing to Pratt, Gould described how several suppliers had dunned him for immediate payment of all money owed: "Everybody seems frightened to death. I could have managed to have got along very well had not this report got abroad, & as we have a note due on the 27th . . . I did not sleep a wink last night for fear we cannot meat [*sic*] it."[7] Ironically, it was into this troubled environment, with prices for everything (including such commodities as leather) falling steadily, that the first tanned hides finally came out of Gouldsboro. Two months later, in December, Jay and his tanners finally got the very last of the bugs out of the wet-spent tan-bark process. Thereafter Pratt & Gould was fully functional, if not yet profitable. Depressed leather prices meant it would take Pratt far longer to get into the black than he had originally planned.

In early 1858, a variety of pressures conspired to disrupt the relationship between Jay Gould and Zadock Pratt. Gould could hardly be blamed for either the slow start of the wet-spent tan-bark method or for the Panic of 1857, but Pratt nevertheless began to reconsider his young protégé. Simultaneously, as Gould learned more and more about the business and became increasingly confident of his own instincts, he began consulting Pratt less often and deferring to him less willingly. A new tension entered the relationship.

Pratt's formerly encouraging letters now took on a dictatorial style, with Pratt roundly criticizing Gould's management and bookkeeping. Gould, however disenchanted he had grown with Pratt's judgment, remained at the financial mercy of his mercurial and increasingly hard-to-please partner, and he responded accordingly to the old man's criticisms. "I am under many obligations for your good advice & useful suggestions," he wrote shortly before Christmas in 1857. "There is an old saying in my scrapbook, 'that it is our best friends that tell us our faults.' . . . I often read over your letters rainy days and always I think I learn something new from their persual [*sic*]."[8] But he was also becoming his own man. Early in the spring of 1858, in a move he knew Pratt would not like, the twenty-two-year-old Gould broke off relations with Corse & Pratt. His new association with one of the Swamp's largest and most influential brokerage houses, that of Charles M. Leupp & Company, allowed him to acquire hides and sell leather on better terms than those offered by Corse & Pratt.

At this juncture the amount of business awarded to Leupp, and lost by Corse & Pratt, was hardly small. Despite what the dissatisfied Pratt continued to classify as Gould's bungled management, the Gouldsboro tannery was destined to produce no less than 60,000 sides in 1858, a number rivaling the output of Pratt's old Prattsville operation in its best year. In a September letter addressed to Pratt as "Dear sir" rather than the "Dear friend" to whom Gould had written so often previously, the junior partner happily—and perhaps a bit smugly—informed the colonel that hides were going through the tannery at a rate of 300 sides per day. On the strength of these figures, a grim Pratt—satisfied with the plant's output, but not with his per-side return nor with the gathering independence of his young partner—continued to advance funds as needed, while also pondering his options.

◇   ◇   ◇

Zadock Pratt, in his later years, hardly ever spoke of his partnership with Jay Gould. In *The Chronological Biography of the Hon. Zadock Pratt*—a mistitled 1868 volume that is far more autobiography than biography—Pratt filled page after page with the names of dozens of partners and tannery enterprises. Nowhere did he mention Gould, Gouldsboro, or Pratt & Gould. (Jay himself commented on the dissolution of Pratt & Gould only once, during Senate testimony many years later, when he summarized the event in one flat sentence: "We carried on the business for a while, and then I bought Mr. Pratt out."[10]) That Pratt came away from the partnership feeling ill used can be verified by letters he wrote after the fact, and by the bitter reminiscences of his daughter, Julia Pratt Ingersoll. That Gould robbed and defrauded a guileless and easily bamboozled Pratt—as so many previous biographers have suggested—cannot be proved with the existing documents and seems, when all the facts are considered, highly unlikely.[11] The popular folklore of the Pratt & Gould dissolution was first recounted in a potboiler biography published just weeks after Gould's death. It was then mindlessly parroted in numerous books, most recently in Charles R. Geisst's *Wall Street: A History* (1997), in which Geisst states categorically that "Gould had been discovered cooking the books at the tannery . . . and siphoning off funds for some use unknown to his elder partner."[12]

The detail of the legend that Geisst and so many other writers have confused with history goes as follows. According to the story, throughout 1858

Gould consistently diverted funds from the Pratt & Gould accounts. As the tale has it, he used some of Pratt's money to speculate in Lehigh Valley lands and to open his own bank in Stroudsburg, where he subsequently deposited even more Pratt & Gould capital for siphoning into additional side ventures. As Robert I. Warshow put it, "The tannery was doing a rushing business, and was always at capacity. Profits, however, were very small. Then Pratt came on one of his rare visits, and went over the books [which he found to contain] very original bookkeeping." Elsewhere Warshow added, "Gould . . . had started a private bank in Stroudsburg, and . . . Pratt had caught him using the firm's funds in its operation."[13] According to Richard O'Connor, who evidently enjoyed a certain telepathy with the dead, "Pratt realized that for the first time in his life he had come across a completely amoral specimen of humanity, a creature as remorseless as a weasel loose in a hen roost."[14] For these reasons, according to the accepted story, a disgusted Pratt announced to Gould during the Christmas season in 1858 that he wished to close their partnership.

The town records of Stroudsburg and the state banking records of Pennsylvania reveal no bank started by Gould, and no bank on the board of which Gould sat, existing in 1857 or 1858. Local land records in the region of Stroudsburg do show some land purchases in Gould's name. These transactions, however, had an investment value of not more than $4,000 to $5,000, roughly the amount Gould is known to have possessed after his Roxbury land speculation. Another gap between the folklore and reality is the image of Pratt as a naive old man taken to the cleaners by a young and crooked upstart. Pratt had not amassed his fortune by being an idiot; and he was known to play fairly sharply himself on occasion. In fact, there is every indication that the breakup of Pratt & Gould represents the first time Pratt failed to get the better of a junior partner.

The habitually incorrect Warshow stumbled into a true statement when he wrote, "The tannery was doing a rushing business, and was always at capacity. Profits, however, were very small."[15] But the reason for the small—in fact, nonexistent—profits was not theft by Gould. In the wake of the 1857 Panic, leather prices remained severely depressed. Margins were tight. Against this backdrop—with his tannery running full tilt, but amortization of his investment slowed by a dismal economy—Pratt apparently sought to improve his personal profit by ousting his partner at a bargain price. The man in the best position to know—one John Gardner, who worked as an assistant to Jay at Gouldsboro—recalled that "Pratt having the largest interest said to Gould you must either sell or buy thinking it impossible for Gould to buy and secretly hoping to force Gould to sell his share thereby enriching himself at Mr. Gould's expense."[16] More precisely, the terms laid down by Pratt were these: Pratt would buy out Gould for $10,000; or else Gould must buy Pratt out for $60,000. In an off-hand manner, Pratt added that the seemingly unbankable Jay could have ten days to decide.[17]

Reason suggests that Pratt's offer to sell his share for $60,000 was a canard pure and simple. Pratt had sunk $120,000 into the operation. Therefore he would have offered to sell at half that amount only if he were convinced there was no way Gould could come up with the necessary funds. The actual deal that Pratt meant to force was Gould's selling out for $10,000. This transaction, had it gone through, would have allowed Pratt to purchase Gould's two-and-a-half years of full-time managerial devotion, not to mention Gould's rights in the enterprise, very cheaply. But Pratt, who perhaps should have known better, had underestimated his young colleague.

In the time allowed him by Pratt, Gould traveled to the New York Swamp, where he struck a fast deal with Charles M. Leupp and Leupp's partner and brother-in-law, David W. Lee. Leupp and Lee agreed to acquire a two-thirds stake (one-third apiece) in Pratt & Gould for a total price of $60,000. Returning to Prattsville, Gould flabbergasted Pratt when he exercised his option to buy the firm, offering letters from his new partners as surety. The deal, finalized on 27 January 1859, left Pratt with a $60,000 loss overall. Simultaneously it left Gould with a one-third stake in a thriving tannery and an alliance with one of the Swamp's most prestigious brokerage firms.

In short, what so many previous writers have described as Gould's first great swindle was in fact his first great coup. Given the facts, Pratt's utter silence in later years regarding his partnership with Gould—an enterprise at the end of which Pratt wound up bettered by a man barely out of his teens—begins to make sense.

Chapter 9

CUNNING LUNACY

THE PRODUCT OF A socially prominent New York family, Charles M. Leupp was just fifteen when he went to work for Manhattan's most success- ful leather merchant—also state legislator, New York City mayor, and De- mocratic congressman—Gideon Lee. Eventually, Leupp married Lee's daughter.[1] After Lee's death in 1841, Leupp changed the name of the firm to Charles M. Leupp & Company while remaining partners with Lee's son David, who served as attorney for the organization. By the time of his asso- ciation with Jay Gould, Leupp was the dominant leather merchant in the Swamp.[2]

Unlike the rustic Pratt, with whom he had done much business in the 1820s and 1830s, Leupp prided himself on being an urbane gentleman, a lover of fine things, and a patron of the arts. Leupp's $150,000 mansion at the corner of Madison Avenue and Twenty-fifth Street, in which he labored to raise his three daughters after his wife's untimely death in 1843, was one of the handsomest in New York. Leupp cultivated writers including the journalist and essayist Nathaniel Parker Willis and artists such as the Hud- son River painter Jasper Cropsey as friends. He was a member of the Cen- tury Club and of numerous artistic societies, and he took a leading role in several charitable institutions, most notably the Episcopal church (to which he was devoted) and the New York Society Library (which he served as trustee). All told, Leupp stood as a central figure in New York's social, financial, and artistic aristocracy. He was a man of impeccable reputation, powerful connections, and great means. Were Leupp alive today, we would call him a "player."

In business, Leupp had long been known as a conservative: He was a solid citizen who calculated his risks carefully and placed only the safest of bets. Therefore one is at first at a loss to explain Leupp's move to purchase a controlling interest in the Gouldsboro concern. The leather merchants of the Swamp generally did not invest directly in tanneries. Thus they avoided overt conflicts of interest that might complicate their buying, selling, and bartering. By going in with Gould, Messrs. Leupp and Lee risked alienating the numerous other tanners on whom they relied for trade, who would now have cause to question the Leupp firm's impartiality in dealing.

Why did the normally conservative Leupp take himself and his brother-in-law into the Gouldsboro enterprise? Few understood at the time what David Lee did: Leupp was mentally unhinged. David Lee would tell friends in later years that he'd noticed severe changes in Leupp's demeanor as early as 1853, when the leather merchant began exhibiting wild, albeit occasional, swings from high elation to deep depression. Things had grown so bad, and the swings so frequent, by mid-1856 that Lee took the reins of the firm for a time, sending Leupp off to travel and revive himself. The convalescence ended abruptly, however, with the advent of severe market conditions in 1857, a financial storm that Lee was unprepared to deal with. The Panic brought Leupp reluctantly back to the Swamp, where, by October 1858, he'd once again fallen prey to mood shifts. Thus the maniacally optimistic speculator who agreed almost instantly to bank Gould against Colonel Pratt soon enough collapsed into nervousness, second guesses, and doubts. Lee said later that he should have guessed that his partner was completely insane. "That Charles was unsound in mind I have seen for a good while [but] how terribly in this have we all (for several of us—friends & physicians were conscious of his unsoundness and watching him carefully) been deceived by the wonderful cunning of lunacy."[3]

Because of Leupp's mental state, the business arrangement between Gould, Leupp, and Lee, which promised to be complicated from the outset, became even more so. Wishing for reasons of both practicality and public relations to distance themselves from the day-to-day management of the Gouldsboro tannery, Leupp and Lee signed a working agreement with Jay on 1 February 1859 that called for Gould to act as the "sole known partner" of the concern. Although Charles M. Leupp & Company would underwrite all of the Gouldsboro tannery's credit going forward (thus allowing Jay to issue "two-named paper" for which he, Leupp, and Lee would be equally liable), the plan as originally proposed called for Jay to make all decisions concerning the running of the Gouldsboro plant. As Gould explained it later, Leupp and Lee wanted their involvement kept as quiet as possible, for they feared that knowledge of their interest "in manufacturing would affect the standing of their paper [credit] in [the] market."[4]

As might be expected, the management agreement called for Leupp & Company to continue to service Gouldsboro as merchants, just as they had done for more than a year. Leupp & Company's standard commission schedule of 5 percent for the purchase of hides and 6 percent for sales of leather remained unchanged. Interestingly, however, the contract obligated Leupp to deliver a monthly minimum of only 1,800 sides, less than half the 5,000 sides per month he'd provided for the voracious and productive Gouldsboro plant through 1858. Perhaps Leupp and Lee, already carrying paper representing their $60,000 initial investment in Jay's operation, thought by this method to limit their overall exposure with regard to the Gouldsboro enterprise. Perhaps, as well, it suited Leupp & Company's purposes (in their representation of other tanneries) to cut back production at the upstart Gould operation, thus upping demand (and pricing) for tanned sides overall. Both these elements of business calculus were most certainly in the air, as was Leupp's increasingly impaired mental state, as Leupp and Lee launched their uneasy relationship with Gould. And all three of these factors, combined with Jay's growing penchant for maximizing his advantage and cutting legal corners, would quickly collide.

Gould read the 1,800-side minimum as just that—a minimum—and proceeded into 1859 with no idea of restricting production at the Gouldsboro tannery (a policy that, although it might have served the purposes of Messrs. Leupp and Lee, could only have hurt Jay's position). Aggressive and expansionist by temperament, Gould argued to Leupp and Lee—diplomatically at first, after several months of tolerating low unit production—that he could and should ship 21,120 finished sides during July, August, and

September of 1859, and that he would increase production to 8,000 sides in June "if you consider it safe & prudent to do so—if not—not." In making his case for maximum production, Gould stated the simple math of static costs quite plainly, as if educating a nitwit son. "We can tan 90,000 sides cheaper pro rata than we can 60,000 as the same tannery & machinery does it & the same men oversee it, so that the cost of supervision is not increased."[5] When Leupp and Lee proved unreceptive to this logic, Gould countered by reminding them that he had, in the past six months, endorsed notes for Leupp and Lee associated with the Gouldsboro tannery amounting to more than $100,000 and had done so only on the assurance that he would always have enough hides flowing from the merchants to cover this debt. As well, Gould added darkly, there were also his own notes *to* Leupp & Company for hides that needed to be covered.

By the summer of 1859, Jay was dealing almost exclusively with David Lee. Starting in July, Leupp descended into hallucinations (an elephant in his living room, a vampire bat on his shoulder) and also began to display symptoms of paranoia. He believed (probably with reason) that his friends were spying on him. He also became convinced that detectives from the New York City police department followed him wherever he went. And he decided, without benefit of diagnosis, that he suffered from heart disease. At the same time that the distracted Lee dictated letters to Gould, he sat with one hand on his partner's wrist, checking the man's pulse, something Leupp insisted he do every ten minutes, "and in this way reassure my poor, haunted brother-in-law that he did indeed remain alive."[6]

An unwilling leather merchant, the lawyerly Lee seems also to have been supremely concerned about spreading Leupp & Company's position too thin with regard to the Gouldsboro tannery. Throughout June and July, Lee became so agitated about Gould's insistence on operating the plant at maximum capacity that he offered to buy Jay's share of the concern for $20,000, an offer Jay flatly rejected before countering with an offer to buy out Leupp and Lee instead. Unwilling to take Gould's note, and unable to convince Gould to leave, Lee instead rectified his and Leupp's chief conflict with Gould by arranging for another leather dealer, Boston's John B. Alley, to replace Leupp & Company as supplier for the Gouldsboro tannery. In this way Gould could move to full capacity without unduly expanding the credit risk of Leupp and Lee, who remained partners in the Gouldsboro operation and so remained liable, with Jay, for its debts. As well, Leupp & Company would also continue to market the leather produced at Gouldsboro. But in the future they would not have the double risk of extending credit to Gouldsboro for hides and sharing indebtedness for those same items.

By early autumn only one dispute remained between Gould and his two partners from the Swamp. Lee insisted that the firm's interest in a large supply of hides delivered before John Alley entered the picture be protected. Jay, in turn, told his partners he considered the hides collateral for all the paper he'd endorsed for Leupp and Lee over the past nine months. Gould and Lee were still negotiating this impasse—politely arguing back and forth in carefully worded letters—that October, when the next and perhaps inevitable scene of the drama played out.

◇ ◇ ◇

On 5 October, a Wednesday, Charles Leupp spent most of the day in his Ferry Street office sporadically dealing with business but mainly complaining to Lee and several secretaries about his terrible health, his faithless associates, and his numerous unnamed enemies. After work, Leupp walked uptown to his home on Twenty-fifth Street, where he ate a silent dinner with his daughters Maggie and Laura. Later on, William F. Cook, one of a dozen or so friends who had lately taken turns dropping in on their troubled associate, stopped by and was invited to share a glass of ale. When Cook lifted his glass and made a toast to Leupp's health, Leupp sighed, buried his head in his hands, and then looked up forlornly with an "unnatural expression."[7]

Cook acquiesced when the agitated Leupp asked that he stay the night. A few hours later, as the guest chatted with Leupp's daughters in an upstairs sitting room, a "wild-eyed" Leupp suddenly rushed in. The daughters, by now quite used to their father's outbursts, did not comment when Leupp embraced and kissed each of them, tears in his eyes, before turning briskly away and stalking back out the door. Moments later, from Leupp's bedchamber, came the crack of a gunshot. Running to the sound, Cook and the girls found Leupp lying on his bed, blood pouring from a wound in his chest, and a double-barreled pistol cast down on the floor. "Poor father shot himself . . . ," Laura wrote the following morning. "It was not his fault. He was insane and has been so some time. . . . He has intended it a long while, don't blame him."[8] Testifying before an inquest on the afternoon of 6 October, David Lee talked at length about his brother-in-law's prolonged "mental degeneration" and stated categorically that "there was nothing in the facts of Mr. Leupp's personal, family, social, property or commercial condition, as far as I am aware, to justify any apprehension or distress on his part."[9]

◇ ◇ ◇

Leupp's suicide is another chapter of Jay's life that several generations of biographers—fixated on demonizing their subject—have gotten utterly wrong. The popular, spurious version of the story lays the blame for Leupp's suicide squarely on Gould and, to make the economics fit the tale being told, changes the date of Leupp's death from 1859 to 1857.[10] Never mind that Leupp and Gould did not even become partners until the very end of 1858. Never mind that both Leupp & Company and Pratt & Gould emerged solvent from the Panic of 1857. And never mind that Leupp was by no means bankrupt when he died. As the story goes, Gould—creating "two-name" paper—had begun speculating wildly in hides, attempting to corner that market, just prior to the Panic of 1857. Then, in the midst of the 1857 collapse, Jay supposedly left Leupp a ruined man, holding the bag for hundreds of thousands of dollars in sharply devalued hides and leather. This in turn led to Leupp's suicide.

According to the version propounded by Richard O'Connor, "Then came the Panic of 1857, in which . . . Gould was caught short in his gamble on leather futures. . . . Meanwhile, Charles Leupp was learning that he had not only invested in the Gouldsboro tannery but his name and credit had been used to finance [a corner on] the hide market."[11] In the tale as related by Warshow, Josephson, O'Connor, and Edwin Hoyt, Charles Leupp and his bookkeepers descended on Gouldsboro at one point in the midst of the Panic. There, like Pratt before him, Leupp supposedly discovered not only his gross liability for Gould's failed speculations, but also large discrepancies in the books. "When the Panic of 1857 occurred," wrote Charles Geisst in his 1997 volume *Wall Street: A History*, "the hide market collapsed and Gould lost nearly everything. Word of the collapse soon reached Leupp, who hastily [went] to confront Gould. The younger man simply shrugged off the loss, which had bankrupted both of them, as bad luck."[12] Hoyt, using vivid details taken from thin air rather than from the official coroner's inquest, wrote that "on leaving the train [after his visit to Gould], Charles Leupp took a cab to his Madison Avenue mansion, walked in the door, marched into his library, locked the paneled doors behind him, picked a revolver out of the desk drawer, put the barrel in his mouth, and pulled the trigger, sending a bullet through his brain. All this happened in the summer of 1857, when Charles Leupp gave himself to history as the first notable ruined man . . . to choose death by his own hand rather than public dishonor."[13]

Thirty years after Leupp's 1859 suicide, a grim Gould—weary of being blamed by uninformed gossip for the leather merchant's sad end—succinctly and somewhat impatiently snapped at a reporter that Leupp was a victim of "his own demons, and nothing else."[14]

Chapter 10

THE GOULDSBORO WAR

W ILLIAM M. EVARTS—the distinguished, Harvard-trained attorney who was destined to act as defense counsel during the 1868 impeachment trial of Andrew Johnson and later serve variously as U.S. attorney general, U.S. secretary of state, and Republican senator from New York—oversaw the long process of settling Leupp's estate in collaboration with David Lee.[1] While these gentleman did their work, Jay did his best to keep the Gouldsboro tannery afloat, a suddenly precarious undertaking given the fact that paper underwritten in whole or in part by Leupp—as were the credit lines maintained by Jay's operation—now became impossible to extend. Indeed, for the short term, Gould's collateral was strictly limited to the market value of the hides and leather he had on hand in the tannery warehouse.

After struggling with this situation for close to two months—at which point the Leupp estate was still not completely settled and the business of Leupp & Company still not reorganized—Gould offered to take the Gouldsboro tannery out of the picture by purchasing Leupp's one-third of the tanning enterprise from his estate and Lee's one-third from Lee. In a detailed letter of proposal to Lee, Gould calculated that a separation at that precise time would benefit all parties, removing a complicating factor from the tangled affairs of Messrs. Leupp and Lee, and also removing credit complications arising for Jay out of his affiliation with Leupp. Just under a year after Leupp and Lee had entered into the Gouldsboro operation with an investment of $60,000, Jay offered to let them out for the same sum. This price, Jay said, was to be paid at a rate of $10,000 per year, the funds for the buyout coming from a joint stock initiative (the Gouldsboro Manufacturing Company) that Jay planned to organize. Through the Gouldsboro Manufacturing Company, Jay proposed to take ownership not only of the tannery but also some $10,000 in hides and leather currently on hand. Lee accepted these terms in a formal document signed 19 December 1859, noting only that his commitment was subject to the approval of Evarts. Nine days later, Evarts objected to the clause giving Gould control of the tannery's inventory. Subsequently the parties signed a revised agreement under which Gould would compensate Lee and the Leupp estate for two-thirds the value of the hides and leather at Gouldsboro.[2]

With everyone finally agreed, Jay was chagrined to receive word from Evarts that the sale could not be completed until the final settlement of the Leupp estate, this still several months away. "The wheels of the Gods," he complained in a letter to his sister Sarah, "turn slow, as do the wheels of the probate court."[3] Forced to continue to do business in the purgatory of quasi ownership and quasi credit, Jay now also found himself having to bicker with Lee as to who would exert management control over the operation until the sale finalized. When Lee insisted that he held authority over the Gouldsboro plant because of his association with the two-thirds ownership block, Jay—grasping tightly his initial management agreement with Leupp and Lee—pointed out that the Gouldsboro property represented the sole holding of a special partnership owned by himself and Leupp & Company, this partnership having been formed under the name Jay Gould, and that the agreement identifying Jay as "sole known partner" and manager remained in force until such time as Leupp's estate was settled. Simultaneous with these discussions, probably in a move to protect himself from too much credit exposure vis-à-vis Leupp & Company, which had suddenly become slow in paying for leather received from Gouldsboro, Jay set himself up as a leather merchant on Manhattan's Spruce Street and started marketing tanned sides from Gouldsboro on his own. (Gould was also, by this time, a silent partner in the Swamp firm of Wilson, Price & Company, Leather

Merchants.) While he did this, he simultaneously pressed Lee to settle Leupp & Company's account, paying all money due the Gouldsboro concern for leather delivered to date, and thus setting the stage for a clean break.

Lee, for his part, had other concerns. Evarts's ongoing investigations of Charles Leupp's assets and debts revealed a bitter truth. While slowly losing his mind, Leupp had allowed his personal financial affairs to slip into disorder. Although he remained quite rich by the standard of his era at the time of his death, the one-time millionaire's total wealth in the autumn of 1859 was just a fraction of what it had once been. "It is positively asserted," reads a credit report that Evarts commissioned from the independent financial reporting bureau R. G. Dun & Company, "that Leupp's means will not exceed $100,000, which is a great deal less than he was thought to be worth."[4] In the wake of this revelation, wishing to do their best for Leupp's three daughters, Evarts and Lee seem—in the early months of 1860, after signing their revised letter of agreement with Gould—to have made a decision to play hardball in settling Leupp & Company's affairs, and to leave no tree unshaken in their quest for dollars for the estate.

After Gould pestered him for weeks to settle Leupp & Company's account, Lee finally acquiesced, making an appointment for Saturday, 25 February. Arriving in Manhattan for the meeting, Gould and his plant supervisor, J. A. DuBois, found themselves put off until Tuesday the 28th, when, after at last gaining access to Lee's office, they were informed that the man had changed his mind about settling accounts, needed to think things over, and would see them again the following morning. When Gould and DuBois returned on Wednesday, a secretary told them Lee was ill and regretted having to cancel their conference.

In fact, having contrived to lure Gould away from the Pennsylvania tannery, Lee had now gone there himself, intent on seizing the property outright. In testimony given several weeks later, Lee would state that his move had been based on Gould's unreliability and inexperience in tanning, and on rumors of mutinous feelings among the demoralized tannery staff. But the notion of Gould's unreliability does not jibe with his record of steady output, nor with a letter addressed to him by Lee, representing Leupp & Company, on 29 December—one day after the signing of the revised sales agreement—in which Lee praised Gould's operation, saying, "Since you have been tanning for our house yours has been the quickest tannage which our books record, showing in one instance the unusual fact of a sale of all the leather before the maturity of the hide notes."[5]

As to the tales of disquiet among Gould's men, subsequent events would show these to be false. Arriving at Gouldsboro, Lee made an impassioned speech about Gould's shortcomings and leveled a charge (unsubstantiated, and never repeated by Lee in the court proceedings that were to follow) of Gould's misappropriating some $25,000 forwarded from Leupp & Company to settle tannery debts. After his remarks, however, he found only about fifteen men willing to take his side in seizing the tannery. Given this unpromising start, Lee sent an agent to Scranton to hire as many armed guards as could be found. The agent returned with ten, after which Lee and his total army of twenty-five barricaded themselves inside the Gouldsboro tannery, prepared for a fight.

As for Jay, his first action was to consult with his attorney, Andrew H. Reeder. The former proslavery governor of the Kansas territory when it was nicknamed "Bleeding Kansas," Reeder promptly urged that Gould take back his property by force. Arriving at the tannery on 5 March, Gould was met at the gates by Lee and his crew, who threatened his life if he did not leave the premises. Early the next day, Gould addressed a crowd of more than two hundred employees and townspeople, persuading some hundred of them to join him in ousting Lee. Gould then invited Lee to surrender in order to avoid bloodshed. Upon Lee's refusal, Jay moved into action.

"I quietly selected fifty men," he told a reporter several days later, "commanding the reserve to keep aloof. I divided them into two companies, one of which I dispatched to the upper end of the building, directing them to take off the boards [of the wall], while I headed the other one to open a large front door." When Jay burst open the door and ran in, he was "immediately saluted with a shower of balls," which forced him to retire temporarily before charging a second and then a third time, at last gaining complete entrée. "By this time the company at the upper end of the tannery had succeeded in effecting an entrance, and the firing now became general on all sides and the bullets were whistling in every direction. After a hard-contested struggle on both sides, we became the victors, and our opponents went flying from the tannery, some of them making fearful leaps from the second story."[6] Three men received wounds. David Lee, whom Jay immediately cast out of Gouldsboro, absorbed a piece of buckshot in one finger.

Gould and Lee wound up in the courts. Suits and countersuits went on for seven years while the Gouldsboro tannery languished and lost all value, incapable of transacting business while the lawsuits progressed. Lee would eventually win a settlement of some thirty-five hundred dollars against Gould, partial payment for Lee and Leupp's share of the hides and leather at Gouldsboro in late 1859. In 1868 Gould would sell his interest in the Gouldsboro property to Lee for a grand total of one dollar, and do so happily, pleased to close that chapter of his career, a chapter that, though tangled, had led him inevitably to the next rung of his life.

After the "Gouldsboro war," Gould was forced to start over both financially and professionally. At the start of 1859, when Leupp and Lee first came in with him at Gouldsboro, he'd estimated his personal net worth at about $80,000—his chief assets being his share in the tannery, 9,000 acres of Pennsylvania forest that he owned outright, and another 30,000 acres for which he controlled the rights to bark. As late as February 1860, just weeks before the battle at Gouldsboro, R. G. Dun & Company described Gould as "a smart, enterprising young man of good character and habits, reliable in his statements."[7] But the publicity of the Gouldsboro fight and Lee's charges of malfeasance, however unwarranted or unprovable, soon worked to undermine both Jay's reputation and his credit. In a memorandum of April 1860, the same credit-reporting firm expressed concern over "unfavorable reports in circulation respecting Gould which have greatly impaired if not destroyed his credit in the Swamp."[8]

Gould eventually closed his Spruce Street establishment. Then his investment in Wilson, Price & Company evaporated when that firm collapsed, at a loss of $60,000, early in the summer of 1860. Soon he was forced to sell his Pennsylvania bark rights and acreage, albeit at a small profit. Thereafter he spent an autumn of discontent in Manhattan, pondering his future, looking for a toehold and a new career.

◇   ◇   ◇

The fact that Gould lived during this period in the exclusive Everett House Hotel, opposite the northeast corner of Union Square at Seventeenth Street and Fourth Avenue, suggests that despite his losses he did not feel overly impoverished. He was also wealthy enough to pay for his brother Abram, now seventeen, to take business courses in Poughkeepsie, where the youngster now lived with the newlyweds Anna and Asahel Hough, who had recently relocated to that town from a church in Tuckahoe, New York.

Jay enjoyed a brief reunion with Abram, Anna, and all the rest of the family that September when he traveled to Pennsylvania—Canadensis, not Gouldsboro—for the marriage of Bettie Gould to George Northrop's partner, Gilbert Palen. John Burr Gould, grim as an undertaker, also made an appearance. The old man did not have far to travel, as he had recently started living with Sarah and George Northrop in their large but crowded home not far from the Canadensis tannery. (In addition to the five children that Northrop brought to the marriage, George and Sarah now had five-year-old Howard, four-year-old Ida, two-year-old Frank, and a new baby, Reid. Four more girls and two more boys were to follow.[9])

Between her youngsters and her father, Sarah had her hands full. The doddering senior Gould—who'd sold his tin shop in 1858 and then gotten rid of the house on Roxbury's Elm Street in 1860—was by this point unpredictable and mischievous. At one moment a benign and beneficent grandfather, an hour later he'd transform into a dark and contrary inebriate, quickly revealing the result of snorts taken from the bottles he hid about Sarah's house in direct defiance of Sarah's and George's outspoken temperance beliefs. (Sarah would not even allow her children to drink cider or root beer lest they develop the habit of going to a keg for a drink.[10]) "Jay looks at father sadly," Sarah wrote a cousin not long after the Palen wedding. "What he sees in that broken man, I cannot tell."[11] What Jay saw, most likely, was a specter of futile pride and broken dreams from which he would spend the rest of his life in flight. "I am trying," Jay wrote James Oliver a few weeks later, "to start myself in the smoky world of stocks and bonds. There are magicians' skills to be learned on Wall Street, and I mean to learn them."[12]

Chapter 11

A PARTICULAR FUTURE

WRITING IN HIS 1908 MEMOIR *Fifty Years on Wall Street*, banker Henry Clews, a Gould contemporary, wryly commented on the geography of New York City's financial district. Manhattan's shabby avenue of cynical dealing and ultimate greed, he noted, started at a church (Trinity, near lower Broadway) and then rushed downhill to the East River waterfront, a hellish neighborhood that trafficked not just in maritime commerce but in lust, drunkenness, and violence. Describing the same landscape in 1860, just when the twenty-four-year-old Jay Gould began to explore Wall Street, an anonymous commentator for the *New York Tribune* wrote that "the road to Hell is not—contrary to popular rumor—paved with good intentions. It is paved instead with cobblestones, beer and broken promises. That is Wall Street, plain and simple, the place where the faithless mingle, where dreams are shattered and fortunes lost and made."[1]

More than two centuries earlier, Dutch settlers had built an east-west wall across this part of lower Manhattan as a barricade against Indians, pirates, and other dangers. In time, the path along the wall became a bustling commercial thoroughfare. Early merchants built warehouses, shops, a city hall, and a church (the aforementioned Trinity). When New York City served as the U.S. national capital, the focal point of the road was Federal

Hall, on the front steps of which George Washington stood for his inauguration as the country's first president in 1789.

The earliest stock exchange in America was founded one year later, not in New York but in Philadelphia, just as Alexander Hamilton, Washington's secretary of the treasury, issued the first federal bonds to pay down the debt of the Revolution. Informal New York trading, routed by couriers to the Philadelphia exchange, commenced soon after. Local brokers transacted business under a buttonwood tree outside 68 Wall Street. Shortly, in 1792, twenty-four of these traders established a formal New York market. The Buttonwood Agreement mandated that signers trade securities only among themselves, that they set trading fees by mutual agreement, and that they not participate in other auctions of securities. The organization launched by the Buttonwood Agreement would evolve into the New York Stock Exchange Board (in 1817) and in 1863 the New York Stock Exchange.

From the start, the Exchange was a clubby affair. Bylaws required that new members be voted in, and a candidate could be blackballed by three negative votes. The average price of a seat in 1817 stood at $25. It had increased to $100 by 1827 and $400 by 1848. Members wore top hats and boasted—with reason, after the state of Pennsylvania defaulted on notes and scores of Philadelphia brokers closed shop during the Panic of 1837—that their Exchange represented the dominant financial market in the United States. Dominant or not, and despite the rules of membership governing the Exchange, Wall Street as a financial marketplace was hardly the habitué of elites when Gould arrived in 1860. Outside the walls of the stuffy Exchange, on the street itself, virtually any "curb broker" could buy and sell securities. These dealers conducted business literally on the curb, also in the lobby of the Fifth Avenue Hotel, at Delmonico's restaurant, on Gallagher's Evening Exchange, and—after 1864—via representatives in the "Long Room" of Broad Street's "Open Board," which in fact frequently did ten times the volume of the Exchange's so-called Regular Board. (Typically, in the early 1860s, the Regular Board might see $7 million in business on any given day, and the Open Board $70 million.)

It was among the hundreds of Wall Street curb traders that Jay Gould trolled during late 1860 and early 1861, searching for opportunities as the United States disintegrated. Whereas the advent of Civil War meant bloodshed and heartache for hundreds of thousands of Americans on both sides of the conflict, for much of Wall Street it meant only an opportunity for profit. "Along with ordinary happenings," recalled Daniel Drew, almost thirty years Gould's senior and well-established by 1860 as the most sinister and self-serving of operators, "we fellows in Wall Street had the fortunes of war to speculate about and that always makes great doings on a stock exchange. It's good fishing in troubled waters."[2]

Drew was, by all accounts, startling to look at: cadaverously thin and stooped, walking about in the same ancient suit day in and day out, using the stripped shaft of an old umbrella as a cane. His hair was as wrinkled as his clothes, and his manners were as rustic as his roots even though he lived in a fine mansion on Seventeenth Street, near Union Square and the Everett House. Born on a farm in rural Carmel, New York, in 1797, Drew began his career working as a roustabout for a circus and then joined the U.S. Army in 1812, at age fourteen, pocketing a one-hundred-dollar bonus but never seeing any action against the British. Following the war he became a drover who purchased cattle from the local farmers in Westchester and Putnam Counties and then brought them down to Manhattan for resale. During these pilgrimages, Drew usually salted his herd to make them ravenously thirsty and then stopped in the village of Harlem to water up his inventory and increase his cows' weight before selling them by the pound to downtown wholesalers.

Settling in Manhattan in the 1820s, Drew bought the Bull's Head Inn at the corner of Third Avenue and Twenty-sixth Street and thereafter acted as an innkeeper and informal banker for drovers. During the 1830s—at about the same time he began his speculations on Wall Street—he entered the steamboat business on the Hudson River, starting the Peoples Line of steamers and making his first acquaintance with Cornelius Vanderbilt. (Drew later branched out with steam lines extending south along the Jersey coast and north through Long Island Sound.) At the same time Drew earned himself a reputation as an outright liar and cheat. On those occasions when he was caught on the bad end of a deal, Drew would routinely "squat"—Street slang for dishonoring a contract—and take cover behind a bombardment of spurious lawsuits.

By the time Gould arrived, Drew—known variously as "Uncle Daniel," "The Great Bear," "The Deacon," and "Ursus Major"—was something of a legend on Wall Street: a completely unscrupulous master of financial poker.

Drew's particular specialty—aside from "watering" the stocks of firms in which he had authority, manipulating their values far in excess of reality by excessive issuances of securities—was the bear raid. During such a raid, Drew would pool with others to short a particular stock, borrowing shares that were then sold at market price. The speculation of Drew and his colleagues was that the value of the security in question would soon drop, allowing them to purchase more shares on the cheap for return to the owner while claiming the margin between the two prices as their own. In the midst of a typical bear raid, once he was sufficiently short, Drew would spread rumors and otherwise push the price of the selected stock lower. On such occasions, he left little to chance. He once told Gould that to speculate on Wall Street without inside information made as much sense as to drive black pigs in the dark.

Both despised and envied, the outwardly reverent, Bible-quoting Drew provided a case study in speculative success for a whole generation of smart young men who—though they may have arrived on the Street with scruples—quickly realized that ethics and ambition could not easily coexist, at least not south of Washington Square. When writers of a later era chastised Gould for his brazen guile, they seemed to forget that he was hardly alone. In fact he was just one—albeit an inordinately talented one—of a pack and was considerably less brazen and cynical than some.

◇　◇　◇

Jay spent his first months on Wall Street nibbling around its edges, doing small deals, winning and losing, and learning from his mistakes. Intent as ever, the young devotee spent long days researching leads with a monklike dedication. He also studied the moves of the sharpest players and learned how instruments might be leveraged to provide either the cash or the credit necessary to make one's desired next step possible. Every morning at the Everett House he rose early and rushed through breakfast. Then he devoured the financial news in the various New York papers. Thereafter he was on the curb and in and out of brokers' offices, buying and selling all the day, until five or six at night, when he retreated to the Everett House, or to some restaurant, for dinner. Later he would visit Gallagher's Evening Exchange, where the hungriest young self-starters—and Jay was certainly one of these—were always likely to be found.

The round stopped only on weekends. Coming out of the Everett House on the morning of Saturday, 20 April 1861, two weeks after the battle of Fort Sumter, Gould would have seen more than 100,000 ardent supporters of the Northern cause rallying in Union Square. Just across the square from the Everett House, at the intersection of Fourteenth Street and Broadway, stood the brick-faced home of millionaire Cornelius Van Schaack Roosevelt, grandfather of the toddler Theodore. Both the Roosevelt home and the nearby Union Square Hotel flew massive American flags from their roofs. In the square itself, a newly installed bronze statue of George Washington sat wrapped in the very flag that had been fired upon at Sumter. The gathering on 20 April, as banker John Austin Stevens later recalled, was meant to provide a forum in which the general population of New York could entrust "the guidance of their action [to] the merchants of the city, the chief representatives of its wealth and influence."[3] One wonders whether Gould stood and listened as a score of speakers—among them Major Robert Anderson, the hero of the Sumter battle—called the city to arms in support of the Union.

Jay Gould's personal feelings about the Civil War are not recorded. No mention of the weighty political and social issues of his age—abolition, secession, or any other—shows up in his personal correspondence. If he ever received a draft notice, he, like so many others, most likely purchased a substitute to serve in his place, for we know that Gould never wore a uniform. Fixated on business and his own future, Jay appears to have cared little about the wider world and the course of history as it paraded before him. It would be a mistake, however, to presume that Gould was completely apolitical. By family tradition he was a Democrat, and most of Gould's closest associates—such as the attorney Andrew Reeder, who had represented him in the Gouldsboro affair—were ardent proslavery Democrats. Gould's domicile in New York, the Everett House, served as the city's Democratic Party headquarters. And many of the New York politicos with whom Gould would ingratiate himself in future years—among them William Marcy "Boss" Tweed—were power brokers associated with the Democratic Tammany machine. Later in life, Gould would cultivate a number of Republicans as well, most notoriously Ulysses S. Grant. But his imbroglio with Grant was still far off.

◇ ◇ ◇

Busy wheeling, dealing, and searching for a foothold, the serious-minded Jay Gould nevertheless found time to socialize. Even this, however, he did with deliberation and without humor. He seems to have approached all things, even his vain stabs at play, with a machinelike intensity that some found hard to take. Henry Clews told the story of what happened when members of Westchester County's socially prominent Cruger family, whom Jay was anxious to cultivate, invited him out for a Hudson River cruise during the summer of 1861. No sooner had the expedition got under way—Jay's hosts pushing their yacht from the pier at Crugers-on-Hudson, near Croton— when Gould began to make himself unpopular, worrying out loud whether they'd return in time for him to catch his train back to Manhattan. Throughout the afternoon the nervous Gould refused to let the topic drop, repeatedly suggesting that his hosts cut their outing short and return to dry land. Eventually—according to Clews, who got the story directly from a member of the sailing party—the senior Cruger decided he'd had enough and would teach his obnoxious guest a lesson. Coming into shore only minutes before Gould's Hudson River line train was due, the elder Cruger purposely left the centerboard down, causing the yacht to run aground. Then Mr. Cruger told Gould he'd have to swim if he wanted to make his train. Not hesitating, Gould quickly stripped down to "aggressively scarlet undergarments" while the young Cruger females "hid their blushes behind parasols." Then, holding his dry clothes over his head, Jay determinedly beat a one-armed breaststroke to land.[4]

Such incidents reveal a socially uncouth young man who, though he may have possessed ambition, had yet to shake off many of his backwoods ways. Given as well his soured reputation after the Gouldsboro war, not to mention his recent career as a lowly Wall Street curb wheeler and dealer, it seems remarkable that Gould was able to cultivate a relationship with one of the flowers of Murray Hill society. Miss Helen Day Miller had been raised in an opulent family home on Seventeenth Street, not far from Jay's residence at the Everett House. Helen's mother, Ann, was a descendant of two of New York City's oldest families, the Kips and the Baileys. Her father, Daniel S. Miller, himself the descendant of prosperous merchants, had since 1853 focused his energies on managing his various investments on Wall Street. Miller worked out of the offices of Dater & Company, a firm in which he held a partnership. A Dun & Company credit report of 1860 described him as reliable, bankable, and "more than ordinarily bent on making money."[5]

We have no precise record of how Jay and Helen, two-and-a-half years his junior, first met. Although they lived near one another, it seems quite out of the question that the very shy Gould would have simply struck up a conversation with a young lady on the street, as some biographers have asserted. Besides, this simply was not done. More likely, Jay had dealings with Helen's father, who, finding him to be a young man of promise, invited him home to dinner. Despite the fact that Jay lacked polish, he possessed qualities likely to interest both Mr. Miller and his daughter. These included modesty, ambition, and smarts. As well, Jay was a sober fellow blessed with great personal discipline. Thus he himself represented a commodity that, as Miller surely knew, remained in perpetual short supply among the would-be millionaires on the Street.

Jay and Helen were not unalike. Each was unimpressive physically. Jay was short and unmuscled. Helen—whom Jay soon took to calling Ellie—was equally small, thin, and rather plain, with a prominent nose. The two were also similar in that they delighted in quiet pleasures, preferring intimate family gatherings and interesting books to galas and recitals. From her few written remains, Ellie appears to have been the classic "gilded bird" of Murray Hill, one completely content with her gilded cage: a strictly traditional Christian lady dedicated to all the proper charities and subscribing to all the popular bigotries. Like her parents, she loved Jesus Christ, Murray Hill, and the Daughters of the American Revolution, in that order. She likewise joined her parents in distrusting Catholics and Jews and in believing that Protestant America would be remiss in overtolerating either. Therefore it seems reasonable to guess that Jay's Puritan background—and the fact that his great-grandfather was the hero of the Battle of Ridgefield—did not work against his cause as he sat in the Millers' living room earnestly courting his Ellie through most of 1861.

Jay proposed in early 1862. Some biographers, among them Edwin Hoyt in his 1969 book *The Goulds,* have claimed that Ellie's father disapproved of the match with a vengeance that forced the couple's elopement. The existence of a printed wedding invitation among the papers of Jay and Ellie's eldest daughter at the New York Historical Society, however, calls this assertion into question. According to the invitation, Jay and Ellie were married at the Miller home on the afternoon of 22 January 1863. Writing in 1897, Jay's sister Bettie Palen recalled being present at the wedding along with her husband, Gilbert, Abram Gould, and Anna and Asahel Hough. Only Sarah and George Northrop, busy tending to the unpresentable John Burr Gould, stayed away.

After the nuptials, Jay moved out of the Everett House and in with Ellie and her parents. Here he and his wife would remain for a full six years; and here their first three children would enter the world.

◇ ◇ ◇

For close to a year after the wedding, Jay continued to study the art of Wall Street as practiced by the most seasoned speculators. In time, he became a master of stock watering, short selling, pooling, bear raids, bear traps (wherein bears short in a stock are forced to cover their short positions at ever-escalating prices), and other standard tricks of the Street, most of which would not be tolerated today but were standard practice in Gould's time. He developed, as well, into a maestro of margins, one of the many Wall Street wizards capable of creating capital out of thin air and gaining control of companies by using just a few dollars reflected in a hall of financial mirrors: funhouses of convertible bonds, proxies, and leveraged cash. Eventually, Gould's skills at fiscal sleight-of-hand were unsurpassed. But unlike the Daniel Drews of the world, Gould valued Wall Street speculation for the most part as a means toward greater and more complicated ends. He sought, in the long run, to take control of companies that he could manage, improve, and merge. It was thus only a matter of time before he focused his attention on the one sector of the marketplace that offered not only the greatest range and flexibility of financial instruments, but also the greatest promise for long-term growth: railroads.

During the autumn of 1863, D. M. Wilson—with whom Gould had briefly partnered in the leather merchandising firm of Wilson, Price & Company—approached the twenty-seven-year-old Jay with an offer to sell $50,000 worth of first-mortgage bonds in the Rutland & Washington (R&W) Railroad. As Gould well knew, the New York General Railroad Act of 1850, which allowed directors of railroads to issue bonds on their own authority to finance expansion, also permitted the easy conversion of these same bonds into common stock and then back again into bonds. Doing the math in his head, Jay must have quickly realized that just a small percentage of Wilson's bonds, when converted, would establish a controlling interest in the R&W.

Founded in the 1840s for the purpose of providing a link between the marble quarries of Rutland, Vermont, and the Hudson River port of Troy, New York, the small R&W ran just sixty-two miles, from Rutland to Salem and Eagle Bridge in New York's Washington County. At Eagle Bridge, the road connected to the Rensselaer & Saratoga Railroad, which owned the track to Troy and beyond.[6] By the early 1860s the R&W was underused and unprofitable. Its tracks and rolling stock were in poor repair, and its staff was demoralized. Anxious to get out of his significant investment in the road, Wilson offered Gould all his bonds at just ten cents on the dollar.

Using some of his own cash, some of his father-in-law's money, and a small amount of speculative paper, Gould transacted the deal shortly after Christmas in 1863. Effective New Year's Day he assumed the titles of president, secretary, treasurer, and superintendent of the road. Thereafter, for a solid year and a half, Jay spent four to five days a week in Rutland working to improve the infrastructure, traffic, and profitability of the R&W. Gould made his office in the Bardwell House Hotel on Rutland's Merchants Row. What he didn't know about the railroad business, which was considerable, he made a point of learning. "I left everything else and went into railroading," he remembered a few years later. "I took entire charge of that road. I learned the business and I was president and treasurer and general superintendent. . . . I gradually brought the road up and I kept at work."[7] After hiring experienced managers and making necessary repairs, he then needed to drum up new freight and passenger traffic now that the quarries were at a standstill: their men at war, and the large construction projects they routinely supplied being on hold for the duration.

Jay issued new bonds as necessary over the course of eighteen months, both to support infrastructure improvement in the line and to help finance payroll in the short term. One Charles Frost—a native of Salem who was to have a lengthy career as a baggage man and conductor on the road (eventually a branch of the Delaware & Hudson Railroad)—began working for Gould as an office boy in 1864. "The duties to which he was assigned were not many or strenuous," wrote Salem town historian William A. Cormier, "and he received in return fifty cents a day. He kept the office clean, ran errands, and at times, went out on the road with his superior." Frost recalled Gould "as a man of small stature and having a countenance of stern and commanding features which were greatly intensified by a thrifty and carefully barbered beard. He chose to remain closely secluded in his private office the greater part of the time when he was in Rutland. . . . He was a man of snap judgment, curt in his remarks, and exacting. Action was ever his hobby, and he was relentless in his efforts to bring about the accomplishment of those things which he set about to do."

At one point when Frost asked for an increase in salary, he was refused on the grounds that fifty cents a day was "big pay for a man." On another occasion, when Frost accompanied Gould to the nearby town of West Rupert, Vermont, for the purpose of measuring wood that had been delivered for locomotive fuel, the famished boy was at first delighted when—in the midst of their ride—Gould proposed a stop for lunch. Disappointment came soon thereafter, however. Instead of taking his assistant to a tavern for a sit-down, Gould picked up his small leather satchel ("such as he was accustomed to carry") and out of it produced an assortment of crackers and dried prunes, which he amiably split with Frost.[8]

Another old local—Elisabeth Hughes, who was interviewed in 1937—remembered that shortly after Gould became involved with the R&W he also made a small investment in the region's burgeoning slate industry (hoping, perhaps, to stimulate freight traffic). "Ben Williams was the quarry boss for Jay Gould," recalled Mrs. Hughes, who had been a little girl at the time, "and every time Jay Gould came to Middle Granville [Vermont] the children would run out to greet him. On seeing us he would say, 'Hold up your pinafore,' and Jay Gould would always drop some copper coins in our aprons for us. I can see him now. He was one of the best-looking men I ever saw. He was always full of pep and dressed so nice." He also—as Mrs. Hughes's story made clear, and as she herself commented—"always loved children."[9]

Early in his career with the R&W, Gould demonstrated his lifelong disinclination to separate himself from family. He always returned to his Ellie every weekend, riding his own trains between Vermont and Eagle Bridge, then continuing to the Hudson River on the Rensselaer & Saratoga line. Frequently he chose to stand in the front engine with the various crews, all of whom he got to know on a first-name basis. Somewhat ironically, given what was to come, most of his journeys on the Hudson between Albany and Manhattan seem to have been on the steamboat *Daniel Drew*. Passing the river towns on the western shore below Albany, Gould routinely got a good though distant view of his native Catskills. But home and hearth for Jay were now quite different from what he'd known in those mountains.

"I am missing my fond wife terribly," he wrote the very pregnant Ellie near the end of January, his first month overseeing the R&W. "I am hoping she is not feeling too delicate or indisposed. I know she is as brave as she is beautiful; and I know the great gift she is about to bestow."[10] Jay was at work in Rutland, after a weekend home in early February, when word came that Ellie had given birth to a baby boy: George Jay Gould. "And how is the little emperor?" Jay asked from Rutland two weeks later, after a lengthy stay in Manhattan to enjoy his new son. "Tell him his father—who misses both he and his mother quite completely—will be home soon, and that the good men of the R&W are quite tired of hearing about his handsomeness. Some say Robert Lincoln is the 'Prince of Rails,' but George's mother and I know better."[11] In a long missive from Pennsylvania, John Burr Gould congratulated the daughter-in-law he would never meet on the birth of a grandson he would never see, but puzzled over where the name "George" had come from. John Gould said he had no recollection of any Talcotts, Burrs, or Goulds who'd worn that stamp. (As he might have guessed, the name came from Ellie's side of the equation, specifically her Kip lineage.) "The boy chirps like a bird," Jay wrote his sister Sarah that May. "We push him in the carriage quite proudly round Union Square and then up to Madison Square and back."[12]

Although not seeing much of them, Gould remained on close terms with all his siblings, writing often. A few months after George's birth, when the Reverend Asahel Hough received word that he'd been appointed superintendent of Methodist missions for the Montana Territory, Jay arranged new accommodations for Abram that would allow him to finish his commercial studies in Poughkeepsie. At the same time, he did his best to help Anna as she prepared to depart for the Montana wilderness. "In 1864, the day before we started on our long trip to Montana," she remembered years later, "I received a long letter from him bidding me 'good-bye' and, fearing our slender purse would not furnish us all the comfort we needed on such a long hard journey, he enclosed a $100 bill. Dear kind brother. How many times in all his busy life he took time to write me a few lines to remind me I was not forgotten and with it sent a generous gift."[13]

◇ ◇ ◇

George Jay Gould, aged fourteen months in April 1865, was a toddler on a sunny day, stumbling along between his two parents whose hands he held. After a block Jay picked the child up and carried him. The date was the 25th, and the parents, if not the happy little boy, were unusually somber as they emerged from the Miller home and strolled three blocks south to view history. Standing at the corner of Fourteenth Street and Broadway, just outside C.V.S. Roosevelt's opulent mansion, the family watched as Abraham Lincoln's funeral procession moved up Broadway and then swung west on Fourteenth. "Georgie rode on my shoulders and giggled," Jay told his sister Bettie, whose first child—a daughter, Anna—was just three weeks older than Jay's boy. "He talked his darling gibberish to all the horses and all the stone-faced drummers, obviously with no idea of the solemness of the occasion. God bless him. Of course, the whole sight was quite profoundly moving for everyone old enough to realize. The papers call Mr. Lincoln the final casualty of the war, and the papers are not wrong. Therein lies the only good news. We are all, north and south, well-quit of this futile fight. Now is the time to bury our animosities with our dead, and get on with constructive business. Enough good meat has been wasted on the dogs of war. This is the moment for new enterprise."[14]

The sister to whom Jay wrote was about to embark upon a new enterprise herself—leaving Canadensis with her husband, Gilbert Palen, for a place some fifty-seven miles to the west: Tunkhannock, Pennsylvania. Here the Palen brothers—without George Northrop, who remained focused on the Canadensis operation—were planning to build yet another tannery. Family correspondence suggests that Gould may have put a small amount of capital into this new venture, but only on condition—readily agreed to by the Palens, who were well aware of Gould's damaged reputation in the Swamp—that his involvement as silent partner remain strictly confidential.[15] The Palens' Tunkhannock tannery, unlike Northrop's Canadensis concern, would remain a going business for decades, closing only in 1931.

While publicly keeping his distance from the Palens' tannery, Gould remained energetically hands-on when it came to the Rutland & Washington

Railroad. During May 1865, he sold control of the R&W to William T. Hart, a Hudson River steamboat entrepreneur who, like those other old steamboatmen Drew and Vanderbilt, saw the future and was now interested in railroads. (Hart already controlled the Rensselaer & Saratoga, the line that connected the R&W to the Hudson.) Jay realized more than $100,000 on this one transaction—his first truly enormous payday. But he was not done. A week later, as had previously been agreed, he and Hart incorporated the Troy, Salem & Rutland Railroad, this representing a consolidation of the R&W with the Rensselaer & Saratoga: a new and dynamic rail operation poised to own its market.

"I believe," the would-be monopolist wrote Hart, "that consolidation will prove both essential and inevitable for a score or more roads in the coming decade. Far better than mere cooperation is tight coordination, close vertical integration, unwatered economy-of-scale, and unchallenged market domination wherever possible. Of particular importance, of course, are routes between major cities; but also vital will be routes linking quarries, forests and other resources with key ports, or water-links connecting to key ports."[16]

Ever since boyhood he'd had a fascination with maps. Now the one-time surveyor scrutinized his maps with a freshly engaged eye. Noting commercial hubs and terminuses along with key resource and factory sites, he studied the small railroads dotting the landscape as one would the pieces of a complex jigsaw puzzle, pondering which among the myriad possible combinations might yield maximum economy and profit.

"We are at a moment," he wrote James Oliver—once his teacher, now his sounding-board—"where there is a particular, inevitable future waiting to be made. I see things very, very clearly. I feel inspired with an artist's conception. Divine inspiration? I cannot say. But my road is laid out before me in the plainest of ways." To this he added that he felt as if "all the wheels" had finally been installed on his life. Not only did he have professional focus, "but also the meaning that is family: a wife and child to fight wars and build castles for. Now that I am at this place, it is a puzzlement to me how I endured before. Everything prior seems to have been boxing in the dark, scraping without reason. Now I have my road to walk and my reason for walking it. Now the pieces fit, and this thing ambition is no longer blind but divine, a true and noble and necessary path."[17]

Work and family would remain his two hallmarks to the end of his days.

MUCH TO GET DONE

THROUGHOUT 1865 AND INTO 1866 Jay spent roughly half his time overseeing the consolidation of the Troy, Salem & Rutland Railroad, all the while impressing William Hart with his powers of organization and his capacity for innovation. On several occasions, when legislative help from Albany became necessary, Gould got back in touch with the attorney and lobbyist Hamilton Harris, sixteen years his senior, whom he'd first impressed twelve years earlier as a boy at work on the Shakersville plank road.

Harris held considerable influence in Albany. His older brother Ira had served fourteen years (1846–1860) as one of the thirty-three elected judges constituting New York's so-called Supreme Court (actually the lowest court in the state). Later, in 1861, the people of New York had elected Ira Harris U.S. senator on the Republican ticket. (Harris's opponents had been William M. Evarts, with whom Gould still dealt on occasion in their efforts to settle the Gouldsboro tannery's accounts, and newspaperman Horace Greeley.) Once in Washington, Senator Harris had become a devoted and close friend to Abraham Lincoln. The senator's daughter Clara, together with her fiancée—and also stepbrother—Major Henry R. Rathbone, shared Abraham and Mary Lincoln's box at Ford's Theater on the night of the assassination. Rathbone received a knife wound trying to stop Booth from escaping. As for Hamilton Harris, by 1865, when Jay Gould reentered his life, the distinguished former district attorney for Albany County chaired the state's Republican committee.

The twenty-nine-year-old whom Harris encountered in 1865 hardly resembled the man-child the attorney had met in 1853. Though still short—just barely reaching five feet—Gould now seemed aged beyond his years. Perhaps to compensate for his receding hairline, the mature Jay hid much of his face behind a beard and mustache. His eyes—which flashed with excitement and energy whenever he talked of business—were otherwise sunken and wreathed with bags. If he ever complained at all about anything, it was tiredness. His lack of physical stamina was perhaps a lingering result of his bout with typhoid fever more than a decade earlier. The attorney remembered that his friend's hands were quite small, almost ladylike, and that Gould nervously rubbed them together, one over the other, while contemplating a problem or enunciating a solution.

"That little exercise," said Harris, "seemed the only form of hyperactivity his frail form would allow outside the parameter of his energetic mind. Of course, he rarely complained about his health or his obvious tiredness. Jay did not choose to waste conversation on so trivial a topic as his physical well-being. . . . Jay seemed intent on husbanding himself, saving himself, for the battles of the marketplace. He suffered neither fools, nor smalltalk, gladly. Although he could be made to chuckle at a well-told joke, he would not, for example, tolerate lengthy, meaningless discussions of the weather. Invariably polite-to and solicitous-of everyone, whether sweeper of the floor or commander of the fleet, he would nevertheless extricate himself quite promptly from any interaction that seemed without point. One got the feeling that he did not believe he had time to waste, that he thought his hours might be short, and that he had much to get done."[1]

Friends, relatives, and business associates noted Jay's economies of action: the way he hoarded his time and his capacity for focus as much as he did his dollars. "We have nothing to spare for subtleties," he would tell an assistant. "We must look at accomplishing big things in big ways." Early in his career, during a meeting with subordinates who exasperated him by bickering about whether a particular move might be too audacious, he insisted that they keep their eye on the ball. "The procedure, gentlemen! The procedure! We need not hesitate about *dimensions*."[2] Just as he demanded prompt and invariable wit from himself—logic that cut to the heart of matters immediately and did not allow itself to get muddled in meaningless detail—so, too, did he respect, admire, and reward the same in others, high and low. "Young Murray, assistant manager of the road from Rutland to Eagle Bridge, surprised me by taking it upon himself to offer limited discount drayage for the corn wholesalers in season," Gould wrote Hart in September 1865. "In this way we suddenly become competitive with the wagon-haulers, and excess capacity that had gone empty is used. Every discounted dollar is pure profit. There will be something special for Mr. Murray this Christmas, and we will do ourselves a favor if we keep him in mind for other things."

Gould's abilities as an entrepreneurial talent scout, selecting the natural leaders from among the naturally led, the innovators from among the drones, would loom large in the making of his fortune. In time he would surround himself with an assortment of lieutenants who had little in common other than their drive, their smarts, their inventiveness, and their humble origins. "The best schools only rarely produce the best men," he wrote. "The school of the street seems the one that teaches the most important lessons to those who have the capacity for learning them."[3] Hamilton Harris had been raised on a farm some hundred miles to the west of Roxbury, in New York's Cortland County. In time, Gould's inner circle would also include a former Vermont peddler, an Italian immigrant whose only formal training was as a deckhand on square-riggers, and a onetime grocery clerk from Upstate New York. Gould's natural friends and allies would always be self-made men, and his natural enemies would be those with generational financial inertia on their side: men of inherited wealth, old ancestral connections, and vast social pretensions.

During the hours when he was not focused on the affairs of the Troy, Salem & Rutland Railroad, Gould continued to play the games of the Street, harvesting dollars and hoarding his capital to fund future plans. Operating out of Dater & Company, he acted rather like a modern day-trader, but without the Internet and without Securities and Exchange Commission regulation. Jay coordinated his business with other bulls or bears—whatever the day's opportunity called for—and joined dozens of speculators just like himself in (as Henry Clews put it) "milking the Street from every tit."[4] This metaphor was more than apropos for a onetime dairy boy like Gould. By the time old John Burr Gould died, on the eve of St. Patrick's Day in 1866, Jay could— if he wished—have purchased the old family farm plus twenty more like it for cash. One wonders if so self-satisfied a thought as this was in Gould's mind as he and his family traveled back to Roxbury to lay John Burr Gould in the old plot near the Yellow Meeting House. Probably not.

John Burr Gould passed away at Sarah's house in Canadensis of "the old Gould disease," tuberculosis. Sarah, George, and their brood came to the Catskills with the corpse, meeting up with the Palens, who came in from Tuckhannock. Anna and Asahel Hough, far off in the west, could not make the trip. Twenty-two-year-old Abram, meanwhile, journeyed to the funeral from Salem, New York, where Jay had recently set him up as a "time-keeper" for the Troy, Salem & Rutland. The large extended clan virtually took over Roxbury's one hotel. In addition to Howard, Ida, Frank, and Reid, the gag-gle of Northrops now also included two more daughters: four-year-old Mary and one-and-a-half-year-old Alice. As well, both Jay and his sister Bettie brought new babes in arms. Ellie Gould had given birth to a boy, Edwin, less than a month earlier, on 25 February, and Bettie Palen had de-livered a son, Rufus, on 6 March. Jay's friend Peter Van Amburgh would re-member Jay's oldest boy, George, and Anna Palen, both toddlers, scampering happily among the headstones during the funeral service.

All told, ten of John's grandchildren were in attendance. The eldest of them, eleven-year-old Howard Northrop, later joined his uncles Jay and Abram—along with Van Amburgh, Abel Crosby, Hamilton Burhans, and Simon Champion—for a walk to the outskirts of town. There the party stopped to chat with the current residents of the Gould homestead, the George Bouton family. Later on, Jay visited Edward Burhans, with whom he'd buried the hatchet with regard to the Roxbury land speculations several years earlier. Since their last meeting, Burhans had served a term (1858–1859) in the New York State Senate as a Democrat representing the Fourteenth Dis-trict. He and Jay talked casually about common Albany acquaintances. Jay likewise gossiped with Edward's daughter Maria, now married to Peter Lau-rens, the man who had succeeded him as clerk in her father's store.

The funeral marked the only time Jay's wife laid eyes on the face of her father-in-law: stiff, cold, and stern in his narrow box, the years of disappointment and dissipation etched clearly on his haggard face. More happily, it also marked Ellie's first meeting with Jay's eldest sister, Sarah. These two were destined to become close friends and allies. Bettie Palen would recall Abram sobbing during the evening after the burial, not so much over the loss of his father as over the fact—as he told them all—that never again were so many of their scattered family likely to be gathered together in the same place at the same time.

It was, most certainly, the closing of a chapter: one they must have looked back on with mixed emotions. Jay's and his siblings' sorrow at the loss of their father was surely moderated by a sense of relief. Writing many years later, Sarah would make a half-hearted stab at emphasizing the positive about her father, saying that it was from John that Jay had inherited, if not his business skill, then at least "his indomitable will."[5] But the truth was that Jay and John Burr Gould could not have been less alike. In his own eyes, and in the estimation of those who knew him best, John Gould had been a failure on all of life's most important fronts. He'd let his children down both economically and emotionally; and his subsequent collapse into alcoholism had provided an all-too-bitter coda. "My father met many unconquerable challenges," Jay commented charitably, long after John Burr Gould was in the ground. "He walked a hard road. The world did not open up for him as it does for some. He was haunted by unfulfilled aspirations, broken dreams, empty hopes. He drank from a bitter cup, and did so more than once. I have tried to make it my business to achieve some of the things that were denied him. In that way, perhaps, I can honor my father with my actions. That has been my philosophy. That has been my best hope. We all give—or should give—the best that is in us; but what he had inside was just not enough. He was not blessed with the stuff of success."[6]

◇　◇　◇

By the time he buried his father, Jay Gould had achieved prosperity but not unrivaled wealth. Approaching age thirty, he was, by the standards of his day, quite rich: worth several hundred thousand dollars. But he was by no means a millionaire. He was also not well known beyond his close circle of business associates. But all that would change soon enough. The stage was already being set for Jay Gould's high-profile career with the Erie Railroad.

Chapter 13

THE ERIE IN CHAINS

E ARLY IN 1867—at about the same time his father-in-law Miller retired from Wall Street and sold his interest in Dater & Company—Jay Gould helped found a new trading firm: Smith, Gould & Martin. His partners were Henry N. Smith, a veteran broker, and Henry Martin, a banker hailing originally from Buffalo. In the midst of daily speculations, Martin usually manned the firm's office while Smith and Gould strode the Street, transacting deals large and small for themselves and a steadily growing list of clients, many of them British investors with large accounts. It was Jay's connection with Smith, Gould & Martin that would bring him into the Erie Railroad's murky boardroom.

The Erie had started off in 1832 as the grandest of visions: a mighty and vital rail link between New York harbor and the Great Lakes. But it took nineteen years for the line—completion of which required cooperation from many distinct municipalities and dozens of local commissars—to finally become a reality. Even then, the Erie fell short of its original inspiration. The "completed" road ran not from Manhattan to Buffalo, as originally planned, but from Jersey City (directly across the Hudson from Manhattan) and Piermont (on the Hudson's western shore some twenty miles above Manhattan) to the small village of Dunkirk on Lake Erie. Worse still, political exigencies related to New York State's financing of the project forced the Erie's rail bed onto many miles of poorly graded terrain in southern New York State. The resulting track infrastructure was at once massively expensive to maintain and inappropriately placed for servicing lucrative freight traffic originating in northern Pennsylvania. Additionally, the Erie was a shambles mechanically. More than thirty major accidents occurred on the line in 1852 alone.

Elected to the board of the Erie Railroad in 1853, Daniel Drew was made treasurer in 1854 after lending the troubled Erie a desperately needed $1.5 million, this amount being secured with a mortgage on the line's rundown engines and rolling stock. Intent on recouping his Erie investment and then some in short order, Drew quickly became adept, under the General Railroad Act of 1850, at using the convertibility of Erie bonds to manipulate the amount of Erie common stock, and thereby the stock's price. With the Erie being traded in several venues on Wall Street—the Exchange, the Open Board, Gallagher's, and elsewhere—Drew (who was quickly nicknamed the Erie's "speculative director") routinely benefited from confusion. He developed the habit of dumping Erie stock and driving down the price in one market while shorting the same stock in another exchange, after which he'd buy back some of the shares on the cheap in preparation for a repeat performance. Drew's interest in the Erie extended only as far as manipulation of its stock. His ambition was to loot his own corporation, squeezing out cash while reducing the firm's equity and allowing the line itself to remain in shambles. Financial pundits soon took to calling Erie stock "the scarlet woman of Wall Street," a whore serving Drew's purposes.

The year 1859 found the company's stock at $8, down $25 from its all-time high of $33, this depreciation largely due to the Panic of 1857 and the games played by the speculative director. As well, the virtually bankrupt firm was in receivership. Numerous creditors stood at the gates, the mercurial and mercenary Drew first in line among these unequals. Given this state of affairs, Erie shareholders breathed a unified sigh of relief in 1861, when the line hired the no-nonsense Nathaniel Marsh as its president. Marsh reined in Drew's speculations and also reorganized the firm in January 1862. Early in his tenure, Marsh converted the Erie's numerous unsecured bonds, together with the accumulated unpaid interest on those notes, into preferred stock. This left the struggling concern with a funded debt of nearly $20 million, common stock in excess of $11 million, and new preferred stock in the amount of $8.536 million. With his financial house in order for the short term, Marsh next began to increase his business: acquiring a new short line to Buffalo, completing an essential "long dock" at Piermont to facilitate freight transfer, and securing an entrance to the rich market of Pennsylvania's coalfields.

More important, Marsh also positioned the Erie to help service the western Pennsylvania fields where oil had been discovered in 1859. Although the Erie did not reach to that region, it connected to the new Atlantic & Great Western Railway (A&GW), which ran close by the oil reserves and thus— it seemed—would be in a position, over time, to greatly impact the business and value of the Erie. Very early in 1864, Marsh contracted to pay the A&GW a bonus for all flow-through eastbound traffic. Additionally, as part of the agreement, he promised to provide the A&GW with some $5 million in rolling stock to increase the A&GW's overall capacity and thus the amount of traffic the firm would be able to route east via the Erie.

In all of these endeavors Marsh was helped—just as Gould had been helped during his eighteen-month-long resuscitation of the Rutland & Washington—by war inflation and the war economy generally, which increased traffic for railroads overall and reversed the extended rate cutting that had cannibalized trunk line earnings nationwide between 1857 and 1860. By the spring of 1864, when the savior Marsh suddenly died, he'd tripled traffic on the Erie and had the firm headed toward long-term solvency. But in the wake of Marsh's demise, and with the end of the Civil War boom, the Erie eventually (in 1866) was forced to borrow almost $2 million in order to fulfill its rolling stock commitment to the A&GW. The lender was none other than Daniel Drew, who demanded that the capital he extended be secured with 28,000 shares in the corporation and $3 million, face value, in bonds convertible to 30,000 shares of stock.

The Erie's floating debt now stood at a massive $3.624 million, and well-founded rumor suggested a general relapse into malfeasance by its treasurer. As early as 1865, the Erie was said to have made a mysterious payment of several million dollars abroad to settle its debt to an unnamed director, most likely Drew. The most astute analysts and commentators of the Street suspected Drew of other pilfering as well. "It is really remarkable," commented the editor of *American Railroad Journal,* "that this road, doubled in value by its connection with the Atlantic & Great Western, should flounder around as it does notwithstanding its enormous receipts."[1]

The editor, although correctly skeptical of the Erie's accounting, had overestimated the value of the Erie's link with the A&GW. The two railroads severed friendly connections in 1866. Directors of each line anticipated an eventual break in all business relations and interchange traffic, when the A&GW—counting on promised foreign investment capital—decided to create its own rival route to the sea. Soon, however, the London financial crisis of that year caused the A&GW's plans to fall through and left it dangerously close to bankruptcy. Worse still for both roads, the A&GW's monopoly on oil traffic was shortly lost when the Pennsylvania Railroad linked Pennsylvania's Oil City with the East Coast via a controlled line, the Philadelphia & Erie. This took a direct route from the oil country to New York City that was far shorter and more cost-effective than the A&GW/Erie route.

To maintain its oil business, the A&GW—and, by extension, the Erie—was forced to slash oil drayage fees and start a price war with the Pennsylvania Railroad. The average rate per ton on the A&GW dropped from $3.70 in 1865 to $2.87 in 1866. Although this drop occasioned nearly a 50 percent increase in the amount of oil shipped via A&GW/Erie, the earnings of both firms suffered severe declines. Rates and earnings dropped even further in 1867, despite another rise in volume, raising concern among Erie shareholders and bondholders that their railroad—which now nursed a floating debt of some $6 million—was on a collision course with disaster. "It cannot be disguised," wrote one industry observer, "that very great uneasiness prevails in interested circles with regard to the condition of this road."[2]

Given the tentative state of the Erie's finances and market position, the firm's executive committee was understandably dubious when Boston banker John S. Eldridge, eager to build a direct line running from Boston to the Hudson, proposed that the Erie guarantee interest on $6 million in bonds for the fledgling Boston, Hartford and Erie (BH&E). As inducement, Eldridge dangled the possibility of the Erie's gaining an annual gross of some $2 million from business linked to the new road, which, he emphasized, would be very direct and efficient, with few short curves and excellent grades overall. As Eldridge pointed out, his line would cross no fewer than eleven other roads, offering maximum potential for delivering the Erie's freight, most especially Pennsylvania coal and oil, to central New England. He added that the line would prove an efficient route for eastbound cargo headed for the port of Boston. What Eldridge left unsaid—and what the Erie directors surely realized—was that the newly proposed line faced established and well-funded competition from the existing Boston & Albany Railroad. Running to the north of and parallel with Eldridge's proposed line, the B&A linked through to one of the best-financed railroads in the country, Cornelius Vanderbilt's New York Central. Efficient and highly regarded, the B&A and the New York Central together represented a total investment of some $17 million, whereas the total capital liability Eldridge proposed for the Boston, Hartford & Erie was an enormous $40 million.

The Erie board hesitated to support the proposed BH&E. When they finally—after much lobbying on the part of Eldridge—voted in June of 1867 to guarantee interest payments of $140,000 annually for $4 million of the BH&E's bonds through 1867 and 1868, their offer included a maze of asterisks. The Erie required that the BH&E must itself sell enough bonds to finish the line to the Hudson and make its own arrangements for satisfying interest on those notes; that it must set aside enough of its gross revenue to match Erie's guarantee, thereby guaranteeing Erie's guarantee, so to speak; and that it must allow the Erie to set rates and fares on interchange business moving eastward.

Unhappy with these caveats, Eldridge began buying Erie stock in order to take control of the corporation. This maneuver, in turn, led to a fascinating conflagration of competing titans.

◇   ◇   ◇

As early as 1857, Cornelius Vanderbilt had begun to buy heavily into the depressed stock of the struggling Erie. His long-term but by no means urgent ambition was to eventually gain a dominant interest in the line. By 1859, Vanderbilt had gotten himself elected to the Erie board, on which he would serve until 1866. After that year, he installed his nephew Frank Work, a devoted if unbrilliant model of diligence and loyalty who would, generations later, gain minor fame as the American great-great-grandfather of Diana, Princess of Wales.

By mid-1867, when Vanderbilt at last decided to make his dominance of the Erie complete, he stood at a very interesting angle to the weary Scarlet

Woman. The Harlem Railroad (acquired in a cornering move by Vanderbilt, one avidly fought by Drew) had given the Commodore a terminal in Manhattan; the Hudson River Railroad (acquired, again, in a hard-fought battle against Drew) extended Vanderbilt's rail empire up the river's eastern shore all the way to Albany; and from Albany, Vanderbilt's New York Central shot up the Mohawk Valley to Buffalo, connecting with the Lake Shore Railroad (of which Vanderbilt owned a significant piece) as far as Toledo. In this way Vanderbilt's combined properties—well financed, well managed, and well maintained—offered shippers and passengers what the Erie could not: a reliable, cost-effective route from Manhattan to the Great Lakes. Through most of 1867, Vanderbilt was largely focused on the next phase of his expansion: gaining control of the Michigan Southern Railroad and its Chicago terminal.

Born just three years apart, Vanderbilt and his Erie colleague Drew were alike in that neither made any pretense of being a gentleman. Each was considered vulgar by New York Society. As well, each was voracious about acquiring wealth. "I have been insane," Vanderbilt once told a reporter, quite unapologetically, "on the subject of moneymaking all my life."[3] But there all similarity ended. A genuine thief when it came to business, the ostensibly devout Drew was pleasant enough in person: gracious, amusing, able to tell a good story. Vanderbilt, although enjoying a well-earned reputation for honesty, was mean-spirited, vain, and blatantly irreligious. He grew increasingly and unaccountably more miserable and bitter with every lurch forward of his fortune, and he delighted in making life torture for everyone around him: not just his employees but also his family. Ironically, the closest thing Vanderbilt had to friends were the old operators—such as the deceitful Drew—with whom he alternately warred and allied himself through the decades, and for whom he eventually developed a certain twisted and quite nonsensical loyalty. Vanderbilt had a long history of chastising such sharp players as Drew one day and then rehabilitating them the next, granting forgiveness and forging new deals.

Born into poor circumstances at Port Richmond, Staten Island, in 1794, Vanderbilt quit school at age eleven to work for his father, a farmer and ferryman. When Cornelius turned sixteen he persuaded his mother to give him a hundred dollars for a boat, with which he launched his own ferry and freight service between New York City and Staten Island, a successful venture that allowed him to pay back his mother the hundred dollars plus a bonus of $1,000 within the year. During the War of 1812, Vanderbilt received a government contract to carry supplies to the forts around New York. Large profits from this venture allowed him to build a schooner and two other vessels for coastal trade. He got his nickname, "Commodore," by commanding the largest schooner on the Hudson River.

By 1817 he possessed $9,000 in addition to his interest in the sailing vessels. Shortly thereafter, however, he sold his sailing ships and—looking toward the future—embarked upon a career in steamboating. During 1818 he placed himself under the employ of one Thomas Gibbons and began operating a steam-ferry service between New Brunswick, New Jersey, and New York City, this being an important link on the New York-Philadelphia freight, mail, and passenger route. Vanderbilt charged his customers one dollar, whereas his rivals—Robert Fulton and Fulton's sponsor in invention, Robert Livingston—charged four dollars for the same trip.

Fulton and Livingston soon sued Gibbons and Vanderbilt, protesting that they had a legal monopoly on Hudson River traffic. The case, now a famous one, eventually reached the U.S. Supreme Court. The 1824 decision in *Gibbons v. Ogden* struck a blow for free trade by nullifying the navigation monopoly New York State had granted Fulton and Livingston and by giving teeth to the constitutional principle that interstate commerce came under the authority of the federal government. Vanderbilt subsequently gained control of much of the shipping business along the Hudson River. During the next eleven years, the Commodore made himself and Gibbons a fortune. Vanderbilt's wife also made money managing the New Brunswick halfway house where all travelers on the Gibbons line had to stay.

Near the end of 1829 Vanderbilt decided to go on his own, giving new competition to Daniel Drew's Peoples Line between New York and Peekskill. Embarking on a price war with Drew, Vanderbilt eventually forced him to withdraw from the New York–Peekskill market. Next Vanderbilt challenged the Hudson River Association in the Albany trade. Once again he cut rates, but this time his competitors paid him to move his operations elsewhere. So he opened service on Long Island Sound to Providence, Boston, and points in Connecticut, once again entering into direct competition against Drew. The Commodore's vessels offered passengers not only comfort but often luxury. By the 1840s Vanderbilt was running more than a hundred steamboats, and his company had more employees than any other business in the United States. Vanderbilt is credited with bringing about a great and rapid advance in the size, comfort, and elegance of steamboats, creating the vessels that were shortly dubbed "floating palaces."

Never satisfied, Vanderbilt always looked for new opportunities, and found them. During the California Gold Rush of 1849, people traveled by boat to Panama, then by land across the Isthmus, after which they boarded steamers for the California coast. Vanderbilt challenged the Pacific Steamship Company by offering similar service via an overland route across Nicaragua, which saved six hundred miles and cut the going price by half. This move netted him over $1 million a year. In the process he improved the channel of the San Juan River, built docks on the east and west coasts of Nicaragua and at Virgin Bay on Lake Nicaragua, and made a twelve-mile macadam road to his west coast port. He also began construction of a fleet of eight new steamers. Vanderbilt's route was not only less expensive but two days shorter than that via Panama. He soon owned that market.

Throughout the 1850s, Vanderbilt also dabbled in the North Atlantic trade, attempting to compete with the Cunard and Collins lines for passenger traffic between New York and Le Havre. When this venture proved unprofitable, he sold his Atlantic line for $3 million just as the first guns of the Civil War sounded. At the same time, he expanded his railroad holdings, having become intent upon building a rail empire to Chicago and points beyond. As Maury Klein wrote, Vanderbilt's strategy in railroading was "as elemental as it was effective: buy a road, put in honest management, improve its operation, consolidate it with other roads when they [could] be run together economically, water the stock, and still make it pay dividends."[4]

Given this straitlaced methodology and his fairly upright (though cutthroat) business practices, it is surprising that Vanderbilt would sit still for Drew as long as he did. Indeed, as the 1867 elections for the Erie board approached, Vanderbilt at one point resolved to remove Drew from the Erie and busily set about marshaling the votes to oust his old compatriot. At the same time, John Eldridge, intent on seizing control of the Erie board for his own purposes, was beating the bushes for the same votes.

◇   ◇   ◇

Much of the Erie's stock at this time was in the hands of British investors, who, as was the habit, left their shares registered in the "street name" of their New York brokers, this being the most efficient way for brokers to buy and sell shares quickly on their clients' behalf, without undue paperwork. Thus most Wall Street brokers were largely free—unless instructed otherwise—to vote stocks as they saw fit, not to vote them at all, or to sell their proxies in auctions during times of peak demand, times such as those involving wars for the control of company boards.

The thirty-one-year-old Jay Gould and the firm of Smith, Gould & Martin did not possess enough proxies to ensure control of the Erie Railroad. Gould did, however, oversee a large enough bundle of votes to attract the attention of John Eldridge, who made sure to line up his support during August 1867. At the same time, Eldridge allied himself in a partnership with Vanderbilt (the latter very much the senior partner) aimed at decapitating Drew. The net result was to disenfranchise Drew, who was voted from the Erie board, and from his treasurer's post, on 8 October.

Abuzz with gossip about this overthrow and the installation of Eldridge as president of the Erie, the financial press was even more astonished by what happened the next day, as was Eldridge. Early on the 9th, Vanderbilt—after a tearful reconciliation with the apologetic Drew—forgave all, arranged for a nonentity on the board to step down, and reinstalled Drew not only to the board but to his treasurer's perch. On the heels of this event, a reporter for the *Herald* speculated about the possibility of future intrigues among the three lions: Vanderbilt (represented by Work on the Erie board), Drew, and the newly elected president, Eldridge. Only these three, in the *Herald's* estimate, bore watching. The balance of the board were nothing more than "a batch of nobodies."[5]

One of those new board members was Gould. Another was an equally obscure player, a small broker by the name of James Fisk, Jr. No one, not even the men themselves, could have guessed that these two unknowns would soon be notorious as the all-time greatest tag team ever to wrestle Wall Street to its knees.

Chapter 14

BLUE FIRE

LOOKING BACK, few commentators would think it inappropriate that Vermont native James Fisk, Jr., had been born on 1 April (Fool's Day) of 1835. Not that Fisk was a fool. But he was a rather gleeful and thoroughly lovable master of the hoodwink: a most amiable fraud, the quintessential noble and endearing bad boy whom women and bankers alike hoped in vain to reform. The journalist Robert H. Fuller—a Harvard graduate and a childhood friend of Fisk's who eventually wound up among a gaggle of reporters covering his and Gould's most flamboyant business outings—wrote that Fisk's "generosity, geniality and open-hearted good fellowship were as pronounced as his capacity as a swindler. Jim never saw a stock he would not water, a fool he would not rob, or a hungry vagabond he would not feed. The part of him that favored two-headed pennies was very much a man of his times busy combating others who sought the same sort of advantage. The part of him that routinely did so generously for others was unique in a coarse, craven, grasping age. As for his many dalliances and indulgences, tell me with a straight face that New York—that town of so many avid spectators—did not delight in them, just as it did in Jim."[1]

Another journalist would note that Fisk, not deeply philosophical and hardly religious, saw life, business, and love simply as elaborate, absurd, and

ironic games of the boardroom and bedroom. "The phenomenon of his existence," noted a reporter for the *Sun* not long after Fisk had suddenly and
violently ceased to exist, "didn't trouble him a bit, but simply titillated him
as a continual joke."[2]

Like Gould, born one year after him, Fisk had only the barest memory of
his mother, who died when the boy was tiny. He was still quite small when
his father, Jim, Sr.—a peddler and, like old John Burr Gould, a dealer in
tin—married the woman Jim, Jr., would always revere as his mother, Love
B. Ryan. Shortly after their marriage, the Fisks moved from Pownal, Vermont, to nearby Bennington, where they would remain until young Fisk
turned fifteen. Here the boy became close friends with Fuller. "Everybody
liked him," Fuller recalled. "He was the leader among the boys in the village
in spite of the fact that his father, who was an unprosperous tin peddler,
owed everybody who would trust him. [Jim] had a fair skin, with red in his
cheeks and wavy chestnut hair that turned brown when he was older. His
eyes were greenish gray and a trifle prominent—the bold kind of eyes. He
had plenty of self-confidence—'cheek' we used to call it. He was smart in
school, especially in arithmetic."[3]

The geography of Fisk's boyhood, like that of Gould's, was eminently pastoral. Fisk commanded Fuller and a pack of other boys in years of adventures
through the woods that draped themselves about Bald Mountain, the naked
granite ledge below which their town sat. Fisk also marshaled his gang on the
unpredictable Walloomsac River, a stream of plunging cataracts interrupted by
long, placid levels that ran along the broad valley to the south. As Fuller recalled, he and Fisk knew not only every foot of the Walloomsac near Bennington, but also, like Gould and Burroughs at Roxbury, all the trout brooks for
miles around. "We swam in the pools and we built rafts to sail on," Fuller
wrote. "We made fires and roasted our fish on forked sticks and ate them. We
got as sunburned as it was possible to be."[4] The river and woods were as well
a refuge in winter. The broad flanks of Bald Mountain seemed made for coast-
ing; and sections of the frozen Walloomsac were perfect for skating parties,
after which the boys gathered by great bonfires on the bank. To the south, on
clear days, they could see Mount Anthony and further, over the line in Massachusetts, Mount Greylock and other heights of the Berkshires.

When Fisk was fifteen, his father moved the family—which now included Fisk's half sister, Minna—from Bennington in southwest Vermont to

the town of Brattleboro, which sat on the banks of the Connecticut River in the southeastern corner of the state. Here Fisk, Sr.—having cleared his debts and saved up his peddling receipts over many years—built the imposing Revere House Hotel, a three-and-one-half-story Greek Revival edifice destined to dominate Brattleboro's downtown until its destruction by fire in 1877. When the teenaged Fisk, Jr., was not busy waiting tables, he traveled the local roads around Brattleboro peddling wares of all kinds in the tradition of his father, for whom he now worked. Both professions helped him develop his gift for blarney. He was, by all accounts, quite an amusing story- and joke-teller, spouting tales honed on the sharp edge of irony, all of them guaranteed to delight.

After his initial foray into peddling, Fisk traveled the Northeast with an outfit known as Van Amberg's Circus, working variously as an animal keeper and ticket salesman. Then he returned to the peddler's life. In 1854, at age nineteen, he married Lucy Moore, four years his junior and a native of Springfield, Massachusetts. The couple would remain married—and, in their way, devoted to one another—for seventeen years. But they would rarely spend time under the same roof. Indeed, during the last six years of their marriage they maintained completely separate and distinct residences in two different cities: Lucy in Boston and Fisk in New York. "She is no hair-lifting beauty, my Lucy," Fisk told one of his numerous lady friends, the actress Clara Morris, "just a plump, wholesome, big-hearted, commonplace woman, such as a man meets once in a lifetime, say, and then gathers her into the first church he comes to, and seals her to himself. For you see these commonplace women, like common sense, are apt to become valuable as time goes on." In the same breath, Fisk praised his wife's discretion. "Never, never, does Lucy surprise me with a visit, God bless her!"[5] (Lucy in fact had little inspiration for jealousy, just as she had little cause to complain about her husband's numerous infidelities. An inescapable fact had revealed itself early in their marriage: Jim was not Lucy's type. Through most of her long years "alone," Lucy would live with Fanny Harrod, a childhood friend and her inseparable companion.)

Around the time he married Lucy, Fisk began expanding his father's peddling business by using publicity and sales gimmicks he'd picked up during his brief tenure with the circus. Dubbing himself "Jubilee" Jim Fisk, he dressed up in a garish uniform that included a ringmaster's striped pants and top hat. Then he painted his wagon to look like a circus coach with a red frame and yellow wheels. (He would always love being the center of attention, the jovial and loud personality around which all else revolved.) Armed with his regalia and a dazzling script of jokes, the handsome and flirty Fisk quickly developed a brisk and profitable trade selling shawls, utensils, and other knickknacks to bored, easily complimented housewives. (His travels covered all of southern Vermont and New Hampshire, northern Massachusetts, and eastern New York.) In the words of one early biographer, "The matrons and maids from one end of his route to the other could never have been brought to admit that Jim Fisk was not the most captivating peddler, the most stylish driver, and the most princely traveler that ever measured silk, cracked whip, or settled tavern bill."[6] As often happened throughout his short life, not a few of Fisk's flirtations led to something more.

So, too, did his career as a peddler. Fisk's supplier—the venerable Eben D. Jordan of the Boston dry-goods franchise Jordan, Marsh & Company—took due note of Fisk's distinction as one of the firm's most successful dealers. In 1860, Jordan offered him a place in Boston representing the firm at the wholesale level. At first, after selling his route and moving to the city with Lucy, Fisk looked to be a failure in his new role. His charms did not help him in negotiations with the hard-nosed merchants who routinely bought from Jordan, Marsh in volume: men who could not be complimented and prodded into overbuying and overpaying. Only when the Civil War erupted did Fisk's fortunes rise, for only then did he find wholesale buyers who *could* be complimented and prodded into overbuying and overpaying.

Targeting army supply officers—agents charged with the expenditure of vast sums not their own—Fisk moved to Washington, D.C., during the summer of 1861 and opened a "hospitality suite" at the capital's finest hotel, Willard's. Here, once again center stage, and quite happy to have left Lucy behind in Boston, the jovial Fisk entertained lavishly. "[Aided by] some Massachusetts members of Congress," remembered Fuller, "and the member from the Brattleboro district, who was a friend of his, Jim got together the men he wanted and he gave them such good things to eat and drink and smoke that they forgot their cares and enjoyed themselves. . . . Jim was the first in the field in providing a snug refuge where government officials on small salaries could always find a welcome, a good cigar, and a drink of the kind of poison they preferred." As well, when necessary, Fisk administered outright bribes in return for government contracts. "Jim knew how to distribute little presents, as he called them, and keep his mouth shut about it. He always attended to such matters himself."[7]

Despite the payola and despite what were plainly inflated prices, Jordan, Marsh & Company nevertheless—unlike so many other suppliers who were busy giving bribes and overcharging—quickly developed a reputation for quality items delivered in a timely manner: facts that went a long way in helping army buyers decide whose bribes to take. Blankets, shirts, shoes, and other essentials moved by the trainload from Jordan's warehouses to the Union forces in the field. In return, rather than quibbling over Fisk's massive expenses at Willard's (which sometimes ran as high as $1,000 a day), Eben Jordan took his young protégé in as partner. Fisk further endeared himself to Jordan (and to starving southern planters) when he devised a successful scheme to circumvent both the Northern blockade of the Confederacy and the Confederacy's own laws forbidding sales of cotton to the Union. The Southern cotton smuggled to hungry northeastern mills made Fisk a small fortune while also providing the raw material for more Union Army blankets and shirts. (Meanwhile, the man who sacrificed most for the cause of contraband cotton was Fisk's father, who suffered a mental collapse of some kind while representing his son on a furtive cotton-buying expedition, after which he had to be committed for a time.)

As generous as he was mercenary, Fisk was frequently driven by a brash and sentimental benevolence. He first came to national prominence as a colorful, good-hearted philanthropist. Fisk happened to be in Boston on a Sunday in the middle of September 1864 when telegrams brought word of the previous day's fight between McClellan and Lee, a savage battle that left 22,000 dead and wounded on the battlefield near Antietam Creek. (This astonishing figure, the greatest single-day accumulation of casualties in the entire Civil War, was greater than the total casualties suffered by both sides during the American Revolution.) Telling Jordan that they simply had to do something to help the thousands of "poor devils" who lay in need of assistance, Fisk anxiously set about collecting donated supplies for shipment to "the boys," both blue and gray.

A Jordan, Marsh & Company employee who worked with Fisk on the project remembered him at Boston's Tremont Temple surrounded by crates,

boxes, and barrels. "Jim was the center of everything. His remarkable orga-
nizational ability and his boundless energy made a great impression on the
beholders. He was a wonder that Sunday. He just threw his whole soul into
it. He did more in an hour than any other three men, and there were some
fast workers there. He looked after everything, gave all the orders and in-
spected everything. Everybody did what he told 'em to do. The whole thing
was his from beginning to end and nobody was able to take the credit away
from him. Was he proud? What do you think?"[8]

Through the end of 1864, as the Confederacy continued to show sure
signs of faltering, Union Army expenditures dropped. At the same time,
with more and more of the South falling into Union hands, Fisk's profitable
sideline of smuggling Confederate cotton up to Northern mills began to
fade. In this environment, he shut down his D.C. operation and—perhaps
recalling his lack of success with Jordan, Marsh & Company before the war
economy took hold—opted out of the firm, selling his share back to his
friend Jordan for the princely sum of $65,000. A bit later, after a few months
of dabbling with other Boston opportunities that proved unsuccessful, Fisk
packed his bags and headed for the place where his instincts told him he was
meant to be, a place in need of a great impresario, a place of unsure rules, a
place—he said—of "great doings." This was Wall Street, to which Fisk came
as a complete novice.

Twenty-nine, rotund, and very much used to high living after his days in
D.C., Fisk was powered not only by his own usual high energy and the remains of his Marsh profits but by an unusually large dose of uninformed
confidence. After just one week in town he opened a gaudily ostentatious
brokerage office on Broad Street. At the same time, he moved into the luxurious Fifth Avenue Hotel at Fifth Avenue and Twenty-fourth Street, on
the western perimeter of where Broadway and Fifth Avenue crossed Madison Square. Said to be the finest hotel in the city, the Fifth Avenue was itself the site for much after-hours trading in stocks and bonds. Thus it was
not only convenient for everyday living and dalliances but for business as
well. (Once again, Fisk traveled without Lucy, who remained in Boston, living for the time being at the Tremont House Hotel.)

Fisk held regular open houses at his Broad Street offices, treating fellow
brokers and speculators to choice liquors. But this time the men he entertained were not quiet clerks with small aspirations. They were, instead,

wolves with no allegiances—wolves looking for profitable kills. Until he learned expensive lessons, Fisk would remain for several months an unwitting financial lamb easily ambushed by self-serving advice dished out by untrustworthy associates. "He was mercilessly hugged by the bears," wrote one early biographer, "and unceremoniously tossed by the bulls, but with indomitable pluck and a blind trust in the possibilities of the future, he held his ground until the Street had swallowed every dollar of his money and he was ruined."[9] When the market suddenly turned bearish that winter, the unsuspecting Fisk found himself dangerously long in a range of falling stocks, and at risk of going under completely. When a subsequent attempt to short falling Confederate bonds on the London Exchange proved successful, he again went long in the Street—taking advice from some of the same players as before—and came a cropper. Unfazed, Fisk told a friend, "I'll be back in Wall Street inside of twenty days, and if I don't make things squirm I'll eat nothing but bone button soup until Judgment Day."[10]

It is emblematic of the serendipity that so often governed Fisk's life that on the train ride back to Boston from his New York disgrace he encountered a gentleman on whom he would, in the long term, make a great deal of money. John Goulding, a native of Maine, was bound back home after his own period of failure in New York, where he'd hoped to market the patent on an improved device for weaving textiles invented by his father. Fisk knew a little about textile processing from his days with Jordan, Marsh & Company. Showing Fisk his drawings, Goulding explained that the device, duly patented in Washington, was already used in numerous New England mills. All it would take was effective lawyering (which Goulding didn't have) to get the textile manufacturers to pay the royalties they owed on the machine. Settling on $20,000 as a price for the rights, Fisk quickly raised this money from Jordan and other investors. At the same time, for a share of the back-end profits, he engaged a team of attorneys to embark upon dozens of infringement suits that would eventually prove quite lucrative.

Still, the Goulding deal did nothing to relieve Fisk's immediate financial need. For this, he turned once again to his most steadfast benefactor. Using funds provided by Eben Jordan, Fisk reestablished himself in New York in late 1865, once again at the Fifth Avenue Hotel. Here he approached Daniel Drew—a frequent participant in the hotel's after-hours trading sessions—with an offer from a group of Boston investors (including Jordan) to buy Drew's Stonington line of steamers: nine ships navigating Long Island Sound between Manhattan and Stonington, Connecticut. The barely profitable enterprise was one that Drew was glad to be rid of. Fisk brokered it to the Boston syndicate for a lordly $2.3 million, earning himself a fat commission in the process and, more important, earning Drew's profitable attention. The two former circus hands got on well. Within months, Drew, always on the lookout for another friendly broker to lend a hand in his manipulations of the Erie and other stocks, helped establish Fisk in business. By the spring of 1866 Fisk was partnered with one William Belden (the son of a friend of Drew's) in the firm of Fisk & Belden, from which office he actively represented much (though by no means all) of Uncle Daniel's buying and selling.

As one-half of Fisk & Belden, Jim Fisk happily participated in a succession of Drew's plays of Erie stock through 1866, making large brokerage commissions and also benefiting from his own insider speculations transacted on Drew's coattails. No longer a lamb, Fisk had transformed himself into the most capable of Wall Street wolves. The broker W. W. Fowler wrote after Fisk's triumphant return to New York's financial district that "the blonde, bustling and rollicking James Fisk, Jr. . . . came bounding into the Wall Street circus like a star-acrobat: fresh, exuberant, glittering with spangles, and turning double-summersets, apparently as much for his own amusement as for that of a large circle of spectators. He is first, last and always a man of theatrical effects, of grand transformations, of blue fire."[11]

By the end of 1866 Fisk was able to build Lucy and her friend Fanny a $75,000 brownstone on Boston's then-fashionable Chester Street. He likewise upgraded himself to the Fifth Avenue Hotel's most expensive suite of rooms and became something of a fixture at the finest eatery in town: Delmonico's, near the financial district on Beaver Street. Champagne breakfasts, the most exquisite silk suits, and gold-headed canes became his permanent norm. So did actresses and chorus girls, a steady procession of them, all dazzled, one gathers, as much by Fisk's joyous wit and manic energy as by the baubles he dispensed so liberally.

◇ ◇ ◇

This, then, was the man, Drew's hedonistic, garish, tempestuous ally, who joined the somber, puritanical Gould on the Erie board during the autumn of 1867. If Fisk was "blue fire," Gould was anything but. Fuller, who knew both men well, wrote that the "contrast between Jim and Gould was complete. Jim was florid and fond of the table, a weakness that was beginning to show in his figure. Gould was abstemious. Jim was loud and self-confident; Gould was silent and seemed diffident. Jim was bold; Gould was cautious. Jim said what he thought; Gould kept his mouth shut. Jim liked to spend his money; Gould kept his. Jim was generous and open-handed; Gould wasn't. But both men had inexhaustible capacity for work and both were unusually intelligent. They made a formidable combination when they joined forces."[12]

Chapter 15

THE ABUSED MACHINERY
OF THE LAW

GOULD AND FISK came to the Erie board at a time of conflicting interests and diverse, often Byzantine, agendas. Just as the new board assembled,
the Erie's major western connection, the Atlantic & Great Western Railway
(A&GW) went into receivership. The Erie itself, two years after the death
of its erstwhile savior Nathaniel Marsh, remained an unmitigated mess. Already carrying a dangerously high floating debt of $6 million, the misman-
aged and physically broken railroad was about to confront, for the first time,
competition from Vanderbilt's newly consolidated, fiscally and physically
sound trunk line extending from the Atlantic Ocean at New York to the
Great Lakes at Buffalo. Adding even more uncertainty to all of this was
Vanderbilt's presumed dominance on the Erie board. For anyone with eyes
to see, Vanderbilt's agenda was clear: to eventually, on his own leisurely
schedule, gain complete control of the Erie and in that way come to dominate most of the main lines entering New York State from the West. Meanwhile Erie president John Eldridge had only one focus and interest: the
Boston, Hartford & Erie (BH&E)—of which, coincidentally, Fisk's old
friend Eben Jordan was a backer. As for old man Drew, he could only be

counted on to do whatever, at any given moment, would put the most green-backs in his pocket. Drew remained, according to the *Herald*, "a wild card."[1]

The notion of Vanderbilt as the Erie's driving force was slow to be challenged, since Vanderbilt's nephew Work acquiesced that October when the Eldridge recruits on the board proposed and passed a measure guaranteeing interest for $4 million of the BH&E's bonds. To Eldridge's pleasure, if not surprise, the offer from the Erie came without most of the caveats that had been attached to the Scarlet Woman's previous guarantee proposal. All the BH&E had to do was meet a January 1870 deadline for rails and rolling stock capable of carrying 300,000 tons of coal annually. Thereafter the BH&E would also be required to set aside for the bondholders' trustees enough revenue from coal profits to pay the interest on the guaranteed notes. At about the same time that this transaction occurred, Work joined the party when several board members (including Drew, Gould, and Fisk) together with a few outsiders (among them Fisk's partner Belden, Gould's brokerage partners, Smith and Martin, and the Commodore himself) formed a pool designed to bull up the price of Erie stock, this pool to be run by the undisputed master of stock manipulation: Drew.

The first intimations that Vanderbilt and Work were not in undisputed control of Erie's helm came in November, when the Erie board rejected an offer from Vanderbilt to participate in another kind of pool. Vanderbilt proposed that the Erie join together with the New York Central and the Pennsylvania Railroad in evenly dividing the earnings of the three trunk lines into southeast New York, thus avoiding the type of ruinous rate war for which Vanderbilt had become justly famous. By the time he approached the Erie, Vanderbilt already had the Pennsylvania Railroad committed to the plan, and he expected the Erie to come over willingly. (In fact, some writers have speculated that the New York Central–Pennsylvania–Erie pool may have been a key part of whatever backdoor deal making had gone into seating the new Erie board that October.) But when the measure came up before the Erie's board, only Frank Work voted in favor, the other members insisting that Erie's share of the proposed pie was not large enough. One month later—in yet another blow to Vanderbilt—the Erie board overrode a protest from Work and entered into direct negotiations with the Michigan Southern & Northern Indiana to gain the Erie a line to Chicago with which it could compete head to head with the New York Central–Michigan Southern interchange.

While this maneuvering went on, the pool masterminded by Drew slogged along but did not yield instant results. Erie stock moved up slowly, achieving a high of $79 per share by late January 1868, only to collapse back down to $71 in one day's trading on 4 February. Vanderbilt and the others who had authorized Drew to orchestrate heavy purchases using pool funds were baffled, unaware that Drew had privately resorted to his old game of converting bonds, dumping stocks, and shorting—a classic bear raid. As a reporter for the *Herald* was to note, on the day of the collapse "the emissaries of the speculative director exerted themselves . . . to create a panic, and told more falsehoods than usual about stocks in general and Erie in particular."[2] Broker William Fowler, who continued trading the stock that evening long after the Exchange and the Open Board had closed, recalled that the "whole strength of Wall Street seemed to have poured into the halls of the Fifth Avenue Hotel. Daniel Drew, with his face pushed into an expression more than usually somber and solicitous, stood near the grand stairway, watching the writhings of his victims, the late exultant bulls."[3] In the end, Drew made considerable profits for the pool, not by building up the stock but by shorting.

Ironically—and perhaps to Drew's delight—one of the victims who sweated late into the evening on the 4th was none other than Frank Work, who had gone so far as to borrow pool funds from Drew in order to do some speculating on his own and thus benefit from what he believed would be the steady rise in Erie shares. Work was subsequently outraged to find that the shares he'd bought had come from the pool's own brokers. Henry and Charles Francis Adams eventually chronicled Work's dilemma in their book *Chapters of Erie,* but they did so without giving away the embarrassed man's identity. The Adamses wrote that the unscrupulous Drew had actually loaned "the money of the pool to one of the members of the pool to enable him to buy up the stock of the pool; and having thus quietly saddled him with it, the controller proceeded to divide the profits, and calmly returned to the victim a portion of his own money as his share of the proceeds."[4]

Afterward, Vanderbilt—who came away unhappy even though he'd personally racked up substantial gains through this round of Drew's unauthorized machinations—realized his mistake in allowing the uncontrollable speculative director to return to the Erie board. Vanderbilt likewise realized that the board contained few members besides Work on whom he could rely. Therefore the Commodore resolved, at long last, to finish up the lethargic

process he'd begun years before and do whatever it took to gain a controlling interest in the Erie sooner rather than later. Ordering his agents to
begin buying up all the shares of the Erie that they could find, Vanderbilt
simultaneously had Work obtain from New York Supreme Court Justice
George G. Barnard—an easily bribed Tammany Democrat operating in
Manhattan—injunctions prohibiting Drew and the Erie directors from issuing bonds, converting bonds, selling Erie stock, or guaranteeing the bonds
of any other railroad. These injunctions, issued first on 17 February and then
extended on 3 March, were supposed to remain in effect pending the out-
come of a suit to remove Drew as the Erie treasurer and force his return of
the 58,000 shares (28,000 units of stock plus $3 million in bonds convert-
ible to 30,000 units of stock) given him as collateral in 1866. Through this
mechanism Vanderbilt sought to protect himself—and those buying Erie
shares on his behalf—from Drew's usual tricks. By manipulating the convertible shares alone, Drew—if left free to do so—would have been able to
expand or contract the number of outstanding Erie securities by more than
20 percent, according to his whim. From his treasurer's throne, Drew could
also—if left free to do so—manufacture as many more convertible bonds as
he saw fit by getting a majority vote of the board.

At the time there was some $17.5 million in Erie common stock out-
standing, and some $8.5 million in preferred stock. Vanderbilt calculated it
would take something in excess of $10 million combined with what he
owned already to gain absolute control of the Erie. This sum represented a
fraction of the Commodore's net worth. But it also represented far more
than he had liquid, since the bulk of his capital was tied up in the stock of
the New York Central. Still, Vanderbilt remained easily the most bankable
buccaneer on Wall Street, and with Drew and his clique of directors apparently neutralized, he set out to corner Erie shares. As well, he arranged for
wealthy friends such as Leonard Jerome to invest along with him.

◇   ◇   ◇

Vanderbilt's errors were two.

For starters, in sculpting the injunctions that he handed to Judge Barnard
for pronouncement, Work had neglected a key nuance of language.
Barnard's order enjoined both Treasurer Drew and the Erie board from
"selling, transferring, delivering, disposing of or parting with" Erie bonds

and stocks.[5] But as Gould, that avid reader of fine print, readily surmised, Barnard's order contained no words limiting the actions of the Erie's executive committee, the latter being empowered by the corporation's charter to act for the Erie in between regularly scheduled board meetings. So in closed session on 4 March, the executive committee—dominated by Drew, Eldridge, Gould, and Fisk—fired a volley against Vanderbilt's takeover of the road. The committee approved $5 million in bonds and voted their sale to Drew's broker, William Heath. Within hours those same bonds were converted into 50,000 shares. Heath combined these with another 10,000 shares Drew had on hand and dumped the lot onto the market that same evening. (Prior to this, some 251,050 shares had been outstanding.) Vanderbilt's representatives eagerly devoured the newly minted Erie shares, buoying the price. Drew, meanwhile, personally shorted Erie on every board in town, to the eventual chagrin of Vanderbilt, who did not yet realize the true number of Erie shares outstanding or the relative inflation of Erie's per-share price above fair value.

On another front, Vanderbilt had either ignored or not realized one painfully obvious fact. The same highly corrupt court system that he had leveraged to bring injunctions against Drew and the Erie board could be exploited just as easily by others.

Despite its name, New York's "Supreme" Court is actually one of the lowest courts in the state, a court of first rather than last resort. The Supreme Court's judges (four to each of the eight judicial districts at the time of our story, except for Manhattan, which had five) were elected every fourteen years, with the combined judges of a district sitting en banc to constitute that district's first-tier appellate court. In this highly incestuous atmosphere, the justices of the Supreme Court—all of them creatures of their party, most often the Democratic Party—were routinely called upon to review decisions made by their local political allies and brothers on the bench: men who, on the morrow, would wield similar appellate authority over them.

The program of elective judgeships had arisen out of the populist fervor that inspired the new state constitution of 1846—a deep Jacksonian faith in the ultimate wisdom of the common man. In practice, however, as the aristocratic Adams brothers eagerly pointed out in *Chapters of Erie*, the electoral approach filled the benches with political hacks. "The system of electing judges by the popular vote," they wrote, ". . . brought forth bitter fruit, and men had been elevated to the bench who should have orna-mented the dock."[6]

In adjudicating commercial disputes, New York judges were bound by a Code of Civil Procedure authored by Manhattan attorney David Dudley Field and approved by the New York State Legislature not long after adop-tion of the 1846 constitution. Eventually the essence of the "Field Codes" would become law at the federal level, in twenty-six states, and in Great Britain. Although generally a model of excellence, the Field Codes never-theless included certain particulars that tended to complicate matters, at least in corrupt New York. According to these Codes, Supreme Court judges, although elected by voters only in the district where they sat, enjoyed authority that extended throughout the state. Furthermore, they were not barred from entering into cases already under adjudication by another Supreme Court justice in a different district. Additionally, the judges pos-sessed vast, unrestrained powers to issue injunctions and appoint receivers in *ex parte* proceedings where—by definition—only one side of a case was heard. These idiosyncrasies of the Field Codes, the New York Supreme Court's odd appellate structure, and the cronyism of the justices would play major roles in the coming battle for the Erie.

The best of New York's attorneys had long mourned the shortcomings of the Supreme Court. Writing in his diary, Manhattan attorney George Tem-pleton Strong complained that "law does not protect property. The abused machinery of law is a terror to property owners. No banker or merchant is sure that some person calling himself a 'receiver,' appointed *ex parte* as the first step in some frivolous suit he never heard of, may not march into his counting room at any moment, demand possession of all his assets and the ruinous suspension of his whole business, and when the order for a receiver is vacated a week afterwards, claim $100,000 or so as 'an allowance' for his services, by virtue of another order, to be enforced by attachment. No city can long continue rich and prosperous that tolerates abuses like these. Cap-ital will flee to safe quarters."[7]

Thus Vanderbilt should not have been surprised, on 5 March, when Gould, on behalf of the anti-Vanderbilt clique, found a judge of his own. Operating out of the Erie County town of Cortland, Judge Ransom Balcom willingly issued an injunction against any further Erie proceedings in Barnard's Manhattan court pending a hearing in Erie County on 7 April.

For good measure, Balcom also suspended Frank Work from the Erie board. On the heels of Balcom's order effectively closing Barnard's court to all matters relating to the Erie, Vanderbilt ally Richard Schell (lately a member of the Erie pool who had joined Work in his unhappy speculations) prompted Supreme Court Judge Daniel P. Ingraham (of Manhattan) to issue an order on the 6th forbidding the Erie board from transacting any business without Frank Work in attendance.

The air of uncertainty around the company did not go unnoticed. The *New York Herald* commented: "The Street is afraid to hold Erie, and the clique supporting it [Vanderbilt and his cohorts, who together, on the morning of 10 March, held some 100,000 shares] has to bear its full weight. . . . There are rumors afloat that the amount of common stock is far larger than is generally supposed, owing to the conversion of old bonds into stock and the issue of new convertible bonds to an extent which is at present difficult to estimate."[8]

Because of the rumors, as reported in the *Herald* and every other paper in town, the price for the stock began to plummet. When several banks hesitated to advance Vanderbilt money on which questionable Erie shares were to be pledged as collateral, Vanderbilt had to force their hand. He threatened to reduce the value of New York Central stock—in which most New York banks held major positions—down from its current market price of $68 to $50 per share and to ruin several institutions in the process, unless the banks immediately advanced him half a million on the Erie at $50. Surrendering instantly, the banks gave Vanderbilt his money, which he immediately ploughed into Erie shares, buoying the value once more.

Vanderbilt evidently believed that since no rival judge had as yet explicitly vacated Barnard's original order, Drew's stock-manufacturing machinery was still shut down. But even as Vanderbilt's soldiers bought up the latest printing of Erie shares, the Erie's executive committee created a second $5 million in bonds, converted them, and tossed the results at the market, while also setting up a $500,000 legal defense fund. At the same hour of the morning on the 10th that the executive committee did its work, Fisk's brokerage partner, Belden, appeared before a Judge Gilbert in Brooklyn. Represented by the demonstrably upright Thomas G. Shearman, superintendent of the Sunday school in Henry Ward Beecher's Brooklyn church, Belden orchestrated an order enjoining "all parties to all previous

suits from further proceedings." Gilbert also ordered that every Erie director, save Frank Work, continue to discharge his duty and continue to convert bonds into stock as necessary.[9] The same morning, Judge Barnard
voided all injunctions except his own.

Gould and friends reveled in the stalemate. "One magistrate had forbidden them to move," wrote Henry and Charles Francis Adams, "and another
magistrate had ordered them not to sit still. If the Erie board held meetings
and transacted business, it violated one injunction; if it abstained from doing
so, it violated another."[10] Edmund Clarence Stedman—a broker, banker, and
minor poet who watched this first Erie War from a front-row seat—pointed
out the convenience of the dilemma faced by Gould, Drew, and Fisk: "Since
they were forbidden by Barnard to convert bonds into stock, and forbidden
by Gilbert to refuse to do so, who but the most captious could blame them
for doing as they pleased?"[11]

The broker William Fowler stood by the Open Board on the morning of
the 10th, watching as Vanderbilt's buyers soaked up Erie stock. "The whole
market hung on one word—Erie. The strident voice of George Henriques,
the Vice president of the Open Board, was heard calling off in quick succession, government bonds, state bonds, Pacific Mail, New York Central,
then a pause, a shadow rippled across his face and a shiver ran through the
hall as he ejaculated in a tone still more strident—Erie! For ten minutes
bedlam seemed to have broken loose. Every operator and broker was on his
feet in an instant, screaming and gesticulating. The different Vanderbilt
brokers stood each in the center of a circle, wheeling as on a pivot from
right to left, brandishing their arms and snatching at all the stock offered
them. As the presiding officer's hammer fell and his hoarse voice thundered
out 'That will do, gentlemen. I shall fine any other offer,' Erie stood at 80.
The crowd, leaving the other stocks not yet called, poured into the street,
where nothing was heard but Erie. Vanderbilt's brokers had orders to buy
every share offered, and under their enormous purchases the price rose, by
twelve o'clock, to 83."

Sometime that afternoon, Vanderbilt ran across shares that, having been
signed by Jim Fisk, were demonstrably new. And only then, with his purchases continuing at fever pitch, did the Commodore realize the trouble he
might be in. By this point, with rumors rampant that an unknown quantity
of new Erie shares had been put into the market, the stock had once again

gone into free fall, standing at 71 by 3 P.M.. Vanderbilt had by this time plunged $7 million completely leveraged dollars into the stock. Understanding instantly that the shares would drop even further if he stopped buying—precipitating a financial collapse that would threaten not only himself but many others—Vanderbilt chose to stay the course. "He never flinched," Fowler recalled admiringly.[12]

The Commodore commanded his representatives to go even longer into Erie. By that evening, he had created enough "demand" so that the stock stood at 76 1/8. As the day's business closed, Vanderbilt owned or controlled almost 200,000 units of the firm, at least half of these of dubious value, their ink still wet. Did this represent a majority of the Erie's equity? Who knew? Certainly not Vanderbilt. (In fact, more than 50 percent of Vanderbilt's shares would be challenged just two days later, when the administrators of both the New York Stock Exchange and the Open Board ruled that Erie certificates dated after 7 March were not valid.)

Adding to Vanderbilt's problem was the inflated rate of interest he had paid on the vast sums he was forced to borrow during the afternoon of the 10th. Early that morning, acting on a suggestion from Gould, Drew had shrewdly moved to drive up the price of credit. Visiting several downtown banks, the speculative director withdrew as cash close to $7 million in proceeds derived from the recent Erie stock sales, which he then placed in the safe at the Erie offices downtown near the foot of Duane Street. This maneuver, as Maury Klein has described in a wonderfully crafted phrase, "precipitated a spasm in the money market" and caused short-term interest rates to suddenly leap.[13] Thus Gould, Drew, and Fisk—with Gould as chief strategist—had Vanderbilt coming and going.

William Fowler was with the three of them at the Erie offices early on the morning of the 11th. "The executive committee of the Erie board," he wrote, "were holding high festival over their triumphs at the offices of the company. . . . Uncle Daniel's corrugated visage was set into a chronic chuckle, Jay Gould's financial eye beamed and glittered and the blond bulk of James Fisk, Jr., was unctuous with jokes." But the mood in the room changed abruptly when messengers arrived bearing word that Vanderbilt's lawyers had been busy. None other than Judge Barnard himself, Fowler recounted, had issued a "process of the court" to "punish them for contempt of its mandates." Barnard's order for the arrest of Drew, Fisk, and Gould "would soon be placed for service in the hands of the high sheriff's spongy officers."[14]

Soon thereafter, according to a reporter for the *Herald*, a police officer walking his beat on Duane Street noticed "a squad of respectably dressed, but terrified looking men, loaded down with packages of greenbacks, account books, bundles of papers tied up with red tape [emerging] in haste and disorder from the Erie building. Thinking perhaps that something illicit had been taking place, and these individuals might be plunderers playing a bold game in open daylight, he approached them, but he soon found out his mistake. They were only the executive committee of the Erie company, flying the wrath of the Commodore, and laden with the spoils of their recent campaign."[15]

None of these men found the prospect of incarceration appealing. Likewise, they realized that to be thrown behind bars would be to cede the ability to manipulate events, cash, and stocks. Thus they determined immediately that they must get out of the reach of New York marshals. The panicked Drew took the very next ferry across the Hudson to Jersey City, carrying with him numerous key files and records of the corporation. Gould and Fisk, meanwhile, stayed behind in Manhattan to clean up a few details with brokers and bankers before fleeing. Although they had dispatched Drew with the files, they themselves hung onto the $7 million from the Erie vault. ("Such a sum," Fisk later told his friend Robert Fuller, "was far safer with myself and Jay than it would have been if left in the hands of Uncle Daniel."[16])

Gould and Fisk were relaxed enough to dine that evening at Fisk's favorite restaurant, Delmonico's, with guards outside watching for the marshals. They were halfway through their meal when their men alerted them to approaching officers of the court. Running out the back of the restaurant and down the alley, Gould lugging the $7 million in greenbacks in a large satchel, the partners hailed a cab to take them down to the waterfront. There they engaged two seamen from the steamer *St. John* to row them across to Jersey City in one of the steamer's lifeboats.

The trip, as Fisk later described it for a reporter, was nothing if not hair-raising. The waters of New York Harbor still ran profoundly cold in mid-March; to submerge in them longer than a few minutes would have meant death. Ocean tides pushing north into the estuary of the Hudson made the work all the harder as the men from the *St. John* endeavored to row in a straight east-west line across the channel. Added to that was the moonless night, the thick pea-soup fog, and the many large, fast steamers and freighters that pushed quickly in and out of sight without warning, their running lights obscured, and their helmsmen frighteningly unaware of the little band of rowers. At one point a large ferry suddenly bore down on the rowboat, "and only the vigorous use of their lungs" allowed them to row out of the ferry's path before being struck. After a second episode much like the first, the party "determined to get some assistance" and hailed a Jersey-bound ferryboat, from which they "could get no response." In desperation, instead, Fisk reached out and made "a clutch" for the housing that covered the ferry's giant, churning paddlewheels, with the result that they "were drawn so near to the wheel as to nearly wash the whole party out of the boat. They however saved her from swamping, and climbed aboard, arriving shortly afterwards at Jersey City, safe and sound, but thoroughly drenched."[17]

Chapter 16

AN ALMIGHTY ROBBERY

G OULD, FISK, AND DREW—together with Eldridge and a few other more minor players—established their headquarters in Taylor's Hotel, right on the Jersey City waterfront. The hotel lay just a stone's throw from the Erie's terminal, adjacent to the town's Long Wharf. Taking an entire floor of rooms for themselves, the Erie clique also set up a reception hall in the hotel's Ladies' Parlor for the comfort of the many reporters who promptly followed them into exile. Fisk's old Vermont friend Fuller—now one of the journalistic throng attached to the traveling Erie circus—remembered Fisk's supplying ample cigars, liquor, and food. Fisk also did most of the glad-handing and chatting-up of the press, a task that Gould—who most people, including Vanderbilt, were slow to realize had begun to displace Drew as the clique's chief tactician—was glad to delegate.

"[Fisk] could manage them [the press] better than Gould could," Fuller wrote. "Gould was always intense and therefore serious. His whole mind was centered upon whatever project he happened to have in hand. He was a stronger character than Jim because he was more tenacious; but somehow he didn't seem to know as much about people." Fisk, on the other hand, served as the consummate salesman and promoter. "The Commodore owns New York," he told the reporters. "The stock exchange, the streets, the railroads, and most of the steamboats there belong to him. As ambitious young men, we saw there was no chance for us there to expand, and so we came over here to grow up with the country." When a correspondent countered that Drew was none too young—was, in fact, of the same generation as Vanderbilt—Fisk answered that "Uncle Dan'l says he feels like a two-year-old now that he's taken the plunge."

What, the press asked, were the Erie's immediate plans? To become a New Jersey corporation, answered Fisk, and after that to capture the Erie for the common man, whose interests would not be served should Vanderbilt be allowed to establish a monopoly of all the railroads linking New York with the West. "The Commodore," said Fisk, "will never be quite happy unless he owns all the railroads and can charge whatever he darn pleases for the freight that comes into New York. He don't care a cuss how much the people of that city pay for their bacon and eggs, not a bit, provided they pay it to him. Well, he isn't going to get hold of the Erie—at least, not as long as the Erie Exiles are patrolling the quarter-deck. We know what to do with pirates when we see one!"[1] Fisk was center stage, and public interest was at a fever pitch. The *Herald* noted that the impeachment proceedings against Andrew Johnson, then going on at the nation's capital, were eclipsed nearly completely in the press by the war over the Erie.[2]

While Fisk did all the talking, it was Gould who had composed the talking points. To him goes credit for the masterstroke of framing the fight against Vanderbilt in populist terms: a high-minded battle against single-minded greed, a war against monopoly. It was also Gould's idea to order up a quick report from the Erie's chief superintendent, which, in order to demonstrate the urgent need for the bonds recently issued, earnestly decried the road's horrendous physical condition. (One year earlier, in an effort to placate federal overseers, this same superintendent had authored a report describing the Erie as "in better condition and better equipped than at any period during the past ten years."[3] But luckily for Gould, the boozy hacks who chronicled the Erie for Greeley's *Tribune,* James Gordon Bennett, Jr.'s *Herald,* and other New York dailies were not inclined to delve too deeply into inconsistent company statements.)

To make their antimonopoly campaign seem more real, Gould and Fisk soon launched a rate war against the New York Central, slashing freight and passenger prices to the extent that the Erie instantly began to operate at a loss. At the same time, they moved to secure the necessary legislation at Trenton to make the Erie a New Jersey corporation—a legal status that would permit the Erie clique to issue even more bonds and stock, regardless of what injunctions might be flung against them from the eastern shore of the Hudson. The recognition by New Jersey also provided the Erie's substantial New York properties with some measure of protection against seizure by Vanderbilt via the New York courts.

But more than mere property stood threatened with seizure. Given their proximity to New York, the personal security of Gould and his allies became an issue, especially after Gould received word of a $50,000 reward supposedly offered by Vanderbilt for the capture and return of the Erie clique to the jurisdiction of the New York courts. The rumor, which was false, metastasized into action on 16 March, when armed bands of thugs began debarking various Pavonia ferries from New York and gathered ominously at the Erie terminal. But this was an eventuality for which Gould had prepared himself. A *Herald* reporter described how "fifteen picked men of the Jersey City police force, armed with revolvers and [nightsticks] under the command of Chief of Police Fowler" commanded the approaches to what was now being called Fort Taylor. Beside Fowler and his men stood a slightly smaller force under Inspector Hugh Masterson, special superintendent of police for the Erie Railroad.[4] Despite all this firepower, it took several hours for the Erie's Masterson to convince the New York horde their errand was useless. Gould, Fisk, and Drew could not be pried from the heavily defended hotel.

On the same day that brought the thugs from New York, Judge Barnard announced that he would indict for contempt any Erie fugitives whom he or his deputies found in New York. Drew, meanwhile, became quickly unhappy in New Jersey. The speculative director, a family man like Gould, missed his wife and hearth just as much as Gould missed his. Additionally, the secretive Drew did not like sharing close quarters with business associates. "Hardly had the Erie confederates been installed in Taylor's Hotel," Fowler wrote, "when [Drew's] younger and more robust associates noticed the workings of his timid, vacillating nature. He had been borne along by their stronger wills and now felt painfully his trying position. He missed his pleasant fireside, where he had so often toasted his aged limbs and dreamed of panics."[5]

Early on, Gould guessed that Drew might seek to profit via a separate peace with Vanderbilt. The Commodore had always forgiven Drew and taken him back in the past. Why not now as well? What was to stop the old allies from striking a bargain that left Fisk and Gould out in the cold? Drew had a long track record of betrayal. As Gould, Fisk, and everyone else on Wall Street knew, in any given situation Drew could always be counted on to do whatever most benefited Drew.

Thus Gould and Fisk were annoyed but not surprised when, a few days into the New Jersey adventure, treasurer Drew—under the constant scrutiny of a tailing detective underwritten by Gould—made his move. The treasurer withdrew the Erie directorate's $7 million from the firm's New Jersey bank and sent it via messengers for deposit in several New York banks, where the funds would instantly become liable to attachment by Vanderbilt. Once apprised of the situation, Fisk and Gould immediately attached Drew's own considerable Erie securities (these still located in Jersey) and demanded that Drew return the $7 million forthwith. Drew did so but remained under suspicion. After this episode, the increasingly tired and forlorn old man was relieved of all treasurer's authority. As the Adams brothers put it, Drew "ceased to be a power in Erie."[6]

Rather than a shaper of events, Drew would from now on be—for the most part, with just two notable exceptions—a prisoner of events. And large events they were. As the *Herald* pointed out, "The great Erie railway stock litigation, at present going on in this city, promises to assume proportions of the most extensive and complicated character ever brought before the civil courts of any country."[7] The weapons deployed by both sides in the quarrel added up to about $120 million in capital. The players contesting for control of the Erie were the sharpest to ever walk on Wall Street.

Only a few days into the commotion, Judge Barnard appointed attorney Charles S. Osgood—one of Vanderbilt's sons-in-law—to serve as receiver for the stock sale that Barnard had previously forbidden to take place. When Gould got a friendly Ulster County judge, T. W. Clerke, to stay Osgood's appointment, Barnard in turn voided Clerke's stay. This exercise in judicial badminton would have continued ad infinitum save for Osgood's recusing himself. (The point was actually moot, since the funds Osgood would have been receiving were in New Jersey. The next appointed receiver—Peter B. Sweeny, chamberlain of Boss Tweed's Tammany Hall ring—therefore had nothing whatsoever to do, save collect $150,000 from the Erie at the end of the day, for services not rendered.) To complicate matters further, Judge Gilbert of Brooklyn—who had previously ordered the continued conversions of Erie bonds into stock—now vacated his own order, announcing that he had been tricked by false facts into issuing his initial judgment.

◇   ◇   ◇

Both Gould and the speculative director made visits to New York on successive Sundays, that Sabbath day which, according to New York law, remained free of marshals, writs, summonses, and subpoenas. Through careful planning—chartering a small vessel to land them on the Battery just after midnight and then returning just before midnight twenty-four hours later—Drew and Gould were able to safely spend a night and one long day and evening with their wives and families every week. From the Battery they rode together with two armed guards—just in case—to their respective homes within a block of each other on Seventeenth Street. One guard stayed with Drew, both to protect the man and to keep an eye on his activities. The other shadowed Gould.

Fisk, on the other hand, had his comforts delivered to him in Jersey. Food from Delmonico's came rolling across the harbor in regular convoys. So did cigars, liquor, and—most important—love, the latter in the form of a music hall actress and onetime whore by the name of Helen Josephine Mansfield. Twelve years Fisk's junior, "Josie" Mansfield had been born in Boston but moved to San Francisco with her parents when she was sixteen. One year later she married an actor, Frank Lawlor, but divorced him in short order after he'd paid both their fares to New York. Once in Manhattan, Josie made her home in a Thirty-fourth Street bordello run by a Miss Annie Wood, whose official profession, according to the *New York Directory* of 1866, was that of actress. It was at Annie Wood's notorious establishment in 1867 that Fisk fell under Josie's spell. He soon set her up in her own suite of rooms at the American Club Hotel and began financing her career on the stage.

At Fort Taylor, as Fuller told it, Fisk installed Josie in a "comfortable room which opened into the same bathroom from which his room connected." Fuller also remembered how Gould, when first presented with the fact of Miss Mansfield in residence, "looked at her and through her with his piercing black eyes and stroked his beard, but made no comment. . . . The newspaper reporters gradually learned about Josie, but they never said a word."[8] Meanwhile Drew, devoutly puritanical when it came to everything but business, was outraged. Already surrounded by liquor, something of which he stoutly disapproved, Uncle Daniel was now confronted with the thinly veiled fact of Fisk's extramarital exploits. "The only Scarlet woman Drew ever had a mind to countenance was the Erie," wrote Fowler. "He did not care to see, be seen with, or breathe the same air as the likes of Miss Mansfield. The founder of the Drew Theological Seminary had no patience or charity for harlots. Not only did he not desire Miss Mansfield's company, he detested it."[9]

Of course, all members of the Erie clique realized that a prolonged stay in New Jersey was impossible. A real solution, either peace with Vanderbilt or a New York law formally legitimizing Erie's recent issues, was clearly necessary. Vanderbilt, still busy financing injunctions from Judge Barnard, seemed in no mood to negotiate. Thus Gould decided to focus his attention on gaining favorable legislation in Albany. Soon, cynical pundits were hailing Gould's Erie Bill, introduced by a friendly Ulster County representative, as a boon to one of New York's most corrupt institutions. The *Herald* described the Erie Bill "as a Godsend to the hungry legislators and lobbymen, who have had up to this time such a beggarly session that their women and bootblacks are becoming insubordinate. As the Erie Bill promises to carry the fight up to the Capitol, the whole army of [politicos], inside and out, are in ecstasies; and numbers of experienced lobbyists, who had left Albany in despair, are packing up their paper collars and making the best of their way back, in the hope of sharing in the anticipated spoils. It is whispered that Vanderbilt is determined to defeat the bill, and fabulous sums are mentioned as having been 'put up' for that purpose."[10]

As early as 20 March, Gould had Hamilton Harris (aided by Erie director John E. Develin) busy trying to lobby (i.e., bribe) that sizable and infamously bribable segment of the New York legislature known as the Black Horse Cavalry. But when Vanderbilt's Albany representative, John B. Dutcher, a director of the Harlem, aided by yet another of Vanderbilt's sons-in-law, Horace F. Clark, outbid Develin and Harris for votes on the Erie Bill, the legislation wound up being reported unfavorably out of the Assembly's railroad committee on 27 March. After this, it crashed and burned on the floor of the Assembly with a vote of eighty-three against, thirty-two for. Word came that the bill might, however, be reconsidered. "The hint," wrote Henry and Charles Francis Adams, "was a broad one; the exiles must give closer attention to their interests" in the form of more generous bribes.[11] (At the same time, a New York State Senate subcommittee recently impaneled to investigate the financial manipulations of the Erie clique came down three to two against the Gould forces. Two of the senate investigators had received bribes from Gould, and two from Vanderbilt. A third senator, A. C. Matoon, took bribes from both camps and then finally sided with Vanderbilt.)

With Harris and Develin having failed to obtain the required results in the Assembly, Gould decided a personal trip to Albany was necessary even though such a journey would have to occur on a day or days other than Sunday. Negotiating via messenger with Judge Barnard, Jay promised to appear in Barnard's court on 4 April but insisted that he be left a free man, unaccosted, until that date. His safety thus secured, Gould departed Jersey City on 30 March with a suitcase full of money and a backup supply of Erie checks. Upon his arrival at Albany, Jay, who'd already decided to pay far more than the paltry $1,000 per vote previously offered by Develin, joined immediate battle against the Vanderbilt representatives. Both parties held open house in equally luxurious suites at Albany's Delavan House Hotel, so that legislators could conveniently stroll back and forth from one cocktail party to the other, watching the value of their votes accumulate. For this round, Vanderbilt was represented by none other than the Grand Sachem of Tammany Hall himself, Boss Tweed, for the moment acting in his role as state senator. Tweed had no less than six bars set up in his seven-room suite, and Gould had almost as many. After a visit to Gould's rooms, a *Herald* reporter wryly described Gould's trunk as "literally stuffed with thousand dollar bills which are to be used for some mysterious purpose in connection with legislation."[12] Each team avidly bid up the price of votes, creating quite a bull market in democracy.

Jay briefly interrupted these proceedings on 4 April in order to return to Manhattan. There he made good on his promise to appear before Judge Barnard. Deferring proceedings until 8 April, Barnard insisted that Gould remain thereafter in the custody of a court officer. Outside the court building, Gould glibly informed his somewhat witless guard that he must return to Albany. When the guard protested, Gould simply replied that he was free to tag along. Thus the chain of custody would be unbroken. On the 8th, Gould pleaded sickness and sent his lawyers to make excuses to Judge Barnard. As the Adams brothers would observe, Gould was "not too ill to go to the Capitol in the midst of [an early spring] snow storm, but much too ill to think of returning to New York."[13]

Reintroduced in the Senate rather than the Assembly, the Erie Bill—meant to legalize bonds ostensibly issued in order to finance repairs—received help from an ironic God on 15 April, when three Erie railway cars ran off a broken rail and tumbled down an embankment at Port Jervis, New York, killing twenty-six. Three days later, greased by many thousands of dollars, the Erie Bill cleared the Senate by a vote of seventeen to twelve. (This time Matoon voted with Gould. "A man more thoroughly, shame-facedly, contemptible and corrupt," the Adams brothers fumed, "a more perfect specimen of a legislator on sale haggling for his own price, could not well exist."[14])

Meanwhile, various newspapers had already come over to the side of the Erie clique by adopting antimonopoly as their editorial slogan. The highly respected *Commercial and Financial Chronicle* stated things unequivocally: "The question that concerns our great trading interests is this—shall the main avenues of our commerce be under the control of a gigantic monopoly, or shall they be stimulated and expanded under the wholesome competition of transportation companies?"[15] James Gordon Bennett, Jr., of the *Herald*—a man who would hardly ever find himself on Jay Gould's team in the future—sang the same tune. "It is obviously contrary to the interests of the public that any one party should have control of the Erie, the New York Central, the Hudson River and the Harlem," Bennett wrote. "Such a monopoly could exact its own rates on fare and freight, except where restricted by legislative enactments, and the results would be deplorable."[16]

With editorial and public sentiment swinging in favor of the Erie clique, some thought it a strategic retreat when Vanderbilt suddenly, four days after the Senate vote, stopped all lobbying and vote buying. One day later, on Monday, 20 April, the environment in Albany had changed completely. "Ere ten o'clock," wrote the *Herald's* reporter, "there was a perfect rush for Parlor 57 at the Delavan House, where the pecunious Gould had been holding forth. It is said that prices came down wonderfully. Those who had been demanding $5000 were now willing to take anything not less than $100. The great Erie coffers were closed, however. There was no longer any need."[17] Later that afternoon, the men of the Assembly—enraged at Vanderbilt, whose apparent surrender had cost them thousands—promptly passed the Erie measure by a staggering anti-Vanderbilt vote of 101 to 5.

Observers wondered why Gould did not appear to delight in this unexpectedly cheap victory. We have no record of exactly when Gould and Fisk realized that both Drew (weary of New Jersey and annoyed at Gould for supplanting him) and Eldridge's Boston group (ultimately uninterested in anything that did not immediately affect the fortunes of the BH&E) had been in secret talks with Vanderbilt. The settlement between Eldridge, Drew, and Vanderbilt was finalized in a meeting at the Manhattan Club on Sunday afternoon, and word must have reached Gould either late Sunday or very early on Monday.

Combining all their shares, the Eldridge group, Drew, and Vanderbilt agreed to three key items. First, much of the stock Vanderbilt had so recently purchased would be bought back from him at a price approximating what he'd paid. Second, Vanderbilt's nephew Frank Work and others hurt by Drew's manipulations of the pool would be compensated and made whole. Last, Drew would withdraw from all future management of the Erie. This final item was actually not a large issue with the old man, who had already been effectively removed by Gould and Fisk.

The two key figures in the late fight were left with very little to show for all their troubles. In fact, the New York courts were still contending with Gould and Fisk on the subject of their freedom. This situation led the pair to descend on Vanderbilt at his Manhattan mansion, 10 Washington Place, in a surprise visit early one morning in May, about a week and a half after the Assembly's passage of the Erie Bill. Testifying in 1869 before the New York State Senate committee investigating the Erie Wars, Fisk recalled that when they arrived unannounced at Vanderbilt's house, Gould "wanted to wait until the Commodore should have time to get out of bed, but I rang the bell, and when the door was opened I rushed up to his room. The Commodore was sitting on the side of the bed with one shoe off and one shoe on." (The embarrassed Gould, meanwhile, lingered discreetly in Vanderbilt's downstairs parlor.) When Fisk—stalking back and forth across Vanderbilt's bedroom—insisted that Vanderbilt call off Judge Barnard's dogs, Vanderbilt in turn insisted that Fisk and Gould join Drew and

Eldridge in relieving him in an "honorable way" of his large supply of Erie stock. Vanderbilt, Fisk recalled, "said I must take my position as I found it, that there I was and he would keep his bloodhounds . . . on our track; that he would be damned if he didn't keep them after us if we didn't take the stock off his hands. I told him that if I had my way, I'd be damned if I would take a share of it; that he brought the punishment on himself and deserved it. He said the suits would never be withdrawn till he was settled with." Confronted by this threat, Fisk agreed to most of Vanderbilt's terms. "I said (after settling with him) that it was an almighty robbery; that we had sold ourselves to the Devil, and that Gould felt just the same as I did."[18]

As it was, Fisk and Gould stood to gain little from their adventure. Nevertheless—and despite a tacit agreement—Drew, Eldridge, and Vanderbilt appear to have made at least one stab at seeing that the pair got nothing at all. When Eldridge failed to appear for a promised meeting with Gould and Fisk early in June, the two went directly to the nearby home of Judge Edward Pierrepont (soon to be appointed U.S. Attorney General under President Grant). Here, according to rumors on the Street, a secret meeting of the Erie board was in progress. Barging into Pierrepont's back parlor, Fisk and Gould found Drew, Eldridge, and Work along with the rest of the Erie board finalizing the details of the agreement with Vanderbilt, an agreement that left no slice of the pie, not even a sliver, for the two new arrivals.

Through fast and loud talk, and not-so-veiled threats of their own court actions, Fisk and Gould endeavored to improve their position to the extent that they could. That is, not by very much, but by some. The final agreement called for Vanderbilt to be relieved of 50,000 Erie shares priced variously at $70 and $80, these amounts to be paid with $2.5 million cash and $1.25 million face value BH&E bonds. Vanderbilt also received another $1 million for a four-month call on another 50,000 shares of the Erie, and two seats on the Erie board. (Over the coming weeks, the total of 100,000 shares was to be eased into the marketplace slowly with an eye toward maintaining the price.) Drew, already out of the treasurer's job, resigned from the Erie board and repaid the road $540,000 in exchange for the dropping of all other claims against him. Eldridge's Boston group likewise resigned their seats on the board and exchanged $5 million face-value BH&E bonds for Erie acceptances. And Frank Work and Richard Schell received $464,250, representing what they'd lost in Drew's manipulations of the pool.

At the end of all this finance, the Erie was left as an empty husk. Mired down by more than $9 million in newly minted debt, the corporation consisted of more than $21 million in outstanding stock, few tangible assets, and a bad reputation. This booby prize, as one reporter called it, now went to the two apparently not-so-smart young men who had orchestrated the late drama. By the close of the meeting Gould had become treasurer and president of the Erie, replacing Eldridge in the latter position. His first act was to appoint Fisk as controller and to form a new executive committee consisting of himself, Fisk, and Erie chief counsel Frederick Lane.

None envied Gould. The Erie seemed hardly worth having. Besides, the thirty-two-year-old man's hold on the road was by no means assured. Gould himself did not own enough Erie stock to guarantee his position. He might well be out when the new board elections came along in October. And even if he stayed, what—exactly—was he president of? "There ain't nothin' in Ary no more, C'neel," Drew told Vanderbilt.[19]

Chapter 17

SCOUNDRELS

ONE OF JAY GOULD'S most valuable acquisitions in the Erie was a thirty-four-year-old Italian immigrant and former seaman named Giovanni Pertinax Morosini. He claimed descent from a prominent and ancient merchant family of Venice. But after coming to the United States in 1850 the physically imposing and naturally intelligent Morosini worked five years as a deckhand on clipper ships. Then fate intervened. Morosini's fortunes changed one summer night in 1855 when he stumbled upon a young man in a suit being beaten by waterfront toughs near New York's South Street. Morosini rescued the teenager, who turned out to be the son of an officer of the Erie. He received as his reward a clerkship in the offices of the Erie auditor. Over the next thirteen years the smart, diligent Morosini rose to the post of assistant comptroller. He also married, started a family, and established a small estate (Elmhurst) in the Riverdale section of the Bronx. As a hobby, he collected medieval armor, sabers, and gold coins.[1] Such was Morosini's situation when Gould, a self-made man with a natural affinity and trust for other self-made men, came into possession of the Erie. Gould swiftly removed Morosini's longtime boss (an old Drew crony) and installed Morosini as acting auditor, formalizing the position a few months later. In time, Morosini would also become Gould's confidential secretary, bodyguard, and sometime broker, remaining a staunch friend and ally of the Gould family until well after Jay's death, and always profiting from the relationship. (Today Morosini—who died in 1908—is still close to Gould, occupying a Woodlawn mausoleum that is nearly as elaborate as Jay's own.)

The financial affairs Morosini found himself auditing were necessarily complex. As Fisk was to recall, the first thing he and Gould found upon their arrival at the top of the Erie mountain was "a very well dusted treasury."[2] To shore up that treasury, Gould and his cohorts avidly took to the printing press throughout the summer, creating some $20 million in convertible bonds that were then instantly made over into stock. "For the issue of $20,000,000," complained the *Commercial and Financial Chronicle*, "there is nothing to show beyond $5,000,000 of bonds of another corporation [the BH&E], the interest of which is guaranteed by the Erie Company, the laying of a new line of rails, some minor improvements of no great consequence, and ordinary repairs which should have been covered by the current earnings."[3] In the end, although Gould did succeed in replenishing the Erie's treasury, he did so entirely at the expense of stockholders, who saw the value of their equity cut by more than a third as a result of the new issues. (Erie stock stood at around $70 in June, before the new issues. By the end of August, with so many certificates on the market, the stock hovered just above $44. All the while both Fisk and Gould personally shorted Erie stock, and made hundreds of thousands.)

At the same time, Gould prepared carefully for the October board elections. Through September, he used some of the Erie's own money to buy proxies. He also made an executive decision to close the Erie transfer books on 19 August, more than a month before they would normally be shut prior to the annual Erie election. It was of course no coincidence that on 19 August, though not necessarily one day later, the bulk of the newly manufactured shares (a plurality more than large enough to control the election) sat on the books of brokers friendly to Gould. Thus, on 13 October, the Erie elected a board of Gould's own choosing. New members included Gould's brother-in-law Daniel S. Miller, Jr., and Boss Tweed, along with Tammany chamberlain Peter Sweeny, the Erie's recent nonfunctioning receiver under Judge Barnard. By recruiting the former Vanderbilt ally Tweed and gifting him some stock, Gould also brought onboard Tweed's entire operation and crew, including the once annoying but now instantly tamed Barnard.

"Barnard's roaring by degrees subsided," commented the Adams brothers, "until he roared as gently as any sucking dove, and finally he ceased to roar at all."[4] (Soon Gould and Fisk would go so far as to name the Erie's newest locomotive, an ornate thing decorated by the famed artist Jasper Francis Cropsey, the *George C. Barnard*.)

The new board dutifully reappointed Gould, Fisk, and Lane as the executive committee, Gould as president, Fisk as controller and chief operating officer, and Lane as counsel. The board also approved a key change that Gould proposed in the language of the Erie bylaws. Henceforth, Erie stockholders would be required to vote *in person* at annual board elections. By eliminating the possibility of proxies, this new rule effectively disenfranchised some of the largest holders of Erie stock who were located abroad. Going forward, Gould would not have to exert himself quite so much to ensure smooth elections. At the end of the day on 13 October, Gould went home jubilant to his family on Seventeenth Street, and Fisk went home jubilant to his mistress. "My dear Josie," he wrote her in a note messengered that morning, ". . . Mr. Tweed and Mr. Lane will dine with us at half-past six o'clock. Everything went off elegantly. We are all *safe*. Will see you at six o'clock."[5]

Feeling quite safe indeed, Gould now—as had always been his custom—reached for a place even higher than the elevated and powerful perch on which he found himself. He and Fisk got in touch with their old mentor Drew and made him a proposition. How would the "Great Bear" like to participate in the ultimate bear trap, one of staggeringly unprecedented proportions? "Drew might have enjoyed life and the consolation of religion on the few millions he had left," commented Henry Clews a few years after the start of Drew's destruction, "if he had retired in company with his Bible and hymn book to some lovely, secluded spot in the peaceful vales of Putnam County; but he was under the infatuation of some latent and mysterious force of attraction, the victim of some potent spell."[6] Bear raids and short selling had become a part of his nature. They possessed an allure and offered an adrenaline rush that he simply could not resist. Besides, what the audacious Gould proposed was quite breathtaking. Drew may have found the plan appealing for its promise of a final great triumph, a fitting Olympian end to his long career.

Gould's idea was a play that involved not just Wall Street but also London's Lombard Street, along with the whole money market on two continents.

Briefly sketched, his plan that autumn was to constrict the U.S. money supply, causing interest rates to rise and, conversely, the price of stocks—the Erie included—to plummet. Armed with some $10 million in Erie cash reserves, Gould had a good head start toward locking up greenbacks. Cash was usually scarce on Wall Street in the fall anyway, as significant amounts were routinely withdrawn for the payment of farmers after harvests. To tie up the $10 million, Gould drafted checks against the Erie funds and then had the checks certified, a mechanism that obligated banks to place these funds in reserve. To further strain the money supply, Jay took the certified checks to still other banks, where he used them as collateral with which to borrow cash over the counter, this to be locked up in deposit boxes. Meanwhile Drew, the erstwhile puppetmaster, was simply asked to add $4 million to a blind pool (directed by Gould) designed to short Erie stock in the bear market that would inevitably follow a rise in bond coupon rates.

Gould did not bother to keep his mechanics a secret. "There has been a mischievous manipulation of the money market for speculative purposes," wrote a reporter for the *Commercial and Financial Chronicle* in mid-November. "A combination, not only owning large private capital, but also controlling several millions of funds in possession of a leading railway company, have withdrawn from the banks and placed in hoard an aggregate of money which cannot be estimated below $10,000,000, and by many is considered to reach $15,000,000. In addition to this withdrawal of funds, these parties are engaged in reckless and demoralizing operations embracing a railroad scheme the full scope of which is not yet apparent, but which it is feared may involve more serious consequences to holders of securities and to the public confidence in corporate management than is generally anticipated."[7]

Stocks fell, the Erie to a low of 38 1/2.

As for Drew, he soon realized that he was incapable of allowing someone else to drive. Having so frequently and wantonly robbed participants in pools of his own devising, Drew simply could not relax with the thought of his $4 million resting in a blind pool directed by Gould, whom he'd taught so many tricks. That Gould and Fisk felt ill used when Drew suddenly demanded all his money back in early November cannot be denied. That Drew also felt ill used when refunded only $3 million of his original $4 million investment—a function of market timing, Gould announced, the cost of cash-ing out at the wrong moment—is also a fact. Intent on recouping his million and then some, on 12 November Drew shorted Erie (70,000 shares at 38) and got ready to ride the stock down, convinced that Gould and Fisk were not done tightening the dollar market and that the Erie (along with Wall Street in general) had considerable sinking to do before it would finally bob to the surface on the back of dollars released by Gould.

Gould and Fisk quickly became annoyed by what they saw as Drew's duplicity. In retaliation, they decided to expedite their schedule a bit and give the dean of stock watering a financial bath. One day after Drew took his short position, the Erie sank to 35 and all seemed well. This was most likely the day Gould's blind pool relieved itself of its short positions, for on the next morning, 14 November, a Saturday, Gould and Fisk unlocked their cash reserves. During the abbreviated weekend session of the Regular Board that followed, the Erie represented half the day's volume of 80,000 shares, and its price rose steadily to close at 52 1/2.[8]

Meanwhile, facing ruin, Drew considered his options. On Saturday afternoon, he paid a call on his sometime associate August Belmont. The venerable Prussian immigrant, twenty years Gould's senior and known for years as "the king of Fifth Avenue," owned 4,000 shares of Erie himself. More important, Belmont also represented many British, French, and German clients (among them the Rothschild family) who were short in the stock. Belmont had recently felt himself slashed by both sides of Gould's sword. In the preceding weeks, with Gould still on the short side of the market, Belmont had seen his own shares lose half their value. Now, with Gould releasing funds and moving the price of the Erie upward, Belmont looked on helplessly as many of the European investors he represented approached ruin. Adding to his frustration was the fact that the stock certificates his distant clients hoped to use to cover their contracts were quite literally on a slow boat to New York. The steamer *Russia* was not due to arrive in Manhattan until 23 November. (Gould had made a point of moving a large number of stock certificates—including some specially prepared ten-share notes—to Europe explicitly to have them out of reach of the bears who would desperately need them when he released currency, allowed the market to buoy, and reaped massive profits from a sudden Erie corner.)

At Drew's urging, Belmont made a decision to sue Gould and Fisk for malfeasance, and to ask that the courts appoint a receiver to take control of

the Erie. Drew pledged his support and even wrote out and signed an affidavit detailing everything he knew about recent Erie operations—which
could not have been much. True to form, however, Drew was in this instance
a double-agent with sworn allegiance to just one interest: his own. Saying he
had to go over it and perhaps reword it, Drew took the affidavit away with
him from Belmont's house. The next day (Sunday), he made a beeline for
the Erie offices on West and Duane Streets, where he accosted Fisk and
Gould.

According to Fisk's account, Drew cried for protection (a loan of stock at
3 percent interest, to cover his short positions) and begged the two younger
men to drum up fresh convertible bonds for prompt metamorphosis into
shares. When Fisk coldly informed Drew that he "should be the last man
that should whine over any position in which you may be placed in Erie,"
Drew then "entered into an explanation as to certain proceedings that he
said were being got up in the courts; he said that he had been in the enemy's
camp." Next, Fisk remembered, Drew delivered a threat: "You know that
during the whole of our other fights, I objected to ever giving my affidavits,
but I swear I will do you all the harm I can do if you do not help me in this
time of my great need." In the end Fisk and Gould, who unlike the veterans
Vanderbilt and Belmont did not nurture a soft spot for old Drew, remained
unmoved. "I am a ruined man," the Great Bear whined in parting, not realizing that he'd provided Gould and Fisk with a vital warning of what was to
come.[9]

On Monday, Belmont's lawyers, the same attorneys who had most recently represented Vanderbilt in Erie-related proceedings, took Drew's affidavit and other evidence before New York Supreme Court Judge
Sutherland, whom they asked to appoint a receiver to oversee the Erie. But
before Sutherland could act, it was discovered that another receiver had already been appointed in connection with yet another suit against the Erie: a
receiver by the name of Jay Gould.

Earlier that morning, Gould, Fisk, Lane, and Morosini had visited
Barnard at his home together with Charles MacIntosh, superintendent of
the Erie's Hudson River ferries and a small shareholder in the firm. "The
policy of the conspirators," commented an outraged *New York Times* reporter, "resolved as they were to control the proceedings, was prompt and
characteristic. One Charles MacIntosh, a hired ferry agent of the set con-

trolling the Erie Company, was caused to bring suit before Judge Barnard on a few shares of stock, in which he praises 'the management,' declares the public is unreasonably disturbing its policy by making troublesome inquires about stock issued and to be issued, tells us that it will be best to let things go on as they are going; . . . that the true remedy—the one he prays for—is that the chief author of the iniquity be appointed receiver; that his associates remain in power; that they bring such suits as they wish before Judge Barnard alone; that Mr. Belmont and everyone else be enjoined from bringing any suit anywhere; that the other judges attend to other business, while this ferry agent, Mr. Jay Gould, Mr. James Fisk Jr., and Judge Barnard, aided by the advice of Mr. Lane, counsel to the Erie Railway Company, attend to the whole of that particular business! If anything could surpass the audacious assurance and effrontery of this scheme set forth in the suit of MacIntosh, it would be the fact that Judge Barnard responded instantly to its demands."[10]

Meanwhile, Drew's contracts were fast coming due, and the price of Erie steadily rose. Wednesday saw it close at 58. Thursday morning brought the stock to 62 in early trading, before it settled back a bit. Thus Drew stood to lose more than twenty dollars on every scarce share he managed to buy, his need being on the order of 70,000 units, and the *Russia* still at sea. Concurrently, as if to make doubly sure that Drew found no way out, newly appointed receiver Jay Gould suddenly expressed doubts as to the legality of stocks issued the previous summer by Erie president Jay Gould. So on Wednesday afternoon Judge Barnard granted receiver Gould permission to buy up to 200,000 shares of the new stock at prices not to exceed par value.[11] Barnard likewise granted Gould permission to use corporate funds for this court-ordered corner of Erie stock. (Although New York State law forbade officers of railroads to use corporate funds for dealing in the company's stock, the law was less clear when it came to receivers, who were officers of the court.)

Gould's one miscalculation in all this was to discount that most nebulous and unpredictable of Wall Street figures, the small investor. Although numerous large blocks of shares were to be found in Europe—or on the slow-floating *Russia*—nonblock Erie shares were abundant in New York and, indeed, throughout the United States. Given the ready availability of Erie stock in small increments, when Gould and Fisk drove down its price through machinations earnestly chronicled by the popular press, they unwittingly created a large subculture of working- and middle-class investors who took small positions in the Erie at its low in the thirties. Now, with both Gould and Drew competing for shares, these bakers and teamsters and clergy came out of the woodwork and sold. By the end of the day on Thursday, Drew had garnered enough stock to cover his contracts, paying a mean average of $57 per share, which added up to a total loss of about $1.3 million. Gould and Fisk, meanwhile, bought all they could at roughly the same price, if only to keep Drew as "cornered" as possible and make him pay as dearly as possible. On Friday, when Drew and Gould stopped buying, the price of Erie fell promptly to 42.

At the end of the affair, Gould and Fisk emerged with an odd negative celebrity as ingenious scoundrels: the only two young men to have ever gotten the better of Daniel Drew, albeit at a cost. At the same time, Fisk and Gould walked away from the episode well liked by numerous minor Wall Street players: all those bakers and shopkeepers who had stumbled into a windfall on their coattails. For the moment, most newspaper editors expressed more intrigue than disdain, and more amusement than outrage, when it came to Gould. It seemed there was little real villainy in making a victim of one such as Drew, especially through a scheme that enriched so many small investors. By mid-November 1868, Gould's was a name well known not only in financial circles, but also among all readers of the general press. It did not yet, however, possess the profoundly negative connotation that was to come.

In appraising Gould's Erie corner, James Gordon Bennett, Jr., of the *New York Herald* expressed slight annoyance mixed with a large dose of envy: "The speculations of the last month have been on a gigantic scale such as never were equaled before in Wall Street, while it is doubtful if they have been surpassed elsewhere. Millions of dollars have been handled as if they were thousands, and the capital employed has been such as to make the outside public gape with astonishment at the daring and boldness of the operators."[12]

Bennett added that the operations of the Erie clique indicated the presence of a financial mastermind. "However questionable these schemes may be, their skill and success exhibit Napoleonic genius on the part of him who conceived them."[13] A writer for the *Commercial and Financial Chronicle* opined that the problem, if there was one, did not lie in the men who trans-acted the business of the Erie so much as it did in the laws governing those men: "The letter of the law is very deficient in its regulation of the manage-ment of corporate interests." Gould and Fisk had done absolutely nothing illegal. And the spectacle of clever fellows exploiting inadequate laws for short-term profit was, quite simply, "nothing new under the sun."[14]

◇ ◇ ◇

"The victors had got the spoils," Clews wrote, "but they paid dearly for them, and had come pretty near being destroyed in the moment of their tri-umph. They had purchased Erie at 'corner' prices, and they were obligated to carry it, for nobody wanted it."[15] Indeed, the Street remained more than wary of Erie. Some two weeks earlier, at the end of October, a group of Wall Street brokers had visited Gould at his office to complain about the murki-ness of Erie stock. Given the vague number of Erie shares outstanding and the seemingly unlimited possibility of new shares being issued, it was nearly impossible, they said, for them to extend credit based on the shares or to allow the shares to be bought on margin. In response, Gould claimed the amount of stock outstanding in the company represented approximately $39.5 million and told his listeners to expect more bonds and more stock conversions to raise funds necessary for maintaining the line and keeping the Erie away from Vanderbilt.

"With unspeakable effrontery," wrote the Adamses, "an effrontery so great as actually to impose on his audience and a portion of the press, and make them believe that the public ought to wish him success, he described how stock issues at the proper time, to any required amount, could alone keep him in control. . . . The strangest thing of all was that it never seemed to occur to his audience that the propounder of this comical sophistry was a trustee and guardian for the stockholders, and not a public benefactor; and that the owners of the Erie road might possibly prefer not to be deprived of their property in order to secure the blessings of competition."[16]

Chapter 18

THE SMARTEST MAN IN AMERICA

As was fast becoming the New York tradition, Belmont's Judge Sutherland and Gould's Judge Barnard squared off with opposing pronouncements and orders at the end of November. On the 24th, the same day the *Russia* at last showed up in the harbor of New York, Sutherland stayed Barnard's order appointing Gould as receiver for the Erie and issued a show-cause order as to why the ruling should not be vacated. One day later he went ahead and vacated Barnard's order and confirmed as receiver retired Judge Henry E. Davies. A few hours after Sutherland rendered his decision, Davies showed up at the Erie offices with another former judge, Noah Davis, and D. B. Eaton, retired counsel to the Erie. An unwitting clerk stationed at the front door allowed them to enter despite orders to the contrary. Davies walked in on an astonished Gould and Fisk huddled in a back office with their lawyers. In short order, Fisk excused himself from the room. But he soon returned with one Tommy Lynch and ten other "rough-looking" Irishmen who, Fisk assured Davies, would be delighted to escort the new receiver out of the building upon the slightest signal from either Fisk or Gould. (Soon these "Thugs of Erie"—headed by Lynch, proprietor of an oyster stand near the Erie terminal in Jersey City—would become constant presences in and around the Erie offices.[1])

The gentlemanly Davies immediately objected to Fisk's tone and the-
atrics, upon which Gould quickly apologized for his partner's threats. At the
same time, however, Gould handed Davies an order by Supreme Court
Judge Albert Cardozo—scion of a distinguished Sephardic Jewish family of
New York and father of future U.S. Supreme Court Justice Benjamin
Cardozo—vacating Sutherland's order. Like Sutherland and Barnard, Cardozo was one of the five New York Supreme Court judges operating in
Manhattan at the time. As Davies was quick to note, Cardozo's order had
been issued on 24 November and thus predated the ruling it purported to
vacate. When Davies protested, Erie counsel Lane actually concurred with
his opinion but nevertheless was able to persuade Davies, with Lynch and
his boys hovering nearby, to defer taking actual possession of the Erie until
later that same week: on Friday, the 27th. Returning on the Friday, Davies
found—as the Adams brothers described it—the Erie directors "fortified
within and himself a much enjoined wanderer without."[2]

Meanwhile, Gould and Fisk were preoccupied with bigger fish than Belmont. Having evened up their score with Drew, they now set about taking
on the other winner in the first of the Erie Wars. Early in December, Fisk
(with Gould's OK) made a grasp for some anti-Vanderbilt publicity by paying a visit to Vanderbilt at his home. Fisk was accompanied by attorney
Thomas Shearman, that lawyer with the impeccable reputation who doubled as a Sunday school teacher at Beecher's Brooklyn church. In a fierce
snowstorm, the two men rode up from the Erie offices to Vanderbilt's townhouse at 10 Washington Place, Fisk carrying 50,000 shares of Erie in a carpetbag. Once inside the Vanderbilt home, Fisk laid the carpetbag at the
mogul's feet. "I told the Commodore," he recalled, "[that] I had come to tender 50,000 shares of Erie and wanted back the money which we had paid
for them and the bonds."[3] In other words, Fisk wanted $70 per share at a
time when the street price stood at about $40. It was also, moreover, a time
when Vanderbilt desired no part of the Erie at any price. Of course, Fisk was
hardly surprised when Vanderbilt gave the predictable answer: an answer
Fisk later fed to reporters. News accounts appeared the next morning, 6 December. The articles detailed Vanderbilt's stock buy-back deal with the Erie,
and the $1-million bonus associated with his dropping of the lawsuits.

As Gould and Fisk must have anticipated, Vanderbilt became enraged at
the reporting and, in his rage, acted unwisely. In a foolhardy and demonstra-

bly false letter to the *Times,* Vanderbilt flatly denied the terms of the spring agreement ending the first Erie war. "I have had no dealings with the Erie Railway Company," Vanderbilt wrote, "nor have I ever sold that company any stock or received from them any bonus. As to the suits instituted by Messrs. Schell and others, I had nothing to do with them, nor was I in any way concerned in their settlement."[4] Within days, a delighted Fisk sent the *Times* a letter of his own, this accompanied by facsimiles of checks endorsed by Vanderbilt. "In as much as it appears from these documents that some-one of the name of 'C. Vanderbilt' received $1,000,000 from the Erie Com-pany, and as it does not appear by any records in the Company's office that Mr. Vanderbilt gave the company any consideration for that sum except the discontinuance of suits over which he now says he had no control, it would seem that some further explanation is needed to relieve Mr. Vanderbilt from the imputation of an enormous fraud upon the stockholders of the Erie Railway Company."[5]

On 10 December, after Vanderbilt once again refused Gould and Fisk's tender offer, the Erie Railroad sued Vanderbilt for breach of promise. This suit, more an attempt to embarrass than to extort money, was eventually dropped. Annoyed but also impressed by Gould, Vanderbilt about this time told a reporter that he considered the younger fellow "the smartest man in America."[6]

◇   ◇   ◇

Shortly before December 1868, Jim Fisk had purchased a majority share in the Narragansett Steamship Company, a small firm running the steamers *Providence* and *Bristol* between Manhattan and the Massachusetts town of Fall River, on Mount Hope Bay. In connection with this enterprise, he ac-quired an admiral's uniform in which he quite proudly had himself pho-tographed. Not long after, Fisk bought Broughman's Theater, at Fifth Avenue and Twenty-fourth Street. This he renamed the Fifth Avenue The-ater and used for hosting performances by the Christy Minstrels along with various comedies and burlesques. Fisk also briefly leased the Academy of Music on Fourteenth Street, where he took a loss trying to stage grand opera. Then, in December, he talked Gould into going partners with him in acquiring Pike's Opera House. This establishment, at the northwest corner of Twenty-third Street and Eighth Avenue, had been built that same year by one Samuel N. Pike at a cost of $1 million. Located considerably further west than most Manhattanites were accustomed to travel for their theater, the opera house had not proved profitable for Pike, who sold it to Fisk and Gould for $820,000.

The partners purchased the building personally, renaming it the Grand Opera House and splitting the investment 50-50. The building's upper floors included a great deal of office space, which Gould and Fisk soon refurbished in grand style, crafting a baroque palace to suit Fisk's elaborate tastes. Eight months and $250,000 later, Gould and Fisk leased the newly decorated space to the Erie Railroad for $75,000 a year.[7] "There are but few places," wrote a reporter for the *Herald* after being given a tour of what the press was already calling Castle Erie, "wherein so rich a *coup d'oeil* could be presented as that of the main offices of the Erie Railway Company." The *Herald's* man praised the carved woodwork, the stained and cut glass of the partitions, the gilded balustrades, the splendid gas fixtures, and the "artistic frescoes" on the walls and ceilings.

Although Gould's personal office seems to have been simple enough, Fisk's featured a desk raised on a dais surrounded by low chairs. The Erie suite also incorporated separate but equally elaborate dining rooms for executives and clerks, with a single kitchen and French chef supplying both. The *Herald* journalist took particular notice of the Erie's enormous safe, which had cost more than $30,000 to install. "It is seven stories high," he wrote, "each [floor] totally unconnected, and is built upon a solid foundation of granite. Rising to the very roof of the main building, this immense safe is so constructed that were the Grand Opera House to be burned to the ground, the safe would stand. It is reared within the house, but in no wise is connected to it."[8] Another observer, the writer Meade Miniegerode, described the new Erie headquarters as "the most fantastic offices ever occupied by a business corporation—a splendor of marble, and black walnut inlaid with gold, and silver name plates, and crimson hangings, and painted ceilings, and washstands decorated with nymphs and cupids."[9] The basement of Castle Erie included printing presses for new bond and stock issues. Meanwhile, Cavanagh's Restaurant, on a diagonal at the southeast corner of the intersection, was the well-known hangout for the Erie's recent ally and current board member, Boss Tweed.

The theater itself remained a theater, featuring six proscenium boxes, twenty-seven boxes in the dress circle, and a total capacity of 2,600. (Removable seating allowed easy conversion into a ballroom.) The stage, the largest in Manhattan, measured seventy feet by eighty feet. The acoustics of the hall were said to be among the finest in the world. Here, in this elaborate space, Fisk soon started staging farces, musicals, and melodramas highlighting the talents of various young actresses in whom he was interested. Most notable among these was his most frequent paramour, Josie Mansfield. Fisk also installed Josie in a townhouse at 359 West Twenty-third Street, half a block from the theater in the direction of Ninth Avenue, where he spent many a night. (His own townhouse, meanwhile, stood a bit closer to Castle Erie at 313 West Twenty-third.) Fisk went on to purchase other adjacent properties, including a fine stable where the "Prince of Erie"—as reporters now called him—kept the animals charged with hauling his ornate brougham coach ("tended by four smart footmen in flamboyant liveries") about the streets of Manhattan.[10]

For all of his self-indulgence and exhibitionism, Fisk was nevertheless quietly devout about his charities. Shortly after the opening of Castle Erie, he instructed bemused police officers at the nearby precinct to send needy people to the opera house when they came begging for food, coal, or rent money. Fisk's personal secretary saw to the handouts as part of his daily duties, the funds coming from Fisk's own wallet rather than from Erie coffers. (Fisk also donated to a struggling black church near the Erie offices and sent five hundred dollars in answer to a plea from the Baptist Church in Brattleboro that it needed a new graveyard fence. "But what in thunder do you want with a new fence?" he inquired in the note accompanying the check. "Those that are in can't get out; and those that are out don't want to get in."[11]) In his numerous small acts of giving, as in so many other ways, Fisk seemed the antithesis of his friend and alter ego Gould. "Jay Gould is the complement—the foil of James Fisk, Jr.," wrote William Fowler at about this time. "He is a short, slight man, with a sable beard, a small, bright, introverted eye, and a cool, clear head. His forte is planning, and he presents the man of thought as Fisk does the man of action. . . . He is the engineer, with his hand on the engine-lever, while Fisk is the roar of the wheels, the volume of smoke from the stack, the glare of the head-light, and the screaming whistle of the locomotive."[12]

Gould tolerated the ragtag line of supplicants in the lobby of the Erie offices just as he tolerated Fisk's other idiosyncrasies. "Gould and other staid souls of Erie," wrote Maury Klein, ". . . trod the rich carpets of the Opera House with the disquiet of monks in a bordello. They cringed at Fisk's unabashed pleasure seeking, at the proximity of Josie Mansfield and the champagne and poker soirees she hosted for Tweed, Barnard, and other politicos."[13] But Jay remained devoted to Fisk, who fulfilled most of the social and public relations obligations of their partnership. In all things, Fisk most often provided the public face for Gould's machinations. Although Gould needed the men of smoke-filled rooms—functionaries such as Tweed and his cohorts—he abhorred their milieu and preferred to let Fisk handle all late-night entertaining. As well, Fisk was far better than Gould at gladhanding, befriending, carousing with, and winning the men of the press. Jay, meanwhile, retreated to his hearth and family every evening with a religious constancy.

By early 1869, Gould's family included not only George and Edwin, in their fifth and third years, respectively, but also a daughter named for her mother, born in June 1868. To avoid confusion, the parents began calling young Helen "Nellie" very early. It was by this name that she would always be known within the Gould family. The couple and their growing clan still lived near Union Square in the mansion of Ellie's parents, where Jay took over a back room as his private study and library. Always devoted to books, Jay now began to collect and, unlike many such collectors, actually *read* antique editions of classic works. His tastes ran for the most part toward the natural sciences. He collected such volumes as Thomas Kelway's translation of Oger Ferrier's *A Learned Astronomical Discourse,* published in London in 1593.[14] He also collected books on botany and spent much time with his children working in a small flower garden he cultivated in the yard behind the Miller home. (When his sister Sarah visited, she guessed at the source of Jay's fascination with beautiful blooms when she recalled, as Jay could not, the extensive gardens their mother had once maintained around the old farmhouse in Roxbury.)

◇   ◇   ◇

While Vanderbilt's New York Central enjoyed a monopoly on passenger trains traveling in and out of Manhattan, Gould and Fisk nevertheless did their best to give Vanderbilt's road some competition for the New York passenger trade. During the summer of 1869, just as the Erie moved into its new headquarters, the railroad commissioned two new 176-foot ferryboats, the *James Fisk, Jr.*, and the *Jay Gould,* which shuttled hourly across the Hudson between the foot of West Twenty-third Street and the Erie's pier at Jersey City, next to the Erie terminal. Passage on these glamorous and elaborate ferries was free each way for Erie ticketholders. Once they debarked in Manhattan, passengers had the option of free carriage transport up West Twenty-third Street, past the Grand Opera House and on up to the Fifth Avenue Hotel at Madison Square. Erie ticketholders could likewise catch a free ride down to the piers from the centrally located hotel. (In the 1920s, George Gould would recall being taken by his father on Sundays for round-trips on the Erie ferry. As each vessel included in its grand saloon a life-sized portrait of its namesake, Jay always made a point of riding aboard the *James Fisk, Jr.*, so as to avoid being recognized.)

Elsewhere, Gould tried in other ways to consolidate the sagging Erie's position and make it as competitive as possible. Towards this end, in the summer of 1869, Jay set his sites on acquiring the Albany & Susquehanna Railroad. The tiny A&S ran 143 miles through the Catskills from the Hudson River at Albany to the Susquehanna River at Binghamton, New York. (Like the Erie, the A&S was a broad-gauge railroad, six feet across, designed and built before a smaller "standard gauge" became the norm nationwide. Thus, like the Erie, the A&S would eventually have to lay an extra line of track within its broad gauge to accommodate narrower, standard-gauge interchange traffic. Vanderbilt's New York Central, on the other hand, was standard gauge for every inch of its mileage.) The A&S possessed just 17 locomotives (compared to 317 owned by the Erie) and 214 cars (compared to 6,643 held by the Erie). But the line's insignificant rolling stock held little interest for Gould. What attracted him was its interchange potential with the Erie, which opened up the possibility of direct competition against the New York Central for traffic between Albany, Buffalo, and cities further west. As well, the A&S's Hudson River railroad bridge at Albany could prove vital in linking the Erie, with all its valuable Pennsylvania coalfield connections, to coal-hungry New England.

Founded in 1852 by Joseph H. Ramsey, the small but profitable A&S remained to some extent under Ramsey's control in 1869. However, full half of the A&S's fourteen directors (led by its vice president Walter S. Church) stood opposed to Ramsey's management, and Ramsey himself had recently announced that either one side or the other would have to leave after the next round of board elections. Church and Gould therefore struck an agreement and made a plan to seize control of the A&S. To this end, Gould started buying what he could of the thinly traded A&S stock. In the process, Gould sent the price up to new highs of about a hundred dollars from its average in the low twenties but failed to tie up enough equity to ensure his dominance in concert with Church's group of directors.

Upon investigation, Gould found that the main reason for the scarcity of shares on the open market was the possession of large blocks by municipal governments along the A&S line. Under New York law, these municipally held shares could be sold by the towns only under very specific terms: at or above par value, and only for cash. Although Gould shortly succeeded in purchasing several hundred shares at par, he still remained short by the end of July, at which point he brought a dozen or so local commissioners from villages and hamlets in the western Catskills down to Manhattan as guests of the Erie Railroad. Gould and Fisk put up the gentlemen (representing some 4,500 shares among them) at the Fifth Avenue Hotel. They treated them to fine meals, took them on a tour of the new Erie offices, and then, on 1 August, made them an offer. If the trustees would vote with Church and Gould at the upcoming annual meeting of the A&S, allowing the Erie to take control of that road, the Erie would then buy all their shares at par value, providing a massive financial windfall to their various governments. The thought that Gould's pledge was not legally enforceable apparently did not occur to the gathered local commissars, all of whom readily agreed to the deal. (Only the representative from Oneonta had the wit to insist that the Erie purchase his government's shares before, rather than after, the A&S's annual meeting. This insistence caused Gould to go into a sprint in order to get the deal done on time, as the A&S subscription books were set to close on 7 August, one month before the 7 September meeting.)

Ramsey, for his part, was not unaware of the intrigue against his authority. A friend and ally of Vanderbilt's who harbored a strong antipathy to Gould and Fisk, Ramsey now took steps to protect his domain. Legislation years before had authorized the issuance of 40,000 shares of A&S stock. However, given the small demand and the general lack of speculation in the stock, some 12,000 shares had never in fact been issued. Now, in collaboration with a few partners, Ramsey subscribed 9,500 new shares at $100 per share, putting down a deposit of 10 percent ($95,000), which he borrowed using $150,000 in A&S bonds as collateral. Subsequently, the company's Ramseyite treasurer did his best to delay the formal transfer of Oneonta's 700 A&S shares to the Erie. On 3 August, after receiving an order from a Supreme Court judge in Owego, the treasurer happily refused to effect the transfer of the shares in the firm's subscription books. But then, twenty-four hours later, Thomas Shearman swooped in and arranged for the suddenly compliant Owego judge to lift his injunction. One day after that, Shearman orchestrated an order from Judge Barnard compelling the transfer of the Oneonta stock. For good measure, Barnard also suspended Ramsey from the A&S board.

Walter Church now planned a meeting for the morning of the 6th where, with Ramsey absent, he would force a vote to fire the treasurer and appoint one favorable to the Erie group. That meeting was just getting under way when several Ramsey attorneys interrupted. The lawyers served Church and three other Erie-friendly board members with injunctions from Albany State Supreme Court Judge Rufus Peckham (father of a future U.S. Supreme Court justice of the same name), suspending *them* from the A&S board. This injunction in effect left the A&S without management, as the accumulated suspensions meant that those board members still standing did not constitute a quorum. Hearing this, Shearman, seasoned by the recent fight for the Erie, immediately realized what the A&S needed: *a receiver.* "Come to New York without fail tonight," read a cable sent the afternoon of the 6th to Judge Barnard, tending the bedside of his dying mother in Poughkeepsie. "Answer care 359 West Twenty-third Street."[15] This was Josie Mansfield's address. Leaving his mother to meet her maker without him, Barnard traveled immediately to Manhattan, where he signed papers appointing Fisk and one Charles Courter of Cobleskill—an Erie-friendly member of the A&S board—receivers for the A&S.

Later that night, Fisk traveled north on Vanderbilt's New York Central, carrying Barnard's order and accompanied by several attorneys and bodyguards. The party met Courter at the Delavan House. There they rested for the night, unaware that Ramsey's judge, Peckham of Albany, had already named one Robert H. Pruyn (a local and a Ramsey protégé) as receiver for the A&S. When Fisk, Courter, and company arrived at the A&S offices near the Albany riverfront the next morning—Saturday, 7 August—they found Pruyn already in possession and his terrain protected by more than a dozen tough railroad mechanics headed by John W. Van Valkenburg, general superintendent of the A&S. Van Valkenburg admitted Courter, an A&S board member whom he could not readily turn away, into the office. But he insisted that Fisk and the various Erie henchmen wait in the antechamber. When Fisk and his toughs tried to advance on the door, Van Valkenburg's more numerous men easily turned them back. Subsequently, one of the A&S mechanics, posing as an Albany detective, pretended to take Fisk into custody. The man marched Fisk all the way to the station house before revealing that he was no officer of the law at all.

After wiring Judge Barnard for more injunctions, Fisk returned to the A&S office, where, unaccountably, an air of civility now dominated. When one of Ramsey's lawyers showed up, Receiver Pruyn "claimed the honor of introducing him to his friend Mr. James Fisk, Jr.," wrote a reporter for the *Albany Evening Journal*. Fisk in turn complimented Van Valkenburg on his thoroughness and manliness and assured him there would always be a place for him with the Erie should he want it. On through the muggy afternoon "the lawyers assembled, and grave efforts were made by all parties to maintain composure and be friendly and genial, which succeeded to a good degree. The hours passed in talking over matters between each other, private consultations, jokes and business."[16] Later, when a freshly minted order arrived from Barnard via telegraph, thus lacking all the requisite signatures and seals, it was seen by everyone in the room as a topic for further discussion rather than an unequivocal rule of law. Barnard's new injunction vacated Peckham's ruling naming Pruyn receiver. It also forbade Pruyn, the Albany County sheriff, the Albany police, and railroad employees from standing in the way of Courter and Fisk. As a means to this end, Barnard issued the sheriff a writ of assistance "commanding him to call upon the whole county as a posse comitatus, if need be, to enforce the writ." But Barnard's order seemed unenforceable, and the parties foresaw no immediate end to their deadlock. Thus they agreed to "rest on their arms till nine o'clock Monday morning, each receiver leaving a personal representative in the office."[17]

Fisk took a late train back to Manhattan, where he conferred with Gould. Returning Sunday by night boat up the Hudson, he carried with him Judge

Barnard's orders formally executed on paper. But these did him no good. Ramsey's support in Albany, where he lived, was quite strong. Few in that town believed Fisk's true-enough assertion that Albany's interests would be advanced by Erie control of the A&S. As John Steele Gordon observed, Fisk and Gould's plan for the A&S involved turning Albany into an important hub. "Because of the Erie's crippling broad gauge, a defect it shared with the Albany & Susquehanna," wrote Gordon, "[the Erie] would have no choice but to break bulk at Albany on the way to New England [while] the New York Central could, and increasingly would, treat Albany as a whistle-stop."[18] But such fine points of railroad strategy were not easily conveyed via the press, at least not quickly with little time to spare.

At 8 A.M. on Monday, 9 August, Van Valkenburg sent messengers out on the A&S local for Binghamton with instructions for stationmasters to ignore court orders siding with Erie control. At the same time, Fisk had Barnard wire copies of his writs directly to Binghamton. There, the Broome County sheriff, acting on Barnard's writs, seized the A&S terminal at 2 P.M. The sheriff locked down three of the four locomotives, the last making a fast escape in the direction of Albany. Thirty minutes later, the sheriff joined H.D.V. Pratt (Receiver Fisk's newly appointed superintendent of the A&S, and no relation to old Zadock) and some twenty Erie mechanics on an Erie train aimed east through the Catskills toward Albany. They traveled at a fast clip, intent on taking possession of each station as they went. On the opposite end of the line, Van Valkenburg ordered all regularly scheduled A&S trains to pull onto sidings. Then he sent a special train headed east toward Binghamton loaded with 150 heavily armed men under the command of attorney Henry Smith. Smith's special stopped at each station, leaving off a contingent of guards to protect the property of the A&S from Erie invaders.

The two engines met at the town of Bainbridge. Smith's train arrived there first. When the Erie train rolled in that evening, Pratt and his cohorts saw the A&S special pulled up on a siding. After a brief pause to ponder the possibilities, Pratt foolishly ordered his train to continue straight ahead. As a more astute commander—perhaps Gould—might have predicted, the Erie engine soon ran into sabotage. A "frog" routing device laid down on the track quickly derailed the Erie train, stranding it where it stood. Pratt then surrendered to Smith, whose men set the Erie engine back onto its tracks before escorting it to Albany. Undaunted by this turn of events, Fisk at the

Delavan House wired his men at Binghamton to prepare another engine. The new train set out on the afternoon of Tuesday, 10 August, with 600 men but little in the way of guns or ammunition: just clubs hastily carved from the trees of the nearby woods. Later that day, at the railroad tunnel near Harpursville, New York, the Erie engine met an A&S train loaded with 450 Van Valkenburg stalwarts.

The Erie train stopped at the sight of the oncoming A&S engine traveling slowly up a steep grade on the eastern side of the tunnel. Thus the collision, when it came, was not overly traumatic. It demolished each engine's cowcatcher and partially derailed the A&S train, from which the well-armed Van Valkenburg forces poured out, scattering the club-wielding Erie defenders, who broke and ran back into the safety of the dark tunnel, their engine backing up behind them. A few minutes later, after the A&S fighters put their engine back on the tracks and proceeded to meet the Erie men at the western end of the tunnel, a full battle broke out. "The conflict was reopened with great fury," reported *Leslie's Illustrated Newspaper*. "The Erie men, occupying their own ground, had no intention of giving it up. . . . The Albany men, flushed with success, attacked vigorously. Pistols were used, with stones, clubs, and fists."[19] This bloody stalemate continued until the Forty-fourth Regiment of the State Militia arrived to quell the riot—at which point all combatants, those of the Erie together with those of the A&S, retreated into the woods to avoid arrest. By nightfall, the Erie train occupied the western end of the tunnel and the A&S train the eastern. Miraculously, no one died, although ten had been shot and many more suffered various bruises.

The next day—Wednesday, 11 August—both sides agreed to the governor's appointment of Major General James McQuade, Inspector General of the State Militia, as interim superintendent of the A&S. Less than a month later, at the annual election of the A&S board on 7 September, there erupted "a perfect meteoric shower of suits, injunctions, and receiverships that has not been surpassed in any of the Erie Wars," continuing the stalemate.[20] A series of court cases followed, amid which—during a brief interlude when the courts gave him and his clique control of the A&S—Ramsey adopted the advice of J. P. Morgan, who recommended that the A&S be leased to the Delaware & Hudson Canal Company, thus effectively insulating it from takeover by the Erie.

In the aftermath of the war for the A&S, more than one commentator noted the absence of Jay Gould from center stage. Some assumed, incorrectly, that the fight had been Fisk's alone, a diversion allowed the Prince of Erie by the railroad's undisputed king. Nothing could have been further from the truth. Gould was in fact preoccupied with another, far more important project at the same—a complex and ultimately flawed scheme that would forever cement his and Fisk's reputations as pirates.

Chapter 19

WHERE THE WOODBINE TWINETH

EARLY IN THE AFTERNOON of 15 June 1869, President Ulysses S. Grant, in office just three months, encountered Jay Gould at the West Twenty-seventh Street mansion of the president's sixty-seven-year-old brother-in-law, Abel Rathbone Corbin.[1] Grant and his wife, Julia, who'd attended the commencement at West Point that morning, were passing through Manhattan on their way to a somewhat belated celebration marking the end of the War Between the States: the National Peace Jubilee in Boston. After an hour or so of cordialities, the Grants, together with Corbin, Gould, Treasury Secretary George S. Boutwell, Atlantic-cable innovator Cyrus Field (brother of Gould's sometime-attorney David Dudley Field), and several other worthies traveled with a military escort down to the Chambers Street pier. There Fisk's Narragansett Line steamship *Providence* awaited. Fisk and Gould had volunteered the vessel to the convenience of the president. Fisk, dressed in his admiral's finery, stood beaming on the gangway. Just behind him, Dodworth's Band, the finest such organization in Manhattan, boomed a rousing march as the president boarded.

Grant's brother-in-law Corbin—the man instrumental in bringing Gould and Grant together—was a widower who'd only recently married Grant's spinster sister, Virginia Paine Grant. Corbin had a gnarled and troubled

history as a somewhat shady lawyer, speculator, and lobbyist. Technically retired, he nevertheless continued to dabble in various Wall Street and real estate investments. It was, in fact, a New Jersey land speculation that had first
brought him into Gould's orbit early in 1869. More recently, Gould had allowed Corbin to join him in an audacious private investment involving gold.

Until the end of 1861, the federal government had contributed only
coinage to the national money supply. All paper currency had emanated
from state-chartered banks, which issued notes backed by their deposits.
Early in the Civil War, however, the National Banking Act and the Legal
Tender Act set up nationally chartered banks with the power to issue currency backed by government bonds. At the same time, the U.S. Treasury
began issuing nonredeemable notes: some $400 million in greenbacks, not
backed by gold, that allowed the government to pay for the Civil War but
caused great inflation. Starting in mid-1865, the government slowly began
to withdraw greenbacks from circulation. This withdrawal led to a fall in the
per-ounce price of gold from nearly 300 in greenbacks in 1865 to 130 by
early 1869. (Of course, in addition to adjusting the amount of currency in
circulation, the U.S. Treasury could also influence the greenback price of
gold through carefully calculated sales from the million-ounce gold hoard in
the Federal Reserve.)

In 1862, traders had set up a formal "Gold Room" right next to the New
York Stock Exchange. Four years later, various members of the Exchange
organized the Gold Exchange Bank, a clearinghouse that by 1869 averaged
$70 million in greenback business every day, the lion's share of this trade
being transacted on margin. As Gould later explained to a congressional investigating committee, "A man with $100,000 of money and with credit can
transact a business of $20,000,000," the latter figure, coincidentally, being
the total gold available in New York City at that time.[2]

Gould did not, at first, attempt to reach this far. During April 1869—
using only the smallest slice of his own capital—he tied up approximately $7
million in gold contracts, purchasing these on margin at rates varying from
a low of 130 (ounce price) to a high of 137. When he sold a few weeks later,
he did so after bulling the price up to 142. A subsequent bull rush in Jay's
wake sent the price even higher, to 145—a number that caused Treasury
Secretary Boutwell to double the weekly amount of gold sold by the government, which promptly brought down the price. Gould, meanwhile, took no-

tice of the Treasury Department's power to shape and move the market. To Giovanni Morosini he commented—as if idly, by way of fantasy—that if one could control or at least have advance knowledge of the Treasury's movements with regard to gold, then one would be in a position to corner the market, reaping a massive return in the process.

Although the United States was slow to get back onto a firm gold standard after the Civil War, the rest of the world had never left it. Therefore all American merchants involved in export were forced to pay for domestic goods and commodities using fluctuating greenbacks, before selling these goods overseas for gold. For American importers, of course, this process reversed itself, but it still involved the same dilemma of exposure to unpredictable greenback values. "To protect themselves," explained Maury Klein, "merchants paid a premium to borrow gold and sold it for the greenbacks needed to make their purchases. After a foreign exchange house discounted his bill, the merchant took the gold paid him and returned it to the loaner. This was in theory the legitimate business function of the Gold Exchange, but it also offered choice opportunities for speculation. Merchants who borrowed in this manner were in effect short of gold. A fall in the price could wipe out their profits on business transactions. However, a sharp rise in gold required merchants to put up fresh margins (in greenbacks) against what they had borrowed. In the process some might go bankrupt before their bills were discounted abroad. If speculators could control the available supply of gold, they could use the frantic buying by merchants who were short to help run the price up."[3]

Going into the summer of 1869, as Gould began to consider a serious move to corner gold, he did so with two agendas. First, of course, he hoped to make a speculative killing. But he also sought to raise chronically depressed commodities prices and thus build up the Erie's farm-freight-hauling business. Taking his cue from James McHenry, a British financier who held stock in the Erie and was also president of the Atlantic & Great Western Railway, Gould realized that a sharp decline in the value of greenbacks against gold would stimulate American agricultural exports by making western wheat and grain—not to mention southern cotton—relatively cheap for gold-based foreign markets to buy and more profitable for American farmers (paid in greenbacks for their crops) to sell. On the other hand, as Gould told Corbin several weeks before their cruise with the president, if the government were to do anything to strengthen green-backs (such as stepping up sales of gold from the Federal Reserve as it had in May), then in the long run American crops would go unharvested, farmers would go bankrupt, boxcars would stand idle, and economic depression would overwhelm the landscape.

Gould ensured Corbin's dedication to the economic national good (that is, escalating gold prices) by providing him an account (recorded in his wife's name) containing certificates for $1.5 million in gold without margin. From that moment on, Corbin (or rather, his wife) would profit $15,000 on every $1 rise in the greenback price of gold. In early June, shortly after the account materialized in the name of Grant's sister, Gould sent Corbin to Washington, there to lobby his brother-in-law on the necessity of tightening the gold supply. And now, as the *Providence* eased away from Manhattan on the evening of 15 June with the Grants ensconced in the ship's bridal suite, Gould prepared to drive home the argument in person.

After a fine dinner followed by whiskey and cigars, Gould broached the topic of federal gold policy with Grant and Secretary Boutwell. "The President was a listener," Gould would recall for congressional investigators. "The other gentlemen were discussing. Some were in favor of Boutwell's selling gold, and some were opposed to it. After they had all interchanged [*sic*] their views, some one asked the President what his opinion was." Gould said later that he was chagrined when Grant discounted his carefully crafted arguments for boosting the price of gold. Grant, much to Gould's surprise, spoke on behalf of sound money and the orderliness of the gold standard. "There is a certain amount of fictitiousness about the prosperity of the country," Grant said, adding that "the bubble might as well be tapped in one way as another." The remark, Gould commented later, "struck across" him and his allies "like a wet blanket." As Gould recalled, "I gave it as my opinion that if that policy were carried out it would produce great distress, and almost lead to civil war; it would produce strikes among the workmen, and the workshops, to a great extent, would have to be closed. . . . I took the ground that the government ought to let gold alone, and let it find its commercial level; that, as a matter of fact, it ought to facilitate an upward movement of gold in the fall." Grant remained unmoved through the rest of the journey, and as Gould said later, "We supposed from that conversation that the President was a contractionist."[4]

With typical fortitude, Gould continued his siege of the chief executive. When Grant returned to New York on 18 June, he attended a performance of Jacque Offenbach's *La Perichole* at Fisk's Fifth Avenue Theater, Grant sharing Fisk's proscenium box with Gould and the Corbins. Jay talked nothing but gold during the intermission. On several other occasions that summer when Grant overnighted at the home of the Corbins, Gould made it his habit to materialize along with a briefcase full of data demonstrating the need for some healthy inflation. Eventually, in early August, an exasperated Grant told Corbin's chief butler to turn Gould away if he showed up, because the Erie president "was always trying to get something out of him."[5]

Gould did, however, make some inroads. When the post of assistant federal treasurer for New York came open in late June, Gould through Corbin lobbied successfully for the appointment of Brigadier General Daniel Butterfield, a retired Civil War officer (and former eastern superintendent of the American Express Company), remembered today as the composer of "Taps." Butterfield was actually Gould's second choice for the job. The first had been Corbin's son-in-law, Robert B. Catherwood, who evidently took himself out of the running when he learned the impropriety of what would be expected of him. "I satisfied myself that I could not fill the bill," Catherwood would tell future president James A. Garfield, chair of the House Committee looking into Gould's gold speculations, "[for] it was understood that if I took the position, Gould, Corbin, myself and others would go into some operations such as the purchase of gold and stocks, and that we would share and share alike."[6] Not afflicted by Catherwood's scruples, Butterfield started as assistant treasurer on 1 July. His new position called for Butterfield to execute all orders for U.S. Treasury transactions in the New York market. By definition, therefore, Butterfield would be the second man after Secretary Boutwell himself to know of any U.S. Treasury moves with regard to gold. Shortly, Gould gave Butterfield a "loan" of $10,000 that was never to be repaid. He also set up a no-margin gold account for Butterfield just as he'd done for Corbin, even though Butterfield would later deny it.

By mid-July, the price of gold stood at 136 and was headed south. This downward movement looked as if it would continue even though Boutwell—surveying Department of Agriculture forecasts projecting bumper crops and at the same time noting steep declines in port grain export receipts—took steps to shore up gold prices by reducing government sales. Two weeks later, at the start of August (as Fisk waged the war for the A&S), Gould bought a controlling interest in New York's Tenth National Bank, many shares of which he soon conveyed to Fisk and several other Erie and Tammany colleagues. Henceforth, the Tenth National would supply Gould with a more than ample line of unsecured credit for his gold speculations, even issuing certified checks for funds not already on deposit. Meanwhile, Gould formed a pool comprising a number of Wall Street brokers and investors, including Arthur Kimber, W. S. Woodward, Russell A. Hills, James Ellis, H. K. Enos, Edward K. Willard, and Charles Quincy.

Fisk, however, bowed out at first. In leaving Gould to his plan, Fisk cited Grant's seeming intransigence and uncontrollability. Although Fisk remained willing to help his partner any way he could, at the outset he kept his own money off the table. "The thing began to look scary to me," he would say later.[7] Indeed, given the many wild cards in play, it seems surprising that the normally careful Gould—always so intent on controlling every aspect of his deals—decided to go ahead with the plan to corner gold. For starters, Gould's pool was barely that. The "members" remained independent, giving Gould no fiduciary authority over their investments. Each player was free to buy or sell according to his own clock. As well, although Gould's "inside" man, Corbin, had succeeded in securing the nomination of Butterfield, it seemed apparent after numerous conversations with Grant that Corbin would be useless in influencing economic policy. (Worried about Corbin's value, Gould soon tried to seduce Grant's military secretary and confidante, General Horace Porter, with a no-margin gold account of $500,000, only to find himself indignantly rebuffed.)

Nevertheless, after a false start during late July when he managed to bull gold up to only 140 before a precipitous fallback to 135 7/8, Gould and his allies began buying in earnest in mid-August. On the 25th, to help his campaign along, Gould arranged for the witless John Bigelow—former ambassador to France and newly appointed editor of the *New York Times* (where he would not last)—to publish an editorial that pretended to present informed details concerning Grant's position on gold. Entitled "The Financial Policy of the Administration," the piece asserted that "until the crops are moved, it is not likely Treasury gold will be sold for currency to be locked up. . . . The President will not send gold into the market and sell it for currency."[8] The next day, feigning ignorance of how the editorial had come to be, Gould wrote Boutwell, "If the *New York Times* correctly reflects your financial policy during the next three or four months . . . then I think the country peculiarly fortunate in having a financial head who can take a broad view of the situation. . . . It is only by making gold high and scarce that . . . we are enabled to compete in the London and Liverpool markets."[9]

One week later, Gould managed another meeting with Grant at Corbin's house when the vacationing president passed through New York on his way from Newport to Saratoga. During their talk, Grant revealed that reports of enormous harvests in the West had brought him round to Gould's point of view. American farmers would need to be able to sell their excess abroad, and the government would have to help them by condoning some well-timed inflation. Writing to Boutwell on 4 September, Grant stated categorically that it was "undesirable to force down the price of gold."[10] Immediately after this chat with Grant, Gould instructed his allies to begin buying gold contracts even faster than before. Pushing most of his personal trades through his old firm of Smith, Gould & Martin, Jay told his colleague Smith to work through a number of subbrokers in order to avoid the appearance of orchestration. By mid-September, Gould's pool controlled contracts far in excess of the amount of gold to be found anywhere in New York outside federal vaults. Gould alone held contracts valued at $25 million, and the other members of his clique possessed contracts totaling $65 million more.

On the 13th, when the president returned to Manhattan en route to Pennsylvania for a visit with relatives of Mrs. Grant, Gould offered the chief executive a private Erie Railroad car to take him to Pittsburgh—thus reinforcing the general view that he had Grant's ear. According to James B. Hodgskin, a broker who headed the Gold Room's arbitration committee, it was common knowledge "that the parties who . . . were manipulating the gold market had in league with them pretty much everybody in authority in the United States, beginning with President Grant and ending with the door-keepers of Congress."[11] But this impression, which Gould certainly wanted to enforce, hardly reflected reality. In fact, Grant was wary of being manipulated by Gould or anyone else. In the same week that he accepted Gould's hospitality on the Erie Railroad, Grant sent a second note to Boutwell in which he commented that "a desperate struggle is now taking place, and each party wants the government to help them out. . . . I think, from the lights before me, I would move on, without change, until the present struggle is over."[12]

By now, the struggle of which Grant spoke involved Gould against some of his own recent pool members. The voracious buying of Gould and his cohorts had driven the gold price to 138 by 8 September, at which point Jay's cabal began to show signs of fragmenting. On that day Corbin, nervous about the prospect for further heights, demanded and got from Jay the profits on the gold purchased for him. Kimber abandoned ship as well, taking profits on his $10 million in gold contracts before switching to the short side of the speculation, joining the numerous bear operators who were anxious to depress prices. Woodward could be induced to stay "long" only after Jay relieved him of $6 million out of the $10 million in his account. During the second week of September the bears had their way, causing gold to slide down to 135, where it remained for several days, a hiatus occasioned not only by Kimber's defection but by the New York market's receipt of fresh certificates from Boston, Philadelphia, and Chicago.

At this time, early in the second week of September, the press began to take notice of the operation. The *New York Tribune*'s Horace Greeley thundered against Gould and the other "goldbugs." Greeley denounced what he called "a vast gold conspiracy." He likewise called upon the U.S. Treasury to sell gold and purchase bonds, thereby relieving the growing currency tension.[13] Concurrently, leading financial writers for all the other major papers (most notably Caleb Norvell of the *New York Times*, Ford Barksdale of the *Sun*, and George Crouch of the *Herald*) now zeroed in on the mechanics of the corner. The *Times*'s man, Norvell, became especially active, that paper still being embarrassed after having been duped into running Gould's proinflation propaganda back in August. Meanwhile, a thousand or more small speculators eagerly placed their highly leveraged bets, long or short, remembering the killing they'd made a year before when Gould had sought to corner the Erie.

Dogged buying by Gould and his remaining associates brought gold back up to 138 on the 15th, at which point Wall Street's numerous advocates of "sound" (uninflated) money began to petition Boutwell for a narrowing of the spread between greenbacks and gold. Next, in a clumsy attempt to counter this lobby, the increasingly nervous Gould embarked upon an action that proved lethal to his cause. Gould instructed Corbin to write his brother-in-law a letter arguing, once again, against federal intervention. Then he had the letter hand-delivered by an Erie employee—W. O. Chapin—who called upon the president in rural Washington, Pennsylvania, eighteen miles outside Pittsburgh. Arriving at the temporary presidential retreat on the morning of the 16th, Chapin watched as Grant read the letter. Grant, however, offered no reply. An hour later, Chapin wired Gould that the letter had been "Delivered. All right." But all was not right. Thinking it odd that his brother-in-law had sent a courier to find him in the wilderness and deliver a plea for support of gold prices, Grant at long last realized that Corbin was an interested party, long on gold and anxious to influence the president to protect his financial position. That same day, when the enraged Grant came upon his wife in the process of writing a letter to his sister Virginia, he gave her a very specific message to convey. "Tell your husband," wrote Julia Grant, "that my husband is very much annoyed by your speculations. You must close them as quick as you can!"[14]

While Julia was penning those words, the Corbins were entertaining Jim Fisk and confidently telling him gold could not fail. The still-skeptical Fisk, seeking reassurance from the Corbins, was being recruited by Gould to replace Kimber and the weakening Woodward as an ally against the growing horde of bears. According to Fisk's later testimony, his loyal friend lied in order to lure him in, saying Grant himself as well as General Porter were full partners in the scheme. "I know there will be no gold sold by the government," the president's sister told Fisk, backing up Gould's story. "I am quite positive there will be no gold sold; for this is the chance of a life time for us; you need not have any uneasiness whatever."[15]

With Gould's and the Corbins' assurance that federal policy was well in hand, Fisk now plunged in, agreeing to help Jay nudge gold up to a comfortable height, at which point they would both exit. According to their plan, Fisk would transact all his purchases independently of Gould, routing them through a network of brokers administered by his old partner Belden. As Jay would later say, "Our interests were entirely separate. He had his own gold and I had mine."[16] In addition to his fresh credit, Fisk also brought to the enterprise something else Gould sorely lacked: personality and panache, which by mere projection could nudge prices higher. "Gold!" Fisk replied loudly to William Fowler's street-corner inquiry about where things were headed. "Sell it short and invite me to your funeral!"[17]

Meanwhile, newspaper editorial-page editors followed Greeley's lead in boosting one side or the other. The *World*, on the morning of Thursday, 16 September, criticized bearish Republican bankers, hinting at their presumed close relationship with the administration at the expense of the common man. "Why even a 'trooly loil' gold-gambler should expect the government to assist him in making money . . . in his gold-gambling operations is a question which the heavily taxed, hard working, non-gambling people may well ask."[18] But the *Herald*, although urging Boutwell not to be unduly influenced by either lobby in the debate, nevertheless chose to err on the side of the judicious inflation endorsed by Gould: "The only people who want gold cheap at this season are the few merchants who [are short in] gold. Those who wish to see gold higher are the great body of produce and cotton merchants [who] desire to market their goods in Europe for the greatest sum of greenbacks possible."[19] In other words, according to the *Herald*'s analysis, in this instance only speculators would benefit from sound money, while working people would benefit from the lack of same.[20]

The following Monday, the 20th, the story of what was going on in the gold market leaped from the editorial and financial pages to the front page, with the *Sun* breathlessly announcing that an "alliance of the most powerful and influential firms in Wall Street, including notorious Erie speculators, has been effected with a view of obtaining the exclusive possession of all the gold in the market."[21] Two days later, the *Times* took issue with Gould's idea that his maneuvering for higher gold prices would help agricultural prices. Caleb Norvell pointed out how the uncertainty over gold had created chaos in foreign exchange and produce markets, causing prices for a host of commodities to drop. "Large export orders for Flour, Grain, Provisions, Petroleum, &c., are held in abeyance on account of the difficulty of negotiating Exchange," Norvell wrote. This problem was bound to continue until "the combination in Gold is broken down." Imports from Europe could do it; so could action by the U.S. Treasury. But something had to happen in short order to create "a free supply of gold which speculation cannot lock up or control."[22]

Despite all this journalistic hand-wringing, the fact is that by the close of trading on Wednesday, 22 September, Fisk and Gould had managed to bull the price of gold up to only 141 1/2. Not very impressive, considering Fisk alone by this point held contracts valued between $50 million and $60 million and other members of the Gould pool had likewise increased their purchases. (Henry Smith wound up with contracts totaling $50 million.) Still, the attempted corner had already had its unintended impact. With the bears fighting back ferociously, scarcity of credit now sent interest rates soaring, making the market for cash contract to a point where it began to affect both the stock and the bond markets. (Stocks, which nearly always moved inversely to gold, were already sinking. In the midst of all their other busy deal making that Wednesday, Gould and Fisk paused long enough to sideswipe their old nemesis Vanderbilt, mounting a quick bear raid of the New York Central that sent that stock down 25 percent in just a few hours.) Meanwhile, in the Gold Room, bulls were paying half a percent per day for the funds needed to carry their contracts. At the same time, some bear operators, after lending the funds for gold, used the return to borrow gold, which they, in turn, sold short.

"There is a panic on Wall Street," Gould wrote Boutwell on Wednesday afternoon, "engineered by a bear combination. They have withdrawn currency to such an extent that it is impossible to do ordinary business."[23] Jay pleaded with Boutwell to increase the currency supply for the general good, but he never once brought up his own personal need for ready credit with which to finance his unique project. Shortly before sending his message to Boutwell, Gould suffered a conversation with the frantic Corbin, whose wife had just received the letter from Julia Grant. After a long discussion, Gould promised Corbin what amounted to a $100,000 bribe if he would just keep Julia Grant's letter confidential. "I am undone," Gould told Corbin, "if that letter gets out."[24] (Ironically, the *Evening Mail* painted a very different picture of how things stood with Gould, and one wonders if Jay himself didn't plant the misinformation: "At no time for months have the bull clique of operators felt more sure of their ground than they were [on Wednesday]. They were even somewhat indifferent as to whether or not Mr. Boutwell came into the market, and boasted that they could put gold up to 150 if they chose to press matters."[25])

The next morning at Castle Erie, Gould did not tell Fisk of Julia Grant's letter to Corbin's wife. He explained simply that Corbin needed money. Later on, the still confident Fisk told his broker, Belden, to put gold up to 144. At the same time, in another office, Jay quietly and without Fisk's knowledge instructed Smith to stop buying and to start selling on a slow schedule, so as not to raise suspicions. Concerned about looming federal intervention if gold went much higher, Jay shifted gears as swiftly as a loco-motive and became a stealth bear. "The only hope," commented Maury Klein, "lay in Jay selling out his holdings in a rising market, which could best be done if Fisk continued to play his role of bull to the hilt. When the price collapsed, Fisk and his brokers would suffer heavy losses but Jay would emerge relatively unscathed. The task then would be to extricate Fisk from the wreckage."[26] This would be done in the usual way: by using the courts as a shield and reneging on obligations.

The Gold Room opened Thursday morning at 141 5/8 and closed at 143 1/4. Fisk and other members of the pool bought frantically while a number of the less solvent bears literally went broke trying to cover their short posi-tions. Caleb Norvell, after looking down from the gallery at the frantic trad-ing below, wrote that the "roar of battle and the screams of the victims" made it seem "as though human nature were undergoing torments worse than any that Dante ever witnessed in Hell."[27] Total Gold Room volume for the day exceeded $239 million, a 66 percent increase over Wednesday's brisk trade. Belden operatives buying for Fisk secured $14 million in contracts in just four hours, and Smith arranged for an unwitting subbroker to acquire $3.4 million in Gould's name as a smokescreen to hide Gould's revised agenda. Another of Smith's subbrokers sold more than $8 million of Gould's con-tracts, the majority of these ironically going to brokers buying for Fisk. "My purchases were very light," Gould said later, describing Thursday's trading. "I was a net seller of gold that day. I purchased merely enough to make be-lieve that I was a bull."[28]

That evening, in Washington, Secretary Boutwell called on Grant, now returned to the White House from Pennsylvania. Boutwell had, in the pre-vious hours, been bombarded with telegrams from merchants and bankers imploring him to sell gold to depress the price. He'd also received reports of the Tenth National Bank's certifying checks for bullish "goldbugs" without requiring deposits to back them up. Boutwell informed Grant that he'd dis-patched examiners to the Tenth National. They would be at the door when the bank opened for business the next morning. He also asked for instruc-tions regarding gold—instructions Grant declined to give. The president said only that the price of gold was a bubble, and that Boutwell should act on the matter however he thought appropriate.

◇   ◇   ◇

On the morning of Friday, 24 September—the day to be known ever after as Black Friday—the *Times*'s Caleb Norvell ran an outraged piece describing Thursday's action.

[Fisk's] presence in the Gold Room was signalized by the rapid rise in gold [and] the other engineers of the movement were not idle. . . . They had not only bulled gold with a will, but talked freely of the warrant which they had from Washington that the government would not interfere with them. The highest official in the land was quoted *as being with them,* and he, of course, controls the actions of the Secretary of the Treasury and the New York Assistant Treasurer. Although this must have been known to be false, there were abundant rumors and suspicions insidiously spread around the street to create the belief or fear with good men that the administration would not interpose by further sales of gold from the Treasury.[29]

At this juncture, Jay himself knew it was only a matter of time before Grant and Boutwell acted against him. And with the *Times* publicly challenging his influence, it seemed that now was the moment to bring things to a head.

Very early in the morning on Friday, Gould visited Butterfield at the Treasury Building, where the assistant treasurer told him that no orders of any kind had yet been received from Washington. Later Gould spent an hour at Castle Erie with Fisk, who by now understood the situation but had agreed to continue to act the part of bull for the sake of appearances. Then, at about 8:30, the two went down to the Broad Street offices of broker William Heath, who'd lately been assisting Belden with his buying. Gould and Fisk would remain at Heath's for the balance of the day, protected by several large Erie Railroad guards and conducting their business out of two separate rooms. Telling Belden that gold would close at 200, Fisk sent him out to the Gold Room with orders to buy all he could at 145. Gould, meanwhile, issued very different instructions via Smith. "Sell, sell, sell," Smith whispered to subbroker Edward K. Willard. At the same time, Willard was to make no contact with brokers buying for Fisk.[30] Shortly thereafter, when the buy-side broker Heath asked Gould for more greenbacks and more margin, Gould scribbled a note instructing the Tenth National to certify some checks and extend some credit.

In the Gold Room, shouted bids well before the formal 10 A.M. opening put the starting price at 150. Belden's subbroker, Albert Speyers, led the bidding, while Belden himself pressured the most desperate bears to either put up more margin or make private settlements. Apprised of the five-dollar hike, Fisk instructed Speyers to continue buying at 150. Meanwhile, Gould sold steadily and slowly through 11 A.M., at which point—upon receipt of two ominous pieces of information—he quickly accelerated his divestitures. What caused Gould to speed his exit? First, returning from the Tenth National, Heath informed Gould that the bank could no longer be of service. Federal auditors had arrived on the premises. Word of impending failure was on the Street, and the president of the Tenth National anticipated a run at any moment. Immediately afterward, Smith reported to Gould that Joseph Seligman—the broker for Assistant Federal Treasurer Daniel Butterfield—had suddenly become a seller rather than a buyer of gold: a fact that indicated Butterfield now had knowledge of an impending federal move. (After taking his profits, Butterfield would shortly—very shortly, in fact—resign.)

Through the morning, the price moved to a high of 162, destroying literally hundreds of bearish brokers and merchants who were forced to settle their margin accounts on terrible terms. (At the same time, banks in San Francisco, where there was plenty of gold, found themselves inundated with pleas from New York for wire gold transfers. These requests were ignored, as the San Francisco bankers feared causing a shortage on the West Coast.) Then, shortly before noon, word came that Boutwell had released $4 million in government gold through Brown Brothers. By 12:30, the price had settled down to 135. Amid the chaos that followed, depending on their position, brokers and merchants hustled to either repudiate or enforce contracts made in the madness at the peak of the high.

The Gold Exchange Bank nearly collapsed under the weight of the transactions (many in dispute) that needed clearing. Down on Broad and Wall Streets, sullen and strangely quiet mobs of ruined men congregated outside the Gold Room, Heath's office, and the Tenth National (which did indeed experience a run). Across the East River in Brooklyn, a militia unit stood ready to move should events in Manhattan's financial district get out of hand (which they didn't). Meanwhile, the chaos in New York drew spectators in financial markets nationwide. Proper Bostonians huddled

Roxbury, New York, photographed at the turn of the century. The perspective is from the west looking east. The Gould farm was some two miles northwest of the village, in the hills to the left in this picture. The square tower of the Jay Gould Memorial Reformed Church—built by Jay's children in the 1890s after his death—can be seen center right. *Collection of the author*

The Gould farmhouse outside Roxbury as it looks today. The rear portion of the building is a modern addition. The original structure was built by Abraham Gould, Jr.—Jay's grandfather, a native of Fairfield, Connecticut—in 1789.

Photo by the author

The obelisk commissioned by Jay Gould in 1880 to mark the graves of his father, mother, two sisters, and two stepmothers in the cemetery of the Yellow Meeting House, Roxbury.

Photo by the author

The Yellow Meeting House, Roxbury. *Photo by the author*

Jay Gould (right) and Hamilton Burhans
photographed in Roxbury, 1855, when Jay was 19.

Photo courtesy of The New-York Historical Society

The Gould home on Vega Mountain Road—the former Elm Street—
in downtown Roxbury, to which the family moved in 1852 when Jay was
16. Nearly half a century later, in 1895, Jay's daughter Helen "Nellie"
Gould purchased the building and made it into a library for the village.
Today it is in private hands. *Photo by the author*

The old Gould tin shop on Main Street, Roxbury, around the corner from
the Elm Street house, now an art gallery. *Photo by the author*

Wall Street as it looked when Jay first went there as a 24-year-old in 1860.

Collection of the author

Jay Gould, photographed
in the mid-1870s.

Collection of the author

Helen Miller Gould—
Mrs. Jay Gould, known as
Ellie—photographed in
the mid-1870s.

*Photo courtesy of
The New-York Historical Society*

Daniel Drew (1797–1879), devious master of bear raids, bull corners, and watered stocks, who joined with Gould and James Fisk Jr. in their 1868 war against Cornelius Vanderbilt for the Erie Railroad.

Collection of the author

Vermont native James "Jubilee Jim" Fisk Jr. (1835–1872). Gould and Fisk together formed the greatest tag team ever to wrestle Wall Street to its knees.

Collection of the author

Cornelius Vanderbilt
(1794–1877), self-made multimillionaire entrepreneur of
steamships and railroads who
despised Gould but nevertheless dubbed him "the smartest
man in America."

Collection of the author

Helen Josephine "Josie" Mansfield
(1847–1931), a music-hall
actress and one-time whore whom
Fisk kept in luxury, and over
whom he was murdered.

Collection of the author

Fisk's onetime friend Edward S. "Ned" Stokes (1841–1901). The unbalanced Stokes became Josie's lover and ultimately murdered Fisk at Greenwich Village's Grand Central Hotel in January of 1872.

Collection of the author

This Thomas Nast cartoon from the February 24, 1872, issue of *Harper's Weekly* shows Gould and some associates—accompanied by a woman depicting "Justice"—standing above Fisk's grave. The cartoon is titled "Dead Man Tell No Tales." Gould says: "All the sins of the Erie lie buried here." Justice responds: "I am not quite so blind." The man seen leaning on Fisk's gravestone, a handkerchief to his face, is "Boss" William Marcy Tweed (1823–1878), Gould's ally and "Grand Sachem" of Tammany Hall.

Collection of the author

Attorney, politico, and financier Augustus Schell (1812–1884). A Tammany crony who succeeded Tweed as Grand Sachem in 1872, Schell was also an insider with the Vanderbilt organization. He partnered with Gould and Vanderbilt's son-in-law Horace Clark to successfully corner the stock of the Chicago & Northwestern during November of '72. Schell and Clark subsequently played key roles in getting Gould into the Union Pacific.

Collection of the author

Financier Russell Sage (1816–1906) served as one of Gould's closest allies for nineteen years. Sage was unlike Fisk in that his talent for business rivaled Gould's. While Fisk had usually been content to follow Gould's lead in speculation, Sage often had his own ideas.

Collection of the author

Oakes Ames (1804–1873), entrepreneur and Massachusetts congressman. Ames did much to orchestrate the Credit Mobilier, via which he lined his pockets and those of other investors through inflated prices for building the pre-Gould Union Pacific. After the scandal-plagued Oakes died of a stroke in 1873, his brother Oliver and his nephew Fred (Oliver's son) became involved with Gould in the Union Pacific and other ventures.

Collection of the author

General Grenville M. Dodge (1831–1916), chief construction engineer for the Union Pacific, to whom (in late 1873) Gould gave assurances that he intended to stay with the UP for the long haul and "make it a big thing."

Collection of the author

Connecticut-born Collis Potter Huntington (1821–1900), one of the main forces behind the Central Pacific Railroad and related properties. Gould's sometime collaborator, sometime competitor, Huntington said of Jay: "I know there are many people who do not like him [but] I will say that I always found that he would do just as he agreed to do."

Collection of the author

Investor, journalist, and industrialist Henry Villard (1835–1900), with whom Gould engaged in a lengthy negotiation over Kansas Pacific bonds through the late 1870s. "I see my friend Gould frequently," Villard wrote in 1877. "One day he talks peace and the next he threatens. But I am not afraid of him." Villard, the power behind the Northern Pacific Railroad, went on to found the Edison General Electric Company.

Collection of the author

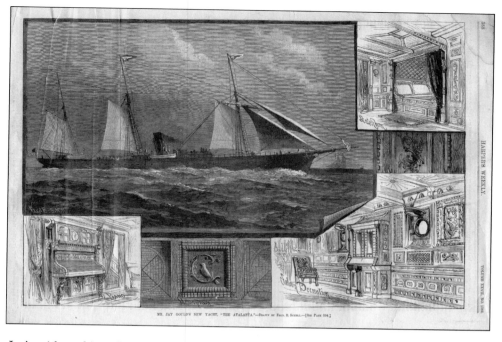

MR. JAY GOULD'S NEW YACHT, "THE ATALANTA."—Drawn by Fred. B. Schell.—[See Page 594.]

Jay's pride and joy: the *Atalanta*, launched in the spring of 1883. This is the vessel as rendered by Fred B. Schell for *Harper's Weekly*. *Collection of the author*

Joseph Pulitzer (1847–1911), who purchased the *New York World* from Jay in 1883 and then promptly made it an organ for his ridicule. Pulitzer wrote that "the mysterious, bearded Gould" was "one of the most sinister figures to have ever flitted batlike across the vision of the American people."

Collection of the author

Charles Francis Adams Jr. (1835–1915): great-grandson of John Adams and grandson of John Quincy Adams. This latter Adams wrested control of the Union Pacific from Gould in 1884, only to see Jay reclaim his prize six years later. Charles and his brother Henry sharply criticized Gould in their *Chapters of Erie, and Other Essays* (1871).

Collection of the author

This 1883 cartoon from *Puck* shows the telegraph monopolist Gould as a treed coon duping the hunter (and would-be regulator) Uncle Sam into leaving him alone.

Collection of the author

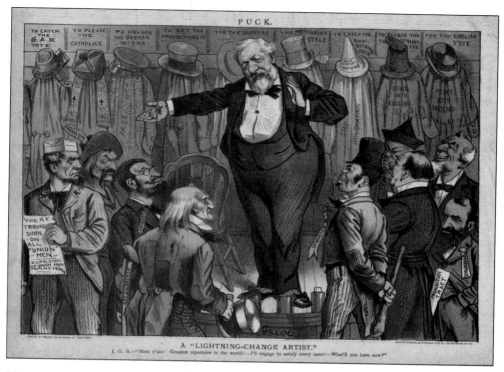

This 1884 cartoon from *Puck* shows Republican presidential nominee James G. Blaine—whom Gould supported—placating diverse constituencies while the diminutive Gould, representing "Monopoly" in the lower right, looks on knowingly. *Collection of the author*

John Pierpont Morgan (1837–1913), with whom Gould and Adams worked in late 1887 and early 1888 to bring order to the American rail industry after passage of the Interstate Commerce Act.

Collection of the author

The Jay Gould Memorial Reformed Church on Main Street in Roxbury. This was built by Gould's children and dedicated in 1894, two years after Jay's death.

Photo by the author

around the wire in the Merchants' Exchange Reading Room, clinging to snatches of news. Investors who gathered on Philadelphia's Third Street became agitated when the gold price indicator at one major bank, this connected directly to the Gold Room via telegraph, went blank. "Boys had therefore to be employed to run from the telegraph office to one broker's office after another, and cry out the premium," reported the *Philadelphia Ledger* the next day. "This added to the Babel."[31] Nearly a thousand individual investors were bankrupted on the day's activity. Fourteen brokerage houses went under, along with several banks. When the dazed Gould and Fisk finally departed Heath's building out a back door on Friday evening, they brought their guards with them and thereafter holed up for two full days at Castle Erie.

"[Jay] has sunk right down," Fisk told Corbin when the latter visited Castle Erie on Sunday. "There is nothing left of him but a heap of clothes and a pair of eyes."[32] Although at the end of the day he turned a small profit on gold, the week's massive decline in stock prices meant that Gould owed significant sums on margin calls for securities. Thus the overall financial result of his gold corner scheme was a net loss for him (though not a loss as extensive as that absorbed by many other players). As well, Gould's gold transactions were stuck in the purgatory of the Gold Exchange Bank's backlog. On Monday, Gould obtained no fewer than twelve injunctions designed to protect his and Fisk's interests, such as they were. One order appointed a Gould-friendly receiver for the Gold Exchange Bank itself. Another enjoined the Gold Room from attaching any contracts purchased by Gould's or Fisk's brokers on Black Friday. Further injunctions protected Gould's man Smith from prosecution and forbade the Gold Room to seek any redress against Fisk or Gould except through the courts. Asked about the injunctions, the Gold Exchange Bank's assistant cashier, Hiram Rogers, replied, "Oh, yes, they came in . . . by the hat full, until finally we did not know what to do. We were enjoined against performing almost every act."[33]

When asked by Congress to explain what had happened to profits from the speculation, Fisk answered that these had gone "where the woodbine twineth."[34] The fragrant woodbine, also known as honeysuckle, was commonly planted about outhouses to mask their odors. Gould's and Fisk's anticipated returns had been, to put it less delicately than Fisk could, thrown down a shithole. And a messy one at that. As Maury Klein wrote concerning the hundreds of lawsuits stemming from Black Friday, Jay "orchestrated them over a period of weeks, months, sometimes years, never intending that any should go to trial on their merits."[35] The last of these would not be resolved until 1877.

In the short term, Jay's attempted gold corner would cost him dearly in at least one other major way in addition to market losses. One of the brokerage houses that failed in the wake of Black Friday was Lockwood & Company. That firm's chairman, Legrand Lockwood, served as treasurer of the Lake Shore & Michigan Southern Line, which ran between Chicago and several up-and-coming towns in Michigan and Ohio. The Lake Shore also owned the Buffalo & Erie Railroad, which connected the Lake Shore to both the Erie Railroad and the New York Central. When his firm collapsed, Lockwood found himself forced to throw his enormous block of Lake Shore stock onto a market considerably depressed in the aftermath of Black Friday. Stressed, and with his own affairs in disarray, Gould could not act swiftly. Instead, it was Vanderbilt who purchased 70,000 shares of Lake Shore at a bargain price, taking control and ensuring that the line would thereafter become an interchange extension of the New York Central rather than the Erie.

But long term, the gold corner was to cost Gould even more dearly in the way of an irretrievably tarnished reputation.

Chapter 20

MEPHISTOPHELES

T HE DEMONIZATION OF JAY GOULD following the shipwreck of Black Friday was strident and fanatical. The juggernaut of negative press launched in late September 1869 has yet to stop, as is evidenced by annual "Today in History" blurbs that routinely damn Gould's soul in newspapers nationwide every 24 September. In Gould's own era, 1869's images of ruined men (with their implicit corollary of once-prosperous families demoted to lives of destitution) formed the bedrock for a lasting reputation as a jackal and betrayer. Gustavus Myers, an early Gould chronicler and critic, wrote that Gould "became invested with a sinister distinction as the most cold-blooded corruptionist, spoliator, and financial pirate of his time. . . . To the end of his days [this image] confronted him at every step, and survived to become the standing reproach and terror of his descendants. For nearly half a century the very name of Jay Gould was a persisting jeer and byword, an object of popular contumely and hatred, the signification of every foul and base crime by which greed triumphs."[1]

The process began with the pot calling the kettle black. In the immediate aftermath of Gould's misadventure in gold, reporters resurrected and burnished a phrase uttered by Daniel Drew one year earlier. At the time of the Erie Corner, Drew had said of Gould, "His touch is death."[2] Thereafter, similar dark metaphors sprang up like mushrooms. The *Times*'s Norvell dubbed Jay "the Mephistopheles of Wall Street."[3] Cartoons depicted him flying on batwings, horns protruding through his top hat as he scowled down on Trinity Church and Wall Street. The same papers, which in the manner of the day did not bother to mask their anti-Semitism, cited standard stereotypes and meditated on the likelihood of a Hebraic background for the covetous, devious financial predator with the Jewish-sounding first and last names. The *Sun* went so far as to suggest a Faustian overtone to Gould's skill: a pact with evil that, though it made Gould formidable in this world, would ultimately destroy him in the next. Wall Street operator James R. Keene, no saint himself, went on record denouncing Gould as "the worst man on earth since the beginning of the Christian era. He is treacherous, false, cowardly and a despicable worm incapable of a generous nature."[4] Meanwhile the *Tribune* chastised Gould for squatting, Drew-like, on the worst of his and Fisk's gold contracts: "They use lawyers' injunctions to prevent the payment of honest debts; obey the rules of the Gold Exchange when they make by it and repudiate when they lose; betray each other's counsels, sell out their confederates and consent to the ruin of their partners."[5]

Throughout October, newspapers revisited early episodes in Gould's career and recast them to fit the contours of a villainous biography. It was now that Charles Leupp's solvency and insanity at the time of his suicide were forgotten and his death moved up from 1859 to 1857, better to coincide with that earlier panic. In subsequent years, the story of Black Friday itself would be remade to include outraged, bankrupted mobs moving through the financial district hunting for Gould, all the while summoning his earlier crime with the chant "Who killed Leupp? Gould!" But according to contemporary reporting no such vigilantism occurred on the day in question, and Leupp's name never came up.[6] It was also now that the darker version of Gould's partnership with Pratt gained currency, even though the old man himself, when sought out and solicited for his opinion, starkly refused to comment on his former associate. (Approaching seventy-nine, Pratt was perhaps preoccupied with his latest wife, aged twenty-eight.)

Reporters at the *Herald* went into their files and, discovering the story of young Jay's first trip to New York, revived and revised it. Now Grandfather More's mousetrap became Jay's invention. It also became a metaphor for all things Gouldian. The *Herald* said the device—merciless, ingenious, and fatally efficient—mimicked its maker, who had gone on to lay such clever traps for other, more speculative mice. (Several cartoons stuck with the rodent-catcher image, portraying Jay as a leering housecat fiendishly toying with wounded prey before the kill.) Looking to scoop the *Herald,* the *Sun* sent a stringer up to Roxbury to collect tales of Gould's early days. From this expedition emerged the anecdote (true enough) of Jay's land deal at the expense of Edward Burhans. The *Sun* also snared Jay's "Honesty Is the Best Policy" essay, which it saw fit to publish in a sidebar beside several columns of blistering ridicule. In this climate, Gould's recent exploits against Vanderbilt took on a new shade, as did the Erie corner and the war for the A&S. Even Fisk's formerly amusing excesses came up for criticism. "The Grand Opera House," intoned Greeley's *Tribune,* "is built on the bones of men sacrificed to the Gods of avarice."[7]

These were gods that the public believed had been fed, and fed well, on Black Friday. Although Gould understood with painful clarity that he'd ended the adventure of the gold corner significantly poorer than when he began it, the everyday man on the street could not have been convinced. In the popular mind, Black Friday was a cataclysm orchestrated superbly and controlled completely by the cunning Gould for the purpose of profiteering. The uneducated majority—who tended to view capitalism as a zero-sum game in which a dollar lost by one player instantly became one gained by another—assumed that the specter of hundreds of bankrupted investors equaled unrivaled (and unconscionable) gains on the part of Gould and his allies. Newspapers went with the flow. Scandals—simple ones summarized in just a few outraged paragraphs devoid of numbing complexities—added up to brisk sales for dailies nationwide. In a market hungry for a one-dimensional arch villain of Wall Street excess, Jay Gould suddenly fit the bill all too well.

That January, while giving testimony regarding Black Friday before the House of Representatives Banking Committee chaired by James A. Garfield, Republican of Ohio, Jay did himself no favors when he appeared evasive. Upon being asked how he'd known the U.S. Treasury was about to sell gold, Gould did not point to Butterfield's personal sales via the Seligmans but instead said, "It is one of those conclusions that a man sometimes arrives at intuitively, that are correct in themselves, and yet, if you undertake to give the evidence by which they are reached, you could not tell how it was done." The committee's investigation focused entirely on discerning the extent to which Grant and other federal officials had been involved. Ultimately, although the Republican-dominated group gave the Republican president a completely clean bill of health, they stopped short of outright exoneration when it came to Butterfield. The committee simply noted that it could not conclusively prove the assistant treasurer had conspired with Gould. The committee also criticized Corbin for practicing the "worst form of hypocrisy," which put on "the guise of religion and patriotism" to manipulate a powerful relative.[8]

Jay's numerous miscalculations in his effort to corner gold, followed by his and Fisk's significant losses overall, should have destroyed the emerging myth of his sinister inevitability. But that clarity went begging in Congress's final summary of events, just as it did in the press. Thus, ironically, amid the debris of Black Friday, the press remained free to craft an illusory image of Gould as malicious, amoral, and unstoppable financial wunderkind. This was publicity Jay himself did nothing to repudiate, thereby entering into the first true Faustian bargain of his life. In the immediate future, his operations with the hopelessly unprofitable Erie would do much to reinforce his popular image as a coldhearted, deceitful financial vampire with a taste for the jugulars of his opponents. Later on, post-Erie, the legend of his audacious bad faith would follow him as he embarked upon his life's real work: taking control of the Union Pacific and the Missouri Pacific, accumulating other major roads in the Southwest, building up the Gould system of railways, mastering the Western Union, and dominating the Manhattan Elevated.

As Maury Klein wrote, Gould's infamy coming off Black Friday "spread like a lethal cloud across every enterprise he touched" for two decades.[9] In the end, no degree of managerial success (and no amount of hard-won profits built up for shareholders over dozens upon dozens of quarters) would ever be enough to mitigate the easy stereotype of the thieving manipulator out to glut himself on spoils flimflammed from unwitting innocents. The presumption of guilt was to go with Jay to his tomb. For the rest of his life, his motives—which, after all, were simply to make money the same as any other capitalist—would be suspect. And to him a higher standard of virtue would always be applied. In time, the press and public came to view the petty ruses and gambits employed commonly by a host of speculators as despised tools of fraud and monopoly whenever adopted by Gould. In part this was because of his reputation for treachery, but it was also because he used the common tools of the Street in strikingly new ways, putting together previously unimagined and fantastically profitable combinations with a dexterity that spawned frustrated envy on the part of bystanders.

Some fifteen years following Black Friday, long after Gould had proved himself a steadfast CEO capable of working in concert with a score of dedicated, long-term allies to maintain and expand several major corporations at once, the *Railroad Times* of London would editorialize, "Mr. Gould's god is his pocket, to fill which he has prostituted every attribute with which he is endowed. Like the Ishmaelite of old, his hand is against every man, and every man's hand is against him. Those who have ventured to look upon him in the light of a friend have invariably found, sooner or later, that they had taken unto their bosom a serpent whose sting is death. But to attempt to sketch the character of Mr. Jay Gould in its true colors would be futile, since no language is equal to the task. His cold, heartless villainy stands alone, like the man himself, who has so ruthlessly swindled those whom he regarded as his 'friends' that he has now none to swindle."[10]

Chapter 21

A SPECIAL STINKPOT

AFTER TAKING HIS POUNDING in the gold speculation, Gould moved swiftly to shore up his personal finances as well as the accounts of his associates. Always, he kept his eye on ancillary deals that might be influenced via his position in the Erie. During a rate war with the New York Central to attract cattle shipments flowing east from Buffalo to New York City, Gould put his per-carload rate down to $75 from Vanderbilt's original high of $125. When Vanderbilt retaliated with a drop to $50, Gould put the Erie at $25, only to have Vanderbilt go to a ridiculous $1 per carload, with a penny per head being charged for hogs and sheep. At first Vanderbilt delighted in reports that while his cars were packed, the Erie trains ran empty. Only later did he learn that Gould and Fisk had bought every bit of marketable livestock coming into Buffalo from points west, which they then shipped to New York via the Central, realizing enormous profits. "When the Old Commodore found out that he was carrying the cattle of his enemies at great cost to himself and great profits to Fisk and Gould, he very nearly lost his reason," Morosini would recall. "I am told the air was very blue in Vanderbiltdom."[1]

Gould also routinely played the stocks of firms such as the United States Express Company, a package and mail delivery service, that relied on the

Erie for its livelihood. He never hesitated, as Erie president, to make ominous noises about severing relations or raising the rates for such a dependent organization. He would then short its stock and reap hundreds of thousands as it tumbled down. Later a more positive word from Gould would revive the company's prospects on the Street, along with its stock valuation, at which point Jay would ride the same security back up. As both Maury Klein and Julius Grodinsky pointed out, such machinations were not uncommon in Gould's day. "While business moralists frowned on such behavior," wrote Klein, "those operators below the rank of saint unabashedly sought corporate positions for the purpose of trading on their inside information. Gould may have been more imaginative than most, but he was no pioneer in the art."[2]

While engaged in such lucrative side deals, Gould also took steps to shore up the Erie's political friendships in Albany and elsewhere. "It was the custom when men received nominations to come to me for contributions," Jay told U.S. Senate investigators in 1873, "and I made them and considered them good paying dividends for the company; in a Republican district I was a strong Republican, in a Democratic district I was Democratic, and in doubtful districts I was doubtful; in politics I was an Erie Railroad man every time." These transactions were plentiful enough so that Jay claimed not to be able to count them off individually. "There has been so much of it; it has been so extensive that I have no details now to refresh my mind; when I went over a transaction, and completed it, that was the end of it; and I went at something else; you might as well go back and ask me how many cars of freight were moved on a particular day, and whether the trains were on time or late; I could not charge my mind with details; I can only tell you what my general rule was; my general rule of action."[3] So far as politics *within* the Erie was concerned, Gould made several key moves to consolidate his position. He'd already, as of May 1869, secured from the New York State Legislature a "Classification Act" staggering the election of Erie directors over a five-year period. Thus, after the annual election of October 1869, he, Fisk, Lane, and Tweed came away locked into their posts until 1874. Jay's brother, Abram—now employed as a purchasing agent for Fisk's Narragansett Steamship Company—also joined the executive committee, although he never attended meetings and gave his proxy to Jay.

The Erie's unaudited annual report, issued in January 1870 for the fiscal year ending September 1869, listed the highlights of the railroad's first twelve months under Gould management. Gross revenues were up 16.3 percent to $16,721,500, and operating expenses declined 4.4 percent. However, once interest on bonds was paid, the Erie had nothing left over for dividends on the 780,000 odd shares of stock outstanding. Unmentioned in the report were the lingering (and largely unsalvageable) infrastructure dilemmas that still afflicted the physically antiquated Erie. The railroad, as Jay noted in a confidential memorandum, had far more problems to contend with than just its broad gauge. High-maintenance wooden bridges (not to mention old and degrading iron tracks) needed to be replaced by steel equivalents. The line also required durable sleepers and costly improvements to numerous grades. The Erie's dilapidated equipment made accidents, many of them deadly, a common occurrence. On top of all this, the Erie possessed only a single set of tracks throughout its course, whereas Vanderbilt's New York Central boasted four and the Pennsylvania a minimum of two, allowing trains to run unimpeded in opposite directions.

These were facts the strategically minded Gould fully understood. Given the physical futility of the railroad, Gould could take it seriously only as a speculative device: a financial shell, an item ripe for manipulation. Bond revenues raised for improvement of the line, though officially spent on the Erie, almost always wound up devoted to the financial betterment of Gould and his cabal. For example, when Gould and Fisk privately purchased the Opera House for $850,000, their down payment of $300,000 came directly from Erie coffers as prepayment of the exorbitant rent to be charged in future. In this way Gould and Fisk spent not a penny out of their own pockets but nevertheless wound up with controlling interest in a major New York address. Similarly, when President Gould decided to expand the Erie's land holdings in Jersey City, it was from real estate speculator Gould that the railroad wound up purchasing waterfront acreage.[4] The proceeds from numerous other bond offerings vanished in similar schemes. Amid all this, as the Erie's securities sank and her debts mounted, shareholders—especially the many British investors who held a clear majority (450,000) of the Erie's outstanding securities, and who recognized and were outraged by Gould's shirking of his fiduciary responsibilities—grew increasingly restless.

Boss Tweed made sure that a representative of the British shareholders—one Joseph L. Burt—received absolutely no satisfaction when, in early 1870, he visited Albany to ask for revocation of Gould's Classification Act. At the same time, down in Manhattan, Judge Barnard fended off Burt's attempts to take the bulk of the British shares out of "street-name" and register them with the New York Stock Exchange under two specially designated British owners—Robert A. Heath and Henry L. Raphael. This move, had it gone forward, would have allowed Heath and Raphael to vote the British shares in the next round of Erie elections and thereby control those elections. Barnard instead placed the British shares in the hands of a receiver and enjoined Burt from any further attempts to register them. So long as Gould controlled the courts and—through Tammany—the Legislature, it seemed the Erie citadel would remain unassailable. But a clock was ticking.

That April, once he'd seen what he could expect from the New York judiciary, Burt went to the federal courts for relief. At first, Fisk and Gould seem not to have realized the threat posed by the federal suit. "Contrary to expectation," said a newspaper account, "no difficulty was experienced in serving the Erie officials with notice of the [federal] suit instituted by Burt's bondholders. Learning that the papers were ready, Fisk dispatched a member of his legal staff to the United States Marshal's office for the purpose of escorting the deputy to the Erie stronghold. Fisk and Gould received the bearer of Burt's challenge to legal combat with the utmost humor and courtesy, and, the ceremony of serving over, [Fisk] entertained the deputy marshal at lunch." Later that day, Fisk told the press, "If these Britishers prefer that their share of the earnings of the road shall be eaten up in lawsuits instead of being distributed in dividends, I can't help it."[5]

During the same interview, Fisk made a recruiting pitch for his latest pet project: the Ninth Regiment of the New York Militia. Fisk, the financial angel of the outfit, had recently been commissioned a colonel. Writing that May, a *Herald* reporter commented that when Fisk wore his uniform, tailored by Brooks Brothers at a cost of $2,000, he "looked for all the world like a pleased school boy let out of school to play soldier."[6] Henceforth, Fisk insisted on being called "Colonel" by all, even Josie. He also purchased new uniforms for every man in the Ninth and offered cash bonuses to those Erie employees who agreed to sign up. After a flashy dress parade down Fifth Avenue at the end of the month, the men of the Ninth made a right turn and marched across Twenty-third Street as far as Eighth Avenue. There, at the Grand Opera House in Castle Erie, they attended a special performance of Fisk's latest theatrical extravaganza, *The Twelve Temptations,* produced at a cost of $75,000.

As its title suggested, *The Twelve Temptations* included a dozen chorus girls dressed, according to one reviewer, "in styles that modesty does not tolerate in good society."[7] The show's elaborate set incorporated a waterfall and several dangerous sulfur magnesium "balls of fire." When juggled by the dancers, the balls cast off showers of dangerous cinders and sparks. (More than one seminude performer wound up singed.) Meanwhile, the chorus line alternated every night between a row of blonds and a row of brunettes. And the show was a smash. Where poor old Mr. Pike had failed to lure New Yorkers to the West Side for high opera and Shakespeare, Fisk attracted them in droves with his *Temptations* and similar spectaculars. "*Spectacles* are proverbially fit for old eyes," wrote the editor of New York's satirical weekly *Punchinello.* "Probably that is the reason why the spectacle of *The Twelve Temptations* is so dear to the aged eyes of the gray-haired old gentlemen who occupy the front seats at the Grand Opera House. . . . Though the dullest of dramas, it is so brightened by brilliant legs that it dazzles every beholder."[8]

Gould did not attend a single performance of *The Twelve Temptations* or any other Fisk-produced extravaganza. By the spring of 1870 both he and his in-laws had vacated the old Miller mansion near Union Square and moved up to larger homes on fashionable Fifth Avenue, the Gould residence being a townhouse at 578 Fifth Avenue, midway between Fifth's intersections with West Forty-seventh and West Forty-eighth Streets.[9] Although Jay created an elaborate library for himself on the first floor of his house, he made his home office for late-night work sessions in an unlovely corner of the basement. Up on the roof, he rigged a simple greenhouse for his flowers: roses, hyacinths, and most especially orchids, with which he'd recently become fascinated. Carpenters built him a small potting shed next to the greenhouse. Here, in addition to his gardening tools, he also kept an ancient trunk (a relic of the old home at Roxbury), packed with botanical reference books. And with this arrangement he was satisfied. "I have the disadvantage," Gould told a reporter at about this time, "of not being sociable. Wall Street men are fond of company and sport. A man makes $100,000 there and immediately buys a yacht, begins to drive fast horses, and becomes a sport generally. My tastes lie in a different direction. When business hours are over I go home and spend the remainder of the day with my wife, my children and books of my library. Every man has natural inclinations of his own. Mine are domestic. They are not calculated to make me particularly popular on Wall Street, and I cannot help that."[10]

Actually, not being sociable came in handy for a man who was not generally welcome in polite society. Jay's lingering newspaper notoriety from Black Friday, combined with his much-publicized contemporary shenanigans manipulating Erie securities at the expense and distress of foreign shareholders, made him a social pariah. Already one of the most despised men in the United States, Gould was well advised to take his pleasures within his family circle. It was a happy coincidence that this was where he'd prefer to be anyway. But even Jay's devotion to family created negative publicity. Newspapers quoted the opinion shared by many rough-and-tumble Wall Street speculators that Gould was a snob willing to spend time with them only when money was to be made. Reporters, themselves no strangers to the after-hours conviviality of Wall Street, tended to take the same view. More than one journalist made a point of contrasting the curt, private Gould with the openhearted and riotously popular Fisk. While one of them was cast in the public role of sinister scoundrel, the other delighted in the part of charming, irrepressible bad boy. In the end, Jay's domestic instincts contributed greatly to the public impression that he had no friends, and consequently no loyalties to anyone other than his kin. The closest Gould came to a nightlife was when he sometimes strolled down to the Fifth Avenue Hotel after dinner, there to observe the after-hours trading and methodically chat with the stock brokers who frequented the establishment's bar and lobby. His conversation was almost always on financial point and without humor, his questions focused and his antenna up for any useful bit of news as he wandered among the traders.

Acquaintances grew used to seeing him linger at the hotel for under an hour every night, only long enough to take the pulse of the market. In turn, they noted no change in Gould's taciturn habits during the summer of 1870, when Ellie and the children went to the beach at Long Branch, New Jersey, for a solid eight weeks. Throughout Jay's long spell of bachelorhood, he still made his evenings early ones. He routinely eschewed the prospect of nymph-filled nights on the town with Fisk, and he made a beeline for Long

Branch every weekend. Crew members recalled him sternly clutching his briefcase as he strolled the decks of the Fisk-and-Gould-owned steamer *Plymouth Rock* plowing between Manhattan and the Jersey coast every Friday afternoon and Sunday evening.

When he boarded the vessel on Friday, 19 August, Gould found himself surrounded by six hundred members of Fisk's militia regiment, all of them headed out to Long Branch for their annual summer bivouac. Decades later, George Gould would recall joining his unsoldierly father on a visit to the Ninth at "Camp Jay Gould," where George, at age six, was permitted to fire a rifle into the waves of the ocean. "As they are to feed at the hotels," the *Herald's* correspondent observed of Fisk's pampered regiment, "they bring no rations with them, encumbering their knapsacks, but fill them with white pantaloons, white gloves, and other dilettante adornments of holiday soldiers."[11] The pious Ellie Gould applauded Fisk for marching his men off to services on Sunday, although the *Herald's* man commented that it was the first sermon Fisk had heard in nine years. "He was greatly moved by the unusual sensation and shed tears. It was better than a play to him."[12]

Part of the reason behind Fisk's sudden need for summer soldiering was the disintegration of his love life back in Manhattan. Shortly before departing for Long Branch with his men, he had received cold treatment from Josie. Thereafter, while Fisk "trained" at Long Branch, Josie entertained a new lover: thirty-nine-year-old Edward S. Stokes, known as Ned. Handsome and married, the socially prominent Stokes served as general manager of the Brooklyn Oil Refinery Company, a firm owned by his widowed mother. According to a contemporary who knew him well, Stokes "had one great fault. . . . His blood was hot, and being of a nervous, sanguine temperament he was liable at any moment to break out when he deemed himself imposed upon or outraged. He had always been sensitive to an insult and quick to resent an injury."[13] A year earlier, when—due to Stokes's own tempestuousness, irrationality, and theft of corporate funds—Brooklyn Oil began to show signs of failing, Stokes had induced Fisk, then his friend, to join the company's board and make a large investment. Later, Fisk ensured favorable Erie Railroad rates for the transport of Stokes's oil between Pennsylvania and New York; and he gave Stokes a de facto monopoly on all of the Erie's sizable oil and kerosene purchases. In return, Stokes stole Fisk's woman. "Miss Mansfield," wrote Fisk biographer R. W. McAlpine, "while she had no real love or passion for Fisk, had received him as her lover, for his money. But Stokes she really loved; or if love be too exalted a word to use in connection with a woman so worldly and designing, it is safe to say that she entertained for Stokes an ardent passion."[14]

Fisk, of course, had routinely conducted a score of affairs with a passing host of actresses and dancers. But Josie always remained the one great constant in his romantic life. As well, all of New York knew of Fisk's indiscreet arrangement with Mansfield, so his sudden banishment from the mansion he'd paid for caused great embarrassment. Josie, for her part, did not appear to understand the concept that when a man kept a woman, he usually expected a fair measure of exclusivity in return. "I was always supplied with silks, wines, food and everything that I could desire," she would later say, "but he would never allow me any freedom."[15] When Fisk returned to Manhattan early in September, he confronted Mansfield and rejected her blunt proposal that in return for his ongoing support she might continue to share herself with Fisk on occasion, while still also seeing Stokes. "It won't do, Josie," he is reported to have said. "You can't run two engines on one track in contrary directions at the same time."[16]

◇   ◇   ◇

The British shares were still tied up in October 1870, when three more Gould-friendly Erie directors (among them Gould's brother-in-law Daniel Miller, Jr.) achieved reelection by large margins. At the same meeting, the Erie board voted to ratify all actions, rules, and programs enacted by management since August 1869. Not long after, as the British suit slowly progressed through the federal courts, Gould took a stab at shoring up the railroad's troubled finances with an issue of consolidated mortgage bonds meant to replace the anarchic mess of the company's previous debt issues. But this time the notorious Scarlet Woman of Wall Street, showing age and infirmities that no amount of rouge could conceal, found it impossible to seduce customers. Gould alone took $3 million at 60. On through the year 1871, the Erie continued to flounder. Never much good as a railroad, it now became increasingly useless as a tool for speculation.

While the Erie wound down, Gould found himself embroiled in a dangerous confrontation with his onetime ally James McHenry. Gould and McHenry had joined forces in 1868 to help salvage McHenry's troubled Atlantic & Great Western Railway (A&GW)—a combination of three broad-gauge short lines connecting Jamestown, New York; Meadville, Pennsylvania; and Franklin Mills, Ohio, via a hub in Cleveland. Leasing the line to the Erie, McHenry and Gould innovated a profitable interchange route for oil moving between Cleveland and the eastern seaboard. However, a subsequent disagreement between the two men caused Gould to unilaterally (and quite illegally) change the terms of the lease in the Erie's favor. During the ensuing court battle, Gould was—as of February 1870—able to control the A&GW on his own terms while McHenry struggled to reorganize the firm and stave off a foreclosure action. Not until October 1871 did McHenry finally regain control.

What he wound up with, however, was of little value without the Erie interchange, and a new lease on favorable terms seemed impossible so long as Gould remained in charge of the larger railroad. Thus, near the end of 1871, McHenry sought to ally himself with the Erie's British investors, their shared goal being to knock Gould off his throne. McHenry likewise teamed up with New York's new reform-Republican attorney general, Francis Channing Barlow, elected November 1871. Though he'd been born and raised in New York, the thirty-seven-year-old Barlow boasted roots in several prominent Boston families. He was also a war hero. After serving with distinction during the battles of Antietam and Chancellorsville, Barlow had been temporarily paralyzed by a rifle shot at Gettysburg while defending a hill subsequently known as Barlow's Knoll.[17] At the time he joined forces with McHenry, Barlow—who'd previously served as U.S. marshal for the Southern District of New York—had already been of help with Burt's federal petition against Gould. He also stood poised, in his new role as attorney general, to collaborate with Samuel Tilden in the state's prosecution of Tweed on charges of corruption.

It was perhaps through Barlow that McHenry's "Erie Protective Committee" secured the services of another Gettysburg veteran, General Daniel E. Sickles. Born in 1819, the ne'er-do-well Sickles was a graduate of the University of the City of New York Law School. His prewar career included stints as a Tammany-entrenched corporate counsel for the City of New York, secretary to the U.S. legation in London, New York State senator, and Democratic U.S. representative from New York. Sickles's two-term career in Congress had been marred by scandal in 1859 when he shot and killed his wife's lover, Philip Barton Key, son to Francis Scott Key, composer of "The Star-Spangled Banner." Sickles's subsequent acquittal involved the nation's first successful plea of temporary insanity, this orchestrated by defense attorney Edwin M. Stanton, later attorney general and secretary of war under Lincoln. During the war, Sickles served in the Peninsula Campaign and fought at Sharpsburg and Chancellorsville before moving on to Gettysburg, where his willful insubordination led to the virtual destruction of the Union's Third Corps. Nevertheless, after losing a leg to a Confederate cannon ball, Sickles wound up with the Medal of Honor. Retiring from the army in 1869, Sickles renounced Tammany, became a Republican, and eventually received Grant's appointment as U.S. minister to Spain. Once in Madrid, the hard-drinking and incessantly unfaithful Sickles quickly gained the nickname "Yankee king of Spain" because of his extraordinarily close relationship with that country's sultry former queen, Isabella II.

Early in November 1871, upon receipt of a $100,000 offer from McHenry, Sickles took a hiatus from his diplomatic duties and returned to New York to help orchestrate Gould's downfall. One month later, he instituted a second suit against the Erie, paralleling Burt's, and assaulted Albany in an attempt to overturn the Classification Act. At the same time, McHenry's committee distributed a broadside informing Erie shareholders of its intention "to break up the whole combination of the Erie ring, without respect to persons."[18] Reading the broadside and realizing the forces arrayed against him, Gould could not have failed to understand how precarious his situation had become. Not only were Erie shareholders in open rebellion, but Gould's support system of cronies also stood in turmoil. Just a few weeks earlier, the Republican reform movement in Manhattan and elsewhere had dealt Tammany a number of conclusive defeats at the polls, leaving reform elements in control of the state legislature. Soon Tweed—recently the target of a *New York Times* exposé and almost daily baiting by Thomas Nast's satirical cartoons in *Harper's Weekly*—would be arrested for fraud, resign from the Erie board, and lose his august post as grand sachem of Tammany. As for Fisk, his unseemly dilemma with Josie Mansfield and Ned Stokes had captured the attention of every newspaper in New York. The negative publicity further threatened Gould's control over the Erie.

◇   ◇   ◇

Throughout 1871, the "special stinkpot"—as George Templeton Strong called it—of the Fisk-Mansfield-Stokes triangle had steadily gained in aromatic force.[19] Shortly after New Year's Day 1871, the jilted and bitter Fisk, still a director of the Brooklyn Oil Refinery Company, had managed to document General Manager Stokes's confiscation of some $250,000 in company funds for personal use. Fisk swore out a warrant for embezzlement and had Stokes put in handcuffs. When Stokes got off on a technicality, he immediately turned around and slapped Fisk with a $200,000 suit for malicious prosecution: an action eventually settled out of court when Fisk agreed to purchase the Stokes family's interest in Brooklyn Oil. (The deal provided the profligate Stokes with a one-time windfall but cut off his access to the Brooklyn Oil Refinery Company's accounts, which he'd previously used as his private bank.) A short while later, Stokes exhibited an egregious degree of unreliability and bad faith when, despite his agreement with Fisk, he revived his action. Later that spring, the two men agreed to take their dispute to a neutral referee. Attorney Clarence A. Seward eventually ruled that Stokes—fast running through the money from Fisk's buyout while trying to support Mansfield in style—had no further claim against the prince of Erie save for an additional $10,000 as compensation for a single night of Fisk-orchestrated imprisonment.

Stokes spent the last of the extra $10,000 in September, at which point he embarked upon yet another run at Fisk's wallet. This time Stokes accused Fisk of stealing corporate funds from both Brooklyn Oil and the Erie, thefts purportedly documented in letters Fisk had written Josie Mansfield before their split. Stokes's game here was to induce Fisk to buy him off. The evidentiary letters did not, in fact, touch on any aspect of Fisk's business life. But they did cover topics far more intimate and potentially embarrassing.[20] Thus, when Fisk's friends urged him to allow publication of the correspondence and be done with it, he refused. "You may laugh at me," he wrote on 27 October, "but I tell you I can't put up on a signboard some of the purest thoughts that ever stirred me. . . . They may curse me for this, and damn me for that, and ridicule me for something else—but, by the Lord, this is my heart that you want me to make a show of, and I won't."[21] Shortly, Stokes made an outright offer to sell the letters to Fisk for $15,000, and Fisk took the bait. Then, after the money had been paid and Stokes once again reneged, Fisk had him arrested on a charge of blackmail.

Fisk interrupted his tiresome contest with Stokes only once that autumn, to organize the gathering and transport of supplies for the relief of Chicagoans after the Great Fire. Just as energetic as he'd been when mobilizing aid for the soldiers at Antietam almost ten years before, Fisk personally drove an express wagon—a sign "Contributions Received Here for Chicago" painted on its side—about the streets of New York on the evening of 10 October. Door to door he went, stopping wherever a hand waved out a window, gathering goods. At the same time, in response to an announcement appearing over Gould's signature in the New York dailies, wholesalers and charitable relief organizations delivered large lots of food, clothes, blankets, and medical supplies to the Opera House. Later that evening, in the lobby of the theater, Fisk supervised more than a hundred volunteers as they organized the goods for transshipping to the Erie terminal at Jersey City and placement on a well-publicized Erie train bound west.

◇ ◇ ◇

Once Chicago was saved, Fisk returned to more basic matters. On 26 November, Josie testified at court proceedings related to Stokes's fraud action. In the process, under skillful cross-examination by attorney William A. Beach, she was made to sound like what she was: a manipulative, money-hungry seductress. Within a few weeks, on 6 January 1872, Justice B. H. Bixbey threw out the Stokes suit altogether. That same morning, a grand jury indicted both Stokes and Mansfield on Fisk's charge of blackmail, issuing warrants for their arrest. After receiving word of the indictments, an enraged Stokes stopped at Josie's home on West Twenty-third Street and then went to Castle Erie, where he demanded to see Fisk. The prince, however, was not on the premises. Fisk, an overly chatty Erie guard informed Stokes, was at luncheon across town, after which he'd be on his way to an appointment at the Grand Central Hotel in Greenwich Village.[22]

Stokes hailed a cab and reached the Grand Central around 4 P.M., shortly before Fisk's scheduled arrival. Richard Wandle, a professional gambler who knew Stokes well, happened to be lounging in front of the Grand Central when Stokes arrived. Wandle saw Stokes jump out of the cab and then dart at "not quite a run, but between a run and a fast walk," into the ladies' entrance, some twenty yards from the main doors.[23] Once inside, Stokes took the ladies' stairs to the second-floor lobby, where hotel employees noticed him pacing back and forth in an agitated state. A few minutes later, Wandle saw Fisk casually step down from a private coach and go in by the same entrance Stokes had used. Then the gambler heard gunfire: two loud rounds with a slight pause between them.

"I saw Edward Stokes at the head of the stairs," the dying Fisk would soon tell a city coroner as part of a dictated antemortem statement. "As soon as I saw him I noticed he had something in his hand."[24] Fisk was halfway up the ladies' stairs when the first shot sliced into his abdomen, sending him tumbling back down to the bottom. Rising, Fisk took a second bullet in the left arm, at which point Stokes, still at the top of the stairs, turned away from his victim. Crossing the second-floor lobby, Stokes tossed his gun, a four-chambered Colt, under a sofa and then walked down the Grand Central's main staircase to the first-floor lobby, where he announced that someone had been shot. "Yes," shouted a bellboy running after him, who'd seen it all, "and you are the man that did it."[25] Stokes, muttering to himself, then sat waiting while the same boy ran to fetch police from the nearby Mercer Street station.

Fisk at first seemed well enough. Leaning on the arm of the hotel's resident physician, he was able to walk up the stairs and cross a short hallway to a private parlor. There the doctor, Thomas H. Tripler, laid him out on a couch. Ignoring the relatively minor wound to Fisk's arm, Tripler cut away the financier's shirt to explore the damage at his gut. The doctor's probe went to a depth of four inches without touching metal. The slug, buried deep in Fisk's intestines, could not be found. Fisk's blood ran black. Informed that his wound was mortal, Fisk asked that attorneys Thomas Shearman and David Dudley Field be called, so that he might dictate his will. He also requested that his wife, Lucy, be summoned from Boston.[26] Captain Thomas Byrnes of the New York City police later recalled that when he escorted Stokes into the room, Fisk "laid there as if he had no pain at all." Stokes, meanwhile, "wore a rigidly dignified air, with a face perfectly immovable, expressive only of intense passion strongly suppressed." When Byrnes asked Fisk to identify his assailant, Fisk nodded and answered, "Yes, that's the man who shot me. That's Ned Stokes."[27]

Fisk died slowly. The indicted Tweed—at liberty on bail of $1 million supplied by Gould—came and joined Shearman and Field in the death-watch, as did Gould. At first composed, the normally unreadable Gould eventually broke down under the strain. "Everyone," noted an observer, "was suddenly startled by seeing [Gould] bow his head upon his hands and weep unrestrainedly with deep, audible sobs."[28] At one point an Erie messenger came and whispered in Gould's ear, after which Gould buttonholed Byrnes and suggested precautions be taken to beef up the guard at the Tombs, the city prison where Stokes had been taken. Rumor had it that the Ninth New York planned to march, seize Stokes, and string him up from the roof of Castle Erie. As a precaution, New York City police superintendent John Kelso posted 250 uniforms about the jail.

By 6:20 A.M. on 7 January, when Lucy arrived from Boston, Fisk was comatose with morphine. He died at 10:45 A.M. A few minutes after that, according to a reporter for the *New York Sun*, a poorly dressed woman carrying a small child showed up at the parlor door. She insisted on paying her respects, explaining that although she'd never met him, Fisk had for six months kept her and her children from starvation.[29] As an editorialist commented at the time, New York was full of people who had either received or were aware of Fisk's many charitable gestures. "They remembered that he had once been a poor, toiling lad who had wrought his success out of hard, earnest effort; that his steps upwards, while decked with a gaudy, semi-barbaric show, were marked by strong traces of liberality and generosity of spirit that threw for the time the faults of his nature in the shade."[30] Meanwhile Mansfield, under protective guard at the house Fisk had bought for her, characteristically focused on herself when giving a comment to the press. "I wish it to be distinctly understood," she said, "that I am in no way connected with the sad affair. I have my own reputation to maintain."[31]

Interviewed at Castle Erie a few hours after Fisk breathed his last, Gould made the depth of his grief clear. "I cannot sufficiently give expression to the extent I suffer over the catastrophe. We have been working together for five or six years and during that time not the slightest unpleasantness has ever arisen between us. He was genial in his habits and beloved by all who had any dealings with him." As to Fisk's tastes for wine and women, Gould commented: "Since the dissolution of whatever tie has existed between him and Mrs. Mansfield, he has been a changed man. He had ceased to practice many of the old habits of which he has been accused, and was in every sense becoming what all who loved him desired he should be. His old associations were being rapidly broken up, and if he had lived some time longer a complete reform would have taken place in his whole conduct, though I do not for an instant say that his improprieties were so heinous as they have been generally represented to be."[32]

The following day, 8 January, Colonel James Fisk's uniformed body lay in state at the Grand Opera House. By the time the doors closed at 2 P.M., 20,000 New Yorkers had paid their respects. A short while later, the soldiers of the Ninth escorted Fisk on the first leg of his trip home to Brattleboro. "As far as the eye could see along 23rd Street," reported the *Herald*, "the sidewalks were lined with people closely packed, and the occupants of the houses along the street, with many invited friends . . . occupied the windows."[33] Only Josie's mansion sat shuttered. A line of coaches followed the hearse. Jay and Ellie Gould sat in the first, along with Lucy. At the old New Haven Railway Station (at Fourth Avenue and Twenty-sixth Street, soon to be the site of the first Madison Square Garden), Fisk's militiamen placed the casket aboard a crepe-covered car pulled by a crepe-covered engine. Nine hours later, when Fisk rolled into his old hometown, 5,000 neighbors turned out in the dead of night to welcome him. He lay in his father's Revere House until noon on the 9th, at which point his kin carried him to Prospect Hill Cemetery, the same graveyard he'd half-jokingly paid to fence a few years before.

Ned Stokes's family hired the best criminal lawyers money could buy. His first trial ended in a hung jury amid charges of tampering. The second concluded with a first-degree murder conviction and a sentence of death, both of which were eventually set aside after aggressive footwork by Stokes's attorneys. A third jury finally found Stokes guilty of manslaughter, for which he served four years in Sing Sing. Thereafter, even though he was not welcome in any respectable club, Stokes remained in New York City, where he died in 1901 at the age of sixty. As for Mansfield, she fled to Europe not long after the murder, there to remain for twenty-five years. She was occasionally an actress, occasionally a whore, and at one point the unhappy wife of a rich but drunken American expatriate, Robert Livingston Reade. The year 1899 found the divorced and aging Josie living off the charity of a brother in Watertown, South Dakota. The brother died ten years later, at which point Josie returned to Europe—specifically, Paris—where she led an impoverished existence for another twenty-two years, dying in 1931 at the age of eighty-three.

Fisk's estate was found to comprise just under $1 million, not nearly as much as some might have guessed, but more than adequate. Despite numerous published accounts to the contrary, Fisk left Lucy set for life. Living in Boston with Fanny Harrod, Lucy routinely turned to Gould for advice in matters of finance. Writing in 1881 to dispel rumors of his neglect, Lucy described Gould as "the only friend of Mr. Fisk who has responded to my actual needs and wants since his death."[34] Lucy died in 1912 at the age of seventy-six. Today she lies with Jim and the rest of the Fisk family at Prospect Hill, beneath an ornate monument created by sculptor Larkin Mead at a cost of $25,000. "On one side of the shaft is cut a portrait medallion of Jim as he looked when alive," wrote Fisk's old friend Fuller in 1927. "At the four corners of the massive base sit four marble young women: one has a locomotive carved on a chaplet which encircles her brow. She represents railroading. The second represents commerce by water. The third figure typifies the stage. The fourth stands for trade in the broadest sense. Thousands of visitors have looked upon the memorial of one of Vermont's sons, and a good many of them have carried home chips of Italian marble which they managed to break off and steal as souvenirs. They have made the monument more fitted to commemorate Jim's career—striking from many aspects, picturesque, but blemished."[35]

After his murder, Fisk received the most gentle treatment by the media. Sensing an appealing human interest story, writers worked industriously to amplify Fisk's persona as a benevolent rake, a generous thief, and the most well-intentioned of frauds. In the process, they continued their habit of contrasting Fisk with his presumed darker half, the latter's reputation sinking further still. At least one editorial went so far as to say the wrong member of the Gould-Fisk team had been shot. The public also chimed in. "We should not judge too harshly of James Fisk," wrote one Colonel J. G. Dudley in a letter published by the *Herald*. "He was a creature of circumstances— a legitimate fruit of the state of public and private morality existing when he began his career. He found legislatures corrupt and he purchased them; he found judges venal and he bribed them; he found a large part of society fond of vulgar display, dash and barbaric magnificence and he gratified the taste of that portion of society. . . . [Nevertheless] the closing scenes of his deathbed condoned for much of the waywardness of his life." But if the writer forgave Fisk for being a product of his time and environment, he did not extend the same courtesy to Gould. "Let the mantle of charity cover [Fisk's] sins—and may it be long before his counterpart [Gould] appear to dazzle and vex the world again."[36]

Later on, some reporters would even claim that it was Fisk who, through his force of personality, had held the Erie together as an enterprise, Gould tagging along as an unwelcome appendage. "The majority of the board of directors," the *Sun* would report, "were enemies of Gould, and were desirous of forcing him from the Presidency. But they were nearly all warm friends of Col. Fisk, and out of respect to his wishes they suffered their opposition to lie dormant until after his death. Stokes's bullet killed Jay Gould's power at the same time it took away Col. Fisk's life."[37]

In fact, things were nowhere near this simple.

Chapter 22

A DAMNED VILLAIN

FISK HAD RESIGNED as vice president and controller of Erie several weeks before the murder. Although he remained on the Erie board, he knew full well that a change was afoot and that soon he would be out. In what seemed a last-ditch effort to maintain control of the railroad in the face of challenges from McHenry and the British shareholders, Gould had written on 11 December 1871 to two of the most respected men on Wall Street with a proposal for a new Erie board of directors. Addressing Levi P. Morton (future New York governor and U.S. vice president) and William Butler Duncan (partner in the eminent Wall Street firm of Duncan & Sherman), Gould suggested a new board contrived to collect "the best railway and financial talent in the country." Such an assembly would, Gould believed, instill new faith in the Erie across world financial markets. Gould's ideal list of board members included Morton, Duncan, and himself along with August Belmont, J. P. Morgan, Erastus Corning (representing Vanderbilt's New York Central), James F. Joy (representing the Michigan Central), Vanderbilt son-in-law Horace F. Clark (representing Vanderbilt's Lake Shore & Michigan Southern), John Jacob Astor, and other worthies. All these gentlemen would have a voice, although Gould would remain at the helm, "the permanent organization of the company to be selected by Messrs. William

Butler Duncan, Levi P. Morton, and myself."[1] Noticeably absent from Gould's roster were the names Fisk, Lane, and Tweed. Also out of the loop were Gould's brother-in-law Miller and his brother, Abram.

At the time that Fisk died, Duncan, armed with Gould's memo plus 280,000 Erie shares controlled by Gould, was abroad in England on a mission to woo large-block British shareholders. McHenry, meanwhile, was in the same country engaged in a far more successful effort to seduce the same elements. McHenry's assistant in this endeavor was a former Gould public relations man. George Crouch had recently jumped his boss's sinking ship, traveled to Britain, and filled the ears of British investors with tales of shady dealings within Castle Erie: fraud, larceny, and an executive committee drunk with both power and greed.

Early in February, Crouch left McHenry in London and returned to New York. There, on McHenry's orders, he worked with Sickles to orchestrate a well-financed coup from within the Erie board. With the Britishers' federal suit in progress and the repeal of the Classification Act just a matter of time now that Republicans controlled the New York State Legislature, a number of Erie board members formerly loyal to Gould sensed that Jay's days were numbered. Thus they sought to carve a profitable surrender with McHenry. Crouch recruited Frederick Lane for a price of $67,500. He snared two other Gould partisans, Henry Thompson and John Hilton, for $67,500 and $25,000 respectively. A former Fisk protégé, M. R. Simons, settled on $40,000 to join the party. Newly appointed vice president O.H.P. Archer also received $40,000. Erie secretary H. N. Otis got $25,000, the same amount being paid Justin White. Charles Sisson, George Hall, and Homer Ramsdell (the latter a former president and current director who'd never been happy with the Gould regime) joined the revolt without charge. Meanwhile Miller and Abram Gould, incorruptible, were not approached. On 27 February, Crouch cabled McHenry in London with the word: "Majority of Erie Directors with us. Gould powerless. Have loaded up in this market at thirty."[2]

Realizing full well that, like himself, McHenry had been buying large blocks of low-priced Erie stock in order to benefit from the rebound sure to follow news of Gould's ouster, Crouch sent another message the following day: "Have you bought all you want? . . . We have moved against the enemy in three columns. One, headed by Sickles, has been diverting him in the

Legislature; another, under the Attorney-General, has been threatening a flank movement in the courts; and the third, under yours truly, . . . has succeeded in undermining the very citadel of Erie. In order to cover my mining operations, I kept up an incessant bombardment in the press."[3] Indeed, Crouch's press bombardment—issued via the *Herald*, where he'd once worked—was quite shrill. "There is no citadel of fraud," that paper shouted on 1 March, "no matter how strongly garrisoned and entrenched, that will not yield in time to the incessant and well-directed blows of an independent and powerful journal. . . . Tammany was an ulcer: Erie is a cancer. It must be rooted out, and at once, and we must make it impossible that it can ever grow again upon our body politic."[4]

On 8 March, nine Erie directors sent Gould a note demanding that he convene a meeting of the board for Monday, 11 March, in order to enact whatever measures might be necessary to counter "the growing distrust which pervades the community in regard to [the Erie's] management."[5] This was a meeting at which, although they did not say so, they intended to fill the two board spots previously held by Tweed and Fisk with men friendly to McHenry. After that, each of the conspiring directors would resign in turn, to be replaced one-by-one with McHenry allies. Gould, however, had been tipped off to the essence of this plot by none other than Lane himself several weeks before, presumably before the Erie's counsel had made his decision to commit to revolution. ("They are counting on me," Lane had told Gould, "but I shall remain true to you, and they have not money enough to change me." This assurance, Gould later commented, he'd taken with "a slight discount, knowing Lane very well."[6]) Thus Gould simply refused to summon the board as requested on the morning of the 11th, at which point Vice President Archer took it upon himself to do so.

Even though Gould quickly got an injunction against the proceedings, the conspiratorial Erie men, together with their poised replacements, gathered in the board room at noon and commenced their business. In short order, the round of carefully scripted appointments, resignations, and elections proceeded according to plan. All this resulted in Gould's firing and the appointment of a new president, John A. Dix, distinguished former general, U.S. treasury secretary, and U.S. senator from New York. Gould arrived on the scene about 12:30, at which point he ordered that the rebelling members be locked in the boardroom and put under guard by several of Tommy Lynch's

men. Then, receiving word that Sickles was on his way with U.S. marshals intent on enforcing the dictates of the new board, Jay barricaded himself inside
his office with Shearman, Morosini, and several Lynch soldiers.

Around 1 P.M., Sickles arrived with the marshals, who pounded on
Gould's door. When Gould refused to yield his chamber, the marshals
opened it with a crowbar and stormed the place. Running from this onslaught, Gould holed up in yet another office—the one that had, an hour
before, belonged to Lane. With him now were Morosini, a roughed-up
Shearman, and a few more of Lynch's boys. They remained there through
the night until early Tuesday morning, when a peace was reached. Sickles
agreed to release both Gould and Fisk's estate from all claims the Erie
might have against them. He likewise agreed to settle all outstanding accounts between Gould and the firm, and to refund loans (approximately $2
million worth) carried by Gould for the Erie. For his part, Gould promised
to step down immediately, if only a new meeting might be held, with him
as chairperson, to replace what Gould called the "illegal" meeting of the day
before.

When Gould finally stepped out of his office, he was, according to a *Sun*
reporter, "very pale and scarce able to walk." Going directly to the boardroom with directors old and new in his wake, Gould promptly brought the
meeting to order. Once again, McHenry's first two appointees were nomi-
nated and confirmed to fill the shoes of Fisk and Tweed. Once again the old
directors abdicated in turn, with carefully crafted votes after each resignation slowly filling up the table with McHenry men. When the long shuffle
was done, Gould announced, "Gentlemen, I herewith resign the office of
President of the Erie Railroad Company." The new board immediately
voted to accept Gould's resignation. Then, for good measure, they approved
a statement endorsing immediate repeal of the Classification Act by the
New York State Assembly and Senate.

After the meeting ended, Gould walked Dix to the president's office.
"You won't find things in very good order," he apologized, waving his hand
across the utterly trashed space.[7] Next, Gould called for Tommy Lynch and
told him to take his men away. Then he himself departed Castle Erie forever. Subsequent newspaper accounts of the altercation in the Erie offices
emphasized Gould's flight from men portrayed as the righteous representatives of order and justice. Cartoonists and pundits painted Gould a weasel-

like physical coward—a bully whose bluff had been called—and delighted in the idea of him being cornered in the most literal sense of the word.

◇   ◇   ◇

Over the next days and weeks, Gould sat at home and watched his fortune soar. He remained the largest single holder of Erie shares. One day following his ouster the Erie rose from 30 to 40 on heavy orders from London. Three days after that, the stock got to 47 1/2. Two weeks later the Erie stood at 67. And by May the price was 75 7/8. Gould reaped millions from his disgrace.

He sold gradually but steadily into each new high, for he had no illusions. He realized the market would figure out soon enough that the Erie remained a financial basket case. In time, examination of the books by the new directors revealed almost $5 million in floating debt, owed for the most part to Gould partisans who now demanded payment. At the same time, hairline cracks developed between various factions within the "new Erie." Burt, representing the interests of the British shareholders, distrusted McHenry, whose main interest, Burt guessed, lay in manipulating Erie stock and propping up the A&GW. It was perhaps for this reason that when the repeal of the Classification Act went through on 16 March, the bill included language forbidding any director of the A&GW to sit as a director of Erie. The repeal document also required a new election of Erie board members in July. When this took place, General Dix—who'd always been seen as an interim president—found himself replaced by Peter H. Watson, an attorney noted for founding the Southern Improvement Company. In the months between repeal of the Classification Act and the election of 9 July, McHenry had made it his business to court the British shareholders, with whom he managed to maintain an uneasy peace. Thus the new president, Watson, and the balance of the Erie board remained very much McHenry partisans going into the summer. In fact, on the very day of Watson's election, the new board approved a $750,000 payment to McHenry for expenses he'd incurred in taking down Gould.

◇   ◇   ◇

Two months earlier, the old bear Drew—now a relatively small and quite obscure operator working on the periphery of the market—had shorted

50,000 shares of Erie for delivery in late December at 55. As his rationale, Drew cited a negative Erie balance sheet. One week after the elevation of Watson to the post of Erie president, the firm vacated Castle Erie (still owned by Gould and the estate of Jim Fisk) and returned to the railroad's original, much cheaper space at Duane and West Streets. After several long nights of study at the Duane and West office, Watson announced that the Erie books for the previous six years were exercises in fiction. Then he authorized a suit against Gould for $10 million, the amount he claimed the former president had misappropriated. At the same time, Watson began proceedings to recover 650,000 shares of Erie stock that he claimed had been fraudulently issued by Gould. In embarking on both these actions, Watson repudiated the promise made Gould by Sickles four months earlier. Adding to the generally litigious atmosphere, Vanderbilt himself lodged a suit against the Erie, demanding payment of the guaranteed interest on the Boston, Hartford & Erie bonds he'd taken as part of his settlement back in 1868, the BH&E having just defaulted.

All of this news conspired to knock the price of Erie back down to size. In August, the stock fell into the 40s. Drew seized upon this drop to close his short, buying 50,000 units at 40 to cover his contracts for sales at 55, thus making himself a quick $750,000. Parlaying this windfall in September, Drew went long in Erie, achieving a brief corner. Drew's trap ensnared none other than Jay Gould himself. Gould and his old brokerage partner Henry Smith had recently been engaged in short speculations concerning both the Erie and the Pacific Mail, a West Coast steamship company. The two had to cough up $400,000 apiece to cover their shorts with relation to the Erie. To Gould the loss of $400,000 was annoying but not, at this stage of his career, devastating. The same could not be said for Smith, who had not done quite so fabulously as Gould after the breakup of Smith, Gould & Martin in August 1870. When Gould refused to cover Smith's losses for him, the latter reportedly closed out their relationship with a threat: "I'll get good and even with you before another year."[8]

◇ ◇ ◇

Reformist Republican housecleaning swept up Gould's judicial protégés Cardozo and Barnard. Cardozo resigned his office in July rather than face impeachment. He would go on to practice law successfully until his death in

1885. Barnard refused to resign. Instead, he surrendered himself to a brief trial before New York's High Court of Impeachment, comprising the State Senate and the Court of Appeals combined. At Saratoga Springs in late August, the High Court voted unanimously to remove Barnard from the bench. He died six years later. As for Tweed, his first trial for embezzlement resulted in a hung jury. At the end of his second trial, in November, Tweed stood convicted and received a twelve-year prison sentence, a sentence later reduced by a higher court. Tweed wound up serving one year. Upon his release, New York State immediately sued him for $6 million and confined him to a debtor's prison until he could come up with half that amount for bail. During December 1875, while enjoying a brief parole to visit his family, Tweed escaped to Spain. There the fugitive worked as a common seaman for a year until, ironically, he was recognized because of his likeness to a Nast cartoon. Extradited to the United States, Tweed died in New York's Ludlow Street Jail on 12 April 1878. On the day of Tweed's funeral, thousands gathered to pay their respects in front of his daughter's house on East Seventy-seventh Street. At the Tweed family plot in Brooklyn's Green-Wood Cemetery, newspaper reporters noted that most of the nearly 1,500 mourners present for the burial were poor New Yorkers, many probably past recipients of Tammany charities. No elected official of importance showed up for Tweed's final rites. Neither did Gould.

◇ ◇ ◇

As he had done when shorting Erie and Pacific Mail shares in his expensive collaboration with Henry Smith, Jay Gould would transact virtually all of his Wall Street business for the balance of his short life through a series of special partnerships with a variety of brokerage firms. This device allowed him the luxury of trading anonymously whenever he cared to, and of trading on both sides of a speculation through different brokers. Eventually, Jay would spread his business over so large a network of Wall Street houses that he became something of a phantom: ever present, but frequently invisible and always inscrutable.

At the time he severed relations with Smith in late September, the latter had seemed intent on hanging tough with his short positions on the Pacific Mail, even though the Pacific Mail's management had just orchestrated a bill in Albany allowing a reduction of the steamship company's capital stock by half. Looking at the situation objectively, Gould saw that with the Pacific Mail buyback afoot, the stock was inevitably bound up and not down. Thus he cut his losses, covered his short positions, and got out. More annoying for the still-short Smith, however, was the fact that Jay then promptly started buying Pacific Mail at market, doggedly bulling up the stock in collaboration with the company's board. During October, Pacific Mail rose from 73 to 103, almost ruining Smith, who came out of the affair even more bitterly incensed by what he saw as Gould's duplicity and malevolence.

Shortly, Smith would have even more to complain about. As Gould well knew, that autumn found Smith conspicuously short in the stock of the Chicago & Northwestern Railroad. (He had, in fact, agreed to sell 30,000 shares at 75.) As Gould also knew, the same could be said for several of the Northwestern's directors as well as Daniel Drew, who personally stood short 10,000 shares at the same price as Smith. This information became valuable to Gould when Morosini, who had followed Jay out of the Erie, brought word of great interest in the Northwestern on the part of Augustus Schell and Vanderbilt's son-in-law Horace Clark. Both men had been buying shares in earnest for many months. Nevertheless, until they spoke to Gould, their former nemesis in Erie affairs, they'd been completely unaware of the extensive short positions in the Northwestern. Now, with Gould, they planned a corner and began bulling up the stock.

Their bulling took a short break right after 11 November, when a large fire roared through Boston and caused markets to pause. Smith, in the meantime, increased his short position by another 10,000 shares at 75, because the year before he'd made a killing in shorts across the board after the fire in Chicago. This time, however, the markets recovered with a terrible swiftness. The Northwestern stood at 95 on Wednesday, 20 November, by which time Smith, Drew, and other bears were scouring the streets, desperate for shares to help cover their positions. But of course—as the bears soon realized—Gould, Clark, and Schell had set a brilliant bear trap and held a secure corner. "In this stock," reported the *Herald*, "the corner had been so carefully and neatly and artistically built up that the victims must either gracefully consent to have their financial throats cut or make one desperate stroke for compromise or revenge."[9]

At this point Smith visited Gould and demanded that he release the stock Smith needed. When Gould refused, Smith issued an ultimatum. The

Erie's $10-million suit against Gould had recently been withdrawn for want of evidence. That evidence, Smith reminded Gould, was to be found in the old Smith, Gould & Martin account books, which had much to tell about Gould's financial manipulations during the years he and Fisk ran the Erie. Smith threatened to turn over the relevant records to President Watson of the Erie unless Gould released his Northwestern stock. Gould, however, seemed unconcerned. "Very well," he reportedly told Smith. "Turn them over. I have no objection."[10]

The Northwestern hit 100 on Thursday, the 21st, the same day Smith delivered his books to Watson. Later that afternoon, Watson filed a suit demanding Gould return the $9,726,541.26 Watson now said he had misappropriated from the Erie, and a judge issued an arrest warrant. Having been forewarned by Smith's threat of Wednesday, Gould was prepared that Friday when a sheriff showed up in the office of Osborne & Chapin, 34 Broad Street, where Gould had been working. Clark and Schell accompanied Gould to the police station. There they met Gould's latest personal counsel, who was also Tweed's—a very young Elihu Root, future secretary of war and secretary of state. Gould's arrest warrant stipulated a bond amount of $1 million, which Clark and Schell supplied in short order. During the half hour Gould was in custody, the Northwestern leaped from 105 to 165. The final bid on the Exchange that afternoon was 200, and there were no takers. During after-hours trading at the Fifth Avenue Hotel, the stock went up to a bid of 210 and an ask of 300.

The Northwestern opened at 150 the next morning, Saturday. Some presumed, mistakenly, that the drop signaled a break in the corner, perhaps precipitated by Gould's arrest. In fact, Gould and his cohorts were simply taking pity on a few smaller operators, allowing them a brief window through which to escape at reasonable prices. Gould's charity, as the *New York Sun* observed, was entirely pragmatic: "This settling with small shorts at whatever they could pay was a good thing for the brokers, and a much better thing for Mr. Gould's party, as it averted failures, and a panic which might have robbed the bulls of the greatest fruits of their brilliant victory."[11] Larger players such as Smith and Drew, however, were on their own. Drew surrendered $1.5 million, and Smith found himself forced to settle at $200, a personal loss of some $5 million. Afterward he shook his finger in Gould's face and ranted, "I will live to see the day, sir, when you have to earn a

living by going around this street with a hand-organ and a monkey." To
which Gould answered, "Maybe you will, Henry, maybe you will. And when
I want a monkey, Henry, I'll send for you."[12] Gould and his colleagues made
in excess of $20 million on the corner.

In the wake of the Northwestern episode, the *Herald* grudgingly congratulated Gould for "one of the most brilliant and successful strokes of fi-
nanciering strategy on record in the annals of Wall Street."[13] But after the
New York Commercial Advertiser commented favorably on the success of
Gould and the rest of "the Vanderbilt party," the Commodore wrote to distance himself from the affair. Vanderbilt's letter to the editor of the *Advertiser* appeared on the 26th: "Sir: The recent 'corner' in Northwestern has
called forth much comment from the press. My name has been associated
with that of Mr. Jay Gould and others in connection with the speculation,
and gross injustice has been done me thereby. . . . The almost constant parade . . . of my name in association with [Gould's] seems very much like an
attempt to mislead the public, to my injury."[14]

One day later, a *New York Sun* reporter asked Vanderbilt to expand upon
his disdain for Gould. Not wanting to go into the details of the past few
years' complex financial dealings, the old Commodore instead said that he
disliked Gould because of his face. "No man could have such a countenance
and still be honest," said Vanderbilt. ". . . God almighty has stamped every
man's character upon his face. I read Mr. Gould like an open book the first
time I saw him. . . . You have my authority for stating that I consider Mr.
Jay Gould a damned villain. You can't put it too strongly." Asked to respond, a bemused Gould suggested that perhaps Vanderbilt, at seventy-
nine, was senile. (Gould was thirty-six.) Then he added, "So far as his
criticism of my personal appearance is concerned, he ought in his piety to
attribute any defects in that respect to the same Wisdom that bestowed on
him his good looks."[15]

◇   ◇   ◇

Jay realized that the case against him by Peter H. Watson and the Erie Railroad, backed by the damning Smith, Gould & Martin account books, was
almost sure to succeed now that judges could no longer be bought. But he'd
also heard through channels that the cash-starved Watson feared a long-
running court fight, dragged out in typical fashion for years by the expert

Gould. After running the calculus of these facts through his nimble mind, in early December Jay embarked upon a series of secret meetings with Watson, their shared aim to arrive at a mutually beneficial understanding. Finally, on 17 December, Gould wrote Watson a formal memorandum proposing terms. In settlement of all the Erie's claims against him, Gould offered various stocks, bonds, and real estate (including Castle Erie) that together, he claimed, were worth more to the Erie company than the total sum claimed. "I do this," Jay wrote, "for the sake of peace, because any litigation of such questions is more annoying to me than the loss of the money involved, and because I am sincerely anxious for the success of the Erie Company, in which I have a large pecuniary interest."[16] The Erie board voted on the 19th to accept Gould's offer, news of which sent Erie stock up to 62.

Gould's current stake in the Erie was not, in fact, great. What he did possess, however, were calls on some 200,000 Erie shares at the market price of 50. Thus the rally after the announcement of the Gould settlement netted Jay $2.4 million on the calls alone. As well, the property he gave up turned out to be worth nowhere near the $9.7 million Jay was supposedly repaying. (Much of the value handed over, including Castle Erie, was not even clear of liens.) But by the time this accounting was complete in early 1874, more than fifteen months after the original settlement, the Erie was in worse shambles than ever under its new management, and Gould was strong again: a financial behemoth, untouchable. As well, the last hope for the Erie's case was shattered early that year when Morosini and Tommy Lynch paid a surprise visit to the New Jersey farm Henry Smith used as a summer residence. There, with Smith away in New York, the two Gould soldiers bullied a caretaker into surrendering a sea chest containing the Gould, Smith & Martin account books. How Morosini learned that Smith had hidden these at his farm is not known. Of course, the records were never seen again.

Chapter 23

TRANSCONTINENTAL

Eᴀʀʟʏ ɪɴ 1873, Jay made the acquaintance of a man who was to become one of his great collaborators over the next nineteen years. Twenty years older than Gould, Russell Sage, like Jay, came from humble Upstate roots. He'd been born on a farm near Oneida in 1816 and started out as a grocer in Troy, where he became active in politics. Sage was elected alderman of Troy in 1845 and served (1853–1856) as a Whig member of Congress, after which he branched out into banking and moved to New York City in 1863. There, six years later at the age of fifty-three, he married the forty-one-year-old Olivia Slocum. Olivia would eventually become a close friend of Jay's wife, Ellie, and his daughter, Nellie. The couple lived just a block south of the Goulds at 506 Fifth Avenue.

Sage could not have varied more dramatically from Gould's previous protégé, Fisk. Although a millionaire many times over, he was personally quite cheap. Jay's niece Alice Northrop would recall Sage proudly brandishing before her uncle a felt hat he'd just bought at a discount price. "One dollar," he bragged to the amused Gould. "Never pay more for a hat. Not worth it. Wear mine as long as yours." Alice likewise remembered her Uncle Jay examining Sage's bargain "closely, politely, though with only perfunctory interest."[1] Slightly taller than Gould at five feet, ten inches, Sage wore secondhand suits and was notorious for never tipping. (After his death in 1906, his wife would make up for his lifelong parsimony by forming the Russell Sage Foundation and giving away roughly half his fortune.) On the Street, Sage was recognized as the innovator of such tools as puts and calls, spreads and straddles. A strict fiscal conservative, he made it a habit to sit on a large cash reserve. Sage was also unlike Fisk in that his talent at business rivaled Gould's. Whereas Fisk had been content to follow Gould's lead in speculation, Sage had his own ideas. In the coming years, Sage and Gould would partner on numerous deals, but they would just as frequently go their own ways and, on rare occasions, work at cross-purposes. Always, however, they remained friends.

Though he liked Sage immensely, Gould sometimes lost patience with his moody friend's frequent outbursts of self-pity and his habit, when feeling low, to overdramatize the petty cares of business. A tale Gould once told to Chauncey Depew of the New York Central illustrates this. During a period in the late 1870s the market went briefly against Sage on a host of fronts, leaving him with large obligations. The commitments in question, though substantial and annoying, in no way touched the largest portion of Sage's wealth. Nevertheless, recalled Depew, the shock "sent Sage to bed, and he declared that he was ruined. Mr. Gould and Mr. Cyrus W. Field became alarmed for his life and went to see him. They found him broken-hearted and in a serious condition. Gould said to him: 'Sage, I will assume all your obligations and give you so many millions of dollars if you will transfer to me the cash you have in banks, trust, and safe-deposit companies, and you keep all your securities and all your real estate.'" The proposition—which by its very insolence demonstrated, as Jay meant it to, the massive net worth to which Sage could still lay claim—proved to be the shock necessary to counteract Sage's panic. He shouted, "I won't do it!," jumped out of bed, and was instantly well again.[2]

Sage was sitting with Gould at Delmonico's on 29 April 1873 when Joseph J. Marrin—an attorney representing several actions against Gould related to Black Friday—walked up to their table, accused Gould of bad faith in negotiations to settle the suits, and punched him in the face. Gould filed a complaint, and Marrin ended up being fined $200. Meanwhile, nearly every New York paper covered the episode with delight. The *Herald* said Marrin deserved a medal. The editors of the *New York Times*, though condemning Marrin's violence, said they understood its genesis. (The previous December the *Times* had embarked on a series of exposés covering Gould and his business practices.) Similar opinions flowed from the *New York Sun, World,* and *Evening Post.* Meanwhile, in all reporting of the episode, it was emphasized that Gould had not behaved "honorably" when attacked, had not stood up to defend himself as most men would, but instead simply retreated with his bloodied nose. Again the image of the skulking coward, the vulture only brave enough to feast on cadavers, was raised. Even as the victim in a case of assault and battery, Gould still wound up demonized.

Only one newspaper roundly condemned the Marrin attack. The *New York Tribune* criticized Marrin for conduct unbecoming a gentleman, even going so far as to compare Marrin to the more lethal Ned Stokes. Picking up on the tenor of the *Tribune's* coverage, the *Times* subsequently cited the *Tribune's* reporting and editorializing about the Marrin affair as an example of Gould's steadily spreading influence over the rival daily. As the editors of the *Times* were at pains to point out, after the death of *Tribune* editor Horace Greeley in 1872, Greeley's assistant Whitelaw Reid had acquired control of the newspaper using funds lent by Gould, who took shares in the *Tribune* company as collateral. Thereafter, all criticism and negative coverage of Gould vanished from the newspaper, and it was widely suspected that Gould planted financial news there to aid his various Wall Street operations. The *Sun* criticized the *Tribune* as a "stock jobbing organ" run by "Jay Gould's stool-pigeon."[3] At one point, the paper's financial editor was physically attacked on the floor of the Exchange by brokers unhappy with the *Tribune's* favoritism toward Gould. When the *Tribune* sought to build a new tower at its headquarters downtown, the editors of the *Times* proposed their idea of an appropriate sculpture: "Jay Gould, under the mask of Mephistopheles, with an armful of *Tribune* shares and an admiring crowd of the purchased legislators of 4 states."[4]

Alice Northrop would one day claim that her uncle cared little about his coverage in newspapers. "Uncle Jay's attitude toward the press," she wrote, "was strictly passive: a mixture of aloofness and disgust."[5] But Alice had this wrong. In fact, Gould was one of the most media-savvy of the early Wall Street moguls. Not only did he harness the *Tribune* for his own purposes, but he would also eventually own the *New York World* outright for four years

(1879–1883), and throughout his career he demonstrated a sharp knowledge of how to strategically work even unfriendly papers to his advantage. "The public heard from him," recalled one editor, "only when he, not the public, would profit by the utterance."⁶ When Gould gave interviews, whether in the *Times* or elsewhere, it was always for a purpose. His statements on these occasions, though overtly truthful, were often masterpieces of misdirection. As well, Gould took care to cultivate quiet relationships with reporters all over town, providing them advice on upcoming moves of various stocks. What Jay offered on such occasions was more than mere news; it was also advance notice of what the reporters should buy and sell for their personal portfolios prior to news publication. "A little W. Union won't hurt you," Gould would tell *Times* reporter William Ward in January 1874. "I think it is the next big card . . . & I would like you to write it up strong."⁷ Through such communications as these Gould nurtured vital alliances with key reporters, providing payola in the form of intelligence while shaping editorial trends to his advantage.

Gould also used the press to nurture the popular image he'd emerged with after Black Friday: the dark, inscrutable, amoral, and ultimately pitiless master of financial markets. Morosini would recall Gould repeating Machiavelli's advice from *The Prince*, that is was better to be feared than to be loved, and explaining that his image as an evil but brilliant wunderkind was his most valuable possession. "There is one man on Wall Street today whom men watch," one newspaper editorialized, "and whose name, built upon ruins, carries with it a certain whisper of ruin. . . . They that curse him do not do it blindly, but as cursing one who massacres after victory."⁸ Not yet forty, Jay already had a notoriety that enabled him to make markets swing on mere rumor. Though the bulk of his contemporaries loathed him, all their eyes were nevertheless upon him. Stocks routinely rose and fell upon whispered news that Jay was long or short in this or that. Brokers competed with each other to gain intelligence about his interests.

Jay's formidable power to influence the Street sprang not just from his presumed skills and savvy, but also from his presumed malignancy. This malignancy was a notion that Jay himself frequently sought to promote and publicize, albeit in subtle ways. When asked by reporters to respond to the enraged Henry Smith's charges that he was a traitor, a Judas, Gould just smiled cryptically and walked away, not bothering to deny anything and appearing not to care one lick about his good name. In this way he left the door open to speculation that he was everything the press made him out to be: not just a brilliant operator, but also a cold-blooded beast delighting in the destruction of others, and not caring who knew it. At about this same time, when rumors again emerged that Gould was of Jewish pedigree, Jay arranged for an editorial in the *Tribune* that said not a word about either him or his religion but defended Jews in general against the cliché stereo-types that were so often applied. A response such as this, in an organ known to be heavily under Gould influence, was bound to incite further speculation as to Jay's background, and he knew it.

According to Morosini, it was to keep up his reputation as a villain that Gould always insisted on anonymity when it came to charitable giving. As Jay's lieutenant was to recall, Gould donated generously to a host of worthy causes throughout the 1870s, 1880s, and early 1890s but routinely insisted that his name not be associated with these gifts lest one of the key pillars of his publicized character—his cold-blooded heartlessness—be undermined. Gould reportedly became annoyed when, during the mid-1870s, the New York politician and editor Thurlow Weed—like Jay, a low-born son of the Catskills region—confided to British reporter W. T. Stead that he served as Jay's philanthropic adviser. "Whenever a really deserving charity is brought to my attention, I explain it to Mr. Gould. He always takes my word as to when and how much to contribute. I have never known him to disregard my advice in such matters. His only condition is that there shall be no public blazonry of his benefactions. He is a constant and liberal giver, but doesn't let his right hand know what his left hand is doing. Oh, there will be a full page to his credit when the record is opened above."[9] As Morosini remem-bered it, Gould expressed relief when papers like the *Times* and the *Herald* refused to either believe or reprint the British report. For good measure, Gould told the *Tribune* to ignore the story while also admonishing Weed, a friend, to please be more discreet in the future.[10]

◇ ◇ ◇

All editors, both friend and foe, were in for a surprise when Jay Gould seized control of the Union Pacific (UP) Railroad in 1874.

Ironically, the UP came to Gould bundled with a history every bit as twisted and unprofitable as the Erie's. In the Pacific Railroad Acts of 1862 and 1864, Congress had set out to inspire and facilitate the construction of a rail line linking the Missouri River with the West Coast. While the UP was charged with extending America's rail system west from the Missouri, the Central Pacific (headed by Leland Stanford and Collis P. Huntington) received the charter to build from Sacramento east, the two lines to meet somewhere in the middle. Whichever company laid track the fastest would wind up controlling the greatest amount of mileage and land. The 1862 and 1864 bills provided land grants (together with title to coal and iron found on those lands) stretching the distance of the proposed line. The bills also supplied capital in the form of subsidy bonds (representing a second mortgage) to be doled out upon the completion of each twenty-mile section of track. They further authorized other private firms to develop branches feeding the UP, which would eventually morph into such lines as the Kansas Pacific, the Denver Pacific, and the Missouri Pacific. To help fund its operations, Congress authorized the UP to issue its own first-mortgage bonds upon approval of its twenty-member board of directors, five of whom were federal appointees.

Irregularities cropped up early. Those who purchased the first-mortgage bonds and converted them to stock—among them Thomas Clark Durant, brothers Oakes and Oliver Ames (who'd amassed a small fortune manufacturing picks and shovels at their factory in Easton, Massachusetts, during the gold rush), Sidney Dillon, and a number of other investors—tended to have hidden agendas. Durant (known widely as "Dr. Durant" because he'd once flirted with a medical career) had formerly been associated with the building of other railroads, notably the Mississippi and Missouri Railroad across Iowa. With regard to the UP, he'd been involved in lobbying President Lincoln and Congress (including Massachusetts representative Oakes Ames) to get the Pacific Railway Acts through. Later, in 1864, Durant purchased numerous UP bonds and secured himself a place on the board. Following a power struggle with the Ames brothers, in which he tried to snare the title of president, Durant wound up as vice president and general manager instead.

In this capacity, Durant made sure the railroad's first exorbitantly priced construction contract (at costs per mile some two to three times higher than necessary) went to one H. M. Hoxie, agent for a Pennsylvania corporation that Durant, Oakes Ames, Dillon, and a few other investors had acquired a year earlier and renamed the Credit Mobilier of America. The Mobilier in turn subcontracted the work, on equally generous terms, to firms owned or controlled by various other UP board members. Three years later, in 1867, the Credit Mobilier awarded a new construction contract to Oakes Ames, who (like Hoxie before him) subcontracted with firms owned by board members to build still more road. Construction profits were later estimated at between $7 million and $23 million. This process depleted generous congressional grants to the UP and left the railroad under a heavy debt by the time of its completion in 1869.

As Maury Klein wrote, by May 1869—when, with great fanfare, representatives of the Central Pacific and the UP hammered in the Golden Spike at Promontory, Utah—the UP's promoters were "balkanized into factions who had blustered and bungled their way through three construction contracts strung together by feeble compromises until their affairs had become hopelessly entangled in litigation."[11] Amid this quagmire, following the Golden Spike ceremony, Durant resigned from the UP board and from his paid position with the railroad. He left in his wake the UP's president of three years, the intense but befuddled Oliver Ames. Although he had no railroading experience whatsoever, it nevertheless now fell to Oliver to deal with the firm's large floating debt ($13 million), rumors of impending default, a falling stock price, and escalating costs for capital based on the company's apparent insolvency. (One 1869 note cost the firm 17 1/2 percent in interest.) Early in 1871, with the UP on the brink of financial collapse, Ames resigned as president while retaining, however, his position on the company's board of directors. Whether Oliver yet smelled the scandal that would soon engulf his brother is not known.

As early as 1869, Charles Francis Adams, Jr., had complained in public about the Credit Mobilier and the perpetual frauds of what he called the "Pacific Railroad Ring." During late 1867 and early 1868, Oakes Ames (still serving as a U.S. representative from Massachusetts) worked to forestall federal investigations into these goings-on by bribing his colleagues in the House and Senate. Ames assigned large blocks of Credit Mobilier stock to specially selected colleagues at par, even though the shares were worth twice as much at the time. Speaker of the House Schuyler Colfax took a taste. So did Massachusetts senator Henry Wilson, Ohio representative James A. Garfield (he of the Black Friday investigation), Senator James W. Patterson

of New Hampshire, and Representatives Henry Laurens Dawes of Massachusetts, John Bingham of Ohio, John A. Logan of Illinois, and William B.
Allison and James F. Wilson of Iowa. Ames also roped in two Pennsylvania
representatives: William D. "Pig-Iron" Kelley and G. W. Scofield. Like
Ames, most of the participants in the Credit Mobilier payola were Republican. The scheme's lone Democrat, James Brooks of New York, served as a
government director of the UP and was thus prohibited by law from owning company shares. No problem: He bought them in his son's name.

The only members of the cabal to eventually get cold feet were Allison
and both Wilsons. They returned their holdings in 1869, Ames buying them
back at par value plus interest. Other members of Congress whom Ames approached, such as Maine's James G. Blaine, declined to get involved. Ames
kept track of all transactions in a little black ledger book. He wrote his associate Henry S. McComb that he had placed the stock "where it will produce the most good to us."[12] Ames subsequently forwarded to McComb
several lists of congressmen who had received or were to receive shares.
Later on, friction between Ames and McComb triggered the publication of
these letters in Charles A. Dana's *New York Sun* during the presidential election campaign of 1872. Two subsequent congressional investigations badly
smirched the political reputations of Schuyler Colfax, by then the sitting
vice president, and most other participants. Oakes Ames and James Brooks
wound up censured. Brooks died of a stroke in April 1873, just one month
before the harried and disgraced Oakes Ames did the same.

Following Oliver Ames's departure as president and a brief flirtation with
Tom Scott of the Pennsylvania Railroad, the UP came under the influence
of Cornelius Vanderbilt, who saw the road's potential as a profitable feeder
for his own Lake Shore & Michigan Southern. By 1872, Vanderbilt held
enough UP stock to force Horace Clark into the organization as president:
a post to which Clark was reelected a year later. During the spring of 1873,
Clark—evidently not concerned about what his father-in-law the Commodore might think—moved to involve Gould in the venture.

Testifying before Congress a number of years after the fact, Jay explained
that Clark and Schell—the latter serving as treasurer of the Lake Shore &
Michigan Southern—had recommended the UP to him as a good stock. It
was sometime in mid-May 1873 that Jay met his partners in the Northwestern corner for dinner at Chicago. Clark and Schell had just finished riding

the length of the UP, inspecting the road. "They spoke so highly of the property that it induced me to send an order down to New York to buy the stock, . . . to begin at 35, . . . buy it on a scale down." In other words, Gould gave his brokers authority to buy virtually any share of the UP priced at 35 or lower. Then he took off with his family for several weeks of holiday in the White Mountains.

As regards what happened next, here is the version Gould told to congressional investigators. Gould was still in the mountains when Clark suddenly became ill. According to Jay's testimony, the market for UP shares dried up almost instantaneously once it became clear Clark was going to die. At the same time, in anticipation of Clark's demise, the dying man's brokers decided to dispose of all his numerous shares. These two factors—the lack of market for the stock and the dumping of the Clark shares—combined and caused the stock to fall precipitously, at which point "my orders caught it." Clark was dead by the end of June. Upon Gould's return from his New Hampshire vacation, he found himself owning 100,000 of the 367,000 UP shares outstanding. "After I got home the stock kept going down, and I got alarmed about it and began to inquire into the condition of the property."[13]

Gould was being coy. That Clark died without much warning in June 1873 is quite true. That Gould issued his scale-down buy order, and then left town, before Clark became sick is also true. But that Gould was surprised by the sharp drop in the price of the UP, and likewise surprised by his own sudden equity in the firm, seems quite unlikely for so cunning and detail-oriented an operator, just as it does not ring true that only after Gould found himself with a substantial interest in the UP did he become familiar with the firm's affairs. For starters, the record shows that Clark's brokers did not sell off his shares in anticipation of his death. Furthermore, the evidence indicates that Clark's sickness and death did not depress the price at all. As Grodinsky noted: "A week after [Clark's] death, the stock after moving down from 26 1/8 to 24 1/2, returned to 26 1/8, but two weeks later it sold at 29. The price declined because of the general market trend, and the threat of legal action by the government. In the midst of [Gould's] buying program, the attorney-general filed a bill against the Union Pacific, its construction company, and a large number of individuals, suggesting that the court, among other things, declare that the Land Grant bonds and the Income bonds had been unlawfully issued."[14]

This action—of which Gould might well have had advance word—influenced the UP pricing, and nothing else. As regards the poor financial condition of the road, this was highly publicized. By simply reading the newspapers Gould would have known about the firm's floating debt and other problems well before buying his 100,000 shares.

At first, Gould, his reputation preceding him, was eyed with significant skepticism by the citizens of the UP board. Men like Oliver Ames and Sidney Dillon—even though they'd already had extensive dealings with the Credit Mobilier, Oakes Ames, and Durant—viewed Gould as something unique: the looter of the Erie. Receiving an initial cold shoulder, Gould was nevertheless able to make peace with a substantial majority of the board over time. Soon Gould included in his camp not only Ames but Ames's son Frederick and other board members, including Elisha Atkins, Ezra Baker, F. Gordon Dexter, and Dillon. (The latter, a onetime farmboy born in 1812 in rural Montgomery County, New York, would—like Sage—become an especially close friend and ally of Gould's through the next nineteen years. Both Gould and Dillon would die in 1892.) Writing after the turn of the century, a banker associated with Gould, David B. Sickels, recalled buying outright control of the road for Jay during the winter of 1873–1874 "by a secret combination with Messrs. Dillon & Atkins, after we had purchased in the open market all the stock available."[15] (Gould eventually came to control some 200,000 shares of the UP.) At about this same time, Gould assured General Grenville M. Dodge, chief construction engineer for the UP, that he intended to stay with the railroad for the long haul and "make it a big thing."[16]

The bulk of Gould's back-end buying of UP during November 1873 and February 1874 was done amid a financial panic that had begun in Europe several months earlier. The turbulence in London and Paris eventually spread across the Atlantic and caused the failure of Jay Cooke and Company of Philadelphia, the country's preeminent investment banking concern. A principal backer of the Northern Pacific Railroad, then still in the early stages of construction between Lake Superior and Puget Sound, Jay Cooke had also handled most of the government's wartime loans. Thus the collapse of his organization touched off a financial domino effect. The New York Stock Exchange closed for ten days. Credit dried up. Foreclosures were common. Banks and investment bankers (among them Wall Street's prominent Fisk & Hatch) failed as factories closed their doors, costing thousands of workers their jobs. Over the course of the two years between autumn 1873 and autumn 1875, approximately 18,000 American businesses would go under. At the same time, 89 of the country's 364 railroads would go bankrupt, and by 1876 unemployment would rise to a staggering 14 percent. Analysts later argued that, more than any other single factor, the extreme overbuilding of the nation's railways had laid the groundwork for the American end of the panic, and for the depression that followed. Full recovery would not come until 1878. In this environment, when Sickels orchestrated the final stock purchases that ultimately sewed up the UP for Gould, he did so at a sliver of the line's actual value.

Along with four of his brokers, Jay joined the UP board in March 1874. During the same meeting, Sidney Dillon, holder of 26,000 shares, became president, a post he would hold for ten years. Atkins stepped in as vice president. In the course of the next twelve months, Gould protected the UP from the fate then being endured by so many other railroads, even though it cost him personally in the short term. As Morosini would recall, the panic left Gould "comparatively a poor man. . . . I doubt if any man parted with more cash and securities than did Mr. Gould by reason of the catastrophe."[17] In one of his first steps after taking control, Gould transformed the UP's floating debt, due to mature that August, into a longer-term bond issue. He also masterminded a refunding of the firm's $10 million in income bonds as new, lower-interest, sinking-fund bonds (issues in which most or part of the issuer's long-term debt is redeemed, according to a strict schedule, prior to maturity). Concurrently, Gould brought suit against the federal government, which, since March 1873, had withheld payments on the movement of government freight—this to recoup partial payment of interest owed on U.S. bonds loaned to help finance the UP's construction. Simultaneously, Gould virtually walked away from another, smaller, unfinished railroad in which he'd been interested since 1872, the New Jersey Southern, selling his interest at a loss of more than $1 million. He apparently felt that he could not shore up two roads at once in the face of the depression, and that he had a larger game to play in the UP.

Once free of the New Jersey Southern, Jay moved to take control of, and thereby suppress, the Pacific Mail Steamship Company's competition with the Central Pacific–Union Pacific interchange. Providing transport between the West Coast docks and the Isthmus of Panama, the Pacific Mail offered the only real alternative to the UP and the Central Pacific for the transcontinental shipment of freight. (Most important in this equation were imports from the Orient arriving at West Coast ports for transshipping to eastern markets, and eastern manufactured goods bound for California and the Orient.) During December 1873 the independent-minded Russell Sage—who'd previously joined Gould in manipulating the stock of the Pacific Mail and served on the company's board—stepped into the Pacific Mail as president. Once installed, he continued the previous management's program of an aggressive price war against the railroads, despite his friend Jay's ascendance at the UP. Throughout the summer and autumn of 1874, the amount of business Sage attracted became frighteningly large.

Early that December, when verifiable revelations of Sage's short-selling of Pacific Mail stock forced his resignation as president, Gould was widely presumed to be the source of the news. Subsequent publicity advertised not only Sage but also several additional board members, along with Gould, as prominent bears in the stock. Accordingly, through early 1875, the price of Pacific Mail slumped to near panic-level prices. Over these same months Gould, though publicly identified as a bear, quietly bought into Pacific Mail through a dozen or more brokers until he'd acquired a controlling interest in the firm at a good rate. On 3 March 1875, Gould and two associates, Ames and Dillon, joined the board of the Pacific Mail. Dillon, already president of the UP, took on the same position with the Pacific Mail, and the rate wars ceased at once. "The Union Pacific, in control of the Pacific Mail, was now free to increase its rates without fear of competition from the steamship route," commented Grodinsky. "With the volume at high levels and moving at monopolistic rates, the earnings picture of the Union Pacific was bright."[18] UP stock, which had stood at 15 in November 1873, soared to 78 by June 1875, despite the ongoing depression.

Profitable news about the taming of the Pacific Mail aside, the Central Pacific's dominant force, fifty-four-year-old Collis P. Huntington, remained uneasy. Shortly before his acquisition of the Pacific Mail, Gould had quite publicly engaged with Huntington in the creation of a railroad-controlled steamship line, the Occidental & Oriental Steamship Company. In retrospect, Huntington realized that mere talk of his and Gould's idea for the new steamship firm had done a great deal to drive down the price Gould had had to pay for the Pacific Mail. When the dust settled, Huntington came away feeling he'd been played as a pawn, though it is not clear he should have felt that way. Gould, Dillon, and Ames owned $2.5 million, $2 million, and $500,000 stakes, respectively, in Huntington's Occidental. What was more, Gould assured Huntington that both steamship lines, not to mention each cooperative end of the transcontinental railroad, could and would be run as one harmonious monopoly. Still, Huntington remained leery of Gould's quiet inscrutability and his penchant for Byzantine endgames. Thus Huntington declined when Gould, in an effort to demonstrate good faith, offered him a seat on the board of the Pacific Mail. He would insist, until proven wrong, on believing that Gould's ambition with the UP and its associated firms was purely speculative, just as it had been with the Erie. In the future, Huntington fully expected Gould to bull up the stock of the UP, sell out, and then go short. Given this assumption, Huntington devised a simple strategy for dealing with Gould in the near term: "Avoid a quarrel with him, and watch for the time when we are ready to control the UP, and then go in and get control of it."[19] But Huntington, along with the rest of Wall Street, was in for an education.

Chapter 24

CONSOLIDATION

FROM THE SPRING OF 1874 onward, Gould's primary personal focus was not stock speculation—although he certainly did some of this, since it always came easily enough—but the management of the Union Pacific as a business. He was the supreme ruler of the UP even though he preferred anonymity and officially held no positions other than his seats on the board and executive committee. Taking authority over President Sidney Dillon, Gould not only strengthened the firm's financial structure but also served as chief strategist in the UP's competitive and political battles. In the course of just a few years he would restructure the UP's chain of management, realign its rates for maximum competitive advantage, and work for the development of properties and resources along the UP corridor. In taking on all these tasks, Jay necessarily immersed himself in the minutiae of the UP's operations, coming to know the UP's road, resources, strengths, and shortcomings every bit as intimately as he had those of the old Rutland & Washington a decade earlier.

Twice a year, Gould would ride the length of the UP's track—as well as tracks controlled by competitors—together with Dillon, Fred Ames, Morosini, and others. His private railroad car, the Convoy, traveled behind its own locomotive, coal tender, and baggage car. Gould insisted on a clip of fifty miles per hour, which was quite fast at the time, and he did not permit any slowing over uneven grades. "During such a trip," reported a correspondent for the *New York Times,* "[Gould] has been known to change seats—from one side of the car to another—not of his own volition, but without changing countenance."[1] As Gould rode, a male stenographer sat at his side jotting down the mogul's running thoughts on maintenance initiatives, possible cost economies, and recommended improvements. All these ideas would later be taken up with Silas H. H. Clark, Gould's chief operational lieutenant for the UP after Dillon. (The man who managed the road in the West as of 1874, Clark was just a few months younger than Gould. He'd been raised on a farm in New Jersey and had spent his entire professional life in railroading. Clark knew Wall Street not at all, but he understood locomotives and freight forwarding intimately. He and Gould shared two traits: They were both workaholics and they both loved books. Gould was to make Clark a rich man.) In the evenings, after Gould's train pulled up onto a siding to rest both the machine and the men driving it, Jay would walk the lonely western towns, make small talk with whoever happened to be about, and quiz local UP employees for their views concerning what the company might do better in that particular neighborhood. "Our men on the ground have intelligence we need. They are our agents, and we fail to know their minds at our own peril," Gould wrote Dillon.[2]

Gould's twice-yearly sojourns led to friendships with various UP customers. For example, the proprietors of the Keith & Barton Ranch in Nebraska came to know Gould well. "For a home ranch they had headquarters at Dexter, a siding near the present town of Sutherland," recalled the editor of the *Lincoln State Journal* in 1930. "Here Jay Gould and Sidney Dillon, of New York, and Fred Ames, of Boston, made their annual visit to the Keith & Barton ranch on their usual tour of inspection over the Union Pacific Railroad. . . . Mr. Barton, knowing of their coming, would send word to his foreman to round up the herd at a certain time and have saddle horses in readiness. He joined the party in their special train at North Platte and accompanied them to Dexter, where all preparations were made for the guests. Gentle horses, with California saddles, stood before them, and, mounting, the party rode among the cattle, crossing hills and valleys, commenting on colors, ages, and beef steer, watching the frolics of the calves jumping around their mothers, and forgetful of Wall Street and the stock market. Later they boarded their train, happy and joyous at the free life of the cattleman, and for miles on each side of the track the big herd would be visible from their car window."³

Jay would usually also stop during his inspection tours to see his brother, Abram. Starting in 1876, Abram, who'd previously worked for the Pacific Mail in San Francisco, found employment under Clark in Salt Lake as manager of the UP's coal department. One year earlier, in September 1875, Jay had served as best man at a ceremony in Salem, New York, when Abram married German-born Sophia Kegler, sister to Fred Kegler, master mechanic for the Rutland & Washington. Sadly, Sophia was to die in 1878, leaving Abram with a small boy, Jay Fred Gould (known as *Fred* within the family) to raise on his own.

◇　◇　◇

Throughout Jay Gould's tours of the UP line, and throughout his long days back at the UP business office in New York, he focused always on core business fundamentals. Memorandum after memorandum stressed essential basics of economy. Earnings had to be kept high, but prices could never rise to the point where they jeopardized the long-term interests of customers, even though the UP had a monopoly position. Only so long as freight clients remained solvent would they remain clients. Jay's general policy was to charge the highest possible local rates for traffic on which the UP held a monopoly, to narrowly beat prices on competitive trade, and to offer steep discounts where necessary to facilitate the growth of new business. In step with all this, expenses had to be monitored constantly and closely—especially the costs of coal, labor, and capital.

With Dillon and Clark, Gould hammered out the efficient running of the UP as a railroad. With the Boston members of the board, especially Oliver and Fred Ames, he shaped the details of finance. It was with Fred Ames, in 1878—one year after Oliver's death in 1877—that Gould worked to craft a key loophole in the Thurman Act: federal legislation requiring the UP to set aside 25 percent of its net earnings for the retirement of debts owed the government. Thanks to lobbying by Gould and Ames, key language in the bill allowed the UP to tap this set-aside sinking fund if the remaining 75 percent of the net was insufficient to pay the interest on the firm's bonds. As a result, the UP could continue to expand even while it declared itself unable to pay back its numerous government loans.⁴

In placing Abram in charge of the UP's coal department, Jay was express-ing vast confidence. Coal was not just a commodity for the UP, but the lifeblood of the line. Before Gould controlled the railroad, the previous cor-rupt managers had, in 1868, leased the UP's own coal lands in Wyoming to two Missouri businessmen, Cyrus O. Godfrey and Thomas Wardell. The UP then agreed to purchase Godfrey's and Wardell's coal on an inflated slid-ing scale ranging from three dollars to six dollars per ton over the next fif-teen years, and to provide the gentlemen with a 25 percent rebate on shipments to other customers. One year later, Godfrey and Wardell—who all along had secretly acted as agents for several UP directors—assigned the contract to a Nebraska corporation called the Wyoming Coal and Mining Company, an operation 90 percent owned by the same UP directors. The end result was a system wherein the UP paid ridiculously high prices for coal mined on its own property. Some bituminous mines Jay owned at Blossburg, Pennsylvania, produced coal at a cost of just $1.25 per ton, so Gould knew substantial savings were to be had. Shortly after coming to power, he moved with typical decisiveness to end the absurdity. With the wave of a hand he abrogated the original contract with Godfrey and Wardell and seized the seven Wyoming mines, sending the executives of the Wyoming Coal and Mining Company to the courts, where their suits would eventually fail after languishing for six years.

The mines Gould started to run in 1874—located in the towns of Rock Springs, Carbon, and Almy, Wyoming—were inefficient and riddled with labor tensions. The miners were for the most part Scandinavians who had been brought to Wyoming in 1871 to replace a previous generation of work-ers then in the process of unionizing. By 1874, however, it was the Norwe-gians and Swedes who talked of solidarity, a sentiment with which Gould, like other capitalists of his day, had no sympathy whatsoever. When these men—whom Gould already thought overpaid at $52 per month—seemed on the verge of a labor action that autumn, Jay reinforced their ranks with Chinese miners at a monthly cost of just $32.50 per head. During Novem-ber, when the white miners finally did go out on strike, Jay instructed Clark to bring in more Chinese. At the same time, Gould issued orders to pur-chase new, modern machinery with which to maximize efficiency. These programs would continue under Abram after 1876. Between 1875 and 1880 production in the UP-controlled mines more than doubled while the cost per ton dropped a total of 65 cents to $1.35, thus laying a vital cornerstone for UP expansion. (During his first year on the job, Abram slashed the cost of the Chinese labor down to $27 a month per head, which his brother nevertheless still thought $2 too high.)

Shrinking the pay for non-Asian labor outside the mines would prove more difficult. In the spring of 1877, Jay briefly allied himself with the heads of other railroads (among them William H. Vanderbilt, now at the helm of the New York Central and the Lake Shore & Michigan Southern after the Commodore's death that January) in announcing a general, across-the-board pay cut of 10 percent for all workers nationwide. Subsequently, strikes and riots erupted at railroad facilities in Pittsburgh, Baltimore, Chicago, Buffalo, and San Francisco. In the end, President Rutherford B. Hayes had to order federal troops to restore order. The Central Pacific, the Erie, and Vanderbilt's roads absorbed considerable costs in lost traffic and damaged property.

Late in July, before any violence afflicted the UP, Jay made some calculations and declared the pay cut a false economy. The workers he'd planned to pickpocket were capable of doing far more than 10 percent worth of damage overall. On 22 July, Gould wired Clark in Salt Lake with instructions to rescind the cut. UP workers held a mass rally the next morning at which they promised to protect the stations, yards, and rolling stock of the UP at all costs. The *Herald*, which had a day before castigated Gould for his mistreatment and betrayal of the working man, now criticized him for betraying his capitalist brethren. That evening, Gould gave an interview to the *New York World* in which he condemned the strikers at the other railroads, saying they represented a "great social revolution" that was likely to end with "the destruction of the republican form of government in this country." Despite his grim message, the *World* noted Gould was "in very good spirits, and seemed to contemplate the coming of the general conflagration as serenely as if he had a complete monopoly of the trade in Lucifer matches and petroleum."[5] In fact, Jay was at the moment busily shorting the stocks of his strike-afflicted competitors, thus his cheerfulness in making the future sound as gloomy as possible.

On another front, Gould made himself busy building up communities and businesses along the UP track. At Laramie, Wyoming, during June 1876—the same month Custer died at the Battle of the Little Big Horn—

Gould made maximum use of local tax concessions, employing them to help finance a steel-rolling mill that soon became the town's largest employer. In a stroke, Jay created a source of cheap rails for the UP while propping up Laramie's sagging economy and inspiring the town's growth. Meanwhile, eyeing the Big Horn Mountains and Black Hills, where gold had recently been discovered, Gould spent an hour with the geologist who'd surveyed that terrain for the federal government. Two days later he wrote a memo forecasting that the region would become profitable not only as a source of gold but as range land. When Clark balked at the danger of extending various lines north after the Custer battle, Gould shut down the debate. As usual, he saw the world with a vivid and heartless clarity: "The ultimate result [of the massacre at the Little Big Horn] will be to annihilate the Indians & open up the Big Horn & Black Hills to development & settlement & in this way greatly benefit us."[6] (Something Gould did not mention to Clark was the fact that his sister Anna and her husband were residents of the region in question. Inhabiting a one-room mud hut that became an oven in the summer and a freezer in the winter, the two suffered greatly on the barren Montana plains, where they would remain, spreading the Methodist gospel to prospectors and Indians, until Anna's health finally broke under the burden. Jay did his best to help them, but with all his wealth he could not revise the harsh realities of frontier living.)

At the same time that he contemplated new branch lines, Gould helped finance a smelting firm in Omaha to handle ore and bullion from western mines, all delivered by the UP. He also micromanaged efforts to market UP lands in western Nebraska and Wyoming. These properties, lying west of the hundredth meridian, were generally not wet enough for farming. Thus Gould sold the grazing rights to ranch interests, sweetening the pot with significant discounts on UP rates for cattle shipments. With these same customers in mind he built a shipping center, a hotel, and yards adjacent to the UP line at Fort Bridger. Then, after making Fort Bridger a destination for cattle drivers and buyers, he did the same thing for the Nebraska towns of Schuyler, Kearney, and Ogallala, all with the aim of capturing northward drives.

◇   ◇   ◇

Besides the western railroads, Gould also had several other games in play. Not the least of these was his investment in the telegraph business and his at first frustrated interest in the Western Union.

Founded in 1851, the Western Union came into its own during the Civil War. In the midst of the bloodletting between the states, the Western seized most of the federal government's telegraph business and absorbed the most viable of its immediate rivals. Between 1863 and its takeover by Cornelius Vanderbilt in 1869, the well-watered Western saw the value of its stock climb from $3 million to $41 million. Of course, much of the Western's commercial viability was tied to its close relationships with railroads. Like other telegraph firms, the Western housed the lion's share of its 12,600 offices in railroad depots nationwide, ran its lines parallel to the tracks of the roads with which it nurtured maintenance agreements, and in return provided those same rail companies with unlimited message service. All such arrangements were made on an exclusive basis.

The Pacific (the Union Pacific, Central Pacific, etc.) roads were among the few rail properties in which the Western did not have itself entrenched. In 1869 the Union Pacific refused to align itself with that firm and instead entered into an agreement with the smaller Atlantic & Pacific (A&P), which one year later reached terms with Huntington's Central Pacific. The Union Pacific's deal with the A&P gave the road 24,000 shares of A&P stock: a controlling interest that, to most observers, appeared to be nearly worthless. One industry observer noted a few years later that whereas the Western Union boasted 154,472 miles of wire, the A&P had only 7,460, not counting the capacity of the tiny, insignificant Franklin Telegraph Company, which the A&P controlled. No one believed the A&P to have much of a future in the face of the behemoth Western Union.

It took Jay Gould, once he came into the Union Pacific, to recognize the potential of the A&P stock as a position from which to leverage influence and, in the long run, a merger with the Western. Soon after taking control of the Union Pacific, Gould induced Levi P. Morton to release recently acquired options on the Union Pacific's A&P shares. Then, in April 1874, Jay instructed Dillon to cancel the A&P's long-standing noncompete agreement with the Western. At the same time, he arranged to shore up the A&P's sketchy physical condition. As well, in December, Gould approached General Thomas T. Eckert, superintendent of the Western

Union, offering him the presidency of the A&P. Eckert had until recently been widely viewed as the Western Union's president in waiting, but that changed when Vanderbilt gave the job to another appointee. Thus the disenfranchised Eckert took Gould's offer seriously and promised to consider it carefully. While Eckert pondered his options, Jay used him to help induce Thomas A. Edison—an inept businessman recently mistreated and underpaid by Western Union president William Orton—to sell to the A&P, rather than the Western Union, his interest in the quadruplex telegraph, this capable of sending four messages simultaneously on one wire, two each way.

Edison was not yet the "Wizard of Menlo Park." He was instead a distracted young inventor, scraping along, hardly holding most of his own patents. What many considered his most significant inventions to date—those related to his automatic telegraph technology, which used perforated paper tape to accelerate the transmission of messages—were held in partnership with former diplomat George Harrington, who had personally financed much of Edison's research in exchange for a two-thirds interest in Edison's machines for a period of five years starting in 1871. Together with the Kansas Pacific Railroad's financial agent, Josiah Reiff, Harrington also controlled the minuscule Automatic Telegraph Company, a firm designed to leverage Edison's automatic patents. (Complicating the matter of patent rights for Edison's quadruplex, however, was the fact that Edison had recently agreed to list the Western Union's chief electrician, George Prescott, as co-owner in exchange for work space in the Western Union's lab. Edison either did not realize or did not care that this agreement directly contradicted his previous contract with Harrington.)

Disrespectful of Edison as a businessman and already believing he controlled 50 percent of the quadruplex's patent through Prescott, Western Union president Orton dickered with the inventor in the worst of faith for the balance of the rights throughout the autumn of 1874. Then, on 10 December, Orton departed for a business trip to Chicago without concluding an arrangement with Edison, whom he incorrectly presumed to be without other options. Orton knew nothing of Edison's arrangement with Harrington, nor that Reiff had recently struck a deal by which Gould would acquire the Automatic Telegraph Company *if*—as Gould insisted—Reiff could also deliver Edison's new quadruplex.

The plot thickened in late December, with Orton still away. Edison re-called:

> One day Eckert called me into his office [at the Western Union] and made inquiries about money matters. I told him Mr. Orton had gone off and left me without means, and I was in straits. He told me I would never get another cent, but that he knew a man who would buy it. I told him of my arrangement with the electrician, and said I could not sell it as a whole to anybody; but if I got enough for it, I would sell all my interest in any SHARE I might have. He seemed to think his party would agree to this. I had a set of quadruplex over in my shop, 10 and 12 Ward Street, Newark, and he arranged to bring him over next evening to see the appa-ratus. So the next morning Eckert came over with Jay Gould and intro-duced him to me. This was the first time I had ever seen him. I exhibited and explained the apparatus, and they departed. The next day Eckert sent for me, and I was taken up to Gould's house, which was near the Wind-sor Hotel, Fifth Avenue. In the basement he had an office. It was in the evening, and we went in by the servants' entrance, as Eckert probably feared that he was watched. Gould started in at once and asked me how much I wanted. I said: "Make me an offer." Then he said: "I will give you $30,000." I said: "I will sell any interest I may have for that money," which was something more than I thought I could get. The next morning I went with Gould to the office of his lawyers, Sherman & Sterling, and received a check for $30,000, with a remark by Gould that I had got the steamboat *Plymouth Rock* [a relic of the Fisk era] as he had sold her for $30,000 and had just received the check.

Although Edison failed to mention it, he also received 3,000 shares of A&P stock along with the title of electrician for the firm. The transaction took place on 4 January 1875 and was oiled by Reiff's assurance to Gould that the Prescott patent claim was indefensible. One week later, Eckert left the Western Union and became president of the A&P. Four months after that, Gould paid Harrington $106,000 for his two-thirds interest in the quadruplex patent, and the sickly Harrington took off for southern Europe. At the same time, however, Gould reneged on his obligations to Reiff re-garding payments for purchase of the Automatic, citing as his reason Reiff's "misrepresentation" of the patent claims held by Prescott. As Gould later pointed out in sworn testimony, the Western Union continued using the quadruplex well after his supposed assumption of exclusive rights. In doing so, the Western cited Prescott's name on Edison's patent: the item Reiff had assured Gould would not be a problem. While withholding payments to the old Automatic board, Gould at the same time assigned the assets of the Automatic to the A&P. The resulting suits and countersuits would linger on this earth longer than Gould himself.

During subsequent interactions, Edison discovered that Gould "had no sense of humor. I tried several times to get off what seemed to me a funny story, but he failed to see any humor in them. I was very fond of stories and had a choice lot . . . with which I could usually throw a man into convulsions."[7] Gould tried in turn to dazzle a blank Edison with detailed discussions of the complexities of railroad interchanges and finance. He brandished maps and lectured on for hours about his particular passion, all to no effect. The two men barely lived on the same planet. Edison soon lost interest in Gould and in perfecting the automatic technology on which both the Automatic Telegraph Company and the A&P had placed large bets.

Unable to compete with the Western Union via exclusives on better technology, Gould turned to more reliable tools. In February 1875 he opened up a rate war. Then in May, he convinced Tom Scott of the Pennsylvania Railroad to run A&P wires along his corridors. Next, Gould arranged for the Union Pacific board to approve the sale of its shares in A&P at 25, Jay taking 16,000 units and the balance going to Sage, Ames, and others of Gould's circle. (Around this time, buying into dips, Gould also personally acquired nearly 50,000 additional A&P shares at prices ranging from 15 to 18.) In July, while offering to discuss the sale or lease of the A&P to the Western Union, Jay bought heavily into Western Union stock as well, all the while encouraging his protégés to do the same. "I don't think an amalgamation of the WU and A&P T. Co.'s far off," he told Ames. "We shall carry through the consolidation of the two telegraph companies in such a way as to make Western Union an active ally of the Union Pacific."[8]

But negotiations collapsed in September, and then in December Jay himself collapsed, retreating to his bed for a month with a recurrence of his old typhoid fever. When he rose like a phoenix in January of 1876, it was to reignite his rate war: a move that caused the Western Union, uncharacteristically, to miss its April dividend. Subsequently Gould recruited John W. Garrett, proprietor of the Baltimore & Ohio (B&O)—at that time engaged in a bitter war with the New York Central for through traffic to the Iowa pool of railroads—to renounce the B&O's Western Union agreement and ally with the A&P. Such was the situation in January 1877 when the Commodore died, leaving William H. Vanderbilt, more of a compromiser, to oversee the family interests.

Gould continued to pressure the Western Union throughout the first half of 1877, succeeding in getting it bounced from various roads in Utah, where the Mormon elites who made the corporate decisions also controlled the courts. As well, Gould leaked to the press that he, as representative of the A&P, was engaged in talks with the Erie, the Northwestern, and the Rock Island. Turning up the heat on William Vanderbilt still more, Jay mounted a series of bear raids on Western Union stock. Conveniently, as Jay had hoped, Western Union's earnings dropped, along with its stock price, while Vanderbilt also confronted a serious profitability problem on his eastern trunk lines due to his ongoing price competition with Garrett.

Vanderbilt's interests were further jeopardized by news in April 1877 that Gould had assumed seats on the Northwestern and Rock Island boards. Soon after, Gould put himself into a position to take control of the Michigan Central. Running parallel to Vanderbilt's Lake Shore & Michigan Southern from Chicago to Detroit, the Michigan Central could pose formidable competition for the Vanderbilt road under the right management, that is, Gould management. But Gould procrastinated in executing the takeover. He dawdled; no one quite understood why. Subsequently, in August, few observers realized what was going on when the Western Union announced it would purchase 72,502 shares of the A&P, mostly from Gould, at 25, a bit higher than the going price on the Street. Less than a year later, Gould allowed Vanderbilt to control the board election for the Michigan Central and become the president of that road.

The result, though it made Gould a tidy sum and solved his problem of what to do with the A&P after he realized he could not grow it to compete significantly with the Western Union, nevertheless left him without what he'd been after all along: a significant interest in the telegraph industry. Shortly after the consolidation, William Vanderbilt stoutly refused Gould's request that he be put on the Western Union's board.

◇ ◇ ◇

At the same time that he struggled against the Western Union, Jay continued to build up and acquire more railroad properties in the West. Initially,
his first interest after the UP was in the Kansas Pacific. Whereas the UP operated from Omaha west through Cheyenne to Ogden (the terminus where
traffic interchanged to and from the Central Pacific), the Kansas Pacific ran
south of the UP, traversing rich farmland from Kansas City to Denver and
then traveling via the Denver Pacific spur line (of which it owned 75 percent) to Cheyenne. At Cheyenne, the Kansas Pacific fed into the track of
the UP, on which it depended for outlets to points west and east. When
Gould first eyed the Kansas Pacific in late 1874, the line was in poor financial condition. The railroad had defaulted on interest payments during the
first stage of the 1873 panic. Early in 1874 this debt was refunded with
long-term bonds, but problems continued. In April 1875, Gould proposed
to the receptive Kansas Pacific president, Robert E. Carr, a St. Louis banker,
that the overcapitalized and debt-ridden Kansas Pacific be merged with the
Denver Pacific and another line, the unprofitable Colorado Central, running
from Denver to Longmont, to form a new entity. This firm would in turn
be managed by the now-profitable UP, which would own half the stock in
the concern. Soon, however, the deal collapsed because of exorbitant demands by William A.H. Loveland, promoter of the Colorado Central. A
number of months later, in November 1876, the Kansas Pacific went into receivership. One year later, Gould made peace with Loveland and extended
the Colorado Central from Longmont to the UP terminus at Cheyenne,
while renewing his overtures to the Kansas Pacific. Carr remained receptive
but now had little power. He was required to obey the dictates of court-
appointed receivers, of which there were two. Carlos S. Greeley, a successful
St. Louis grocer, had been charged to look after the interests of a minority
group of St. Louis investors holding a substantial block of the road's junior
secondary securities. Greeley's counterpart representing the majority first-
mortgage bondholders, most of these being German investors, was Henry
Villard: a formidable individual with whom Gould would have significant
dealings from this time forward.

One year older than Gould, Villard had been born in Bavaria. In 1853 he
emigrated to the United States, married a daughter of William Lloyd Gar-

rison, and started work as a journalist. By the time Gould encountered him, Villard had moved into railroads and steamship companies both as an individual investor and as an agent for German bankers. In 1875 he helped reorganize the Oregon and California Railroad and the Oregon Steamship Company. One year later he became president of both firms, while also taking on receiver responsibilities for the Kansas Pacific.

Of the three classes of investors in the railroad—the stockholders, the secondary bondholders represented by Greeley, and the first-mortgage bondholders represented by Villard—the last constituted by far the largest and most significant investment in the Kansas Pacific. Thus Gould needed to deal with Villard in order to achieve genuine control. Ideally, what he wanted out of Villard was a substantial reduction in the face value and interest rate on the first-mortgage bonds as part of an overall restructuring to make the Kansas Pacific solvent. But Villard was not biting.

The two men liked one another personally. Gould took to dropping by Villard's office on Nassau Street in Manhattan for long discussions on topics other than finance. "They spoke," wrote Villard's great-granddaughter, Alexandra Villard de Borchgrave, "of Germany and Goethe, the Civil War, language acquisition, and the American economy, and each appraised the other's weaknesses and strengths." (De Borchgrave added that "Villard admired Gould's daring, his skill, and the cultured opulence of his private life."[9]) Of course, they also spoke of business. "I see my friend Gould frequently," Villard wrote in 1877. "One day he talks peace and the next he threatens. But I am not afraid of him."[10] In other words, Villard had considerable backbone in the face of an onslaught.

During the fall of 1877 Gould signed a contract with the Iowa pool (a group of independently owned railroads merged as a practical matter through a revenue-sharing agreement) to encourage the movement of freight via Omaha and away from the Kansas Pacific. Soon thereafter, during one of his friendly drop-ins at Nassau Street, Gould let slip that he was thinking of moving the bulk of the Colorado traffic under control of the Union Pacific east to Kansas City via the Atchison, Topeka & Santa Fe. All the while he also conducted a rate war against the Kansas Pacific and pursued other leads. At one point, when learning of a large block of Denver Pacific bonds held by Dutch investors, he chartered a yacht and made a two-week-long dash to Amsterdam, where he bought the securities. As he told it later, in order to acquire "$2 million of Denver Pacific [bonds] at seventy-four-cents, I went over and got to Amsterdam in the morning; washed and had my breakfast. I saw them [the bondholders] at eleven; bought them out at twelve, and started back in the afternoon."[11]

Concurrently, Gould convinced the cash-starved Kansas Pacific's directors to refinance the road's floating debt with a mortgage underwritten by himself, Ames, and the Union Pacific. The collateral for this note was to include the Kansas Pacific's stock in the Denver Pacific. Thus any default would make Gould and his colleagues the de facto owners of that road. As well, Gould personally bought numerous Kansas Pacific income bonds at bargain multiples and lent the firm $85,000 from his own cash reserve. Finally, in April 1878—as Villard unblinkingly continued to defend the interests of his clients and hold out for favorable terms on the German-owned first-mortgage bonds—Gould organized holders of Kansas Pacific junior securities (including most of the St. Louis bondholders represented by Greeley) into a pool that, as the largest holder of junior securities in the group, he immediately moved to dominate. Gould also got the Kansas Pacific's board, led by Carr, to deposit their personal holdings in the pool by offering to assume their share of the railroad's floating debt. Through this device, Gould achieved equity control of the Kansas Pacific. On 2 May, Gould, Dillon, and Fred Ames became members of the Kansas Pacific board. In one move, Jay had succeeded in making himself a Kansas Pacific insider while isolating Villard, to whom he subsequently, and somewhat surprisingly, offered a reorganization agreement with terms the astute Bavarian found acceptable.

With visible relief after a long struggle, Villard turned his authority in the Kansas Pacific over to Dillon on 20 June. But later that same day—just as Villard was preparing for a long-delayed trip to Europe with his family—word came that the Kansas Pacific board, meeting in Lawrence, Kansas, had decided to revise the settlement with the German bondholders on terms much less attractive than those originally agreed to. Canceling his trip, Villard explained to his wife that "the scamp Gould" and "the rascally St. Louis people . . . have formed a regular conspiracy in the West to break the contract and cheat the bondholders."[12]

Eventually, after Villard made it clear he would stick to his guns, Gould masterminded a successful coup, having him removed as receiver. Nevertheless, at the German bondholders' direct request, Villard remained in control of those securities. Villard refused to settle even after Gould offered him, in Villard's words, "a profitable participation in the syndicate to be formed for the reorganization of the Kansas Pacific."[13] This stalemate went on for another year and a half. Then, in early 1879, amid the first great Wall Street boom after the panic of 1873, Gould finally realized that Villard would never bend. "Gould appeared in Villard's office," writes de Borchgrave, ". . . declared himself weary of fighting, and agreed to comply with all the concessions and conditions that Villard's bondholders required. This time Gould kept his word."[14]

As usual, in his surrender Gould made yet another fortune and improved his strategic position overall. Kansas Pacific stock rose immediately and dramatically upon news of the settlement with Villard. Gould's own personal stock profits soon amounted to approximately $10 million. Some of this Gould used as leverage to help acquire a small feeder, the Central Branch, in the autumn of 1879 and, later that same year, the property that was to become the hub of his personal railroad empire, the Missouri Pacific, running from St. Louis to Kansas City. (This road included among its subsidiaries the Kansas Central and another small Kansas road.) Around this same time, Gould also acquired the Wabash and the Kansas City. Of course Villard joined Gould in profiting from the Kansas Pacific transaction, and like Gould he was destined for even more success. In the coming years Villard would come to own both *The Nation* magazine and the *New York Evening Post* (both acquired in 1881). Villard would also control and complete the Northern Pacific Railroad on its challenging course through the Northern Rockies before losing the road in '83 and reacquiring it in '89. The year 1889 would likewise see Villard cobble together the Edison General Electric Company from two smaller firms.

◇   ◇   ◇

Not one of Gould's ancillary roads—neither the Missouri, the Kansas, the Denver Pacific, nor any of the smaller properties—was acquired as a subsidiary of the UP. Gould and his closest allies (men such as Dillon, Fred Ames, Sage, and Cyrus Field) controlled these routes not as officers of the UP but as individual investors. Just as Gould used his dominant position with the Pacific Mail to effect changes favorable to the UP, so did he use his status in the Kansas Pacific, Denver Pacific, and Missouri Pacific, as well as other smaller feeder roads, to complement and accommodate the functioning of the UP. At the same time, however, the holdings Gould controlled independent of the UP gave him an extra power base: an avenue for potential competition with which to threaten any members of the UP directorate (and there were a few of these) hesitant to follow his lead in key matters. Gould and his closest associates, in turn, also controlled, separate from the UP, various branch lines in development through Colorado, Utah, and elsewhere. Their reason for independently administering the lines under construction, however, was less opportunism than necessity. The UP's narrow federal charter expressly forbade construction of branches, although the firm was allowed to acquire them once they'd been built.

Gould's careful amalgamation of rival lines came to a head at the very end of 1879, when he proposed to his fellow UP directors that his Kansas Pacific–Denver Pacific combination be merged with the UP. Gould's proposal called for the stocks of the two firms (the Kansas Pacific and the UP) to be swapped at par ($1 face value per share) regardless of the fact that the Kansas Pacific (selling at $13 per share) was earning nothing while the Union Pacific (selling at $60 per share) earned and paid 6 percent a year. As a carrot, Gould offered to throw in all the capital of the Denver Pacific. As a stick, Gould threatened—should his fellow UP directors turn down his offer—to extend the Kansas Pacific as far as Ogden, where it would link with the Central Pacific and gain an independent connection to the West Coast. After a few weeks of consideration (during which time most UP directors loaded up on as many shares of the Kansas Pacific as they could buy), the UP directorate agreed to Gould's terms. A contract was signed on 4 January 1880. Gould, who held close to half the Kansas Pacific's stock, later estimated that he had personally netted $40 million on this one transaction, so long in the making. He was not yet forty-four. As Grodinsky noted, "In these negotiations, Gould resumed the trading position he had so often occupied on the Erie—that of representing both buyer and seller."[15]

Gould maintained independent control of the Missouri Pacific, as well as such feeder lines as the Kansas Central and the Central Branch. He told intimates he planned to use these properties as the foundation for a new and vital railroad combination. His Missouri Pacific was free of the governmental restrictions that hindered the UP. It was free as well of the crushing debt that, thanks to Villard's shrewd negotiating, still afflicted the Kansas Pacific. Jay was to follow through on this vision. On the day of his death in 1892 the Missouri Pacific would remain the jewel in the crown of the Gould system of railroads.

◇ ◇ ◇

Despite Gould's steadfast and detail-oriented management of the Union Pacific and the other roads in which he was interested, the press and the public continued to view him as nothing more than a supremely talented, and ultimately villainous, corporate raider. Jay said nothing to dissuade them. If people believed he was spending all his hours rigging Wall Street, laying bear traps, pilfering corporate treasuries, and defrauding widows and orphans, then they were distracted from his real agenda.

Not only did the press of Jay's own era presume Gould to have no entre-preneurial devotion to the firms with which he was concerned, but several generations of scholars—relying on contemporary newspaper accounts for their research—were to adopt the same view. "Few properties on which this man laid his hand escaped ruin in the end. . . . He was not a builder, he was a destroyer." So wrote Alexander D. Noyes in his 1909 book *Forty Years of American Finance*.[16] Robert Reigel, commenting in *The Story of the Western Railroads* (1926), pronounced a similar verdict: "Gould was the type of man who would not have been content in the development of his properties and the waiting of dividends. He wanted more action and larger returns." Reigel added that Gould's "control was always exercised from the East, and it is probable that he never saw some of his properties, owing to his infrequent western trips. . . . Gould made a fortune, but the roads he touched never quite recovered from his lack of knowledge and interest in sound railroad-ing."[17] In his 1965 book *Burlington Route*, railroad historian Richard C. Overton insisted that "Gould was first, last, and always a trader. His special talent, amounting to a compulsion, was for detecting opportunities to seize control. . . . His countless deals involving the Union Pacific are legendary; he nearly ruined the road."[18] Elsewhere, Overton explained that "Gould was a speculator [who] cared little for the quality of his railroads as transporta-tion machines, and even less for building up the territory through which they passed; his eye was continually out for quick profits."[19]

After Jay was gone, only a select few—Morosini and Ames among them—would remember the long trips across desert and mountains, Gould demanding that he be shown each and every trivial branch and spur. Only they would recall the plethora of maps stacked up on tables in Jay's office— the maps that had so bored Edison—all of them annotated in Gould's own hand with detailed data on mineral deposits, grades, population centers, and the like. Only they would remember his clearly enunciated vision that the creation of the Gould system of railways in the West constituted his most important life's work, his monument, his contribution. And only they would recognize as truth the simple words Jay spoke, offhandedly and wearily, to a *World* reporter in 1887: "I have been interested in railroads ever since I was a boy. I now think a railroad train is one of the grandest sights in the world. I like to see the great driving-wheels fly around."[20]

Chapter 25

EVERYTHING BUT A GOOD NAME

By THE WINTER OF 1879–1880 Gould, at age forty-three, already seemed old. His diminutive frame carried not a pound of extra flesh. Gould's head was bald, his beard speckled with gray, and his frail body always poised to betray him, as when he'd lain abed for a month in 1875. In addition to the 1875 typhoid, he also suffered from other complaints: insomnia, and neuralgia in his face and eyes. There were times when the general impression Jay evoked was of a highly focused mind tolerating the presence of a body out of mere necessity. ("His concentration was so intense that you noticed it," recalled his niece Alice Northrop. "When he spoke, he became perfectly oblivious of everything around him. When he listened, his eyes would never leave the speaker.") Jay clothed the luggage of his small, skeletal arms and legs in the simplest, most basic suits of unremarkable cut, always either black or gray. During the fall, winter, and spring he wore a conventional felt hat out of doors. In summer, he sometimes became relaxed enough to don a white panama. "He never wore jewelry of any description," Alice remembered, "unless the term could be applied to his modest watch and chain. When you looked at him your impression was that of a small, dark, yet somehow strikingly powerful man who, unlike many commanding men of slight stature, had neither the need nor taste for display."[1]

After he was gone, those who loved him most would recollect particularly his frequent exhaustion: routine episodes of profound tiredness that his wife, Ellie, became expert at dealing with. Returning punctually at five every evening from the wars of Wall Street, Jay entered into a cloistered world that Ellie sculpted carefully for his comfort. Alice wrote that her aunt "managed the household with an adroit and also an exceedingly firm hand. Uncle Jay's home . . . was his solace. And when he returned, weary, seeking quiet and repose, Aunt Helen made sure that he had it. Servants melted from view as through mysterious trapdoors when their functions had been performed. Often, at the table, Uncle Jay was too exhausted or preoccupied to speak. Sometimes he would not give utterance to a word during the entire meal. . . . I used to wonder if he knew what he was eating. At such times, Aunt Helen, with a look, enforced the strictest silence."[2]

But after a silent dinner, Jay would invariably regroup, reenergize, and reengage with his family. Jay was always, Alice remembered, "a devoted father [and] a thoughtful and considerate husband." In fact he delighted in spending time with his children, of which there were now six. In addition to George, Edwin, and Nellie, the clan also included Howard (born 1871), Anna (1875), and Frank (1877). Late in life, George Gould would recall his father reading aloud from books (among them the increasingly popular collections of nature essays written by his old friend John Burroughs), telling tales of family, and instructing all who were interested in the intricacies of his garden. Always he did so in the gentlest of manners, as a soothing and just paterfamilias. "Uncle Jay," Alice wrote, "was exceedingly quiet. His words were both few and carefully chosen. He was perfectly poised, always. In my many months of residence as one of his family, I never once saw him give way to anger. Self-control, I should say, was one of his most pronounced attributes. In matters connected with running the household, he was both fair and considerate. . . . As a result, there was not a man or woman on the place but held it an honor to wait on him, genuinely wished to please him. . . . It has often been repeated that Jay Gould was a man who took little pleasure in life; that the very magnitude and uniformity of his success robbed existence of flavor. . . . The truth was that he derived unlimited pleasure, satisfaction, from many things, but that his enjoyment was deep, contemplative, appreciative in quality."[3]

Unlike most women of her class, Ellie refused to delegate the upbringing of her offspring. The Gould home, though it included a cook and several butlers and housekeepers, employed no nanny and no nursemaids. With regard to Mrs. Gould and her children, Maury Klein wrote: "There is no doubt she was the dominant figure in their childhood. Although Jay was an affectionate, even doting father, the pressures of business limited his presence. The children learned early to obey him at once and not to disturb him unless invited, but it is misleading to view Gould as a stern Victorian patriarch. The trials of his own childhood instilled in him a devotion to family that was his true religion. He had no other creed and did not pretend otherwise."[4]

Thus he was not usually a member of the party when, every Sunday, Ellie marched her sons and daughters to Fifth Avenue's Episcopal Church of the Heavenly Rest. On Sunday mornings, while Jay's pious wife prayed for his reclamation, he worked with his flowers or read. One wonders whether he, or the woman who prayed for him, noticed when the *New York Times*, which rarely found words to praise Gould for anything, praised his honesty when it came to spirituality. "We do not like Mr. Gould," wrote the editors. "We do not think he is a good man to have around. But it is much to his credit that he is wholly free from hypocrisy in the matters of religion."[5]

On Sunday afternoons, the Goulds entertained. Frequent guests included the Russell Sages, Ellie's parents, and others of Gould's inner circle, including Sidney Dillon, Jesse Seligman, and Cyrus and David Dudley Field. The wives conversed with Ellie while the men spoke, for the most part, of their one great bond: finance. With Morosini, however, Jay seems to have shared a somewhat closer relationship. Both enjoyed collecting antique editions of books, and this proved fertile common ground for nonbusiness conversation. Another genuine and good friend of Gould's from his business life, whom he did not see very often but for whom he nourished a great and reciprocated fondness, was Silas Clark, a chronic hypochondriac with whom Jay commiserated on matters of health. After family, and after old friends from the Catskills whom he saw less often than he would have liked, it was within this clique that Gould was most at home, most relaxed, most at peace. (Boston's Fred Ames, it should be said, does not seem to have spent much time at all with Jay outside boardrooms, except for joining him on inspection tours.)

Beyond members of the inner circle, Jay and Ellie did not socialize much. Jay's nearly routine condemnation by the press and by those on the losing ends of his speculations made him something of a social outcast. This fact does not seem to have bothered Gould a great deal, as his banishment from polite society dovetailed nicely with his penchant for solitary avocations and the quiet insularity of family. On those rare occasions when Jay and Ellie received an invitation to a dinner, ball, or some other "inescapable" (Gould's phrase), he would insist on a late arrival and an early departure. Ellie, on the other hand, desired a social life, welcomed what few "inescapables" came up, and did not appreciate being shunned. After having been weaned within a social class that defined itself wholly by whom it allowed in and whom it kept out, Ellie felt the profound isolation of Jay's pariah status far more keenly than the Catskills farmboy ever would or could. As Edwin Hoyt wrote, "Jay was not particularly interested in parties or high life. He did not drink. He did not smoke. He did not sail small boats or shoot billiards. His passions were moneymaking, reading, walking, and the enjoyment of nature."[6]

In response to his wife's distress, however, Jay did what he could. During the early 1880s, he joined with William K. Vanderbilt (grandson of the Commodore, son of William H. Vanderbilt) and other non-Knickerbocker millionaires in funding the new Metropolitan Opera House. The Goulds—along with the Vanderbilts, Goelets, Whitneys, Drexels, Rockefellers, Morgans, and Huntingtons—had previously been denied dress circle boxes at the Academy of Music on Irving Place, where old families like the Astors, Livingstons, Schuylers, and Beekmans reigned supreme. Now they subscribed boxes in the "Diamond Horseshoe" dress circle of the new opera house. "All the *nouveaux riches* were there," said the *Dramatic Mirror* in reporting on the opening night in October 1883. "The Goulds and Vanderbilts and people of that ilk perfumed the air with the odor of crisp greenbacks. The tiers of boxes looked like cages in a menagerie of monopolists. When somebody remarked that the house looked bright as a new dollar, the appropriate character of the assemblage became apparent. To the refined eye, the decorations of the edifice seemed in particularly bad taste."[7] Ellie, who had thus wheedled her way into the right theatrical seating, was nevertheless shunned that same year when the William K. Vanderbilts, after having been denied entry into Mrs. Astor's famous "Four Hundred," announced their own ball to include New York's elite "Twelve Hundred" and then left the Goulds off the list.

◇ ◇ ◇

It was the walker, horseman, and gardener in Jay who insisted every summer on a number of weeks in the country. After various stints not just at Long Branch but also spots more to Gould's preference, places like the White and Green Mountains, Jay finally found a country retreat he liked well enough to make permanent. During the summer of 1877, Gould rented a walled, three-hundred-acre estate overlooking the Hudson River at Irvington (near Tarrytown). The place, not far from the estates of Cyrus and David Dudley Field, had formerly been the home of George Merritt, a once-prosperous New York merchant who had died in 1873. Gould rented from Merritt's widow. Named Lyndhurst (originally Lyndenhurst, but later shortened) after the linden trees to be found on the property, the property featured the very finest example of Gothic Revival architecture to be found anywhere in the United States. The noted architect Andrew Jackson Davis first conceived and built the asymmetrical collection of fanciful turrets, finials, buttresses, and trefoils for Lyndhurst's first owner, William Paulding—a former mayor of New York City who called the place Knoll— in 1838. Twenty-six years later, Davis returned to double the size of the already large home, adding a new wing and tower at Merritt's behest. Thereafter, the house resembled nothing so much as a dark and elaborate Gothic castle: quite a suitable home for a financial Dracula. (During the 1960s, the supernatural soap opera *Dark Shadows* would be filmed here.) But that was only the impression from the outside. The interior was open, welcoming, and flooded with light from numerous strategically placed windows. The Goulds loved the place.

The chief appeal for Jay, however, was the grounds. Broad lawns—framed by stands of ancient linden, elm, beech, birch, and pine trees—sloped down to the river from the house. Along the shoreline, the long lawn stopped at the tracks of the New York Central, which held a right of way. From the house, large vistas across the Hudson provided beautiful views of the Palisades to the south and the Tappan Zee to the north. Here Jay would play croquet with his children. Here he would also walk at twilight or sit on a bench with one of his books. Lyndhurst likewise included large stables, allowing Jay and his boys to engage in their passion for riding. But most important for Jay, just north of the castle stood the largest greenhouse in the United States: 380 feet long by 37 feet wide, with 60-foot wings on either end and a high dome rising 100 feet in the air. On a clear day, standing atop the dome on a platform reached by stairs, one could look northward and see not only the Hudson Highlands but also the distant blue of Jay's native Catskills, which he would point to and describe to the children as "home." (Gould often waxed nostalgic about his old days and friends in the Catskills and continued to make the occasional appearance there.)

Three summers at Lyndhurst so enthralled the Goulds that in 1880 Jay bought the estate from Mrs. Merritt, paying $250,000. Not long after the closing, he made a large second-floor billiard room into a gallery where he hung his growing collection of paintings by members of the Barbizon School. At the same time, he seized two more rooms on the main floor to create a private library with glass cabinets. As for the greenhouse, which had sat empty since Merritt's death, Jay ordered the German landscape designer and master gardener Ferdinand Mangold—imported by Merritt in 1864— to fill the place with large supplies of rare roses, orchids, and other treasures. Every evening that summer, after coming home on the New York Central and sharing dinner with his family, a quietly pleased Gould would shuffle off to the greenhouse wearing his business suit and carpet slippers, there to work happily with Mangold, sorting and planting. By the time Jay and his clan returned to Fifth Avenue that autumn, he'd spent more than $40,000 on various varieties of flowers and plants. Through that fall he was frequently to be found at Lyndhurst on the weekends, playing with his roots and bulbs.

Thus Jay was understandably shattered when, on the morning of 11 December, a fire, perhaps set by an arsonist, destroyed the greenhouse and everything in it. His response, however, recalled his reaction to the destruction by fire of his Delaware County history so many years before. Within weeks—working with an independent architect and the famous solarium makers Lord and Burnham—Jay finalized plans for a replacement structure of equivalent size that would stand complete by early 1882: the nation's first steel-framed greenhouse. Jay's new Eden included a grapery at its west end along with a cold house for rhododendrons, camellias, hyacinths, and bulbs. On the other side, the eastern wing featured individual houses for carnations, roses, orchids, azaleas, and other flowers. Jay's favorite was the orchid house, which he eventually filled with the most significant collection to be found anywhere in North America: 8,000 plants, 150 species. The greenhouse's semicircular central section, meanwhile, featured a large fountain surrounded by exotic palms.[8] Beyond the greenhouse, Gould added to his domain until he possessed 500 acres total, much left to woodland but some converted for farming. Ironically, the boy who'd despised life on a dairy farm now took avidly to dairying. Gould kept fifty cows and three prize bulls. Through the efforts of a twenty-man staff overseen by Mangold, Lyndhurst produced 250 tons of hay and plenty of milk annually.

In addition to its comforts and luxuries, the walled Lyndhurst offered security and a degree of freedom Jay and his family could not find elsewhere. The fact was that the Goulds had to be constantly on guard against a never-ending supply of crackpots, con men, and would-be assassins. Jay, as has already been noted, was once attacked at Delmonico's. On another occasion, while walking near the intersection of Exchange Place and New Street in 1877, he became the target of a muscular Wall Streeter by the name of A. A. Selover, who punched him in the face, grabbed him by the seat of his pants, and hurled him down some steps leading to a basement barbershop. (It speaks to the steadfastness of Gould's infamy that Selover's great-grandson, reached by telephone, expressed pride in the memory of his forebear's battery.) After that, Gould traveled nowhere in public without the robust Morosini or an alert Pinkerton guard by his side. The same went for his kin. Alice Northrop wrote of the "secrecy and precautions which surrounded, pervaded, the family's doings, accepted, inevitable, a part of every day living."[9] Murder and kidnap threats abounded, as did attempts at extortion. Some of these came from extreme members of radical labor movements, others from opportunists trying to make a buck, and still more from simple cranks who imagined themselves instruments of God's righteous justice, out to get the infamous Gould.

Alice remembered being at Lyndhurst, sitting with her uncle beneath a grove of birches in the early summer of 1881, when a servant brought Jay a telegram. "Alice," he half-whispered after reading it, "Garfield has been shot, President Garfield has been shot." Jay turned "very white. . . . He put his head back to rest, and rally that iron will."[10] As a congressional representative, Garfield had investigated Jay's activities with regard to Black

Friday, but in the years since Gould had come to know and like the man. Indeed, he'd supported—albeit quietly, lest hatred of Gould metastasize into hatred for Garfield—the Republican's candidacy for the White House. "No man is safe from the ultimate theft," a reflective Gould told Morosini not long after the lingering Garfield finally succumbed to his wound on 19 September. One day that same autumn, Alice arrived at Lyndhurst with Nellie to find both her aunt and uncle "deathly pale" and her uncle "perceptibly shaking" as the girls entered the house. A gun-toting stranger had managed to penetrate the grounds, and all the family were instructed to remain indoors until he was found by the men Alice characterized as Lyndhurst's "armed auxiliaries." Soon Jay's detectives found the interloper hiding in a clump of shrubbery. A little later, the shaken Gould returned to the library, where the family waited. "The crank and his arsenal," he told them, "are being well taken care of."[11]

◇ ◇ ◇

During the same year that he opened the new greenhouse, 1882, Gould also moved his Manhattan home from 578 Fifth Avenue to a larger townhouse across the street. Number 579 sat on the northeast corner of Forty-seventh Street and Fifth. Jay followed the lead of his neighbor Darius Ogden Mills, the mining and banking magnate who lived one block to the north at 634 Fifth Avenue, when he hired the prominent Herter Brothers to redo the interior of the house. Contemporary photographs show a large, if not palatial, four-story, three-bay home with a central entry. The Goulds took up seven bedrooms on the second and third floors, with the fourth story and basement reserved for staff. Jay and Ellie shared large, adjoining second-story bedrooms fronting on Fifth Avenue. The second floor also included Gould's elaborate, fireplaced library, housing a large collection of books that was not redundant with that found at Lyndhurst.[12]

At both 579 and Lyndhurst, Jay's siblings and their families were always welcome. The widower Abram Gould routinely sent young Fred to spend long summers with his cousins at the grand estate on the Hudson. Likewise the children of Bettie Gould and Gilbert Palen—Anna, Rufus, and Gilbert, Jr., the last born in 1870 and destined for a career as a prominent physician—visited from their comfortable home in Germantown, Pennsylvania, some sixty miles from the prosperous tannery owned by their father and their Uncle Edward. (Another Palen son, Walter Gould Palen, died suddenly in 1877 at age two.) Most important, however, Jay and Ellie Gould made their homes open to Jay's sister Sarah Northrop and her large brood.

George Northrop had not had an easy way of it in later years. Eventually his tannery failed, after which Jay set him up with a general store in a Pennsylvania village not far from the Palens. But Gould's generous charity didn't, in the end, do anything to help Northrop. Past sixty, inconsolable over the collapse of his business, and with his health in decline, the proud man ultimately chose to take his own life. "Don't worry Sarah," Jay cabled his sister immediately after receiving word of the tragedy. "I will help you."[13] Soon thereafter, Sarah received a long, handwritten letter from Jay in which he gave her detailed instructions on exactly how she should close the store. In the same note, he explained that he would pay any and all debts George had left behind, and that henceforth Sarah would receive substantial quarterly checks for the support of herself and the children.

By now, the five sons and daughters George Northrop had sired with Caroline Palen before he'd married Sarah were grown and gone, but Sarah was still left with nine surviving youngsters of her own. (Her youngest and tenth child, Anna, died at age ten in 1880.) With regard to these offspring, Jay stressed that every one of them was to continue in school, and that their grade reports should be sent to him for consideration. From the outset, Jay made it clear that he intended to be considerably more than just a signer of checks for Sarah and her family; he would also be a surrogate father. "Uncle Jay," Alice Northrop recalled fondly, "came into the lives of my brothers and sisters and myself as infinitely more than an uncle. He kept the family together in our great emergency, helped financially as one by one we got on our feet. His help came quite unsought. He took, moreover, in many ways, during his remaining years, the place vacated by father."[14]

After Sarah's eldest daughter, Ida, graduated from Vassar and expressed an interest in opening a preparatory school, Jay moved the Northrops to Camden, New Jersey—George Northrop's hometown—and financed the operation. The school he built there included a twelve-room residence for Sarah and those younger Northrops who remained attached to her apron strings. In time, one of the sons, Reid Northrop, would make a career with American Refrigerator Transit, a Missouri Pacific subsidiary. After Alice suffered an accident at Wellesley that left her lame and forced her to withdraw from college, Gould comforted her with tales of his own youthful dis-appointments and how he'd always overcome them. Then he treated her to fifteen months of rest and recovery in France, after which she returned with-out a limp and began teaching French at Ida's school.

On the emotional first Christmas after George Northrop's death, Jay and Ellie insisted that all the Northrops join them at 579. At the outset, Sarah warned the children not to expect too much; after all, Uncle Jay had already been more than generous. But on Christmas Day each child faced a chair or table loaded with wrapped gifts. Alice's first present turned out to be a monogrammed gold Swiss watch from her aunt, at which point she ex-claimed, "Oh, this is Christmas enough for me!"[15] Alice also received a star-shaped brooch set in pearls from her cousin Edwin, and so on, all culminating with a large check from Jay. After the gifts were opened, the family partook of a massive dinner. The long dining-room table stood dec-orated with vases of scarlet anthuria and poinsettias from the Lyndhurst greenhouse. The menu featured terrapin, oysters, turkey with stuffing, pota-toes, cranberries, and vegetables, all topped off with plum pudding. (In the kitchen, the staff enjoyed the same feast. Each butler, maid, and cook like-wise received a generous check from Mr. Gould, as did every worker at Lyndhurst.) When night came, the children sang carols in the library before the large Christmas tree. Then each girl and boy was handed a box of candy and one more present before bed. (On another Christmas, Alice found her-self whisked off to the family's dress circle box at the Metropolitan Opera. Throughout the performance, she noted a large number of opera glasses aimed in the direction of the Goulds rather than at the stage. She guessed the attraction might have been her aunt's Christmas present that year: pearls and a pendant once owned by Napoleon's Empress Josephine.)

◇   ◇   ◇

Jay and Ellie's own children were a mixed bunch, a gaggle of unique and contradictory personalities. The eldest boy, George, came to be imperious and demanding at an early age. Regularly chastised by his parents for treat-ing servants badly, George was filled with a sense of entitlement. This was something Jay had always found distasteful and foolhardy in those scions of second- and third-generation wealth against which he maneuvered on the Street. When it came to George, however, the adoring father was blind not just to the child's unearned aristocratic sensibilities, but also to his inclination for self-indulgence, his lack of discipline, and his numerous shortcomings when it came to native wit. Unquestionably rational and coldly practical in assessing most things and people, Jay Gould nevertheless insisted—despite all evidence to the contrary—that his eldest son would, in time, possess the prowess and dedication necessary to take over the various Gould enterprises.

George's brothers, on the other hand, were not only smarter but more amiable and somewhat better motivated than he. Edwin, the next eldest, resembled his father in that he was quiet, studious, and disciplined. As well, he loved the outdoors and nature. An avid canoeist, Edwin energetically explored the Hudson River near Lyndhurst as a child and later, as a young man, would win some local note in New York by paddling all the way around Staten Island solo. His best friendship of youth, with the son of one of the Lyndhurst groundskeepers, was one he maintained for the rest of his life. (In this and other things to be mentioned later, Edwin mimicked Jay's fundamental lack of snobbishness.) The next boy in line, Howard, joined Edwin in being naturally brighter than George. But he struck many as being undermotivated: a fine specimen of salmon who, despite ability, refused to swim upstream. As for Frank, he inherited Jay's natural dexterity in advanced math, mechanics, and engineering. When he was just seven he unearthed his father's old surveying gear and insisted that Jay teach him how it worked.

Of the two girls, Nellie demonstrated an early propensity for puritanism, probably inherited from her mother. When she attended the opera with her parents, she always averted her eyes from the short ballet that usually preceded the main event. When Jay inquired why, she told him she did not approve of risqué displays and thought the ballet immoral. Always buttoned up from head to toe, as a teenager Nellie devoted much time to doing good works through Christian mission societies. With the greatest zeal, she sewed blankets for the homeless, purchased Bibles for inebriates, and lent her efforts to all manner of moral reforms. She despised ostentation and at times showed visible embarrassment at displays of Gould wealth. Rarely did she interest herself in the young men of her age who sought her out so diligently. (She told Alice Northrop that compared to her father, they all seemed mere pygmies.) Nellie's sister, Anna, on the other hand, delighted in the rich world of Fifth Avenue and Lyndhurst and displayed a sense of entitlement similar to George's. When at Lyndhurst, Anna slept in the high tower bedroom and acted in every way like the princess one would expect to inhabit such a space. Pampered and self-absorbed, she was, like George, quite capable of being short with the staff that waited upon the family. Like him, she was frequently reprimanded for such outbursts. She was similarly dismissive of her Northrop cousins, whom she tended to view as charity cases and, as such, only slightly better than the servants.

"I am devoted to you children," Jay wrote Nellie in the early 1880s, during one of his western sojourns. "I want the world for you all and happiness for you all."[16] There was never any doubt among Jay's sons, daughters, nieces, and nephews—or among those intimates who observed him with them—that Gould's most important possession, his greatest treasure, was his family. Therefore it was perhaps natural that, over time, Gould would become concerned about what he'd wrought in the way of reputation. "I much fear," he told Morosini, "that I will be able to leave them everything but a good name."[17]

Chapter 26

WIRES AND ELS

THE GOULD WHO PURCHASED LYNDHURST in 1880 had not only just finished merging the Kansas Pacific, Denver Pacific, and Union Pacific but also still maintained independent control of the Missouri Pacific, which he expanded through acquisitions of the Wabash, the Iron Mountain, and other smaller lines crossing the country west to Omaha, east to Toledo and Detroit, and north to the Great Lakes and Chicago. As well, Gould leased the Kansas & Texas (dubbed the Katy) and would by April 1881 purchase the Texas & Pacific from the Pennsylvania Railroad's Tom Scott in a deal that also included the *New York World* newspaper, a subsidiary of that road. Other smaller roads likewise became absorbed in Gould's ever-expanding web of properties. These combined assets—the newly expanded Union Pacific together with the Missouri Pacific and other lines in the Gould system of railways—represented some 15,854 miles of track, roughly one-ninth of the railway mileage in the country.

In acquiring these key positions, Gould had stepped on dozens of powerful eastern toes, most notably those of Boston's venerable John Murray Forbes, who held major interests in the Michigan Central, the Burlington, and the Hannibal & St. Joseph. Forbes, against whom Gould competed for freight in several markets, was reportedly flabbergasted when Gould outflanked him in seizing the lease on the Katy during January 1880. Thereafter, the Brahmin loudly told all who would listen that Gould was no gentleman. (Forbes told their mutual associate Fred Ames, "I, of course, can do nothing with Gould. . . . The last time we met only mischief came of it. I know he don't like me and I certainly don't like him."[1])

Nevertheless, Forbes and others watched Jay's machinations with awe. "He veils his movements in a mystery as profound as that of an African sorcerer," commented the *New York Times*. "When he condescends to speak, men listen as they would listen to the Sphinx which looks across the lifeless deserts of Egypt."[2] A reporter for the *New York Stockholder*, describing Jay's plots, counterplots, and plots within plots, hinted correctly at the complexity of his grand strategy: "In his mind it is mapped out into a series of chessboards, set with curves and parabolas, as well as squares and corners,— chessboards which run into each other curiously, although a separate game goes on upon each. Pawns, knights, castles slip deftly from one to another in kaleidoscopic confusions, out of which only one pair of eyes in the world evolves orderly and coherent plan."[3]

But sometimes the discussions of Gould's dark inscrutability—his brilliant combinations, and his penchant for misdirection and pulling unsuspected rabbits out of previously unnoticed hats—was a bit overdone. The most reasonable of his critics were quick to note the absurd extremes to which some went in both vilifying Gould and extolling his genius. As early as 1875, the *Times* pointed out that nothing seemed to happen anywhere in the nation without "straightway we are assured that 'JAY GOULD' is at the bottom of the whole affair, as he is said to be at the bottom of everything that goes on nowadays. We strongly suspect that he will yet be found . . . to have had something to do with the hard Winter, frozen water-pipes, and plumbers' extravagant bills. He doubtless formed a 'ring' with the plumbers sometime last Summer, and then produced the recent severe cold, so as to get his machinery to work."[4] Forbes found the *Times's* irony amusing. Still, he insisted, within the popular image of Gould as the weaver of Byzantine webs lay a seed of truth.

Forbes would never willingly give any ground to Gould. But with numerous players other than Forbes, Gould enjoyed more amicable relations based on their shared attraction to pragmatic, strategic, and profitable compromise. When Collis P. Huntington invaded Texas in 1881, laying track for his

Southern Pacific toward El Paso and at the same time buying up a small Louisiana trunk line, he posed a large competitive threat to Gould's Katy and Texas & Pacific. Huntington's line, when completed, would offer attractive alternate routing for goods moving between San Francisco and New Orleans, goods heretofore monopolized by the Gould railroads connecting to the Union Pacific and then Huntington's Central Pacific. As well, there was nothing to stop Huntington from eventually building lines north to Kansas City or St. Louis.

The battle was joined when Gould realized Huntington had inadvertently built a section of his new road on land granted by Congress to the Texas & Pacific. While lawyers squabbled in court, construction crews for Gould's Texas & Pacific frantically built a line west toward the oncoming Southern Pacific, with which it would eventually, if things didn't change, run parallel. Meanwhile, the calculating Messrs. Gould and Huntington thought twice. The terrain in question, roughly ninety miles of desert, offered little prospect for local business and thus could not, of itself, be counted on to help support one rail line, let alone two. Confronted with this prospect, Gould and Huntington sat down together at Gould's townhouse on Thanksgiving Day 1881. Over a snifter of brandy that Gould smelled and looked at more than he drank, the pair came to an agreement.

During the coming weeks, their construction crews would change course subtly and build toward one another with the idea of meeting. Thereafter, Gould, Huntington, and their assignees would share the problematic ninety-mile course of railroad. They would likewise divide equally the earnings on through business from California. As well, Huntington dropped his threat of building competing roads north and east. The agreement was to remain almost entirely intact for forty-six years. Eleven years after the 1881 agreement, once Gould was in his casket, Huntington would comment, "I know there are many people who do not like him [but] I will say that I always found that he would do just as he agreed to do."[5] Indeed, it was Huntington, not Gould, who would at one point violate the spirit of their truce by creating a through-line to New Orleans.

◇ ◇ ◇

The Gould who purchased Lyndhurst also still had a hand in the country's wireless business. Back in August 1877, following the merger of the West-

ern Union with the A&P, William H. Vanderbilt had gruffly and loudly refused Gould a seat on the Western Union board. In response, nearly two
years later, Gould formed the American Union, with an eye toward using
this new firm as leverage for wounding and then taking over the Western.[6]
General Thomas Eckert, the former Western Union superintendent whom
Gould had lured over to serve as president of the A&P, now served as president of the American Union. Morosini came on as treasurer. And John W.
Garrett, the proprietor of the Baltimore & Ohio who'd previously played
ball with Gould with regard to the A&P, joined the board. The firm capi-
talized at $10 million to start. Then, through the Gould-organized Central
Construction Company, it began to grow at a swift rate. In repeated newspaper interviews, Gould positioned his American Union as necessary for
democracy and waxed eloquent about how a telegraphic monopoly must not
be allowed to dominate the Republic. Most editorial writers, however, were
skeptical. "We agree with Mr. Gould," said the *Herald*, "that telegraph monopoly is a bad thing in the same way that all monopolies are bad things.
But we doubt very much that the great monopolist himself is a likely knight
to do true battle against this or any other combination. Gould's end-game,
whatever that might be, will most assuredly benefit the Gouldian good more
than it will the public good. Gould has been called many things, but never
a patriot."[7]

Taking these by-now standard criticisms in stride, Jay focused on growing his new firm. He not only built new wires nationwide but also leased
those of the Dominion Telegraph of Canada and entered into agreements
with the Union Pacific and the Kansas Pacific (over which property Gould
had only recently reconciled with Villard). He could not, however, dislodge
the Western Union from the Missouri Pacific—Vanderbilt resorting to the
courts to maintain that franchise and hold the Missouri to previously nego-
tiated contracts. Nevertheless, Gould was able to keep the Western Union
off most of his other properties, including the Wabash. After a year of operation, the American Union had established more than 2,000 offices connected by some 50,000 miles of wire. During the same year, the Western
Union's gross business dropped by $2 million. Sticking to his usual script,
Gould not only supplied competition for the Western Union but also
formed a pool (including Sage and Dillon) to mount bear raids on Western
Union stock, beating the formerly blue-chip item down to depths it had not

known in years. By the close of 1880, Western Union had dropped to below $90 for the first time since its founding. Early in 1881, when the stock stood at 78 and Gould personally controlled 90,200 shares (in excess of $7 million worth), William H. Vanderbilt surrendered. In the year and half since the American Union was founded, Western Union had, at least on paper, lost some 25 percent of its value: more than $10 million.

A memorandum ratified by the Western Union board on 15 February 1881 contained the details of the reorganization and consolidation. Both the American Union and the A&P, the latter having been operated by the Western Union as a separate subsidiary, would be folded into the main company. Western Union issued $15 million in stock to exchange for American Union shares, and the exchange took place at what observers calculated to be twice the American Union's original cost. Western Union also issued another $8.4 million in stock to cover outstanding A&P shares at 60, along with a stock dividend of $15.5 million for all preconsolidation shareholders (Gould near the head of the line). In short order, when rumors of the deal leaked out, shares of Western Union went above 116 and American Union went past 94. In the end, the reorganization left the Western Union capitalized at $80 million. For his part, Gould personally walked away with some $30 million in value over what he'd possessed before the merger, and he emerged with control of the corporation. In under two years' time, Jay had accomplished the nineteenth-century equivalent of creating a start-up Apple Computer and leveraging it to force a merger with an IBM. He was now the key figure in the two most important, cutting-edge sectors of the U.S. industrial scene: transportation and communications.

"The country finds itself this morning at the feet of a telegraphic monopoly," the *Herald* mourned on 16 February 1881, one day after the memorandum of agreement was announced.[8] Even the Gould-friendly *Tribune* expressed concern that the Western Union consolidation was too much and might trigger a massive retaliation by the federal authorities. The *Tribune* argued that the largeness and totality of the Western Union's dominance might eventually tend toward a "control of the telegraphic system by the Government as complete as its control of the mails."[9] On other fronts, the New York Board of Trade—New York's futures marketplace—issued a statement against the merger, the Anti-Monopoly League organized a protest meeting, and the New York State Assembly passed a bill designed to prevent the transaction. (Gould's old Albany protégé Hamilton Harris made sure the measure never reached the floor of the New York State Senate.) When a group of Western Union shareholders tried to sue to stop the merger, Gould gave no ground in cross-examination by the shareholders' attorney—the notorious agnostic Colonel Robert G. Ingersoll—completely baffling him with truthful but arcane double-talk concerning the nature of the consolidation. "I do not believe," Ingersoll said later, "that since man was in the habit of living on this planet anyone has ever lived possessed of the impudence of Jay Gould."[10]

Gould, Sage, Dillon, and Eckert joined the Western Union board. During the first week of March, Gould moved into an office on the top floor of the Western Union's beautiful and relatively new building at 195 Broadway. This was to be his main business address in Manhattan for the rest of his life. Western Union president Norvin Green—who'd replaced Orton after the latter's death in April 1878 and then won Gould's respect as William H. Vanderbilt's chief operative during the fight against the Gould takeover—was allowed to stay. As for Eckert, in addition to joining the board, he became the Western Union's vice president and general manager. Gould, meanwhile, oversaw everything and, some thought, began using the Western Union wires to eavesdrop on his competition at rival railroad lines and brokerages, virtually all of whom were now forced to use the Western Union to relay confidential messages. Of course, Gould's own antimonopoly rhetoric quickly faded. All his roads entered into ironclad agreements with the Western Union. At the same time, New York attorney general Hamilton Ward, a Gould ally, announced that he had no legal grounds on which to contest the merger in court.

The impact of the consolidation was felt most quickly by the operators of the transatlantic cables. Heretofore, the American Union, the A&P, and the Western Union had each maintained separate agreements with three distinct Atlantic cable companies for their links to Europe. (The first Atlantic cables had been laid in 1858 and 1866, under the watchful managerial eye of Gould's sometime associate Cyrus Field.) The American Union was linked with a French cable firm, the A&P with Direct Cable, and the Western Union with Anglo-American Cable. Immediately upon coming to power after the consolidation, Gould severed the A&P and American Union contracts. Later on, in September, Gould's own experiment in

transcontinental cable—built under the Gould-controlled American Telegraph & Cable Company while Gould thundered to the press about American business no longer being hostage to foreign-controlled cable
operators—at first broke down. But the cable proved operational enough by
1882 for Gould to force a pool with the other three companies, each agreeing to uniform rates and the division of earnings.

◇   ◇   ◇

It was in the offices of the Western Union that Gould first made the acquaintance of a thoughtful, bright, well-trained stenographer whom he
made his personal secretary and sought to mentor. One year later, when the
nineteen-year-old Edwin Bok—destined for a long and highly successful
career in magazine and book publishing—gave Gould his notice, the mogul
offered him a large raise to remain with the firm. In answer, Bok explained
that the salary, although of importance, did not interest him so much as his
desire to secure a position in another trade to which he aspired. "And what
business is that?" Gould asked. "The publishing of books," replied young
Bok, who years later wrote up the conversation in his Pulitzer Prize–
winning memoirs, *The Americanization of Edward Bok.* "You are making a
great mistake," Gould answered. "Books are a luxury. The public spends its
largest money on necessities: on what it can't do without. It must telegraph;
it need not read. It can read in libraries. A promising boy such as you are,
with his life before him, should choose the right sort of business, not the
wrong one." Nevertheless, after Bok insisted, Gould wished the young man
well and even gave him a bonus check as a going-away gift.

Seven years after that conversation, fate led Bok to another encounter with
Gould. During 1889, Bok was helping sail a yacht on the Hudson one afternoon when the sight of Jay Gould's Lyndhurst "awakened the desire of the
women on board to see [the] wonderful orchid collection" housed in Gould's
famous greenhouse. Upon hearing this, Bok explained his previous association with the financier and offered to recall himself to Gould in an attempt
to gain access to the grounds. Soon one of the young men of the party, not
Bok, rowed to shore bearing a note for Gould, and shortly the answer came
back that they were welcome to visit the greenhouse. Jay himself received the
sailors. Then, after placing the balance of the group under the personal care
of his chief gardener, Mangold, Gould pulled Bok aside for a chat.

"Well," said the financier, once the others were gone, "I see in the papers that you seem to be making your way in the publishing business." When Bok expressed surprise that Gould had followed his work, Gould answered: "I have because I always felt you had it in you to make a successful man. But not in that business. You were born for the Street [Wall Street]. You would have made a great success there, and that is what I had in mind for you. In the publishing business you will go just so far; in the Street you could have gone as far as you liked. There is room there; there is none in the publishing business. It's not too late now, for that matter."[11] Bok declined the offer. He was always more than content with his career in the world of literature, just as he was always grateful for Gould's genuine interest in him and his prospects.

Another young man of promise who received a bit of help from Jay Gould was the future congressman W. Bourke Cockran. Having opened an office in Manhattan in 1878, the twenty-four-year-old Cockran—who, as a mutual acquaintance had advised Gould, was both smart and struggling—received one day a request to call at Jay's office the following morning. The next day, sitting across from Gould, the Irish immigrant confronted a tiny, taciturn, and to-the-point gentleman of business. "Young man," said Gould, "I should like to retain your service for any jury trials that may come up in my business for the next year. Will you accept a retainer?"[12] After Cockran nodded in the affirmative, Gould wrote out a check, blotted it, folded it, and handed it across the table. Intensely interested to know the amount he'd just been handed, Cockran nevertheless feigned nonchalance as Gould talked at him for more than an hour, dishing out advice on the habit and practice of law. Not until Cockran got outside onto the street did he unfold the piece of paper and find he'd just been given $5,000. Subsequently, even though Gould needed a great deal of lawyering that year, as in any other, he never called upon Cockran once. The check was not in fact a retainer but a leg up for a motivated, entrepreneurial young fellow working to make a start in life. It was to such young men, above all others, that Gould could best relate.

◇ ◇ ◇

The third and last pillar of Gould's empire, after the cross-country railroads and the Western Union, was New York's elevated railroads. All three businesses were embryos that held great promise. All three constituted what, during the Gilded Age, would have been considered the new economy. All three had histories that were both brief and troubled, characterized by inefficiency, fraud, and failed grasps at grand ambition.

Two early attempts to create elevated lines in Manhattan had sunk in the depression that followed the panic of 1873, leaving half-finished routes run by individual private entities: the New York Elevated and the Metropolitan (formerly the Gilbert) Elevated. The New York ran up Ninth Avenue from western Greenwich Village to Thirtieth Street. The Metropolitan ran from Rector Place, in New York's financial district, up to Sixth Avenue, and then on up Sixth to Central Park. Two years following the panic, in 1875, the New York State Legislature created a Rapid Transit Commission empowered to consolidate and improve these lines, create new routes, and plan construction for an integrated system. After study, the commission gave the New York Elevated leave to expand its truncated line all the way to Harlem, down to South Ferry, and over to Third Avenue. It also licensed the Metropolitan Elevated to run parallel to the New York Elevated on Sixth and Second Avenues. As a prod, a third, newly formed company—the Manhattan Elevated—was empowered to build any line not completed by either the New York or the Metropolitan Elevated within specific dates.

Promoters behind the New York Elevated—among them Governor Samuel J. Tilden of New York—persuaded Gould's friend Cyrus Field to buy into the New York Elevated in May 1877, after which Field became the firm's president. Within two years, the New York Elevated would grow from six miles of track to thirty-one miles. The Metropolitan—dominated by Gould's acquaintances Commodore Garrison, his son William, George M. Pullman, Horace Porter (whom Gould recalled from the days of the gold corner), and a Spanish investor named Jose de Navarro—experienced trouble with landholders along its intended routes. Nevertheless, the Metropolitan managed to open its extended Sixth Avenue line by June 1878.

Both the Metropolitan's and the New York Elevated's construction was handled by the New York Loan and Improvement Company. This firm, organized by the directors and chief investors of the two elevated companies, allowed them, in a way eerily reminiscent of the Credit Mobilier, to award themselves contracts and profit doubly from the exercise. (As an example, work on the Metropolitan Elevated, worth about $9.7 million, was done for a fee of $21.5 million in securities.) Subsequently, with both firms moving along punctually against the benchmarks laid down in the charter of the Manhattan Elevated, the latter found itself with nothing to do.

In due course, the graft-swollen interests behind the Metropolitan and the New York Elevated elevated lines began to think that a consolidation—expressly forbidden by their New York State charters—might be desirable. And it was now, during late 1878, that the Manhattan Elevated emerged as a convenient vehicle for working around the charter restrictions. Each elevated company leased its lines on a 999-year basis to the Manhattan, also providing $9 million with which the Manhattan was to complete the last phases of construction. (This task would be accomplished by 1880.) In return, the Manhattan gave each company, the New York Elevated and the Metropolitan Elevated, $6.5 million of its own stock, agreed to pay interest on the bonds outstanding for each firm, and guaranteed a 10 percent dividend on the stock of each firm. This odd business formulation meant that the Manhattan was a holding company with only two assets: its leases. It owned no securities in either of the two firms it "held," firms to which it owed strict payments. The Manhattan possessed a monopoly on New York's elevated rails, but the overhead inherent in the structure of the lease meant that it was virtually impossible for the Manhattan to render any dividends on its own stock.

Still more complexity lay ahead. Once the lines stood complete, Field and his New York Elevated cohorts grew restive. The New York quickly proved far more profitable than the Metropolitan. But since the two lines were pooling their receipts, Field and his partners began to feel they were carrying the Metropolitan. The Metropolitan group soon created even more bitter feelings when they sold off all their Manhattan stock. In response, Field liquidated his 13,000 shares of the Manhattan and resigned from the board, after which Tilden dumped his Manhattan investment along with his long-term interest in the New York Elevated.

Meanwhile, in Albany during the spring of 1881, a bill empowering the state to legislate elevated fares nearly became law. After this threat was averted, managers of the Manhattan barely had time to express relief before a court ruled that property owners along the elevated lines were within their rights to sue for damages related to smoke, foul odors, cinders, and other side effects of rapid transit. On the heels of this ruling, a court of appeals ruled that the Elevated's structures were taxable as real estate, a decision that dealt a potentially fatal blow to the Manhattan's bottom line. Watching this quagmire develop, Gould sensed his favorite kind of opportunity: a wounded property of vast potential waiting to be absorbed at a bargain rate.

In late April—within weeks of Gould's buying Scott's Texas & Pacific and its subsidiary, the *New York World*—the *World* began printing a series of items criticizing the Manhattan's operating structure, management, and capital position: all stories designed to drive down the price of the stock. Despite the Manhattan management's protests that they and their firm were being unfairly portrayed, by early May the Manhattan—which had claimed a high of 57 in 1880—was bottoming at 21. (The facts of the Manhattan's position hardly mattered. The constant rebukes by the *World* signaled Gould's interest—either a long interest or a short interest, most betting on the latter—which was enough to scare buyers away and influence the price of the stock.) Two weeks later, New York attorney general Hamilton Ward sought and received permission from the New York State Supreme Court to nullify the Manhattan's charter—an option he never used, since Gould's goal in having Ward obtain the order was merely to strike fear into the hearts of Manhattan investors and drive down the price of the stock still further.

At this point, Russell Sage—already well known on the Street as a close Gould ally and frequent Gould functionary—stepped forward, picked up vast piles of the security on the cheap, and published a plan whereby he would guarantee the Manhattan's meeting its lease obligations for the coming twenty-four months. Concurrently, Gould and other associates purchased still more shares of the Manhattan privately and quietly while also waging bear campaigns against both the New York Elevated and the Metropolitan. In June, when whispers about Gould's activities began to circulate, he halfheartedly moved to shut down speculation. "The rumor," stated the "Wall Street Gossip" column of the *World* for 15 June, "that Mr. Gould's party is largely interested in the Manhattan and Metropolitan Companies has been put forward merely to make a market on which to sell the stock of these companies."[13] In more than one financial neighborhood, the *World*'s denial of Gould's involvement only served to confirm that involvement. Gould himself did not care. Confusion about his movements and goals achieved his most immediate ambition: keeping people guessing. At the same time, other newspapers, including dailies like the *New York Times* and the *Herald*, which had no interest in helping Gould, inadvertently did so by issuing cold analyses of the Manhattan's financial position. This, most agreed, looked genuinely dire, given the unprofitability of one-half of its business (the Metropolitan), the enormous burden of the newly taxable infrastructure assets, and the unsoundness of the firm's fundamental organization (a holding company that did not own the assets it held). The financial writer for the *Philadelphia North American* positively asserted that the Manhattan's stock would soon be "worth fully the ragman's price for the paper on which it is printed, but hardly more."[14] A solution really did have to be found—and Gould and Sage, soon joined by Cyrus Field, were only too happy to supply it.

Early in July, Attorney General Ward applied to the New York State Supreme Court to put the Manhattan Elevated into receivership. Sitting in Albany, Judge Theodore R. Westbrook, a former Gould attorney, approved the application without hearing arguments from any of the Manhattan's management. Westbrook appointed A. L. Hopkins and John F. Dillon as receivers. Hopkins was an executive with Gould's Wabash Railroad. John F. Dillon, not related to Sidney Dillon, was one of many Gould attorneys. Simultaneously with the appointment of Hopkins and Dillon, Gould joined the board of the Metropolitan Elevated, continued to buy the beaten Manhattan at prices ranging between 16 and 20, and took care to gain influence on the board of the New York Elevated.

At the same time, Gould, Sage, and Field evolved a party line—soon echoed in every paper where Gould had influence as well as every paper where he didn't—that the Manhattan Elevated was nothing but a corrupt and hollow shell that must be done away with. As the *World* editorialized on 23 September, "We are informed on very good authority this afternoon that the New York and Metropolitan Elevated Companies have decided to unite their forces in an attack upon the Manhattan Company, with a view to getting their roads into their own hands. Should they succeed—and we see no reason why they should not—Manhattan will be wiped out as a thing of the past."[15] Both firms sued for their freedom. Then, in September, after Gould's resident judge (Westbrook) approved an application from Gould's resident receivers (Hopkins and Dillon) to issue certificates with which to raise money to pay some of the Manhattan's bills—all of which must have been done with Gould's personal approval—Gould attacked the certificate issuance in a widely published affidavit. "The Manhattan Elevated," he said speaking as a director of the Metropolitan, "is hopelessly and irretrievably insolvent, and the borrowing of money by its receiver will be a most desperate expedient which can at most afford to said company only a temporary relief from its fatal embarrassments."[16]

As Gould spoke, his bear raid on the Manhattan continued. On 8 October—the date of the close of the Manhattan's transfer books, thirty days prior to the firm's annual meeting—Gould held 48,000 of 128,000 outstanding shares. Combined with shares owned by his allies, these gave him control of the company. In the election one month later, Gould, Sidney Dillon, Sage, and Field all joined the board, and Gould emerged as president. (Field, who'd hoped not for this result but rather to liberate the New York Elevated from its bondage to the Manhattan, was placated not just with a board seat but with a timely tip regarding an anticipated rise in Western Union securities. However, Field was to quickly get under Gould's skin when he publicly protested a planned doubling of the fares on the Manhattan from five cents to ten. Organizing minority shareholders during December, Field beat back the idea. In the long run, Field's collaboration with Gould in the Manhattan Elevated would not have a happy ending.)

As for the Manhattan itself—damned by Gould just a few weeks before as suffering from "fatal embarrassments"—its prospects suddenly seemed brighter so far as Jay and his coterie were concerned. Judge Westbrook brought the firm out of receivership and simultaneously denied a motion from the board of the New York Elevated for return of its lines. (In the weeks to follow, a young reform assemblyman named Theodore Roosevelt would try without success to make the truth of Gould's alliance with Westbrook and Attorney General Ward public. Roosevelt's lobbying resulted in a formal inquiry by the New York State Assembly's Judiciary Committee that quickly devolved into a whitewash.) A week after the seating of the new board, Manhattan Elevated stood at 55. In short order, Jay sewed up majority positions in both the Metropolitan and the New York Elevated. Later that November, the Manhattan board authorized the issue of $26 million in new Manhattan stock. Eleven million dollars went to shareholders of the Manhattan, $7.8 million to shareholders of the New York, and $7.2 million to shareholders of the Metropolitan. Then, once he was done watering the

Manhattan's stock for quick cash, Gould took a few key steps to improve the Manhattan's operating position for the future. He arranged legislative compromises to ease the tax burden of the two firms. After this, he renegotiated the terms of the Manhattan's leases on the New York and Metropolitan Elevated, all to the profound advantage of the Manhattan.

In the wake of Gould's takeover, the *New York Times* published an exposé headlined:

PUBLIC TRUSTS BETRAYED

The Stock Jobbing Scandal of the Elevated Road

How the Gould Clique Gained Their Present Control

Ignoring its own factually accurate critiques of the Manhattan and its position, the *Times* ranted that the "daily sheet" owned by Gould, "making pretensions to influence as a newspaper," had been "used to hammer down Manhattan stock and deprecate the value of the elevated railways generally." The *Times* went on to say: "There is no more disgraceful chapter in the history of stock jobbing than that which records the operations of Jay Gould, Russell Sage, Cyrus W. Field and their associates in securing control of the system of elevated railroads in New York City. . . . There is nothing specially surprising in the fact that Mr. Gould and his accomplices should resort to any means in their reach to gain control of other people's property by stock jobbing devices which should frighten or force its possessors to yield it up at a sacrifice. We have never been led to expect that they would have a fastidious regard either for the rights of other men or the interests of the public where an opportunity was presented for putting millions of dollars into their own pockets. . . . But what is both surprising and disgraceful is the facility with which they succeeded in using the Attorney General's office and the Supreme Court of this state to further their object."[17]

Amid this by-now standard harping on and criticism of his operations, Gould could sit back and see the three key pillars of his great, long-term fortune locked into place: the western railroads, the Western Union, and the Manhattan Elevated. This golden triangle of holdings would form the nexus of his wealth and power for the brief eleven years remaining to him. Also standing strong, however, was a hoary, dark, and impossible-to-miss relic of hungrier days. Less needed now than ever before, but impossible to dislodge, Gould's vile reputation persevered, shadowing him and stalking him with a single-minded diligence to be matched only by the Grim Reaper.

Chapter 27

AMBITION SATISFIED

THROUGHOUT THE 1880S, Gould was a tired soul: first just weary, then weary and sick. "I sometimes think," he told a reporter for the *Commercial and Financial Chronicle* in early 1882, "I should like to give up business entirely. The care and worriment attending large business interests are very great, but besides that fact the manner in which motives are impugned and characters assailed is very unpleasant."[1] Another journalist commented that Gould looked "somewhat careworn and weary."[2] That same spring, confronted with unfounded rumors of his impending financial collapse, he summoned Sage, Field, Frank Work, and other interested parties to his office. There he had Morosini dump on his desk an enormous pile of securities—representing the Missouri Pacific, Western Union, Manhattan Elevated, and lesser properties. The items totaled a par value of $53 million, which amounted to a Street value well in excess of that. All of the securities were unsigned, an indication that they'd never been transferred or borrowed against. The witnesses declined when Gould offered, laconically, to produce $30 million more of the same.

One year later, talk of retirement emerged again when Gould sold the *New York World* to Joseph Pulitzer (who promptly made the paper an organ for Gould's ridicule). Simultaneously, Gould commissioned the building of an enormous steam yacht to be launched in June 1883. (A fatalistic man who'd always felt the need to make haste, he named his new vessel *Atalanta*, after the swift hunter-goddess of Greek myth.) "I am going to try a little play," Gould told an interviewer as the yacht began to take shape at a Philadelphia dry dock. "I did not have an opportunity when I was young, and I must do my playing later in life. If I like it I may keep it up."[3]

The *Atalanta*, 233 feet long, was launched from Cramp's Shipyard on 7 April 1883. Young Nellie, not quite fifteen, broke a bottle of champagne against the bow as the massive craft began its roll down into the water. On the 25th, Jay appointed veteran mariner John W. Shackford to outfit the vessel and make her seaworthy. Shackford would eventually command a crew of fifty-two. In its report of the launching, the *New York Times* took the opportunity to editorialize: "Mr. Jay Gould protests that he . . . will quit the world (which is Wall Street), and will wreck no more railroads, rig no more markets, and buy no more newspapers. . . . The wily little man has many devices. This penitential game is one of them."[4] No one at the *Times*, or elsewhere, believed Jay's frank talk of retreat. "I have been in the harness a long time and want rest," he told George Miller of the *Omaha Herald*. "My ambition was long since satisfied and I am ready to go into quiet retirement and hope ere long I shall have the opportunity."[5]

He spoke of making an around-the-world cruise, in part to escape the constant innuendo and speculation of the press. When business made it impossible for him to get away, his repeated, well-meaning promises of imminent departure became something of a joke in the *Times* and other papers. In the near term, the *Atalanta*—capable of crossing any ocean of the world—went only as far as Newport, Rhode Island, and coastal Virginia. Day-to-day, Jay used the yacht to commute between Lyndhurst and Midtown Manhattan in season. He also made a halfhearted attempt at joining the yachting community. When his low birth and lower reputation kept him out of the prestigious New York Yacht Club, he founded his own organization. The American Yacht Club operated out of a Midtown clubhouse until 1887, at which point Jay and several associates purchased twelve waterfront acres at the tip of Milton Point on Long Island Sound in Rye, New York, where the club remains to this day.

Did Gould contemplate retirement because he believed it offered the promise of longed-for obscurity? Comments to friends and family seem to hint at this motive. But retirement remained elusive. Early in 1884—the same year Gould's public support for the Republican presidential candidate James Blaine backfired following a garish gathering of Blaine-boosting plutocrats in New York—few accepted at face value his emphatic declaration that he would soon leave Wall Street for good. Pundits pointed to Gould's special partnership in Washington Connor & Company, a brokerage house headed by Jay's longtime friend "Wash" Connor, who'd once played a role in the old William Belden & Company. Connor's concern handled a large amount of Gould family business. Morosini was another special partner. Here Jay's eldest son, George, had been employed since January 1883. Gould's agreement with Connor was set to expire at the end of 1884, but as reporters noted, Jay wound up extending it. As a practical matter, no matter how many partnerships he ended or thought of ending, an exit from Wall Street was not to be had. The empire he'd built was too enormous, his affairs too complex, to allow withdrawal. There would always be positions that needed defending, capital that needed to be raised, and bets that needed to be covered. This was the prison Gould had built for himself. He controlled a slice of the U.S. economy that was far too large to ignore or, in the end, delegate—though delegate he would try. On George's birthday in 1885, Jay gave the freshly minted twenty-one-year-old his power of attorney, combinations for all his private safes, and keys to his deposit vaults. Two years later he did the same with Edwin, who dropped out of Columbia University to come into the family business. Edwin's privileges came with just one caveat: George was the boss. In time, the boys ascended to posts on numerous Gould boards.

◇　◇　◇

By 1881, Gould—who'd always stayed on the offensive, attacking, seizing, and manipulating corporations—had reached a plateau from which the only war left to wage was a good defense. Although he still occasionally sought to expand his operations, especially his railroads in the Southwest, he would henceforth spend most of his days, Vanderbilt-like, on guard against upstart challengers to his franchises. The largest retrenchment occurred in 1884, amid a bear market that led to depression. This was the point at which Charles Francis Adams, chairman of the government directors of the Union Pacific, successfully undermined Gould's dominance in the UP and emerged as president, replacing Sidney Dillon. Abram Gould now departed the UP, along with Dillon and Silas Clark, and took on the task of heading the purchasing department for the Missouri Pacific: a job he would keep for the rest of his life. He also served on the boards of several of Jay's western roads. Clark eventually joined the Missouri Pacific as well, while Dillon involved himself with various affairs, some Gould-related and some not.

Amid the market doldrums of 1884 Gould temporarily lost control of two other roads: the Wabash and the Texas & Pacific. But unlike the cash-strapped and regulation-ridden UP, these were roads Gould urgently worked to reorganize and restore to his fold, where they continued as feeders for his Missouri Pacific. At the same time, on the telegraph front, Gould confronted a host of would-be competitors, such as the Mutual Union, Bankers & Merchants, American Rapid, and Postal. Some of these he swatted like flies. Others he moved to lease or otherwise control. But increasingly, his dominance was put to the test. Even in New York, where the now profitable elevated railroads hummed along in his daily sight, he had to keep his guard up.

In mid-1886, Cyrus Field attracted Gould's attention when he and his son Edward began, without explanation, to acquire enormous slices of Manhattan Elevated stock, evidently with an eye toward seizing control. By October, the Fields' purchases had helped bull the price of Manhattan up to 175. Despite this rise, and not suspecting that the bemused Gould was laying a trap, Field and his boy borrowed aggressively to acquire still more Manhattan at sharply escalating prices. The Fields' buying continued until June 1887, when Gould released several thousand of his own shares in a flood, making the price collapse down to 125. The Fields' creditors then invoked margin calls that forced them to sell from their large reserves. This in turn made the market for Manhattan go down even further, invoking still more cascading margin calls. In the end, Gould wound up purchasing the Fields' roughly 75,000 shares, bought by the Fields at an average price of 175, for 120.

Some subsequently accused Gould of willfully and maliciously attempting to ruin Cyrus Field. Others saw Field's actions as self-destructive. Alice Northrop recalled being at Lyndhurst on the day Field came to beg Jay's assistance. Field looked "physically sick . . . a drowning man beseeching a rope from shore . . . a picture of abject despair." Alice's mother told her later that "the failure of Mr. Field would have brought down several stock exchange houses and one National Bank, involving large losses to Wall Street, possibly producing a panic, and it was largely that knowledge which caused [your uncle] to render the assistance which he did. It was a matter of great mortification to him, and of disappointment also, that he should be allowed to rest under the imputation that Mr. Field had been unjustly treated by his hands."[6]

Of course, Jay's role was not so benign as his adoring sister made out. But the game played on Wall Street was as deadly serious then as it is today. Jay could not allow the fumbling Field to seize the Manhattan. Nor could he allow himself to be seen in the marketplace as not punishing a challenger who came against him so blatantly, boldly, and ineptly. Still, Jay's loyalty to the old innovator and entrepreneur remained steadfast. After the affair was over, Field himself told the press that Gould had behaved "throughout the transaction in a perfectly straightforward manner" and "the most friendly feelings" lingered between them.[7] Even the *New York Times* chose to defend Gould in the way he had handled the matter. "The truth," editorialized the *Times*, "is that Mr. Field's speculation in Manhattan was so wild that a smash was inevitable. It was carried on against the protests of his associates; and when the final and expected end came, Mr. Gould, though he pricked the bubble, took care to do it in such a way that . . . Mr. Field was left with something. Had he gone on to the inevitable catastrophe, he would have been stripped of everything."[8]

Defending against would-be corporate raiders, Gould also found himself playing defense against organized labor. He emerged victorious in 1883 after a month-long strike launched at the Western Union by the Brotherhood of Telegraphers. In later congressional testimony before the U.S. Senate Committee on Labor and Education—this focused not on Gould himself but on labor relations nationwide, with Gould appearing in the role of expert witness—he asserted that the "poorest part" of one's labor force could usually be found at the bottom of any strike. "Your best men do not care how many hours they work. They are looking to get higher up; either to own a business of their own, or to get higher in the ranks."[9] Commenting on Gould's demeanor as he gave his testimony, Frank Carpenter of the *Cleveland Leader* described the diminutive multimillionaire sitting "with a tired look on his face, answering the questions being put to him. He speaks easily in tones as soft as a woman's, and there is nothing ostentatious or aggressive about him. A couple of his detectives sit nearby, and his lawyer is at his back to give advice when it is needed. But Gould himself answers the questions, and he exhibits no fear as he reads his denunciation of the railroad strikers with a display of feeling."[10]

This was the third and last time in his life that Jay gave testimony on Capitol Hill. His first deposition had been before Garfield's committee looking into Black Friday back in 1869. A few years after that he'd been summoned to testify concerning his management of the Union Pacific, in which the federal government maintained a significant financial interest. But it was during his 1883 appearance before the Senate Labor and Education Committee, under friendly questioning from senators sympathetic with his opposition to labor unions, that he gave the account of his early history—his rough start in the Catskills—that has been quoted earlier in this volume. The message inherent in Gould's tales of his early strife was that one did not need a union, just drive and ambition, to get ahead. Ironically, numerous pundits and legislators who frequently criticized and demonized Gould as a nefarious criminal when it came to his dealings with Wall Street bankers and brokers stood with him when he chose to go up against organized labor. In this battle, at least, Gould was seen by his fellow elites as an upright soldier waging the good fight for the defense of something they all held dear: capital.

Two years after the Western Union trouble, in 1885, Gould did not fare quite so well when the railroad brotherhoods and the Knights of Labor struck to protest depression-driven pay cuts on the Missouri Pacific. The 1885 strike brought a halt to the Missouri's business and eventually forced the railroad to retract the pay cuts after the governors of Missouri and Kansas insisted on arbitration. One year later, Gould—still smarting from his loss on the Missouri—refused to back down on layoffs in the face of a strike by 9,000 employees of the Texas & Pacific. "I beg to say that I am yet a free American citizen," he wrote Terence Powderly, leader of the Knights of Labor. "I am past forty-nine years of age. I began life in a lowly way, and by industry, temperance, and attention to my own business have been successful, perhaps beyond the measure of my deserts. If, as you say, I am now to be destroyed by the Knights of Labor unless I sink my manhood, so be it."[11] Confronting vandalism on his line, Gould suspended service. At the same time, his publicists astutely turned the resentment of a greatly inconvenienced public onto the Knights. By year's end, the strikers—starved out—capitulated. Gould endured no more labor unrest on his roads in his lifetime, though he walked away from the affair widely despised by America's working class.

Like Rockefeller, Carnegie, and other moguls who'd beaten back militant unionism with strenuous, sometimes violent opposition, Gould nevertheless remained a frequent, pragmatic benefactor of numerous worthy causes, all of which he supported with brusque, precise efficiency. Many of his charities were quite personal. In addition to the generosity he extended to relatives, Jay also retired his boyhood pastor to a cottage not far from Lyndhurst. He likewise made frequent contributions to the Five Points Mission, run by his old Roxbury friend Rice Bouton as of 1884. One other intriguing aspect of Jay's benevolence has heretofore escaped notice by biographers. On several occasions he funded scholarships for men and women of the household and grounds staffs at 579 and Lyndhurst. In this regard, Jay reserved his largesse for younger employees: candidates whom he triaged in an interesting manner. After an invitation was made, those who availed themselves of Gould's personal libraries with some frequency on their off hours were in turn spoken to by the master and offered help in continuing their education. Thus more than one job scrubbing Gould floors, tending Gould gardens, or driving Gould carriages eventually morphed into a career in schoolteaching, the law, or accounting. A pattern emerges: Jay never came across a candidate for bootstrapping whom he did not wish to applaud and help.

Beyond his household, his family, and his friends, Gould's charitable endeavors were wide-ranging. At the time of the Memphis yellow fever epidemic, in 1879, Gould wired the acting head of the benevolent Howard Association in that city: "I send you by telegraph $5,000 to aid the Howard Association. I am certain the generous people throughout the country will contribute liberally to aid your stricken city. At any rate keep on at your noble work till I tell you to stop, and I will foot the bill. What are your daily expenses? Answer."[12] Upon receiving word that costs equaled $1,000 per day, Gould supplied that amount until the crisis subsided. On another occasion, when visiting George Washington's old home of Mount Vernon, Gould surveyed maps of the estate and inquired of the site's superintendent why a prominent parcel northwest of Washington's mansion was not part of the property. When informed that the owners of the house and grounds, the Mount Vernon Ladies Association, desired the hilly lot but were forbidden by their charter to invest directly in adjacent lands, Gould immediately offered to buy the plot and donate it, only requesting that his name not be used in publicity.

Early in his career, Jay's penchant for anonymity when it came to charitable giving was a function of his wanting to maintain his reputation as a not very nice guy. Later in life, when he was truly a prisoner of his legend and would have gladly escaped it if he could, the anonymity became necessary for other reasons. The fact was that on the few occasions when the press got wind of Jay's giving, he usually suffered the indignity of finding himself ridiculed and his philanthropy mocked. Early in 1890, Gould heard of two Irvington churches threatened with the building of a tavern on the vacant lot between them. Though not solicited, Jay took it upon himself to buy the lot and deed half to each church. When the *Times* heard of this, the paper's headline ran "GOULD SOOTHES HIS CONSCIENCE."[13] About this same time, after Jay donated $25,000 to help the University of the City of New York purchase a new campus in the Bronx, he came away rebuked yet again. He told Alice Northrop, "I guess I'm through with giving. . . . It seems to cause nothing but trouble, trouble. Everything I say is garbled. Everything I do is purposely misconstrued. I don't care especially about myself, but it all comes back so on my family."[14] In fact he continued to donate, but quietly, as before.

◇   ◇   ◇

Early in 1884, Morosini's daughter Victoria stunned New York society when she eloped with a coachman recently fired from her family's employ. Not long after, Jay's horrified wife, Ellie, spoke at length to Alice Northrop about how terrible it would be if any of the Gould or Northrop girls ever married a member of the servant class. Then Ellie's son George went that dire prospect one better. Just a few weeks after Victoria's adventure, George announced that he'd commenced a two-year betrothal to a beautiful young actress, Edith Kingdon, the product of an impoverished Brooklyn family. According to Alice, Ellie found the idea of George's marrying a woman of the stage "utterly distasteful, such a terrible, completely crushing blow! [But] if she placed too much importance on 'family' and social distinctions, she simply could not help it. Steeped in old (shall we say 'Murray Hill'?) traditions, these things were inbred in her."[15] Memories of the gold-digging Josie Mansfield must have filled Ellie's head as she loudly protested the impropriety of the match, only to be politely but firmly shushed by her husband, who came from a modest background himself and thus did not make a habit of holding such things against people. "She went on the stage to earn her own living and to support her mother," Jay told a *New York Times* reporter the day after the couple's marriage on 14 September 1886, "and that, I think, was very much to her credit. I honor her for it."[16]

The wedding took place at Lyndhurst in a discreet family ceremony designed to spare Ellie the embarrassment of a large, public extravaganza. Edith's mother represented her side. George's parents and siblings, along with the house staff, represented his. A Gould housekeeper, Margaret Terry, described the scene to Alice Northrop not long after. "Your uncle surprised everyone by asking us to come down to the parlor," the maid recalled. "He simply announced, 'George is to be married.' When I reached the parlor George and Edith were there, and your uncle and aunt and the other children. The minister, Mr. Choate [pastor of the Presbyterian Church in Irvington] performed the ceremony. I was asked to sign my name as a witness. Your aunt already had disapproved the marriage and she stood there looking as if the world had come to an end. I am sorry myself that George had to pick out an actress. . . . I did feel sorry for Edith, though, too. She kept up pretty well till it was all over, then she put her head down on George's shoulder and gave way. George had his arm around her and your uncle came forward and kissed her as a sign of his blessing. He stood by George. After the ceremony two carriages drove up. George and Edith drove away in one and Mr. Choate in the other. That was all."[17]

The couple moved into a large house provided by George's parents directly behind 579. One year later, in August 1887, Edith presented Jay and Ellie with their first grandchild, a boy named Kingdon. By that time, however, all the family had noticed a marked decline in Ellie Gould. Not yet fifty, she suffered long bouts of listlessness and weakness, endured fevers, and lost weight. The precise nature of her distress remained undiagnosed, but in October Jay made the decision that both he and his wife, together with the four younger children, needed a solid rest. A European tour was in order—at last, the cruise he'd long been threatening.

On 25 August, the *Atalanta* departed for Marseilles, where the Goulds would catch up with her in a matter of weeks. Four days later, Jay and his family—Ellie along with Nellie, Howard, Anna, Frank, and one of Ellie's sisters—boarded the *Umbria* for the transatlantic journey. A *New York Times* journalist noted that Gould, about to set off, "looked as he generally does, a trifle shabby as to clothes." [18] Jay was seen on deck chatting with well-wishers, among them Sage, Dillon, and J. P. Morgan, the former two charged with keeping a watchful eye on George and Edwin, who would be "running" things while their father was away. Later on, a smiling and relaxed Gould surprised the gathered reporters by coming down the gangway to shake hands. "What will you boys do without me?" he joked. Asked if he would take along a physician, he responded that he had no more need of one than the average reporter. When the *Herald*'s man inquired about the situation in the stock market, Gould shrugged and replied, "Some people say that the market goes up when Gould goes away. Good-bye."[19] Then he retreated back to the ship.

During their five months abroad, the Goulds visited London and Paris before departing on the *Atalanta* for a slow cruise of Mediterranean ports: Nice, San Remo, Florence, Naples, Rome, Sicily, and Greece. After this, the yacht stopped at Gibraltar and the Canary Islands. Then she steered for the West Indies and Florida, where the family waited out the New York blizzard of March 1888 before returning to Manhattan. Ellie, despite the relaxation and the warmth, did not improve. And even Jay himself, upon his return, seemed somehow more drained, exhausted, and skeletal than before. Though it is hard to say for sure, it was probably during the spring of 1888—not long after the end of the cruise—that Gould's physician, John P. Munn, informed him he'd come down with tuberculosis: the disease that had killed his father and so many others of his kin on the Gould side. That May, confronted not only with his wife's decline but his own, the fifty-two-year-old Gould instructed the proprietors of Woodlawn Cemetery to step up the pace and make an end to work on the elaborate mausoleum he'd commissioned several years before.

Gould's diagnosis, a death sentence, triggered the start of the most elaborate charade of his career. Dr. Munn was sworn to secrecy. Gould insisted that the already fragile Ellie not be told. The same went for the children and, most important, the Street. As of that spring, Munn's attendance on

Gould became a full-time job to the nearly complete exclusion of other pa-
tients. Whenever Gould traveled, Munn went with him lest Gould find
himself having to consult with other, more talkative physicians while away
from New York. For the next four-and-a-half years, Gould would mount a
Herculean effort to mask his symptoms while also holding up under a massive workload—a load made all the more complex and vital by his certain
knowledge that he must, with some urgency, pack up his tangled affairs as
neatly as possible for the next generation.

That May, Gould headed west onboard a newly acquired and plushly appointed railroad car: an elaborate rolling palace named after the same god-
dess honored by his yacht: *Atalanta.*[20] Later in the month he made unwanted
headlines when he became ill near Kansas City. When queried, his offices
identified Gould's ailment as a return of his old chronic complaint, neuralgia, for which his physician had prescribed mountain air. Thus the *Atalanta*
detoured to Pueblo, Colorado, where Gould was spotted being driven about
town in an open wagon. A few days later, a reporter bumped into the mogul
on a train platform at Carondelet. In the journalist's estimation, Gould
seemed weak, listless, and unsteady. He "never once straightened his head in
the old defiant state." When approached and asked how he felt, Gould explained, softly and almost apologetically, "We have had a tiresome journey."[21]
Two days after that he made a stop in Memphis, to inspect a newly acquired
road, but was back in New York—where he found his condition the topic of
much discussion—by 16 June. Amid a public debate over whether he might
soon die, Gould dispatched Sage to quell the rumors. Sage sternly warned
reporters that Gould would "show some of these folks down here in Wall
Street before long that he is very much alive."[22]

Gould remained secluded at Lyndhurst with his family and his flowers
throughout the early summer. There, in mid-July, he gave an interview designed to calm fears. A reporter for the *Philadelphia Times* described Jay
emerging from the famous greenhouse, his arms cradling two large pots of
infant rose bushes. Gould wore a straw hat, a blue flannel suit, and felt slip-
pers. He looked thin and pale but seemed chipper. "They make me out a
hopeless case," he chuckled. "Well, it isn't bad as that. I am more miserable
than actually sick." He rehearsed his history of neuralgia and his long-standing problem with insomnia, adding that luckily he found himself twice removed from the concerns of business these days. His sons, especially his

eldest boy, George, in collaboration with Mr. Sage and Mr. Dillon, were proving themselves to be quite capable financial lieutenants. Gould now considered himself "a gardener first, last and nearly all the time." He intended to steer clear of commercial stresses for the balance of the summer and wait on the appearance of his second grandchild, due in August. "I won't undertake to say that my mind is free of thought about my enterprises—a man can't leave his intellect in his office and bring nothing but his body home—but I am diverting myself."[23]

Two weeks later, Jay traveled to Saratoga with Ellie, several of the children, Alice Northrop, and Munn. There, the Gould party moved into two large cottages on the grounds of the United States Hotel. (Morosini, his wife, and their youngest daughter, Guilia, arrived several days after the Goulds, taking rooms in the hotel proper.) Gould declined to immerse himself in the waters that had made the town famous, but he relaxed nonetheless. The multimillionaire snoozed quite publicly on the hotel's piazza, ate his dinners in the large community dining room, and strolled every evening with Morosini. When the circus came to town, he maneuvered his chair on the piazza to gain an excellent view of the parade. Acquaintances among the hotel's guests—these including Frank Work and Henry Clews—told reporters that Gould, though chatty enough when it came to nonfinancial topics, was steadfastly refusing to talk shop. (The hotel's management at the same time confirmed that Gould had turned down an offer to have a private wire installed in his cottage.) "If ever a man were careless of stocks and stock market fluctuations," noted the *Times*'s man on the scene, "Jay Gould just now is posing as that man."[24] Operating from a somewhat closer perspective, Alice observed what reporters could not: Her uncle "had to lie on his bed and rest before he could go anywhere."[25] Munn never strayed far from his side. Meanwhile, Ellie continued her own slow fade, suffering a mild stroke while the family was at the resort.

After Saratoga, Ellie returned to Lyndhurst. Jay, however, insisted on making a side trip to Roxbury with Nellie, Alice, Howard, Anna, and Frank. Jay had last been back to his old home one year earlier with Ellie. Before that he'd come alone in 1880 to install a marker above the grave of his parents and sisters. Now he was intent on showing John Burr Gould's grandchildren their place of origin. Staying in town for several days, the party operated out of Gould's *Atalanta,* pulled up on an Ulster & Delaware siding near the Roxbury station. From there Jay—sans bodyguards, who were not needed here—guided the young people around the village on foot. He showed them the former Gould home downtown, pointed out the tin shop, and introduced them to such worthies as Hamilton Burhans and "cousin" Maria Burhans Lauren. Later on, Jay hired wagons and took the children to the graves by the Yellow Meeting House. They also went to the old Gould farm, visited the school where Jay long before had wrestled with John Burroughs, and ascended to the summit of Utsayantha Mountain. On another day, with boyish glee, Jay took time to fish for trout at Furlow Lake near the town of Arkville: a beautiful stretch of land and water just a few miles from Roxbury. (George subsequently bought the place, planning to build a rustic lodge that he hoped his father would enjoy.) "I have never seen Father so merry," Nellie wrote her mother. "[He] has been so different, the old memories and the old friends have quite brightened him up."[26] Appropriately, while Jay was visiting the place of his birth, word came of the arrival of his latest grandchild: a boy to be named Jay Gould II. (George and Edith were to have two more children in Jay's lifetime, daughters Marjorie and Vivien.)

Of Jay's numerous old friends, perhaps none was a more welcome sight than Peter Van Amburgh, who clambered aboard the *Atalanta* one rainy night with his hat pulled down over his eyes. Despite the hat, Jay recognized Peter immediately. "You needn't try to disguise yourself," he laughed, "I know you."[27] The following day, Gould and the children visited Van Amburgh's farm, where they dined on homemade bread, butter, and honey. After the feast, Jay and Peter spent a good hour walking Peter's fields, reminiscing about old times and people. Then, as Gould climbed back into his carriage, he invited Peter to visit him at Lyndhurst anytime he liked. Earlier, Jay had boasted about his fine, award-winning cattle. Now he added, temptingly, that if Peter came to call he'd let him have his pick of any animal from the Lyndhurst herd.

Lured by this offer, the thrifty Van Amburgh, dressed in his Sunday best, turned up at Lyndhurst one month later. The two spent a morning together, Jay escorting Peter on a tour of the castle and the greenhouse. Then, setting off to take care of some business in the city, Jay handed Peter off to Mangold, with instructions that they go look at Lyndhurst's "beasts of the field." When Jay returned later that evening he found Van Amburgh smiling and Mangold beside himself. "Picked out our prize Jersey," the groundskeeper complained, "that's all. Just the finest one of the lot." Gould, according to his niece, who witnessed the exchange, laughed so hard he could hardly breathe. "Peter," he said, once he'd composed himself, "I always said you were a smart one, and now I think Mr. Mangold agrees with me. The cow is yours. I will send you her pedigree papers and pay for transportation."[28] Van Amburgh spent much of the balance of the night sitting up with the sleepless Gould, talking over days long gone, and agreeing that one's oldest friendships were one's best friendships.

That was in October. On 6 November, Ellie suffered a second stroke. The stroke left her completely paralyzed, able to utter only a single word: Yes. Doctors offered no hope for recovery. The household removed from Lynd-hurst to 579 for the deathwatch. Munn at first predicted that Ellie would not last a week. But she tarried for more than two months, a feeble wreck of her former self, nearer dead than alive. Gould spent long hours by her bed-side day and night, retreating only when he needed rest himself or—as fre-quently happened—when business demanded his presence elsewhere.

◇   ◇   ◇

At this time, Gould's chief professional priority was the same as that of other railroaders around the country: to curb the ferocious price competition stemming from the 1887 Interstate Commerce Act. By breaking up the pools with which railroads had previously worked among themselves to co-ordinate competition, support prices, and ensure some measure of profitabil-ity, the 1887 act had led to a series of bitter rate wars from which no major road had emerged unscathed. As Charles Francis Adams summed things up in his diary, "We [the railroads] need law and order. We resemble nothing so much as a body of Highland clans,—each a law under itself,—each jeal-ous of its petty independence, each suspicious of the other, but all uniting in their dread of any outside power which could compel obedience. . . . In other words, a railroad Bismarck is needed."

On 20 December the nation's leading bankers, railroad owners, and in-vestors gathered at the home of J. P. Morgan on Madison Avenue for the start of a two-day conference to address the problem. There Gould, Adams, John Crosby Brown of Brown Brothers, George Magoun of Kidder-Peabody, and other worthies drew up a document in which they agreed to cooperate on rates and thereby support pricing nationwide. Although voicing skepticism, Gould nevertheless signed. So, too, did Adams, even though he criticized the agreement as an unenforceable effort to bind the railroads together "with a rope of sand." After adjournment, pending further deliberations the next morning, Adams wandered up Madison Avenue with his nemesis, whom he later described as appearing "dreadfully sick and worn." Gould wearily concurred when Adams expressed his dissatisfaction with the agreement. Then he sprang to life when Adams suggested that the overseers of the Interstate Commerce Commission be made a part of the process, to give the arrangement teeth. "Yes!" said Gould, suddenly enthusiastic, "and why not call the Commissioners in now; invite them to meet us, and cooperate in developing a scheme?" This, Gould knew, would not only force compliance but also eliminate the scent of collusion, price-fixing, and monopoly. He promised to bring the idea up the following morning.

Did Adams realize that Jay, exhausted, was totally preoccupied with his dying wife? We don't know. Probably not. Ellie's sickness had not been publicized, and Jay was not one to divulge such personal information. In any event, Adams was underwhelmed the following morning when Gould, arriving uncharacteristically late, lacked his normal force and focus. Adams recalled that Gould "suggested the idea [of involving the ICC], but in so weak and vague a way that it made no impression." Subsequently Adams drove the point home more persuasively, and in the end most agreed to the notion. They came away from the table having decided to maintain rates for two months, and to reassemble at Morgan's place after Christmas to hammer out a final plan. But the second round of meetings, held on 8–10 January, yielded little progress, and Gould—embarked upon the final week of his deathwatch—seemed to Adams "worn, reduced and nervous, with a tired film on his eyes."[29]

Gould had little to say when Charles E. Perkins of the Burlington grumbled he would not attend a meeting at which the ICC commissioners were present. At the end of the grueling sessions, the parties finally agreed to form something called the Interstate Commerce Railway Association (ICRA)—a collection of presidents who would meet regularly, arbitrate disputes, and maintain rates. But the organization was doomed from the start. Within months, Adams himself would begin boycotting the meetings, saying that in the ICRA his worst fear (that agreement without enforcement was no agreement at all) had become realized. Adams eventually defied the spirit of the agreement when, late in 1889, he instituted an alliance with the Northwestern on behalf of the Union Pacific, effectively making the two roads one for the purpose of conducting through traffic. Meanwhile, Gould's Missouri Pacific suffered a pricing assault from the Rock Island. In January 1890, just one year after the launch of the ICRA, Gould would ask Clark, "Is it worth while for us to be represented at the meeting of the President's Association in Chicago, or shall we simply send flowers for the corpse?"[30]

◇ ◇ ◇

Two days following the last of the Morgan meetings of January 1889, Ellie lapsed into a coma. One day after that, on the 13th, she died. "When the end came," stated an uncharacteristically sympathetic report in the *World*, "it found Mr. Gould sitting at his wife's bedside holding her hand. She did not recover consciousness and passed peacefully away. During her entire illness Mr. Gould was at her side or within call, except when matters of vital importance called him away."[31] In the weeks and months after the funeral, it was Nellie, naturally spinsterish, who plunged in to become her father's hostess, the family's household manager, and the dominant force in the lives of the younger children. As for Jay, it took him several weeks to recoup, after which he returned glumly to work.

A small crisis erupted in February when one of Jay's key associates, A. L. Hopkins, abruptly quit. Hopkins had come into Jay's organization a dozen years earlier when Gould took control of the Wabash, and since then he had become one of Gould's closest confidants in business after Sage. "The smooth and plausible story," commented the *World*, "which George Gould put in circulation . . . to the effect that Mr. Hopkins had retired because he wanted to rest, was laughed at. Well-informed men have learned during the past two years something of what manner of man young Gould is. . . . They point out that the young man is animated, just as his father used to be, with a belief that he can run all the diverse and gigantic enterprises . . . and conduct all his speculations without any assistance from able and trusted lieutenants. . . . Mr. Gould, it is pretty well known, discarded G. P. Morosini to please his son. Mr. Morosini felt the treatment very keenly, but he never uttered a word against Mr. Gould."[32] The *World* overstated Morosini's separation. Gould had withdrawn from his special partnership with Morosini and Connor at the end of 1886, and George had departed the firm before that.

Nevertheless, Washington Connor & Company continued to transact much of the Gould family's trading business and even had offices in the Western Union building. As well, Morosini, like Hopkins, continued to serve on several Gould boards. But clearly, some housekeeping was going on in the Gould camp as Jay, racing a ticking clock, rushed to groom George and, to a lesser extent, Edwin, for leadership.

At the same time, amid dismal market conditions and price wars that continued to depress rates for freight and passenger traffic nationwide, Gould fixated single-mindedly on cutting the overhead on his Missouri Pacific and related lines. In this connection, he sent Clark a barrage of missives ("blue jays" as they were called, handwritten on Jay's personal blue-tinted letterhead) packed with detailed instructions for layoffs, pay cuts, and other economies on the Cotton Belt, the Wabash, and every other property that looked fat. No level of micromanagement escaped Gould's studious insomniac eye as he labored through the long nights, poring over payroll sheets and similar key data. Other executives besides Clark received compliments and slaps on the wrist as warranted. When Jay's nephew Reid Northrop—recently made president of a Missouri subsidiary called American Refrigerator Transit—began a small reorganization without consulting Clark in St. Louis, a blue jay quickly flew with a reprimand. The young man was to run the firm subject to Clark's directions, "and it is my wish that you confer with him freely and accept his directions as law."[33]

◇　◇　◇

As time went on, Jay's physical exertions became less and less while his mind rushed ahead of his competition at an ever more rapid pace. Casual onlookers could not guess the strenuous activity of the marketplace in which the frail, wheezing man was daily and nightly engaged. Likewise, few imagined that the emaciated magnate had in him one more great play, one more sudden and majestic move on the chess board.

During the summer of 1890, markets fell and the Union Pacific, mired down in massive floating debt, began to founder under the captaincy of Adams. By autumn, banks were calling in notes, triggering the most severe panic to hit Wall Street since May 1884. In this climate, during November, Gould briefly reentered the market with a view toward saving—or, some said, confiscating—the railroad he'd lost to Adams six years earlier. At first, few suspected Gould was behind the bears who hammered UP. As well, early on, no one guessed Gould might be the source of an idle comment— nothing more than a slim bit of rhetorical wallpaper—picked up and repeated by numerous financial pundits: "A general feeling prevails in railroad circles that Union Pacific is managed by Harvard graduates who have big heads and small experience."[34] Shortly another unsourced bit of gossip appeared and was reprinted: Gould's mysterious ailment had been miraculously healed. He was his old self again, at the top of his game once more, and could "make or break railroad rates in the West [and] the prices of stocks at will."[35] Monday, 10 November, saw an unprecedented sell-off in which all the railroad issues received a pummeling, especially the UP. "One thing is apparent," Adams told banker R. S. Grant, "that is, that the whole pack, headed by Gould, are now at work to pull me down."[36]

At this point, the gods, perhaps urged on by Atalanta herself, intervened on the side of Gould. On the 15th, word came from London that Baring Brothers had shut its doors. Although this news gave life to the general panic for a few more days, damaging all values for the short term, it posed an even greater problem for Adams, who'd recently been relying on sterling loans from Baring Brothers to oil the precarious UP cash flow. On the heels of this intelligence, early on the morning of the 17th, Jay suddenly announced he was going into UP. Acting like the Gould of old, he bounded from the wings to grab his prize, buying aggressively and seizing control, at the same time buoying the price.

Ames and Morgan met with Gould briefly that afternoon. After getting a view of Gould's plan, Ames wrote Adams that Gould's ambition was to work the UP "into some enormous, vague scheme he is meditating of a railroad combination which is to solve the problem, do away with competition, make everyone rich and, at one stroke, reduce chaos to order."[37] In short, Gould sought to make himself the Bismarck that Adams had once hoped for. On the 20th, Adams visited Gould's office to surrender. The men set the following Wednesday as the date to formalize the transition. On that day, Gould, Sage, Henry B. Hyde of Equitable Life, and banker Alexander E. Orr were elected directors, while Dillon returned to the post of president. In a prepared statement read by an assistant, Gould pledged to do everything necessary to prop up the cash-strapped road. When asked by a *World* reporter why he'd returned to the UP, he replied in a breathy whisper, "There is nothing strange or mysterious about it. I knew it very intimately when it was a child, and I have merely returned to my first love."[38]

◇ ◇ ◇

It was his last hurrah. Through late 1890 and into 1891, Jay's physical decline accelerated. He spent most of the winter of 1891 out west, and then holed up at Lyndhurst through the summer. At the annual meeting of the UP board in October 1891, Gould suffered a physical breakdown. Standing to respond to criticisms of the annual report voiced by his friend Sage, he spoke only two or three sentences before losing his stream of thought, sitting down, and covering his face with his hands, "his whole frame quivering with . . . great excitement."[39] Periods of confusion and excitability are common in the latter stages of tuberculosis, but the *World* and other papers reported that Gould's problem was not organic: "The whole trouble arises from shattered nerves and this condition of his nervous system affects his stomach."[40] An officer of the UP told Adams how Gould "would physically collapse while trying to do business."[41] His meetings and interviews were now carefully orchestrated, with subordinates doing much of his talking for him, and every session kept short. Some days were better than others.

Three weeks before Christmas, Gould received a shock when word came of Sage's near murder. A madman named Henry Norcross had walked into the financier's office in the Western Union building and demanded $1.5 million. After Sage told him to go to hell, Norcross activated a bomb he carried in a valise. The explosion killed the bomber and one of Sage's clerks but barely touched Sage, who arose from the wreckage intact. George Gould, sitting in the office of the Manhattan Elevated next door, heard the bomb go off and experienced a rain of plaster, as did Connor and Morosini in their digs one floor below. In short order, George got word to his father, who immediately walked down Fifth Avenue to the Sage home, there to comfort Mrs. Sage and wait with her until her husband was brought home. Sage would recall that Gould could not be dissuaded from staying with him in his room as the doctor attended to his minor cuts and scrapes. "It seemed very strange to me at that time that this little man, who was anything but robust himself, could do so much and insist upon doing it."[42]

In February 1892, Gould suffered another tubercular crisis. On Sunday, the 21st, he felt well enough to spend half an hour in the lobby of the Windsor

Hotel across the street from his home. There he gossiped with the brokers and journalists who frequented the place. In the midst of his chatter, he mentioned casually that he would go south in a matter of days. On the Tuesday following, he bowed to a request from Nellie that he host a meeting of the Church Extension Society and present the organization with a $10,000 donation. Subsequently, as the week dragged on and Gould did not depart, rumors began to circulate. The word was that he'd fallen ill shortly after the church meeting. An anonymous source, probably a member of the household staff, told a *World* reporter that from Tuesday night onward Gould had seemed to improve, but on Friday he began to hemorrhage. "Mr. Gould was coughing violently, and his handkerchief was flecked with blood."[43]

Dr. Munn insisted that Jay's problem was a bad cold, nothing more. At the same time, Gould's *Atalanta* was attached to a flyer, Gould helped aboard, and the train pointed toward the dry air of El Paso. Nellie and Anna went along. Howard, currently enrolled at Columbia, would soon follow. Once he was out west, Gould's appetite improved and his cough dried up. In May, when the heat became uncomfortable, he relocated to the mountains near Pueblo. Reading the papers as his train rushed through the countryside, he could not have missed the obituaries of old friends. Rice Bouton had died the previous September. Now Gould noted the deaths of Bishop John Sharp, a Mormon leader who'd been active with the Union Pacific for years, and New York merchant Edward Jaffray. On 9 June, the sickly Dillon—only recently elevated to the post of UP chairman to make way for incoming president Clark—went to his last rest at Woodlawn, within view of the Gould mausoleum and the future site of the Morosini crypt. Not long after, in July, Cyrus Field closed his eyes.

Gould got back to New York in midsummer and spent several weeks at Lyndhurst, seeing only family and close advisers. Returning to 579 in September, he was observed on several occasions, late at night, strolling back and forth by lamplight in front of his townhouse, guarded by a sleepy retainer. Every now and then he would pause, embark upon a fit of coughing, and hack up bloody sputum into a handkerchief. Whenever one of the boys from the Windsor lobby strolled across to greet him, he'd smile and shake hands but remain silent. Then he'd wander back inside, where his diversions were few. Sometimes he played bezique with Nellie. He also enjoyed it when she read to him from his favorite authors: Dickens, Thackeray, and his old friend John Burroughs.

Jay attended his last meeting of the Missouri Pacific board on 11 October. Two weeks after that, on the 26th, he appeared, beaming, at Edwin's wedding to Sarah Cantine Shrady, the stepdaughter of a prominent physician. That Thanksgiving, when Alice Northrop came to 579 for several days, she found her uncle a ravaged shell of his former self. Early in her visit, as she sat with him, he stunned her when he leaned over and confessed, out of the blue, "Alice, I am not afraid to die. I am not afraid to die. But the younger children—well—I don't like the thought of leaving them." Two nights later, Alice was chatting with Nellie when Jay walked slowly and unsteadily into the room, "sat down heavily" in his favorite armchair, and leaned his head against its back. His face was completely drained. He'd been out with Munn in the carriage. "Uncle Jay," Alice said. "You look so tired!" "Yes," he whispered, breathless. "I am tired. I stopped in for a little at Madison Square Garden to see the horse show. They had some wonderful animals. It was worth going to—but I think I have taken cold."[44]

Later that evening, Jay hemorrhaged severely for several hours, after which Munn announced that it was just a matter of brief time before the end. Still, the secret was kept. Jay lay abed a full week before word of his condition hit the street, appearing in newspapers on the morning of Thursday, 1 December. All through that day, reporters gathered on the cold sidewalk outside 579, watching as Gould's children and intimates came and went. Across the street at the Windsor, Gould's acquaintances—speculators, brokers, and hack reporters—calculated the market ramifications of his last breath and laid their bets. The family, meanwhile, said good-bye. Gould regained consciousness for the last time at about 2 A.M. on Friday, the 2nd. He whispered to Munn that he wished to bid farewell to the household, after which he spoke briefly to each of his children in turn and talked as well with every member of the staff before closing his eyes and lapsing into a coma. He died at 9:15 A.M. The reporters hovering on Fifth Avenue scattered the moment they saw Margaret Terry hang a black knot of crepe on the door. A few hours later, when Munn published the death certificate, the press finally learned the details of the ailment that had stalked Jay Gould for years.

Around the world, editorials condemned the dead man. The *London Standard* eulogized Gould as a "wrecker of industries and an impoverisher of men."[45] The *News*, of that same city, described him as "less a man than a machine for churning wealth."[46] In his own town, the *Times* reminded readers that Gould's fortune was based on his talent for "intercepting the earnings of other people and diverting them from their original destination."[47] And the *Herald* confided that there had been "much quiet rejoicing" down on Wall Street once news of Gould's death circulated.[48] Nearly all these papers printed a report, spurious, that a stock ticker had been installed close by Gould's deathbed. Uninformed gossip had it that the machine clicked away as he breathed his last, providing an oddly appropriate counterpoint to the dying millionaire's death rattle. Even in death, Jay found no escape from the popular romance of his evil.

EPILOGUE

The Goulds after Jay

J AY GOULD'S WILL, a complex and in some ways ingenious document, proved the downfall of his family. Or at least it proved the downfall of the cohesive, dynastic, and eminently solvent version of family Jay had so long dreamed of leaving in his wake.

At the time of Jay's death, the appraised value of the estate stood at $72 million, some $2 million of this being in real estate. (In fact, $72 million represented an extremely conservative estimate made for tax purposes. The actual value was more like $125 million.) By the terms of the will, each of the children received a sixth interest in the amount, but not free and clear. The millions were to be put in trust, and residual income would be paid to every son and daughter for life. As for the core capital of the trust, Jay called for this to be invested and administered by the six cooperatively as trustees, with the two youngest, Anna and Frank, coming into their own as full voting partners once they reached the age of twenty-one. In an attempt to protect Nellie and Anna from gold diggers, Jay stipulated that, should they marry, control of their votes could not transfer to their husbands. In the event of a disagreement among trustees, George was to hold final authority.

Last, any unmarried heir who wed without the approval of a majority of his or her fellow trustees would forfeit half his or her share.

Jay made a few special bequests. Until Anna and Frank reached their majority, George and Nellie were to serve as their guardians, and the young people were to make their home with Nellie. To accommodate this situation, Jay gave both 579 and Lyndhurst to Nellie for her life use, along with an income of $6,000 per month until Frank, the youngest, turned twenty-one. Additionally, as compensation for his senior position and increased responsibility, Jay gave George an extra $5 million of the capital as part of his share. Other unique gifts included $500,000 for the second grandson, Jay Gould II, evidently a bonus for being the only namesake.

As well, Gould's sisters and Abram each received $25,000 plus an annual income of $2,000 for life. (Sarah was to die quite soon. Abram would pass in 1899, at age 56 just like his brother, while still employed as purchasing agent for the Missouri Pacific.[1] But Anna Hough, now retired to Los Angeles with her husband, and Bettie Palen, in Germantown, went on a bit longer, Anna living to age ninety.) Jay also gave Sarah Northrop the school, house, and lots in Camden that he'd long held in his name for her use. At the same time, Jay bequeathed Edwin title to the house behind 579 that George and Edith had once called their own, and in which Edwin and Sarah had recently been living.

Not one nickel went to anyone outside the family. Not one dime went to charity. Any of Jay's children who cared to save the world with the income from his or her share of the estate was free to do so, but Jay's sole ambition seems to have been to gift his fortune in a secure manner to those he loved most.

Each one-sixth share of the trust was to pass intact to blood descendants per stirpes. In other words, children, grandchildren, and great-grandchildren of any one of Jay's sons or daughters would benefit from, and share, the residual on just one-sixth of the estate, no matter how much any one line multiplied. The only possible exception to this rule would be if one of the bloodlines died out, in which case the core would afterward be divided into fifths, then fourths, and so on, thus increasing the percentage for each surviving line.

All this might have worked splendidly if George had been up to the task of maintaining and enhancing the value of the core funds, and had Jay

Gould's children collectively demonstrated an ability to simply get along. George's lack of wit, combined with his laziness, laid the foundation for his undoing. Not inclined to do homework or to spend any more time in the office than was absolutely necessary, George instead indulged himself with a massive estate at Lakewood, New Jersey, called Georgian Court.[2] There, at his mansion on Fifth Avenue, and up at the large Catskills house he built on Furlow Lake called Furlow Lodge, George and Edith entertained lavishly. At Georgian Court their balls included chess games played on boards that took up the size of an entire casino room. Live chess "pieces," decked in full regalia, walked glumly from square to square at the command of millionaire players.

While champagne, indulgence, and ostentation ruled George Gould's home life, the little time he spent on business was defined by inattention combined with delusions of grandeur. When he eventually overreached and engaged in battle with the brilliant, indefatigable W. H. Harriman to see who would create America's ultimate transcontinental system, George's surrender in 1911 cost him the presidency of the Missouri Pacific. It also lost many millions for the Gould family trust. The trust suffered more still when, two years later, George overruled everyone but the compliant Nellie and divested the two remaining cornerstone properties from Jay's time: the Western Union and the Manhattan Elevated.

By 1919, Anna and Frank had become so alarmed at the decline of the core that they brought suit against George for mismanagement. Their motion requested that George be removed as chief executor and trustee. It also asked that George personally render payment of $25 million to Frank and Anna to compensate them for losses suffered during the time of his control. The suit went on for eight years. By the time it was settled, in 1927, George was dead and a circus tent full of lawyers had devoured some $2.7 million in fees. The value of the trust, which dwindled down to $52 million under George's control, had recently rebounded to $66.5 million on the tide of a booming stock market (still well below the approximately $125 million in real-world value that Jay had left on the day of his death). In the end, the courts divided the estate into six separate units (each with a base amount of a little over $11 million) to be administered by four separate trust companies (one working for Nellie and for George's heirs, one working for Edwin, one working for Howard, and one working for Frank and Anna). These independent firms were charged with investing the principal and paying income to qualified claimants through succeeding generations.

George and Edith Kingdon Gould's vigorous marriage produced seven children, but by 1913 Edith's fine figure had disappeared and she was obese. This led George to begin eyeing young female performers at various Manhattan theaters. The woman he wound up with was Irish, in her twenties. Although a humble "Gaiety Girl" dancer in a musical entitled *The Girl on the Film,* Guinevere Sinclair actually came from a prominent background. Her grandfather, Sir Edward Sinclair, had been Provost of Trinity College, Dublin. George bought Guinevere a large townhouse on Seventy-fourth Street in Manhattan and an even larger Tudor mansion in Rye, near the American Yacht Club, where he could conveniently visit aboard the *Atalanta.* A son, George Sinclair, arrived on 15 April 1915. A daughter, Jane, came along in 1917. Then another girl, Guinevere, showed up in early 1922. George was not discreet about his relationship with Sinclair or about his second set of children. His wife realized the facts, and his eldest legitimate offspring, now grown, frequently muttered darkly about "George's bastards."

As all this went on, Edith Gould made earnest, heartbreaking attempts to slim down. Her manic weight-reduction program involved massages, steam baths, and daily games of golf with her husband on Georgian Court's nine-hole golf course. One warm morning in November 1921, as Edith and George were in the midst of a round, she suddenly dropped dead of a heart attack. Edith was later found to be wearing a suffocatingly tight rubber suit beneath her golf clothes, this designed to make her appear thin. George wed Guinevere at Georgian Court six months later, after which the couple moved to a leased castle in Elginshire, Scotland. They hadn't been married quite a year, however, when George died of pneumonia while on holiday at Mentone, France, during the spring of 1923. He was fifty-nine.

George Gould's mishandling of the Gould estate, combined with his squandering of his share, meant that after his death his seven children with Edith received just under $1 million apiece after taxes. Each also received a one-seventh share in the residual on George's one-sixth stake in the much-diminished family trust. They, in turn, had children of their own. In the future, virtually all of George's offspring had to either work for a living, make their own fortunes, or rely on money they'd married into. At the same time, "George's bastards" received just $1 million among them. (They'd been destined for more, including a portion of George's residual from the family trust, but this plan changed when George's children by Edith contested the will wherein George formally recognized each of the three Sinclairs as his legitimate blood heirs.)

Within a year of George's death, Guinevere married the Viscount Dunsford, George St. Johns Brodrick, heir to the Ninth Viscount and First Earl of Midleton. Following the marriage, Guinevere bought Eastwell Park, a large estate near Ashford in Kent. George, Jane, and Guinevere were in turn adopted by the viscount, and their names changed. The elder Guinevere died in 1976, one year after divorcing her eighty-seven-year-old husband of fifty years. (The Tenth Viscount and Second Earl of Midleton promptly married a younger woman.) The last of the Sinclair "bastards" to die was George, for most of his life known as George Brodrick. He passed away at age eighty-eight in 2003 after a long and distinguished career as an Eton- and Cambridge-educated soldier, farmer, and gentleman. His three children have never met any of their numerous Gould cousins.[3]

◇   ◇   ◇

Edwin Gould fared much better in business, and in life, than did his elder brother. Through the turn of the century he worked in various capacities within Gould-controlled companies. Later on, after tiring of George's inept authority, he struck out on his own. By shrewdly investing the bulk of his yearly residual, Edwin built a considerable personal fortune outside the family trust. Like his father, he also pursued the happiest of marriages. Edwin's two sons—Edwin, Jr., and Frank Miller Gould—shared his passion for the outdoors and adventure. Early on, Edwin and his two boys became members of the Shattemuc Canoe Club at Ossining on the Hudson River. Then, in 1913, Edwin purchased two airplanes and learned to fly. With his sons, he hunted and fished in the countryside near the family's two homes: Agawam, at Ardsley-on-Hudson, and Chichota, on Georgia's Jekyll Island.

It was at Jekyll Island that twenty-three-year-old Edwin, Jr., died in 1917, the victim of a freak hunting accident. He thus became the first of several children and grandchildren to join Jay and Ellie Gould in the large crypt at Woodlawn. After their son's death, Edwin and his wife, Sarah, literally abandoned their Jekyll Island home. Originally built in 1897 around a spacious swimming pool, the mansion had been purchased by Edwin in 1900.

Eventually Edwin added a boat dock and boathouse. He also built for his in-laws another Italian Renaissance mansion, Cherokee Cottage, across the road during the years 1904–1907. Cherokee Cottage remains, but not Chichota. Allowed to fall into disrepair through the twenties and thirties, it was razed in 1941. Today, two carved Corinthian lions mark what used to be the front steps. Nearby lie the ruins of the swimming pool. (In 1928, Edwin's son Frank Miller Gould built yet another home on the island, which he named Villa Marianna, after his daughter. This still stands.)

On the heels of Edwin, Jr.'s death, Edwin, Sr.—despite his age (fifty-one) and his millions—volunteered for duty in the U.S. Army during World War I. Edwin served as a supply sergeant. His son Frank also enlisted. Taking a sabbatical from Yale, Frank began a reserve career that would continue into World War II and earn him a captaincy. Edwin himself remained active in the National Guard after the war. Other Goulds filling the U.S. ranks in World War I included two of George's sons: Jay Gould II, who volunteered as a machinist's mate first class in the navy, and Kingdon Gould, one of the first 1,000 privates to get their training at Fort Dix. Kingdon rose through the ranks to corporal, sergeant, staff sergeant, and battalion sergeant major, but eventually turned down a chance to attend officers' training school on the grounds that he'd prefer to stay with his unit. George Gould, Jr., attempted to enlist but was found to be 4-F. Both Edwin and Nellie, meanwhile, were major contributors to the American Volunteer Ambulance Corps for which, ironically, Henry Villard's grandson—yet another Henry Villard—served as a driver along with his friend Ernest Hemingway.

At the end of World War I, Edwin sold his Ardsley estate and built a new mansion on Long Island at Oyster Bay. Thereafter, working out of an office in Manhattan, he occupied himself with investments (match companies, New York City real estate, and railroads). At the same time, he became a pillar of New York philanthropy, establishing homes and charitable relief organizations for underprivileged youngsters under the umbrella of the Edwin Gould Foundation for Children. Edwin named the organization not after himself, but his lost son. Previously, even before young Edwin's death, the father had been active in various endeavors to help young people, chief among these being Camp Woody Crest, in which he partnered with Nellie. In all these activities, Edwin gave more than money. "The thing that fascinates me," says Michael Osheowitz, recent president of the Edwin Gould

Foundation, "is the personal interest that he took in the kids that he was helping. Here's a guy of immense wealth and privilege who had an interest in helping these kids and got to know and mentor many of them."[4] Demonstrating a devotion similar to that which Jay exhibited in his administration of the Northrop family, Edwin personally worked in and around the grounds of the foundation's various schools and orphan homes and came to know many of the children on a first-name basis.

Upon his death in 1933 at the age of sixty-seven, Edwin Gould left one-half of his considerable fortune to his foundation, which continues to this day. The other half, along with a much smaller amount constituting Edwin's residual share of the Jay Gould fortune, went to Edwin's sole surviving son, Frank Miller Gould, who had two children.[5]

◇   ◇   ◇

Nellie rivaled Edwin in the doing of good works. She made numerous generous gifts to church mission societies and other devout organizations worldwide. She likewise supported one of her father's favorite institutions: the University of the City of New York, renamed New York University four years after Jay's death. In this connection Nellie commissioned none other than Stanford White to design the stunning Gould Library, along with other buildings (including a Hall of Fame for Great Americans) at NYU's Bronx campus, now the Bronx Community College. (Among those employed at the Bronx campus at the turn of the century was Dr. Charles Henry Snow, Ph.D., Dean of the School of Applied Science, whom Alice Northrop married in 1897. Like her brother Frank, who studied at NYU under Dr. Snow, Nellie herself was an NYU alumna of sorts. During the 1890s she funded and attended several informal, noncredit law seminars for women conducted at the all-male NYU Law School.)

Just as Nellie's interest in NYU arose from her father's habit of giving to that institution, so, too, did another of Nellie's charitable endeavors stem directly from Jay. Shortly before his death, Jay had promised to help rebuild the Reformed Church of Roxbury, recently destroyed by fire. After Jay died, his children, led by Nellie, moved to make good on his commitment. Built at a cost of $100,000, the Jay Gould Memorial Reformed Church stood complete by mid-1894. Two years later, Nellie—who already possessed life use of both Lyndhurst and 579—purchased a small old house next to the church, which she substantially enlarged to incorporate twenty-two bed-rooms, fourteen baths, twelve maids' rooms, six dens, a large kitchen, two dining rooms, and a dining porch. Thereafter she called her home Kirkside.

Subsequently, more than one annual gathering of local Mores and Goulds was held on the grounds abutting Nellie's home. These eleven acres were ones on which Nellie, with the help of Ferdinand Mangold from Lyndhurst, created a beautiful park (Kirkside Park) for the enjoyment of townspeople. (Today the opulent fields and woods, recently restored and embracing a pic-turesque portion of the East Branch of the Delaware, remain gems. Helen's Kirkside, meanwhile, survives as a retirement home.) In addition to creating the park for the town, Nellie—encouraged in part by Jay's old friend John Burroughs, who now summered in Roxbury—funded the creation of a pub-lic library in the home on Elm Street (now Vega Mountain Road) once owned by John Burr Gould. Then, in 1911, she built a beautiful Greek Re-vival structure next door to the library to house the town's YMCA. (Today the old YMCA serves as the Roxbury Arts Center, home to the Roxbury Arts Group. As for John Burr Gould's tin shop on Main Street, that is today a local center of contemporary fine art: the Enderlin Gallery.)

Once Nellie and George established summer homes in the Catskills, it was just a matter of time before other family members returned as well. Alice Northrop, whose marriage to Charles Henry Snow took place in the Jay Gould Memorial Reformed Church, purchased a residence for summer use right across Main Street from the church and Nellie's Kirkside. It was here, working with her son Henry Nicholas Snow, that Alice wrote her book of the early 1940s, *The Story of Helen Gould*. She died in 1947. Thirteen years later, her daughter Helen Gould Snow bought a place on Roxbury's Lake Street. As well, Anna Palen, a daughter of Bettie and Gilbert Palen and therefore another niece of Jay Gould, lived at Roxbury for several decades before dying in 1944. Her house was close to Alice Snow's, across from Nel-lie's Kirkside on Main Street. There she was followed by her brother, Dr. Gilbert J. Palen, a Philadelphia ear, nose, and throat specialist who'd once owned a farm outside the village and who died in the house on Main Street in 1958, aged eighty-eight. (His son, Dr. Gilbert M. Palen, grandnephew to Jay Gould, spent most of his adult life in the Catskills. This Dr. Palen founded the Margaretville Hospital and then pursued private practice in Walton before dying in 1986 at the age of seventy-three.) Meanwhile, though he did not live in or frequently visit the community, Frank Jay Gould nevertheless demonstrated a persistent interest. At one point he purchased a large bell for the tower of the Roxbury High School. On another occasion, in 1948, he underwrote a new furnace for the Jay Gould Memorial Reformed Church.

Nellie was forty-four when, in January 1913, she surprised her family, the world, and perhaps even herself by taking a husband. Finley J. Shepard was a handsome, debonair executive with the Missouri Pacific. The son of a minister, he shared Nellie's passions for Scripture, anticommunism, and the defense of besieged Victorian values. As it happened, he was also a Burr descendant: a seventh cousin to the Goulds. Too old to have children of their own, Nellie and Finley instead adopted three (Finley Jay Shepard, Helen Anna Shepard, and Olivia Margaret Shepard, the latter destined to marry John Reed Burr, close kin to Finley, Sr.). The couple also became legal guardians for another orphan, Louis Seton. All four were raised personally by Nellie and Finley in a manner that was quite loving but also tedious in its constant piety.[6] All four went to the best schools. And all four played with their father and mother on the private nine-hole course Nellie eventually built on lands adjacent to Kirkside Park. The course, which includes a manmade lake and a stone clubhouse, remains in use to this day as a private facility open to the public.

Nellie died in late 1938 at age seventy. Finley passed away in 1942. Some of their adoptive descendants remain in the neighborhood of Roxbury at this writing.

◇   ◇   ◇

Howard Gould—who like Edwin and Frank was much sharper than their older brother—nevertheless continued after Jay's death to work for a time under George, with whom he co-owned *Vigilant*, the Herreshoff-designed America's Cup defender for 1893. But tensions arose when Nellie, with the support of George, shut down Howard's attempt to marry an actress. Howard subsequently became incensed when Edith Kingdon Gould, who should have known better, denounced yet another actress as completely unacceptable. This time Howard hit back. He married the second woman, Viola Kathrine Clemmons, known as Kathrine, in 1898, not caring that in his rebellion he effectively cut his portion of the estate in half. At the same time, Howard broke away from George in business and set about building a fortune of his own, investing much of the yearly residual on what was now a one-twelfth share.

Howard's marriage to the spoiled, tempestuous Kathrine proved unhappy. It was for her that he built the elaborate Castle Gould on lands that today comprise the Sands Point Preserve of Long Island's North Shore. After the castle's completion in 1904, Kathrine declared the place unsuitable. Trying to please, Howard immediately set about converting Castle Gould into stables and servants' quarters, at the same time commencing work on yet another home a few hundred yards away. By 1912, when the Tudor-style Hempstead House with its forty rooms and eighty-foot tower finally stood finished, Howard and Kathrine had already been separated four years. Howard sold the estate to Daniel Guggenheim in 1917. Then he relocated to a rural mansion in England, where, after twenty years of bachelorhood, he remarried in 1937, only to divorce again ten years later. Howard died in 1959 at age eighty-eight, after deliberately taking not even the slightest precautions to shelter his enormous fortune. The British government devoured $52 million of Howard's $67 million in net worth. His eighty-eighty heirs, the children and grandchildren of his brothers and sisters, wound up getting approximately $170,000 apiece. Not a bad sum, but with just a little planning they could have had much, much more. Howard just didn't care.

◇ ◇ ◇

Self-consumed and self-indulgent, Anna Gould was not yet twenty when she abruptly broke off an engagement to Oliver Harriman, nephew to George's future nemesis E. H. Harriman. Anna's new suitor, seven years her senior, was a penniless womanizer and adventurer, the Count Marie Ernest Paul Boniface de Castellane, known as Boni. According to Boni, he found Anna to be "excessively shy . . . childish, and a trifle malicious; but she possessed charm, and—what is always delightful to a man—possibilities." Boni added that "Miss Gould's fortune played a secondary part in her attraction for me."[7] Astonishingly, George approved of this match, along with Anna's necessary conversion to Roman Catholicism, the latter being more a matter of form than of faith. The couple were married at George's Fifth Avenue mansion in March 1895. During the ten years that followed, Boni ran through Anna's money at a pace that astonished and outraged even the free-spending George. Making matters worse, Boni devoted no small amount of the cash to entertaining other women. Finally, in 1905, after bearing Boni two sons and a daughter, Anna left him. Eventually her lawyers settled Boni's multitudinous debts at thirty-five cents on the dollar.

Later on, after purchasing an annulment from the Vatican, Anna married one of Boni's cousins, the Duc Hellie de Talleyrand-Perigord. Hellie was not only rich in his own right but devoted. This happier union produced two more children, a boy and a girl. Anna's first husband, Boni, passed away in 1932, fifteen years after succeeding to his title and becoming the Marquis de Castellane. The Duchess de Talleyrand's three children from her first marriage all died relatively young, although the eldest son, Boni, Jr., lived long enough to come into the title of marquis. He married a beautiful half-American woman named Yvonne Patenotre. When he died at age forty-nine in 1946, he left a daughter, Elizabeth, who married Jean Comte de Caumont La Force. With La Force, Elizabeth had three children: two boys and a girl (Anna's great-grandchildren), who in turn married and had children. Elizabeth's half uncle—Anna's third son, Howard, born of Anna's second marriage—died by his own hand in 1929 after the collapse of a love affair with an older woman. Anna's second husband, Hellie, passed away in 1937. And Anna's lone surviving child from her second marriage, a daughter, married Count Joseph de Pourtales, with whom she had children. Thus Anna's descendants today remain entirely French in their language, sensibilities, and allegiances.

The champagne-sipping, irreverent Anna had avoided the teetotaling and devout Nellie for some thirty years, but she rushed back to the United States on the heels of Nellie's death to buy Lyndhurst from the estate. During World War II, Anna divided her time between Lyndhurst and a suite at the Plaza Hotel. Then, after returning to France in the autumn of 1945, she made the castle on the Hudson her summer residence. There, every July and August, she slept in the tower bedroom she had used as a child. Anna died in 1961 at the age of eighty-six. In her will she gave Lyndhurst to the National Trust for Historic Preservation, together with a fund for its upkeep. After Anna's French heirs contested the will, the National Trust forfeited the fund but kept the house. Today the estate (severely reduced to just sixty-seven acres from Jay's five hundred), the mansion, and the remains of Jay's wondrous greenhouse remain open to the public.

◇ ◇ ◇

Frank graduated from NYU in 1898 with a degree in engineering. Thereafter, following a familiar pattern, he worked briefly for George. But in time, like his brothers before him, he came to disagree with George's handling of affairs. So he, too, pursued his own personal and quite successful program of investments. Frank's marriage to his first wife (the socially prominent Helen Kelly, granddaughter of one of Jay Gould's early Wall Street allies) broke down in 1904. After that, Frank gained custody of his two daughters, married a showgirl, and purchased a chateau on the French coast at Normandy. No one knows what caused Frank to suffer an emotional breakdown some ten years later, but his behavior became destructive and erratic throughout the years of World War I. During this period, Frank drank heavily and became a regular at Parisian bordellos. His second wife left him in 1918. Four years later he met the woman who would prove his savior.

Frank married Florence La Caze, a strong-willed former actress from San Francisco, in 1923. He was forty-six, she twenty-eight. Florence dried him out and turned him back toward business. Frank invested in casinos and hotels at Antibes, Juan-les-Pins, Nice, and Vagnoles-de-l'Orne, establishments frequently visited by his high-rolling sister Anna, to whom he remained close. Although Frank eventually became known as the "king of croupiers," he in fact concentrated only on the real estate aspects of his enterprises, leaving the details of casino, nightclub, and hotel management to others. (For example, Frank built his Palais Mediterranee in Nice at a cost of $5 million; then he licensed the building to the Monte Carlo Company for thirty years at $1 million per year, during which time he enjoyed a healthy run-up on the value of the property while also collecting the hefty rent.) By 1930 Frank's holdings on the Riviera alone were worth more than $20 million. Florence, meanwhile, founded a literary salon at Juan-les-Pins, where she hosted the likes of F. Scott Fitzgerald and Jean Cocteau.

Frank remained in France throughout World War II. In his sixties and in poor health, he was viewed by the Nazis not as an enemy alien but rather a benign, elderly Frenchman. Seven years after the conclusion of the war, Frank gave New York University $1.5 million with which to build a student

center. Two years later, in 1954, the seventy-seven-year-old Frank—
prompted by his cousin-in-law and former dean, the ninety-one-year-old
Charles Henry Snow—presented the university with yet another $1 million,
this to be followed in 1956 by the deed to an estate at Ardsley-on-Hudson
that Frank had not visited in years.

Charles Henry Snow died in 1957 at age ninety-four. Frank Jay Gould
died at Juan-les-Pins in 1958, aged eighty-one. The bulk of Frank's substantial estate went to his wife, Florence; his two married daughters; and his
daughters' children. Florence went on to help found the International Jazz
Festival. This world-renowned event has been held annually ever since 1960
at Juan-les-Pins in the amphitheater of the Frank Jay Gould Pine Grove.
Florence, who died in 1983, also founded the Florence Gould Foundation,
an organization that supports French cultural events (such as art exhibitions
and music concerts) throughout the United States. In September 2003, by
way of recognizing the foundation and its founder, the Cultural Services Division of the French embassy in New York dedicated a new Florence Gould
Garden at its headquarters, 927 Fifth Avenue.[8]

◇ ◇ ◇

George Gould's second eldest son by Edith, Jay II, became a champion at
court tennis, the ancient sport of kings transacted on a walled court. In
twenty years of top-level competition, Jay II lost only once in singles and
once in doubles. He won the U.S. amateur championship for the first time
in 1906, when he was only seventeen, and he held this title through 1925
except for 1918 and 1919, when there was no tournament and Jay II was in
the service. Gould also won a gold medal in the 1908 Olympics, where his
sport was called *jeu de paume* on the official program. In 1914, he became
the first amateur ever to win the world championship. Subsequently, he and
various partners won a total of fourteen national doubles championships. Jay
died relatively young, at age forty-six in 1935, leaving children who in turn
had children.

The balance of George and Edith's offspring led widely varied lives. Their
eldest, Kingdon Gould, attended Columbia, became a business executive,
and enjoyed a happy marriage to a former family maid. George and Edith's
middle daughter, Vivien Gould, married an Irish nobleman—John Graham
Hope De La Poer Horsley-Beresford, Fifth Baron Decies—in 1911. She

died in 1931. (Her son, Arthur George Marcus Douglas de la Poer Beresford, Sixth Baron Decies, passed away in 1992. Her grandson, Marcus Hugh
Tristram de la Poer Beresford, Seventh Baron Decies, born 1948, is a Dublin
attorney.) George Gould, Jr., George and Edith's fifth child and third son,
became a stock broker, married, and had two sons: George Jay Gould III and
Maugham Carter Gould, about whom little is known. George, Jr., and his
wife divorced when the boys were still small.

Marjorie, the eldest of George and Edith's daughters and their third
child, married Anthony Drexel of the banking family. (It was Anthony who
gave George, Jr., his brokerage job at the firm Liggett, Drexel & Company.)
As for Edith, George and Edith's third eldest daughter and fifth child, she
led a brief life of dissipation, during which she squandered much of her
small inheritance, divorced her first husband (Carroll Livingston Wain-
wright, a descendant of Peter Stuyvesant by whom she had three children),
and remarried before dying at age thirty-six. (Her son, Stuyvesant Wain-
wright II, served as a Republican member of Congress from a district in
eastern Long Island from 1953 through 1961.) Gloria, George and Edith's
youngest daughter, suffered a similar fate to Edith's. After years of unhappi-
ness and alcoholism, she drowned while swimming drunk at her home near
Phoenix in the 1940s, leaving a daughter.

◇   ◇   ◇

If there is one among the current generation of Goulds who most closely re-
sembles Jay in most things, it is great-grandson Kingdon Gould, Jr. This
Gould is the holder of two Purple Hearts and two Silver Stars earned while
serving with the U.S. Army during World War II. He is also a Yale-educated
attorney and a longtime developer of real estate in the Washington, D.C.,
area, an endeavor which has proved enormously profitable. Kingdon spends
his summers at George Gould's old Furlow Lodge by the trout lake on Dry
Brook Road not far from Roxbury, where he is surrounded by several other
Gould homes (one of them owned until recently by his sister Edith Gould
Martin, who passed away in the summer of 2004).

Kingdon is the first son of a first son of a first son after Jay. In addition
to his career in business, he has served with distinction as U.S. ambassador
to Luxembourg (1969–1972) and the Netherlands (1973–1976). A former
chair of the John F. Kennedy International Field Hockey Tournament and

a presidential counselor at Johns Hopkins University, Kingdon speaks five languages, is an avid sportsman, and serves on numerous boards. He is also a devoted family man. Kingdon and his wife, Mary—who together were founders of the prestigious Glenelg Country School in Howard County, Maryland, which marked its fiftieth anniversary in 2004—boast nine children, twenty-eight grandchildren, and numerous great-grandchildren. The couple, both amateur actors, sometimes perform *Love Letters*—A. R. Gurney, Jr.'s romantic comedy—for the benefit of worthy causes. In May 2004 they gave one such performance for the Roxbury Arts Group in the building Nellie built so many decades ago as a gift to Jay's old hometown.

What would Jay think of Kingdon's keen talent and perseverance in business combined with his love of family and his sensitivity to the Goulds' Catskills heritage? One imagines that he would find it all quite satisfying.

ACKNOWLEDGMENTS

My friend and agent, Chris Calhoun, was the first person, after my wife, Christa, and myself, to have faith in this project. He was quickly followed by my even older friend, but new editor, Bill Frucht. Both Chris and Bill—together with Chris's capable assistant Diana Thow and Bill's equally estimable associate David Shoemaker—have proven wonderful accomplices. I would also like to thank Joe Bonyata, the Perseus Group's director of editorial production, for invaluable support.

Many thanks to the good people at Lyndhurst and the New-York Historical Society. I'm also grateful to the special collections staffs at the University of Rhode Island, New York University, Boston University (Mugar Library), the Library of Congress, the University of Michigan (Clements Library), Rutgers University (Alexander Library), the Morgan Library, Clemson University, the Harvard Graduate School of Business Administration (Baker Library), the Denver Public Library (Western Historical Collection), and the Newberry Library.

Numerous individuals have offered various brands of support. Carolyn Bennett, probably the world's leading authority on Gould's mentor and early business partner Zadock Pratt, read and commented on key slices of the manuscript. Peg Ellsworth, official historian for the town of Roxbury, New York, did the same and spent time with me in Jay's natal village. William A.

Cormier, official historian for Salem, New York, helped me track down Jay Gould's early railroad venture on the Vermont–New York border and also put me on the trail of Jay's previously lost brother, Abram, who married a Salem native and lies buried in that hamlet. Another previously lost remnant of the Goulds—the late George Brodrick, illegitimate grandson of Jay Gould—jovially welcomed inquiries from a stranger and willingly filled me in on essential details concerning the latter days of his father, George Jay Gould. Debbie Allen of Black Dome Press—who published my biography of Jay Gould's great friend from boyhood, the naturalist John Burroughs— and her soulmate Bob Hoch offered encouragement, contacts, and shelter in the Catskills. Chris Bentley read my first draft manuscript from stem to stern, offering essential criticism. Other interested parties—among them John Perry Barlow, Doug Brinkley, Eileen Charbonneau, Ben Cheever, John Gable, Arthur Goldwag, Phil Roosevelt, and Artie Traum—cheered and offered needed encouragement from the sidelines. Tweed Roosevelt, true to form, provided shelter in his guestroom during research forays to Boston.

I'm also thankful to Richard Snow, who allowed me to write about America's robber barons for the October 2004 edition of *American Heritage*.

As usual, my wife, Christa, and our two children—Bill and Katherine— have tolerated my distractedness, my preoccupation with a century other than that in which we find ourselves, and my hours locked away in the study. I hope they find the result to be worthwhile.

EDWARD J. RENEHAN, JR.
Wickford, North Kingstown, RI
9 December 2004

NOTES

PREFACE

1. Gould and Rockefeller held each other in high regard. Gould once commented that Rockefeller possessed America's "highest genius for constructive organization." Rockefeller, in turn, categorized Gould as the greatest businessman he had ever met. What was more, the two shared similar lifestyles as devoted family men. Rockefeller would not think nearly so highly of Gould's eldest son and chief heir, George Jay Gould, a self-absorbed dilettante and poor financial tactician by whom Rockefeller eventually lost approximately $40 million in bad investments during the first decade of the twentieth century.

2. *New York Tribune*. 14 December 1892.

3. Gustavus Meyers. *History of the Great American Fortunes*. London: Stationer's Hall. 1909. 115.

4. Matthew Josephson. *The Robber Barons*. New York: Harvest/Harcourt Brace. 1995. 126.

5. Two other worthy books, though not full biographies, focus on key slices of Jay Gould's story: Kenneth Ackerman's *The Gold Ring: Jim Fisk, Jay Gould, and Black Friday, 1869*. (Dodd-Mead, 1988) and John Steele Gordon's excellent *The Scarlet Woman of Wall Street: Jay Gould, Jim Fisk, Cornelius Vanderbilt, the Erie Railway Wars, and the Birth of Wall Street* (Grove Press, 1988).

6. Robert Riegel. *The Story of the Western Railroads*. New York: Macmillan. 1926. 231.

7. *New York World*. 4 October 1891.

8. Robert I. Warshow. *Jay Gould, or The Story of a Fortune*. New York: Greenberg. 1928. 47.

9. Michael Klepper and Richard Gunther. *The Wealthy 100: A Ranking of the Richest Americans Past and Present*. New York: Carol. 1999.

CHAPTER 1: THE MYSTERIOUS BEARDED GOULD

1. *New York Times*. 6 December 1892.
2. Giovanni P. Morosini. "Memoir of Jay Gould." Helen Gould Shepard Papers, New-York Historical Society. (Hereafter *HGS.*)
3. *New York Herald*. 3 December 1892.
4. *New York Times*. 3 December 1892.
5. *New York World*. 3 December 1892.
6. *New York Times*. 5 December 1892.
7. *New York World*. 4 December 1892.
8. *New York World*. 3 December 1892.
9. Henry Adams and Charles Francis Adams, Jr. *Chapters of Erie and Other Essays*. Boston: James Osgood. 1871. 31.
10. Giovanni P. Morosini. "Memoir of Jay Gould." HGS.
11. *New York World*. 4 December 1892.
12. *New York World*. 14 January 1889.
13. Alice Northrop Snow and Henry Nicholas Snow. *The Story of Helen Gould*. New York: Fleming H. Revell. 1943. 196.
14. *New York Times*. 7 December 1892.
15. *New York Tribune*. 13 June 1874.
16. Julia Pratt Ingersoll. Diary Note. 9 December 1892. Ralph Ingersoll Papers, Mugar Library, Boston University. (Hereafter *Ingersoll.*)

CHAPTER 2: ANCESTORS

1. *New York Sun*. 28 November 1880.
2. Daughters of the American Revolution lineage records. Vol. 28, p. 297, #27811.
3. Major Nathan Gold was born 1625 in Langley, Herts., England, the son of John and Judith Gould.
4. Nathan Gold first married Martha Harvey, who died in 1658 without issue. He then married Sarah Phippen, a native of Dorset, England, in 1660. They had six children, of whom Nathan Gold, Jr., was the only son. Nathan Gold died in either 1693 or 1694 in Fairfield.
5. Nathan Gould, Jr., was born 2 December 1663 in Fairfield and died 3 October 1723.
6. The children of Nathan, Jr., and Hannah included Hezekiah, who became a minister. He graduated from Harvard College in 1719 and died in 1761. He was married to Mary Ruggles, the daughter of Rev. Thomas Ruggles, Sr., of Guilford and seems to have spent most of his adult life in Guilford. Hezekiah had a son, also named Hezekiah, who graduated from Yale in 1752 and went into the ministry. This Hezekiah spent most of his life in Cornwall, Conn., and died in 1790. Nathan, Jr., and Hannah also had a daughter, Abigail, who married Thomas Hawley in Fairfield in 1712.
7. Samuel Gold died 11 October 1769 in Fairfield.

8. The children of Samuel and Esther Gold were Daniel, born 11 July 1717 in Fairfield, died in 1775 in that same town; Esther, born 13 October 1719 in Fairfield, died 1 August 1770 in that same town; Abigail, born 27 April 1724 in Fairfield, with no death information available; Abel, born 14 September 1727 in Fairfield, died 11 November 1789 in that same town; Abraham, born 12 October 1730 in Fairfield, died six weeks later on 26 November 1730 in that same town; and then another Abraham, great-grandfather of Jay Gould, born 10 May 1732 in Fairfield, died 25 April 1777 in battle at Ridgefield.

9. Elizabeth Burr was born 7 April 1732 in Fairfield, Conn. She died in that same town on 5 September 1815. Like her husband and most of her offspring, Elizabeth rests in the Old Burying Ground, Fairfield. The Gold/Gould genealogy for this generation is fairly laced with Burr connections. Abraham's eldest brother, Daniel, married Elizabeth's cousin, Grace Burr. Another brother, Abel, married yet another of Fairfield's numerous Burrs, Ellen, the daughter of Samuel Burr.

10. Abigail Gould was born in October 1755 in Fairfield. She died in that same town on 2 November 1795. Elizabeth Gould was born 5 February 1759 in Fairfield. She died on 19 June 1812 in that same town. Deborah Gould was born on 25 July 1763 in Fairfield. She died on 28 July 1785 in that same town. Anna Gould was born 5 December 1768 in Fairfield. She died at Hobart, Delaware County, N.Y., on 2 October 1821.

11. This Hezekiah Gould was born 9 December 1756 in Fairfield. He died 30 October 1785 in New York Harbor, drowned. John Burr Gould was born 7 April 1761 in Fairfield. He died at sea on 2 January 1781. Daniel Gould was born 16 July 1776 in Fairfield. He died on 28 December 1796 in a storm off the coast of France.

12. Jason Gould was born in 1774 in Fairfield. He died in that same town on 17 June 1810. In 1840 his son, Captain John Gould, owner of a fleet of schooners plying the China trade, replaced Elizabeth Burr Gold's rebuilt Revolutionary-era house with a large mansion. This he eventually left to his two daughters, the last of the Fairfield Goulds, both of whom died in 1908 without issue. From 1908 through 1977 the Jason Gould mansion, known as the Gould Homestead, provided, under the terms of the daughters' wills, a free vacation home to working women of Fairfield County. For more information on the Goulds of Fairfield see the Gould Family Papers at the Fairfield Historical Society. The elaborate home of Elizabeth Burr Gould's cousin Thaddeus Burr still stands in Fairfield, where it is owned by the town and administered by the Fairfield Historical Society.

13. Abraham Gould, Jr., was born 28 January 1766 in Fairfield, Conn. He died 23 December 1823 in Roxbury, N.Y.

14. W. W. Munsell. *History of Delaware County, 1757–1880.* New York: W. W. Munsell. 1880. 72.

15. Jay Gould. *History of Delaware County and the Border Wars of New York.* Roxbury: Keeny & Gould. 1856. 102.

16. Abraham Gould, Jr.'s sister Anna Gould, together with her husband, Eben Silliman, followed Abraham to West Settlement in 1810.

17. *New York Times.* 15 August 1888.

18. John Burroughs. *Pepacton and Other Sketches*. Boston: Houghton Mifflin. 1881. iv.

19. All told, the children of Captain Abraham Gould, Jr., and Anna Osborne were Elizabeth Gould, born 17 May 1790 and died 11 July 1867; John Burr Gould, born 16 October 1792, died 16 March 1866; Anna Gould, born 20 August 1794, died 9 March 1828; Abigail Gould, born 20 June 1796, for whom no death information is available; Polly Gould, born 27 April 1798, died 3 April 1811; Katherine Gould, born 20 March 1800, died 25 January 1837; Jason Gould, born 23 November 1802, died 3 January 1864; Abraham Gould III, born 3 November 1803, died 9 May 1812; Daniel Gould, born 4 October 1801, died 3 January 1849; and Sally Gould, born 13 September 1810, died 25 November 1824. Daniel, who appears to have reverted to the old "Gold" spelling of the family name, achieved some success as deputy clerk of the Assembly of New York State, and later, at the time of his death, deputy clerk of the U.S. House of Representatives. Jason Gould emigrated to Canada, where many of his descendants still reside.

20. Robert Irving Warshow. *Jay Gould, or The Story of a Fortune*. New York: Greenberg. 1928. 18.

21. Born 5 January 1775, Jay Gould's maternal grandfather, Alexander Taylor More, died 11 March 1854. He is buried, along with a vast collection of Mores, in the so-called Old Cemetery at Grand Gorge, near the Methodist Church.

CHAPTER 3: TWELVE LINES BY NIGHT

1. Clara Barrus. *John Burroughs: Boy and Man*. Garden City: Doubleday. Page. 1920. 97.

2. Sarah Gould Northrop. "Reminiscences." HGS.

3. Anna Gould Howe. "Mrs. Howe's Reminiscences." HGS.

4. Sarah Gould Northrop. "Reminiscences." HGS.

5. Anna Gould Howe. "Mrs. Howe's Reminiscences." HGS.

6. Eliza's maiden name is unknown. The Gould family marker at the Old School Baptist Church Cemetery indicates her passing on 19 December 1841 at the age of 29.

7. Sarah Gould Northrop. "Reminiscences." HGS.

8. Jay Gould. *History of Delaware County and the Border Wars of New York*. 115.

9. Ibid. 120. Additional detail for the tale as presented here come from Hamilton Burhans's manuscript memoir "Early Days of Jay Gould." HGS.

10. Elizabeth Gould Palen to Anna Palen. 25 March 1893. HGS.

11. John Burroughs. *My Boyhood*. Garden City: Doubleday, Page. 1922. 40.

12. Clara Barrus. *John Burroughs: Boy and Man*. 211.

13. John Burroughs. *My Boyhood*. 37.

CHAPTER 4: A DELIBERATE STUDENT

1. Sarah Gould Northrop. "Reminiscences." HGS.

2. Hamilton Burhans. "Early Days of Jay Gould." HGS.

3. Sarah Gould Northrop. "Reminiscences." HGS.

4. Anna Gould Howe. "Mrs. Howe's Reminiscences." HGS.

5. John Burroughs. *My Boyhood*. 114.

6. Jay Gould. *History of Delaware County and the Borders Wars of New York*. 320.

7. Frank Allaben. "Was Jay Gould Misjudged?" *National Magazine* (May-June 1893). 84–85.

8. Robert Irving Warshow. *Jay Gould, or The Story of a Fortune*. 22–24. This same essay is also published in *Angell v. Gould*. New York: Privately printed. 1897. *Angell v. Gould* contains extensive research underwritten by the Gould family in the late 1890s in order to combat a spurious paternity suit involving Jay Gould. In connection with their investigation, Gould lawyers and detectives scoured the Catskills interviewing old friends, acquaintances and relatives of Jay Gould, gathering written testimony and archival documents from same.

9. Sarah Gould Northrop. "Reminiscences." HGS.

10. The building that housed the tin shop still stands on Roxbury's Main Street and is now the Enderlin Gallery. Around the corner, on Vega Mountain Road, the house involved in the swap still stands as well.

11. Sarah Gould to Edmund More. 29 February 1852. HGS.

12. Abel Crosby to Helen Gould. 20 May 1897. HGS.

13. Sarah Gould Northrop. "Reminiscences." HGS.

14. *Report of the Committee of the Senate upon the Relations Between Labor and Capital, Senate Hearings*. 41st Congress, Vol. 28. 1063–1064.

15. *Angell v. Gould*. 163–167.

16. Ibid. 177.

17. Ibid. 185–189.

18. Ibid. 642–645.

19. J. W. McLaury. "Reminiscences Composed for Miss Helen Gould." HGS.

CHAPTER 5: RAT TRAPS AND MAPS

1. *Angell v. Gould*. 767.

2. At Union College, Rice was a student of the eminent Eliphalet Nott (1773–1866).

3. *Angell v. Gould*. 769.

4. Anna Gould Howe. "Mrs. Howe's Reminiscences." HGS.

5. Abel Crosby to Helen Gould. 20 May 1897. HGS.

6. Robert Irving Warshow. *Jay Gould, or The Story of a Fortune*. 34.

7. Jay Gould to John D. Champlin. 6 December 1853. HGS.

8. Robert Irving Warshow. *Jay Gould, or The Story of a Fortune*. 31.

9. *Angell v. Gould*. 702.

10. Ibid. 480.

11. Ibid. 226–227.

12. Ibid. 776–784.

13. Ibid. 660–669.

14. Polly Gould to Sarah Gould Northrop. 22 July 1854. HGS. One of the few existing copies of Jay Gould's Delaware County map is today on permanent display in the stairwell leading to the basement of the Jay Gould Memorial Reformed Church in Roxbury, N.Y.

15. Polly Gould to Sarah Gould Northrop. 2 August 1854. HGS.

16. *Angell v. Gould.* 669–671.

17. Ibid. 456.

18. Ibid. 672–676.

19. "The Railroad King Dead." *Stamford (New York) Mirror.* 5 December 1892. *Stamford Mirror* publisher and editor, Simon Champion, who had previously served the same role for the *Bloomville Mirror,* quoted much from their early correspondence in his version of Jay's obituary.

CHAPTER 6: HIDDEN MYSTERIES OF LIFE AND DEATH

1. Jay Gould to Simon D. Champion. 29 March 1855. HGS.

2. John Burroughs to Helen Gould Shepard. 7 July 1914. HGS.

3. Numerous previous biographies of Jay Gould cite this gentleman's name as *McLany.* Existing records of the old Roxbury Academy, as well as contemporary newspaper pieces, the Dartmouth College archives, and McLaury's own memoir in the Helen Gould Shepard Papers at the New-York Historical Society suggest otherwise.

4. J. W. McLaury. "Reminiscences Composed for Miss Helen Gould." HGS.

5. Alice Northrop Snow and Henry Nicholas Snow. *The Story of Helen Gould.* 61.

6. Hamilton Burhans. "Early Days of Jay Gould." HGS.

7. *Angell v. Gould.* 300.

8. Ibid. 295.

9. Elizabeth Gould Palen to Anna Palen. 25 March 1893. HGS.

10. Hamilton Burhans. "Early Days of Jay Gould." 6. HGS.

11. *Angell v. Gould.* 641.

12. Clara Barrus. *John Burroughs: Boy and Man.* 210.

13. John Burroughs. *My Boyhood.* 39.

14. J. W. McLaury. "Reminiscences Composed for Miss Helen Gould." HGS.

CHAPTER 7: GOULDSBORO

1. For details on the Palen family and their tanning history, see D. S. Rotenstein. "Tanbark Tycoons: Palen Family Sullivan County, New York Tanneries, 1832–1871." *The Hudson Valley Regional Review.* 15(2). 1–42.

2. Although many different trees contain tannic acid in their bark, the variety of tannic acid found in the inner bark layers of the hemlock are preferred, as they leave pelts with a distinctive and highly desirable red tint.

3. Henry David Thoreau. Manuscript journal, 1844. Thoreau Papers. J. Pierpont Morgan Library.

4. The best overall consideration of Zadock Pratt and his career is to be found in Patricia E. Millen's *Bare Trees: Zadock Pratt, Master Tanner and the Story of What Happened to the Catskill Mountain Forests* (Hensonville, N.Y.: Black Dome Press, 1995). See also *Chronological Biography of the Hon. Zadock Pratt of Prattsville, NY* (New York: Shoe and Leather Press, 1868), which was largely dictated by Pratt himself.

5. Zadock Pratt. "Autobiographical Outline." Zadock Pratt Papers, New-York Historical Society. (Hereafter *ZPP*.)

6. Patricia E. Millen. *Bare Trees*. 15.

7. Carolyn Bennett to Edward J. Renehan, Jr. 19 March 2004.

8. J. W. McLaury. "Reminiscences Composed for Miss Helen Gould." HGS.

9. Elizabeth Gould Palen to Anne Palen. 25 March 1893. HGS.

10. Peter Van Amburgh to Helen Gould. 19 December 1892. HGS.

11. Jay Gould to Zadock Pratt. 5 September 1856. Ingersoll. The original site of the tannery is not in today's Gouldsboro, but 9.5 miles to the west, in the village now known as Thornhurst.

CHAPTER 8: OUR BEST FRIENDS TELL US OUR FAULTS

1. Jay Gould to Zadock Pratt. 24 December 1856. Ingersoll.

2. Jay Gould to Zadock Pratt. 15 August 1857. Ingersoll.

3. Jay Gould to Zadock Pratt. 12 October 1857. Ingersoll.

4. Zadock Pratt. "Autobiographical Outline." ZPP.

5. Jay Gould to John Burr Gould. 7 August 1857. HGS.

6. Jay Gould to Hamilton Burhans. 26 September 1857. HGS.

7. Jay Gould to Zadock Pratt. 22 October 1857. Ingersoll.

8. Jay Gould to Zadock Pratt. 11 December 1857. ZPP.

9. Jay Gould to Zadock Pratt. 15 September 1858. Ingersoll.

10. *Report of the Committee of the Senate upon the Relations Between Labor and Capital,* Senate Hearings. 41st Congress, Vol. 28. 1065.

11. Maury Klein was the first to document this clearly in his *Life and Legend of Jay Gould.*

12. Charles R. Geisst. *Wall Street: A History.* New York: Oxford University Press. 1997. 58. That Geisst got this and other Jay Gould–related stories so wrong is remarkable given that Maury Klein, the first to get most of the history of Gould's tanning enterprises right, published his *Life and Legend of Jay Gould* in 1986, a full eleven years before Geisst's volume appeared. Klein's seminal book is not referenced in Geisst's pages. My discussion of the Pratt & Gould dissolution, though differing from Klein's in a few details, derives in a large way from Klein's investigations of the 1980s.

13. Robert I. Warshow. *Jay Gould, or The Story of a Fortune.* 46–47.

14. Richard O'Connor. *Gould's Millions.* 28.

15. Robert I. Warshow. *Jay Gould, or The Story of a Fortune.* 46.

16. Statement of John Gardner. HGS.

17. These figures comes from Hamilton Burhans's manuscript memoir, "Early Days of Jay Gould," in the Helen Gould Shepard Papers at the New York Historical Society. Burhans must have gotten the numbers from Gould himself near the time of the actual event.

CHAPTER 9: CUNNING LUNACY

1. Gideon Lee's papers are in the Clements Library of the University of Michigan, Ann Arbor.

2. Charles M. Leupp's papers are to be found in the Leupp Family Collection, Alexander Library, Rutgers University, New Brunswick, N.J. (Hereafter *LFP.*)

3. David W. Lee to Thomas G. Clemson. 11 October 1859. Thomas G. Clemson Papers, Clemson University Library. (Hereafter *Clemson.*)

4. "Local Accounts of the Gouldsboro War." HGS.

5. Jay Gould to Leupp & Company. 13 June 1859. LFP.

6. David W. Lee to Thomas G. Clemson. 11 October 1859. Clemson.

7. *New York Herald.* 7 October 1859.

8. Laura Leupp to Mrs. Thomas B. Clemson. 6 October 1859. Clemson.

9. *New York Herald.* 7 October 1859.

10. As with so many other aspects of Gould's business history, the first writer to get the essential facts of Jay's relations with Leupp & Company set down on paper correctly was Maury Klein in his 1986 volume *The Life and Legend of Jay Gould.* My analysis of the Leupp-Gould affair, like my analysis of the Pratt & Gould dissolution, draws in large part from Klein's version of the story, although differing in some details.

11. Richard O'Connor. *Gould's Millions.* 30–31.

12. Charles R. Geisst. *Wall Street: A History.* 59. Once again, it needs to be pointed out that Geisst was writing eleven years after Klein documented the true story in his *Life and Legend of Jay Gould.*

13. Edwin Hoyt. *The Goulds.* New York: Weybright & Talley. 1969. 23.

14. *New York Tribune.* 16 September 1889.

CHAPTER 10: THE GOULDSBORO WAR

1. Somewhat ironically, given Evarts's representation of Andrew Johnson during the 1868 impeachment proceedings, Evarts's great-grandson Archibald Cox served as the first special prosecutor named in the Watergate investigation a little more than one hundred years later.

2. Jay Gould to Leupp & Company. 27 December 1859. LFP.

3. Jay Gould to Sarah Gould Northrop. 11 January 1860. HGS.

4. R. G. Dun & Company. Collection, Baker Library, Harvard Graduate School of Business Administration. (Hereafter *Dun.*) New York City branch files. 193:655.

5. Leupp & Company to Jay Gould. 29 December 1859. HGS.

6. *New York Herald.* 16 March 1860.

7. Dun. New York City branch files. 193:660.

8. Ibid. 347:737.

9. The Henry Davenport Northrop who wrote the potboiler biography *Jay Gould, The Wizard of Wall Street* (Philadelphia: National Publishing, 1892) was no relation.

10. *Angell v. Gould*. 145.

11. Sarah Gould Northrop to Taylor More. 6 October 1860. HGS.

12. Jay Gould to James Oliver. 5 November 1860. HGS.

CHAPTER 11: A PARTICULAR FUTURE

1. *New York Tribune*. 17 October 1860.

2. Bouck White. *The Book of Daniel Drew*. New York: Doubleday. 1910. 160.

3. Edwin G. Burrows and Mike Wallace. *Gotham: A History of New York to 1895*. New York: Oxford University Press. 1999. 869.

4. Henry Clews. *Fifty Years on Wall Street*. 176.

5. Dun. New York City branch files, 201:420. David Murray's *Centennial History of Delaware County: 1797–1897* mistakenly identifies Jay Gould's father-in-law as the David S. Miller who resided in the Catskill Mountains town of Greenville during the mid and late 1800s. This is incorrect.

6. In 1847 the Rutland & Washington Railroad was granted a charter by the Vermont legislature to build a line from Rutland to the New York State line. Two years later, the Troy & Rutland Railroad was granted permission by the New York State Legislature to build a line from Troy to Poultney, Vt., and to connect to the Rutland & Washington. The two lines merged shortly thereafter.

7. *Report of the Committee of the Senate upon the Relations Between Labor and Capital, Senate Hearings*. 41st Congress, Vol. 28. 1063–1064.

8. William A. Cormier. *The Back Shop and Other Tales: Railroading in Salem, New York, 1852–1995*. Salem, N.Y.: Privately published. 1995. 8–9.

9. Ibid. 10.

10. Jay Gould to Helen Miller Gould. 27 January 1864. Jay Gould Papers, Library of Congress. (Hereafter *JGP.*)

11. Jay Gould to Helen Miller Gould. 20 February 1864. JGP.

12. Jay Gould to Sarah Northrop. 13 May 1864. HGS.

13. Anna Gould Hough. "Mrs. Howe's Reminiscences." HGS.

14. Jay Gould to Sarah Northrop. 26 April 1865. JGP.

15. Elizabeth Gould Palen to Anna Palen. 25 March 1893. HGS.

16. Jay Gould to William T. Hart. 27 June 1865. JGP.

17. Jay Gould to James Oliver. 2 September 1865. Kansas State Historical Society. (Hereafter *Kansas.*)

CHAPTER 12: MUCH TO GET DONE

1. *Angell v. Gould*. 272.

2. Richard O'Connor. *Gould's Millions*. 47.

3. Jay Gould to William T. Hart. 15 September 1865. JGP.

4. Henry Clews. *Fifty Years on Wall Street*. 243.

5. Sarah Gould Northrop. "Reminiscences." HGS.

6. *Report of the Committee of the Senate upon the Relations Between Labor and Capital, Senate Hearings*. 41st Congress, Vol. 28. 1064–1065.

CHAPTER 13: THE ERIE IN CHAINS

1. *American Railroad Journal*. 30 September 1865. 942.

2. *American Railroad Journal*. 9 June 1867. 555.

3. *New York Tribune*. 23 March 1878.

4. Maury Klein. *The Life and Legend of Jay Gould*. 78.

5. *New York Herald*. 9 October 1867.

CHAPTER 14: BLUE FIRE

1. Robert H. Fuller. *Jubilee Jim: The Life of Colonel James Fisk Jr*. New York: Macmillan. 1928. 127. Although an invaluable source on Fisk, Fuller's volume must be read—and facts taken it from it—very selectively. Shaping his narrative in the form of a biographical novel rather than a straight biography, Fuller took it upon himself to re-create many scenes and conversations to which he could not possibly have been privy. On the other hand, he likewise retold numerous scenes in Fisk's life, most notably, Fisk's childhood and adventures during the Erie Wars, to which he was himself a witness. In these matters, Fuller's account is nearly always the most informed and eloquent available.

2. *New York Sun*. 8 January 1872.

3. Robert H. Fuller. *Jubilee Jim*. 4.

4. Ibid. 14.

5. Clara Morris. *Life on the Stage*. New York: McClure, Phillips. 1901. 308.

6. R. W. McAlpine. *The Life and Times of Col. James Fisk Jr*. New York: New York Book Company. 1872. 24.

7. Robert H. Fuller. *Jubilee Jim*. 62.

8. Ibid. 68.

9. R. W. McAlpine. *The Life and Times of Col. James Fisk Jr*. 45.

10. W. A. Swanberg. *Jim Fisk: The Career of an Improbable Rascal*. New York: Scribner's. 1959. 21.

11. Ibid. 26.

12. Robert H. Fuller. *Jubilee Jim*. 119.

CHAPTER 15: THE ABUSED MACHINERY OF THE LAW

1. *New York Herald*. 12 October 1867.

2. *New York Herald*. 5 February 1868.

3. William W. Fowler. *Ten Years on Wall Street*. 496.

4. Charles Francis Adams and Henry Adams. *Chapters of Erie*. 16.

5. *American Law Review*. October 1868.

6. Charles Francis Adams and Henry Adams. *Chapters of Erie*. 159.

7. Allen Nevins and Milton H. Thomas, eds. *The Diary of George Templeton Strong*, Vol. 4. 264.

8. *New York Herald*. 6 March 1868.

9. *American Law Review*. October 1868.

10. Charles Francis Adams and Henry Adams. *Chapters of Erie*. 29.

11. Edmund Clarence Stedman. *The New York Stock Exchange*. New York: Stock Exchange Historical Press. 1905. 202.

12. William W. Fowler. *Ten Years on Wall Street*. 500—501.

13. Maury Klein. *The Life and Legend of Jay Gould*. 82.

14. William W. Fowler. *Ten Years on Wall Street*. 501.

15. *New York Herald*. 14 March 1868.

16. Robert H. Fuller. *Jubilee Jim*. 145.

17. *Harper's Weekly*. 17 April 1868.

CHAPTER 16: AN ALMIGHTY ROBBERY

1. Robert H. Fuller. *Jubilee Jim*. 147–148.

2. *New York Herald*. 15 March 1868.

3. Edward Harold Mott. *Between the Ocean and the Lakes: The Story of Erie*. New York: Collins. 1899. 156.

4. *New York Herald*. 17 March 1868.

5. William C. Fowler. *Ten Years on Wall Street*. 505.

6. Charles Francis Adams and Henry Adams. *Chapters of Erie*. 57.

7. *New York Herald*. 12 March 1868.

8. Robert H. Fuller. *Jubilee Jim*. 161.

9. William C. Fowler. *Ten Years on Wall Street*. 507.

10. *New York Herald*. 21 March 1868.

11. Charles Francis Adams and Henry Adams. *Chapters of Erie*. 49.

12. *New York Herald*. 3 April 1868.

13. Charles Francis Adams and Henry Adams. *Chapters of Erie*. 51.

14. Ibid. 50.

15. *Commercial and Financial Chronicle*. 7 March 1868.

16. *New York Herald*. 21 March 1868.

17. *New York Herald*. 21 April 1868.

18. Henry Clews. *Fifty Years on Wall Street*. 134.

19. Edward Harold Mott. *Between the Ocean and the Lakes: The Story of Erie*. 161.

CHAPTER 17: SCOUNDRELS

1. Some of Morosini's collection is today at the Metropolitan Museum of Art, bequeathed by his daughter Giulia in 1932.

2. George Crouch. *Erie Under Gould and Fisk*. New York: Privately printed. 1870.

3. *Commercial and Financial Chronicle*. 31 October 1868.

4. Charles Francis Adams and Henry Adams. *Chapters of Erie.* 41.
5. W. A. Swanberg. *Jim Fisk: The Career of an Improbable Rascal.* 74.
6. Henry Clews. *Fifty Years on Wall Street.* 141.
7. *Commercial and Financial Chronicle.* 14 November 1868.
8. Edward Harold Mott. *Between the Ocean and the Lakes.* 161.
9. *New York Times.* 19 November 1868.
10. *New York Times.* 23 November 1868.
11. For bonds, par value is the amount that the issuer agrees to pay at the maturity date, also called the maturity value or face value of a bond. For common stocks, par value is an arbitrary dollar amount assigned to each share by the company's charter. Par value has little or no impact on the actual market value of a security. However, it is important in the case of preferred stocks and bonds, since the preferred dividend and interest are often based on the par value assigned to each issue. For example, an 8 percent bond is a promise to pay that percentage of the bond's par value (100 percent of face value) annually.
12. *New York Herald.* 18 November 1868.
13. *New York Herald.* 19 November 1868.
14. *Commercial and Financial Chronicle.* 31 October 1868.
15. Henry Clews. *Fifty Years on Wall Street.* 144.
16. Charles Francis Adams and Henry Adams. *Chapters of Erie.* 71.

CHAPTER 18: THE SMARTEST MAN IN AMERICA

1. *New York Herald.* 26 November 1868.
2. Charles Francis Adams and Henry Adams. *Chapters of Erie.* 84.
3. Henry Clews. *Fifty Years on Wall Street.* 140.
4. *New York Times.* 7 December 1868.
5. *New York Times.* 11 December 1868.
6. Richard O'Connor. *Gould's Millions.* 64.
7. The Grand Opera House stood until 1960, ending its days as an RKO Theater. In the years between Jay Gould and demolition, the theater hosted performances by such greats as George M. Cohan and Fred Astaire.
8. *New York Herald.* 18 January 1871.
9. Meade Minnigerode. *Certain Rich Men.* New York: Putnam. 1927. 201.
10. Allen Nevins and Milton H. Thomas, eds. *The Diary of George Templeton Strong*, Vol. 4. 340.
11. W. A. Swanberg. *Jim Fisk.* 117.
12. William W. Fowler. *Ten Years on Wall Street.* 483.
13. Maury Klein. *The Life and Legend of Jay Gould.* 92.
14. The rare and highly collectible volume, with Jay's bookplate from the period intact, recently came up for sale at an auction in New York.
15. W. A. Swanberg. *Jim Fisk.* 95.
16. *Albany Evening Journal.* 7 August 1869.
17. *Albany Argus.* 7 August 1869.
18. John Steele Gordon. *The Scarlet Woman of Wall Street.* 246.

19. *Leslie's Illustrated Newspaper.* 28 August 1869.

20. *New York Times.* 8 September 1869.

CHAPTER 19: WHERE THE WOODBINE TWINETH

1. Abel Rathbone Corbin was no relation to John Burr Gould's third wife or any of the other Roxbury Corbins.

2. *House Report Number 31.* 41st Congress, 2nd Session. 148. (Hereafter *House Report 31.*)

3. Maury Klein. *The Life and Legend of Jay Gould.* 101.

4. *House Report 31.* 3.

5. Ibid. 246.

6. Ibid. 249.

7. Maury Klein. *The Life and Legend of Jay Gould.* 103.

8. *New York Times.* 25 August 1869.

9. W. A. Swanberg. *Jim Fisk.* 136.

10. Maury Klein. *The Life and Legend of Jay Gould.* 104.

11. *House Report 31.* 35.

12. W. A. Swanberg. *Jim Fisk.* 137.

13. *New York Tribune.* 15 September 1869.

14. *House Report 31.* 252.

15. Ibid. 174.

16. Maury Klein. *The Life and Legend of Jay Gould.* 105.

17. William W. Fowler. *Twenty Years of Inside Life in Wall Street.* New York: Orange Judd Company. 1880. 528.

18. *New York World.* 16 September 1869.

19. *New York Herald.* 16 September 1869.

20. Gold closed at 136 5/8 on Friday, 17 September, having gained only a single point for the week despite earnest buying by Gould, Fisk, and their associates.

21. *New York Sun.* 20 September 1869.

22. *New York Times.* 22 September 1869.

23. W. A. Swanberg. *Jim Fisk.* 142.

24. *House Report 31.* 257.

25. *New York Evening Mail.* 23 September 1869.

26. Maury Klein. *The Life and Legend of Jay Gould.* 108.

27. *New York Times.* 24 September 1869.

28. *House Report 31.* 259.

29. *New York Times.* 24 September 1869.

30. Maury Klein. *The Life and Legend of Jay Gould.* 110.

31. *Philadelphia Ledger.* 25 September 1869.

32. W. A. Swanberg. *Jim Fisk.* 154.

33. *House Report 31.* 217.

34. Ibid. 221.

35. Maury Klein. *The Life and Legend of Jay Gould.* 115.

CHAPTER 20: MEPHISTOPHELES

1. Gustavus Myers. *History of the Great American Fortunes*. New York: Modern Library. 1936. 542. The first edition of this work, published in three volumes, appeared in 1909.

2. Maury Klein. *The Life and Legend of Jay Gould*. 3.

3. *New York Times*. 3 October 1869.

4. Richard O'Connor. *Gould's Millions*. 169.

5. *New York Tribune*. 28 September 1869.

6. The most recent published version of this spurious tale is in Denis T. Lynch. *The Wild Seventies*. Westport, Conn.: Praeger. 1971.

7. *New York Tribune*. 9 October 1869.

8. *House Report 31*. 272.

9. Maury Klein. *The Life and Legend of Jay Gould*. 4.

10. *Railroad Times* (London). 12 July 1884.

CHAPTER 21: A SPECIAL STINKPOT

1. Giovanni P. Morosini. "Memoir of Jay Gould." HGS.

2. Maury Klein. *The Life and Legend of Jay Gould*. 96.

3. *Report of the Committee of the Senate upon the Relations Between Labor and Capital, Senate Hearings*. 42nd Congress, Vol. 26. 962–964.

4. *Heath et al. v. Erie Railway Co. et al.,* Circuit Court S.D., N.Y., 27 April 1871. Bill of Complaint.

5. *New York Herald*. 12 May 1870.

6. *New York Herald*. 14 May 1870.

7. *New York Herald*. 28 May 1870.

8. *Punchinello*, Vol. 1, No. 6. 7 May 1870.

9. The Millers lived a block away at 518 Fifth Avenue.

10. Edwin P. Hoyt. *The Goulds: A Social History*. 65.

11. *New York Herald*. 20 August 1870.

12. *New York Herald*. 22 August 1870.

13. *New York Herald*. 18 January 1871.

14. R. W. McAlpine. *The Life and Times of Col. James Fisk Jr*. 329.

15. *New York Herald*. 18 January 1872.

16. W. A. Swanberg. *Jim Fisk*. 209.

17. Rising through the ranks from private to general during the course of the war, the youthful Barlow became known as the "boy general."

18. Erie Protective Committee broadside dated December 1871. New-York Historical Society.

19. George Templeton Strong. Diary. 12 November 1871.

20. Every one of the thirty-nine letters was published in its entirety by the *New York Herald* on 14 January 1872, a week after Fisk's death.

21. E. H. Mott. *Between the Ocean and the Lakes*. 421.

22. Perhaps appropriately, given its macabre association with Fisk, a significant portion of the former Grand Central Hotel (later named the Southern and then the Broadway Central, to avoid confusion with Vanderbilt's Grand Central Station) ended its days in the twentieth century as the Mercer Arts Center, a conglomeration of performance spaces large and small. (The balance of the building, sadly, became a welfare hotel.) The entire place collapsed suddenly in August 1973, killing four people and injuring many others. The building was located on Broadway at Third Street.

23. W. A. Swanberg. *Jim Fisk*. 271.

24. R. W. McAlpine. *The Life and Times of Col. James Fisk, Jr.* 356.

25. Ibid. 336.

26. The will Fisk devised in collaboration with Field and Shearman named Eben Jordan as executor and left Fisk's entire estate (save for annuity payments of $3,000 a year for his father, stepmother, half sister, and several other dependents) to Lucy.

27. W. A. Swanberg. *Jim Fisk*. 274.

28. *New York Herald*. 8 January 1872.

29. *New York Sun*. 10 January 1872.

30. *New York Herald*. 8 January 1872.

31. *New York Sun*. 9 January 1872.

32. *New York Herald*. 8 January 1872.

33. *New York Herald*. 9 January 1872.

34. Maury Klein. *The Life and Legend of Jay Gould*. 122.

35. Robert H. Fuller. *Jubilee Jim*. 564.

36. *New York Herald*. 21 January 1872.

37. *New York Sun*. 12 March 1872.

CHAPTER 22: A DAMNED VILLAIN

1. E. H. Mott. *Between the Ocean and the Lakes*. 180.

2. Ibid. 191.

3. Ibid. 192.

4. *New York Herald*. 1 March 1872.

5. John Steele Gordon. *The Scarlet Woman of Wall Street*. 348.

6. E. H. Mott. *Between the Ocean and the Lakes*. 186–187.

7. *New York Sun*. 12 March 1872.

8. *New York Herald*. 27 September 1872.

9. *New York Herald*. 25 November 1872.

10. E. H. Mott. *Between the Ocean and the Lakes*. 210.

11. *New York Sun*. 25 November 1872.

12. *New York Times*. 13 December 1872.

13. *New York Herald*. 13 November 1872.

14. *New York Commercial Advertiser*. 26 November 1872.

15. *New York Sun*. 27 November 1872.

16. E. H. Mott. *Between the Ocean and the Lakes*. 212.

CHAPTER 23: TRANSCONTINENTAL

1. Alice Northrop Snow and Henry Nicholas Snow. *The Story of Helen Gould*. 67.
2. Chauncey M. Depew. *My Memories of Eighty Years*. 216.
3. Bingham Duncan. *Whitelaw Reid: Journalist, Politician, Diplomat*. Athens: University of Georgia Press. 1975. 49.
4. *New York Times*. 12 May 1873.
5. Alice Northrop Snow and Henry Nicholas Snow. *The Story of Helen Gould*. 182.
6. Henry Davenport Northrop. *The Life and Achievements of Jay Gould*. Philadelphia: National Publishing Company. 1892. 316.
7. Jay Gould to William Ward. 9 January 1874. JGP.
8. *New York World*. 1 September 1873.
9. W. T. Stead. "Jay Gould." *American Review of Reviews*. January 1893.
10. Jay Gould to Thurlow Weed. 5 May 1875. Thurlow Weed Papers, University of Rochester. (Hereafter *Weed*.)
11. Maury Klein. *The Life and Legend of Jay Gould*. 138.
12. *House of Representatives Reports*. 42nd Congress, 3rd Session. Nos. 77 and 78.
13. United States Pacific Railway Commission, Testimony, Executive Document No. 51. Senate, 50th Congress, 1st Session. 1887. 446.
14. Julius Grodinsky. *Jay Gould: His Business Career, 1867–1892*. 118.
15. Maury Klein. *The Life and Legend of Jay Gould*. 140.
16. Grenville M. Dodge to Nate Dodge. 27 March 1874. Grenville M. Dodge Papers, Western Historical Collection, Denver Public Library. (Hereafter *Dodge*.)
17. Giovanni P. Morosini. "Memoir of Jay Gould." HGS.
18. Julius Grodinsky. *Jay Gould: His Business Career, 1867–1892*. 127.
19. Maury Klein. *The Life and Legend of Jay Gould*. 144.

CHAPTER 24: CONSOLIDATION

1. *New York Times*. 27 October 1877.
2. Jay Gould to Sidney Dillon. 12 September 1875. JGP.
3. "Memories of the Old West." *Lincoln State Journal*. 2 March 1930.
4. Gould's overall attention to the details of the running of the UP is documented in the large collection of his letters to Silas Clark. These are in the collection of Jay's great-grandson, Kingdon Gould, Jr., at the latter's summer home in Arkville, N.Y. Duplicates of these items are housed in the Maury Klein Papers, University of Rhode Island, Kingston. Klein gave an in-depth description of Gould's interaction with Clark in his *Life and Legend of Jay Gould*.
5. *New York World*. 23 July 1877.
6. Maury Klein. *The Life and Legend of Jay Gould*. 157.
7. Frank Lewis Dyer and Thomas Commerford Martin. *Edison: His Life and Inventions*. New York: Harper Brothers. 1929. 217.
8. Jay Gould to Oliver Ames. 24 and 25 July 1875. Union Pacific Railroad Archives. (Hereafter *UP*.)

9. Alexandra Villard de Borchgrave and John Cullen. *Villard: The Life and Times of an American Titan.* New York: Doubleday. 2001. 301.

10. Henry Villard to William J. Endicott. 6 April 1877. Letterbook 16, Private Correspondence. Villard Papers, Baker Library, Harvard Business School. (Hereafter *Villard.*)

11. United States Pacific Railway Commission, Testimony, Executive Document No. 51. Senate, 50th Congress, 1st Session. 1887. 450.

12. Henry Villard to Fanny Villard. 25 June 1878. Villard.

13. Richard O'Connor. *Gould's Millions.* 109.

14. Alexandra Villard de Borchgrave and John Cullen. *Villard: The Life and Times of an American Titan.* 302.

15. Julius Grodinsky. *Jay Gould: His Business Career, 1867–1892.* 179.

16. Alexander D. Noyes. *Forty Years of American Finance.* 127.

17. Robert Riegel. *The Story of the Western Railroads.* 223.

18. Richard Cleghorn Overton. *Burlington Route: A History of the Burlington Lines.* New York: Knopf. 1965. 131.

19. Richard Cleghorn Overton. *Gulf to Rockies.* Houston: University of Texas Press. 1956. 220.

20. *New York World.* 2 July 1887.

CHAPTER 25: EVERYTHING BUT A GOOD NAME

1. Alice Northrop Snow and Henry Nicholas Snow. *The Story of Helen Gould.* 115.

2. Ibid. 119.

3. Ibid. 118.

4. Maury Klein. *The Life and Legend of Jay Gould.* 214.

5. *New York Times.* 8 August 1883.

6. Edwin P. Hoyt. *The Goulds: A Social History.* 72.

7. *Dramatic Mirror.* 23 October 1883.

8. In 1900, Nellie Gould donated 230 orchids and palms from Lyndhurst to the new conservatory at the New York Botanical Garden, where descendants of Jay's collection still reside.

9. Alice Northrop Snow and Henry Nicholas Snow. *The Story of Helen Gould.* 276.

10. Ibid. 282.

11. Giovanni P. Morosini. "Memoir of Jay Gould." HGS.

12. The best source for details on the architecture and furnishings of 579 Fifth Avenue, now demolished, is the catalog developed for the sale of the home's furnishings a few years after the death of Nellie Gould. *The Entire Contents of 579 Fifth Avenue [The Jay Gould House]. Superb Paintings Including Masters of the Barbizon School.* New York: Kendel Galleries at Gimbel Brothers. 1942.

13. Sarah Gould Northrop. "Reminiscences." HGS.

14. Alice Northrop Snow. *The Story of Helen Gould.* 22. Alice did not acknowledge her father's suicide in her book, only his death. Confirmation of Northrop's

suicide, however, comes from numerous sources, including the memoirs of Gould's sisters Sarah and Bettie.

15. Ibid. 37.

16. Jay Gould to Helen "Nellie" Gould. 21 March 1882. HGS.

17. Giovanni P. Morosini. "Memoir of Jay Gould." HGS.

CHAPTER 26: WIRES AND ELS

1. John Murray Forbes to Fred Ames. 8 September 1880. Burlington Railroad Archives, Newberry Library, Chicago. (Hereafter *Burlington*.)

2. *New York Times*. 3 December 1879.

3. New York *Stockholder*. 20 August 1878.

4. *New York Times*. 19 February 1875.

5. Maury Klein. *The Life and Legend of Jay Gould*. 490.

6. The date of incorporation was 15 May 1879.

7. *New York Herald*. 2 September 1879.

8. *New York Herald*. 16 February 1881.

9. *New York Tribune*. 10 March 1881.

10. Richard O'Connor. *Gould's Millions*. 132.

11. Edward Bok. *The Americanization of Edward Bok*. New York: Scribner's. 1921. 67–68.

12. James McGurrin. *Bourke Cockran: A Free Lance in Politics*. New York: Scribner's. 1948. 39–40.

13. *New York World*. 15 June 1881.

14. *Philadelphia North American*. 30 June 1881.

15. *New York World*. 23 September 1881.

16. Richard O'Connor. *Gould's Millions*. 141.

17. *New York Times*. 27 December 1881.

CHAPTER 27: AMBITION SATISFIED

1. *Commercial and Financial Chronicle*. 25 March 1882.

2. *New York Tribune*. 7 May 1882.

3. *New York Sun*. 3 October 1882.

4. *New York Times*. 8 April 1883.

5. *Omaha Herald*. 3 February 1884.

6. Alice Northrop Snow and Henry Nicholas Snow. *The Story of Helen Gould*. 320.

7. *New York Times*. 9 July 1887.

8. *New York Times*. 8 July 1887.

9. *New York Sun*. 18 August 1883.

10. Francis Carpenter, ed. *Carp's Washington*. New York: McGraw Hill. 1960. 72.

11. Richard O'Connor. *Gould's Millions*. 195.

12. "Memphis Under Quarantine Rule." *Frank Leslie's Illustrated Paper*. 20 September 1879.

13. *New York Times*. 8 July 1890.

14. Alice Northop Snow and Henry Nicholas Snow. *The Story of Helen Gould*. 204–205.

15. Ibid. 354.

16. *New York Times*. 15 September 1886.

17. Alice Northrop Snow and Henry Nicholas Snow. *The Story of Helen Gould*. 354.

18. *New York Times*. 30 October 1887.

19. *New York Herald*. 30 October 1887.

20. Jay Gould's private railroad car *Atalanta* is today on display at Jefferson, Texas.

21. *New York Times*. 11 June 1888.

22. *New York Tribune*. 24 July 1888.

23. *New York World*. 17 July 1888. (Reprinted from the *Philadelphia Times*.)

24. *New York Times*. 3 August 1888.

25. Alice Northrop Snow and Henry Nicholas Snow. *The Story of Helen Gould*. 169.

26. Helen [Nellie] Gould to Helen [Ellie] Gould. 2 September 1888. HGS.

27. Alice Northrop Snow and Henry Nicholas Snow. *The Story of Helen Gould*. 165.

28. Ibid. 165–166.

29. Charles Francis Adams. "Memorabilia 1888–1893." 23 December 1888, 13 January 1889, 24 February 1889. Charles Francis Adams Papers, Massachusetts Historical Society. (Hereafter *CFA*.)

30. Maury Klein. *The Life and Legend of Jay Gould*. 440.

31. *New York World*. 14 January 1889.

32. *New York World*. 10 and 11 February 1889.

33. Maury Klein. *The Life and Legend of Jay Gould*. 432.

34. *New York Herald*. 7 November 1890.

35. *New York Herald*. 9 November 1890.

36. Charles Francis Adams to R. S. Grant. 13 November 1890. UP.

37. Charles Francis Adams. "Memorabilia 1888–1893." 23 November 1890. CFA.

38. *New York World*. 27 November 1890.

39. *New York Times*. 2 October 1891.

40. *New York World*. 3 October 1891.

41. Charles Francis Adams. Memorabilia 1888–1893. 13 November 1891. CFA.

42. *New York World*. 5 December 1891.

43. *New York World*. 27 February 1892.

44. Alice Northrop Snow and Henry Nicholas Snow. *The Story of Helen Gould*. 193.

45. *London Standard*. 3 December 1892.

46. *London News*. 3 December 1892.

47. *New York Times*. 3 December 1892.

48. *New York* Herald. 5 December 1892.

EPILOGUE: THE GOULDS AFTER JAY

1. See Abram's obituary in the *Washington County (New York) Post*, 30 June 1899. Abram died at the residence of his brother-in-law, Fredeick Kegler, in Salem, N.Y. Today he lies buried in Evergreen Cemetery, Salem, beside his wife, Sophia.

2. The estate is today the campus of Georgian Court College.

3. See George Brodrick's obituary published in the *London Daily Telegraph* on 27 February 2004, some two months after his death on 12 December 2003.

4. "Gould Foundation Carries Out Work of Its Founder." *Journals News, Rockland County.* 29 September 2001.

5. Frank Miller Gould's daughter Marianne married a man named John Wright McDonough, heir to a Texas ironworks. The couple settled in Galveston, Texas, where Marianne had a son in 1947. Marianne's brother, Edwin Gould III, established the New York investment firm of Edwin Gould & Company. Like his father and grandfather before him, this Edwin spent a great deal of time out-of-doors (hunting and deep-sea fishing) while also focusing his professional energies on sound investments that built his fortune safely.

6. For an amusing portrait of Helen Gould Shepard as a mother, see Celeste Andrews Seton's affectionately critical memoir entitled *Helen Gould Was My Mother-in-Law.* New York: Thomas Y. Crowell. 1953.

7. Marie Ernest Paul Boniface de Castellane. *How I Discovered America.* New York: Scribner's. 1924. 14–15.

8. Frank Jay Gould's daughter Dorothy married a Swiss baron, Roland Graffenried de Villars, in early 1925. Their marriage ended in divorce but produced two children (Roland, born 1925, and Dorothy, born 1927). During the early 1940s, while visiting Cuba, the elder Dorothy met her second husband, Archibald Burns, a Mexican national born of Scottish parents. She and Burns married in 1944 and settled in Mexico City, where she died in 1969. Dorothy's daughter wed Alexandre Borgia in 1947; the marriage ended in divorce without issue. Nothing is known of the son Roland. As well, nothing more is known of Frank's other daughter, Helen, except that she married into the Marat family of France and lived in Lausanne, Switzerland, at the time of her father's death.

A&GW (Atlantic & Great Western
    Railway)
  Erie's link with, 97–98
  McHenry manipulates Erie stock,
    207
  McHenry vs. Gould, 192–193
  in receivership, 115
A&P (Atlantic & Pacific) wire,
    235–239
A&S (Albany & Susquehanna)
    Railroad, 155–156
Academy of Music, 151
Adams, Charles Francis, Jr.
  1887 Interstate Commerce Act and,
    288–290
  controls UP in 1884, 277–278
  loses control of UP in 1890,
    291–293
  Pacific Railroad Ring and, 221
Adams, Henry, 3
Albany & Susquehanna (A&S)
    Railroad, 155–156
Albany Academy, 26–28
Albany County survey, 31–35
Alley, John B., 64–65
American Refrigerator Transit, 291

American Telegraph & Cable
    Company, 265
American Union, 262
The Americanization of Edward Bok
    (Bok), 265
Ames, Frederick, 224, 231
Ames, Oakes
  joins board of Pacific Mail, 226
  UP Railroad and, 220–222
  view of Gould, 224
Ames, Oliver, 220–222, 231
Archer, O.H.P., 204
Atalanta steamship, 276, 284
Atkins, Elisha, 224
Atlantic & Great Western Railway. *see*
    A&GW (Atlantic & Great
    Western Railway)
Atlantic & Pacific (A&P) wire,
    235–239
Automatic Telegraph Company, 236,
    238

B&O (Baltimore & Ohio), 239
Balcom, Judge Ransom, 120–121
Bardwell House Hotel, 83
Baring Brothers, 292

Barlow, Francis Channing, 193
Barnard, Judge George C.
  A&S Railroad war, 157–159
  Erie's British shareholders and, 188
  first Erie War, 118–119, 122–124,
    129–130, 133–134
  Gould allies himself with, 140–141,
    149–150
  Gould's bear trap and, 144–145
  impeachment of, 209
Battle of the Little Big Horn, 233–234
Beach, William A., 196
Beechwood Seminary, 17, 22–24
Belden, William, 112, 121–122,
  175–176
Belmont, August, 143–144, 149–150
Bennett, James Gordon, Jr., 2, 134, 146
BH&E (Boston, Hartford and Erie)
  Railroad, 98–99, 115–116, 136
Big Horn Mountains, 234
Bigelow, John, 168
Bixbey, B. H., 196
Black Friday
  actions against Gould, 216
  Capitol Hill testimony, 280
  overview of, 175–178
  reputation ruined after, 179–183,
    218
Black Horse Cavalry, 132
Blaine, James G., 222, 277
Bloomville Mirror, 32
"blue-jays", 291
Bok, Edwin, 265–266
Boston, Hartford and Erie (BH&E)
  Railroad, 98–99, 115–116, 136
Bouton, Orrin Rice, 30–31, 43, 294
Boutwell, George S.
  Black Friday, 176
  events leading to Black Friday,
    169–174
  Gould meets President Grant, 163
  US Treasury gold policy and, 167
Bradley, Esther (great-great
  grandmother), 8–9
Brink, Peter, 26

Brodrick, George, 301
Brodrick, George St. Johns, 301
Brodrick, Guinevere, 301
Brodrick, Jane, 301
Bronx Community College, 303
Brooklyn Oil, 195
Brooks, James, 222
Broughman's Theater, 151
Burhans, Edward
  disagreement with Gould, 40–41
  Gould demonized about, 181
  Gould helps in romance, 40
  Gould's employment with, 37–38,
    40–41
Burhans, Hamilton, 24, 40–41, 43
Burhans, Maria, 40
Burhans, Mary More, 30–31
Burlington Route (Overton, Richard
  C.), 245
Burr, Aaron, Sr., 8
Burr, Sarah, 8
Burroughs, John
  boyhood friendship with Gould,
    17–19, 38
  dropping relationship with Gould,
    42
  Roxbury and, 10
Burt, Joseph L., 188–189
Butterfield, Daniel
  as assistant federal treasurer, 167
  Black Friday and, 175–176, 181–182
  Gould's no-margin gold account for,
    166
Buttonwood Agreement, 76

Calico Indians, 16–17
California Gold Rush, 102
Camp Woody Crest, 302
Canadensis, 45–46
Cardozo, Judge Albert, 150, 208–209
Carpenter, Frank, 279–280
Carr, Robert E., 240, 242
Castellane, Boni, Jr., 307
Castellane, Elizabeth, 307

Castellane, Ernest Paul Boniface
   "Boni" de, 306–307
Castellane, Yvonne (Patenotre), 307
Castle Erie, 152–154, 213
Castle Gould, 306
Catherwood, Robert B., 167
Catskills, 45–46
Cavanagh's Restaurant, 152
Central Branch Line, 243
Central Construction Company, 262
Central Pacific, 226–227, 244
Champion, Simon D., 32, 34–36, 43
Champlin, John, 32–33, 42
Chapin, W. O., 171
Chapters of Erie (Adams), 117,
   119–120, 122
Charles M. Leupp & Company. *see*
   Leupp, Charles M.
Cherokee Cottage, 302
Chicago & Northwestern Railroad,
   210–212
Chicago Fire, 196
*The Chronological Biography of the Hon.
   Zaddock Pratt*, 58–60
Church, Walter S., 156–157
Civil War
   Erie helped by, 97
   gold prices following, 164
   Gould's feelings on, 79, 86
   James Fisk and, 108–110
   profiteers in, 56
   Vanderbilt's railroad strategy, 102
   Wall Street and, 76–77
   Western Union and, 235
Clark, Horace F., 222–223
Clark, Silas H.H., 230–234, 249, 291
Classification Act, 186–187, 204, 207
Clemmons, Viola Kathrine, 305–306
Clerke, T. W., 130
Clews, Henry, 80
Cockran, W. Bourke, 266
Colfax, Schuyler, 221–222
Colorado Central Line, 240
Commercial and Financial Chronicle
   on Erie bonds, 140

   on Erie settlement, 134
   on Gould's money market
      manipulations, 142
   on success of Erie manipulation,
      146–147
Connor, Washington, 277
Convoy railroad car, 229–230
Cook, William F., 65
Corbin, Abel Rathbone
   economic policy influenced by, 168
   gold market exit of, 170
   Gould bribes, 166, 173
   Grant meets Gould through,
      163–164
   Grant sees self-interest of, 171
Corbin, Mary Ann, 15
Corbin, Virginia Paine (Grant), 163
Corse & Pratt, 53–55, 57
Courter, Charles, 157–158
Credit Mobilier of America, 221–222
Cropsey, Jasper, 61
Crosby, Abel, 31, 43
Crouch, George, 204–205

Dark Shadows, 251
Dater & Company, 80–81, 91–92
Davies, Judge Henry E., 149–150
Davis, Andrew Jackson, 251
Davis, Noah, 149
De Borchgrave, Alexandra Villard,
   241
Delaware & Hudson Canal Company,
   160
Delaware & Lackawanna Railroad,
   50
Delaware County survey, 32–35
Delevan House Hotel, 133
Democratic Party, 79, 186
Denver Pacific Line, 242, 244
Depew, Chauncey, 216
Develin, John E., 132–133
Dexter, Gordon, 224
Dickerman, Beda, 48
Dickerman, Esther, 48
Dillon, John F., 270

Dillon, Sidney
  as board member of Pacific Mail,
    226
  buying and converting UP bonds,
    220
  death of, 294
  as president of UP, 225, 231, 292
  relationship with Gould, 224, 249
Dix, John A., 205–207
Dominion Telegraph of Canada, 262
down-renters, 16–17
Drew, Daniel
  Erie stock manipulation, 96, 112,
    117–118, 208
  Erie stock manipulation and demise
    of, 141–147
  feelings about Gould, 179
  Northwestern Railroad and,
    210–211
  puritanical values of, 132
  unscrupulous reputation of, 77–78
  Vanderbilt vs., 100, 103, 120–124,
    127–131, 135
Drexel, Anthony, 310
Drexel, Marjorie (Gould), 310
Du Bois, J.A., 71
Duncan, William Butler, 203–204
Durant, Thomas Clark, 220–221
Dutcher, John B., 132

Eaton, D. B., 149
Eckert, Thomas T., 235–237, 262, 264
Edison, Thomas A., 236–239
Edwin Gould Foundation, 302–303
Erie Bill, 132–137
Erie Railroad, 141–147
  A&S war, 155–161
  adding ferryboats, 155
  background of, 95–96
  BH&E and, 98–99
  British suit against, 188–189,
    192–196, 203–207
  Drew ousted and reinstated, 103
  Duane and West office, 208
  Erie Bill, 132–137

executive board fights against
    Vanderbilt, 127–132
executive board uses law against
    Vanderbilt, 118–125
framing British and Wall Street
    shareholders, 141–147
framing British shareholders,
    187–188, 192–196
Gould settles all claims against him,
    212–213
Grand Opera House offices,
    152–154
near-bankruptcy of, 96–98
Northwestern Railroad strategy,
    210–212
Vanderbilt tries to corner shares,
    116–118
Vanderbilt/Eldridge compete for
    control, 98–99, 102–103, 115–116
Eldridge, John
  competing for control of Erie,
    98–99, 102–103
  Erie agenda of, 115–116
  as Erie president, 103
  Vanderbilt and Drew settlement, 135
elevated railroads, 266–273
Empire State survey bill, 26–27, 31
Evarts, William M.
  background of, 69
  running for U.S. senator, 89
  settling Leupp estate, 70
Everett House Hotel, 73–74

ferryboat business, 155
Field Codes, 120
Field, Cyrus, 163
  attempt to control Manhattan
    Elevated, 278–279
  death of, 294
  as president of New York Elevated,
    267–268
Field, David Dudley
  death of James Fisk, 197
  Field Codes, 120
  Gould's relationship with, 249

Fifth Avenue Hotel, 110, 111
Fifty Years on Wall Street (Clews), 75
Finley, Nellie. *see* Gould, Helen
    "Nellie" (daughter)
Fisk & Belden, 112, 121–122, 175–176
Fisk, James, Jr., 105–113
    boyhood of, 106–107
    Chicago Fire and, 196
    comparing Gould with, 113
    creating "Thugs of Erie", 149
    creating Fisk & Belden, 112
    death of, 195–199
    Edward Stokes and, 191–192,
        195–199
    Goulding deal, 111
    Grand Opera House partnership,
        152–154
    Josie Mansfield and, 131–132,
        191–192, 195–199
    marriage of, 107, 197–200
    peddling business of, 107–108
    side businesses of, 151
    start on Wall Street, 108–112
Fisk, James, Jr., Erie
    A&S Railroad war, 157–160
    abusing law as board member,
        115–125
    bear trap with Gould, 141–147
    as board member, 141
    federal suit vs., 188–189
    fight against Vanderbilt, 127–137,
        150–151
    New York Central and, 185
    resigning as vice-
        president/controller, 203–204
    stock manipulation, 140
Fisk, James, Jr., gold purchases
    Black Friday. *see* Black Friday
    bulling up price, 171–173
    Gould's move to stealth bear,
        173–174
Fisk, James, Jr., personal qualities
    benevolence of, 105, 109–110,
        153–154, 198, 200

    as consummate salesman and
        promoter, 108–109
    hard-work and intelligence of, 113
    love of military, 188–189, 191
    managing press, 127–128
    memorials after death of, 200–201
    physical appearance of, 112–113
    popularity of, 105–106, 190
    self-indulgence, exhibitionism,
        112–113, 152–153
    as swindler, 105, 146
    theatrical nature of, 112
Fisk, James, Sr., 106–107, 109
Fisk, Lucy (Moore)
    death of James Fisk, 197–199
    estate of James Fisk, 200
    marriage to James Fisk, 107–108
    relationship to Fanny Harrod, 112
Fisk, Minna, 106–107
Florence Gould Garden, 309
Forbes, John Murray, 259–261
Forty Years of American Finance (Noyes),
    245
Fowler, William, 122–123
Frank Jay Gould Pine Grove, 309
Franklin Telegraph Company, 235
Frogtown, 45
Frost, Charles, 83–84
Fuller, Robert H., 105, 106, 108–109
Fulton, Robert, 101
Furlow Lake, 6

Gardner, John, 60
Garfield, James A.
    Gould's gold speculations and, 167
    Gould's testimony on Black Friday,
        181–182
    murder of, 253–254
    UP Railroad and, 221–222
Garrett, John W., 239, 262
Garrison, Commodore, 267
Garrison, William, 267
George C. Barnard locomotive, 141
Gibbons v. Ogden, 101
Gibbons, Thomas, 101

Gilbert, Judge, 121–122
Glenelg Country School, 311
Godfrey, Cyrus O., 232
Gold Exchange Bank
    Black Friday, 176–177
    function of, 165
    setting up, 164
gold speculations, 163–178
    Black Friday, 175–183, 216, 218, 280
    bulling up price, 171–173
    commodity price manipulations and,
        165–166
    federal policy manipulations and,
        166–170
    first speculation in, 164–165
    Gold Exchange Bank and, 164–165,
        176–177
    reputation ruined, 178, 179–183
    as stealth bear, 173–174
    Tenth National Bank and, 168, 176
    Ulysses S. Grant and, 163–164,
        166–170
Gold, Abraham (great-grandfather),
    7–9
gold, Civil War and, 164–165
Gold, Esther (Bradley), great-great
    grandmother, 8–9
Gold, family name change to Gould, 9
Gold, Nathan (ancestor), 8
Gold, Nathan, Jr. (ancestor), 8
Gold, Samuel (great-great
    grandfather), 8
Gold, Talcott (cousin), 9
Gould Library, 303
Gould, Abraham (grandfather), 9–10
Gould, Abram (brother), 231
    birth of, 15
    farm work and, 23
    Gould educates, 74
    Gould's homes open to, 254
    inheritance from Gould, 298
    Missouri Pacific career of, 278
    Union Pacific career of, 232–233
Gould, Anna (daughter)
    father's estate, 297–298

    at Gould's death, 4
    life after death of father, 306–308
    personality of, 257–258
Gould, Anna (Osborne), grandmother,
    9, 10
Gould, Anna (sister)
    on birth of Jay, 14
    closeness with Frank, 308
    on Gould driving her to church, 31
    on Gould's health problems at
        eighteen, 35–37
    Gould's help to, 85–86
    Gould's reunion with, 74
    inheritance from Gould, 298
    on mother, 15
    suit vs. George for mismanagement,
        299–300
Gould, Bettie (sister)
    on the aftermath of Civil War, 86
    on Gould's friendship with John
        Burroughs, 17–19
    Gould's homes open to, 254
    inheritance from Gould, 298
    marriage of, 74
    on Pratt's Kingston speech, 49
    as schoolteacher, 23
Gould, Captain John, 30
Gould, Daniel (ancestor), 9
Gould, Edith, 310
Gould, Edith (Kingdon), daughter-in-
    law
    children of, 309–310
    death of, 300
    George's marriage to, 282–283
    indulgence and ostentatiousness of,
        299
Gould, Edwin (son)
    good works after father's death,
        301–303
    Gould grooming to take over for
        him, 291
    at Gould's death, 4
    inheritance from Gould, 298
    personality of, 257
    wedding of, 295

Gould, Edwin, Jr. (grandchild), 301
Gould, Eliza, 15
Gould, family name changed to, 9
Gould, Florence (La Caze), 308–309
Gould, Frank (son)
  at Gould's death, 4
  Gould's estate, 297–298
  interest in Roxbury, 305
  life after death of father, 308–309
  suit against George for
    mismanagement, 299–300
Gould, Frank Miller (grandchild),
  301–303
Gould, George Jay (son)
  birth of, 85
  death of, 300
  estate of, 300–301
  financial talents of, 286
  Furrow Lake and, 6
  Gould grooming to take over for
    him, 291
  at Gould's death, 4
  as guardian of Anna and Frank, 298,
    306–307
  indulgence and ostentatiousness of,
    299
  lives led by children of, 309–310
  marriage to actress, 282–283
  mismanagement as chief executor of
    estate, 297–300
  mistress of, 300–301
  personality of, 256–257
  second set of children of, 300–301
  Washington Connor & Company
    career, 277
Gould, George Jay III, 310
Gould, George, Jr. (grandchild), 302,
  310
Gould, Gloria, 310
Gould, Helen "Nellie" (daughter)
  after mother's death, 290
  birth of, 154
  good works after father's death,
    303–305
  at Gould's death, 4

  as guardian of Anna and Frank, 298
  marriage of, 305
  personality of, 257
Gould, Helen (Kelly), 308
Gould, Helen Day "Ellie" (Miller), wife
  birth of George, 85
  death of, 4, 288
  declining health of, 283–284, 286
  friendship with Sarah, 93
  Gould's devotion to, 84–85
  marriage, 80–82
  on Ninth Regiment of N.Y. Militia,
    191
  personalities of her children,
    256–258
  qualities of, 248–250
  reaction to George marrying actress,
    282–283
  trip abroad, 284
Gould, Hezekiah (ancestor), 9
Gould, Howard (son)
  at Gould's death, 4
  loss of fortune after death of father,
    305–306
  personality of, 257
Gould, Jay, 43–44
  ancestors of, 7–12
  birth, 7, 12, 14
  boyhood friendship with John
    Burroughs, 17–19
  death of, 1–6, 293–296
  death of Ellie, 4, 288–290
  education at Albany Academy,
    26–29
  education at Beechwood, 17, 22–24
  education at Hobart, 22
  education in mathematics, 21, 24
  father of, 74, 93
  Fifth Avenue homes, 189, 254
  gives up plans for college education,
    27–31
  Gouldsboro named after, 51
  health problems at eighteen, 34–37
  last will and testament, 297–298
  Lyndhurst and, 251–254

marriage to Ellie, 80–82
mother, 11–15
mousetrap incident, 29–30
near murder of Russell Sage and,
   293
old friends of, 43–44
personalities of children, 256–258
reputation after the Gouldsboro war,
   73
reputation as ingenious scoundrel,
   146
threats to life of, 253–254
trip abroad, 284
tuberculosis and, 284–285
wrestling skills, 18
Gould, Jay, career on Wall Street,
   80–82
  1887 Interstate Commerce Act
   conference, 288–290
  A&S Railroad, 155–161
  brokerage firm partnerships, 210
  Chicago & Northwestern Railroad,
   210–212
  cross-country railroads, 240–245,
   259–261
  elevated railroads. *see* elevated
   railroads
  elusive retirement of, 275–277
  Erie Railroad. *see* Gould, Jay, Erie
   Railroad
  financial worth in 1882, 275
  gold. *see* gold speculations
  Grand Opera House partnership,
   152–154
  learning tricks, 74, 82
  mentoring relationships, 265–266
  as modern day-trader, 91–92
  prosperity at time of father's death,
   92–94
  Russell Sage collaboration. *see* Sage,
   Russell
  Rutland & Washington Railroad,
   82–84, 86–87
  self-start as curb wheeler, 78–79
  Smith, Gould & Martin, 95

Tenth National Bank, 168
testimonies on Capitol Hill, 280
Troy, Salem & Rutland Railroad, 87,
   89–90
Union Pacific Railroad. *see* UP
   (Union Pacific) Railroad
Watson and Erie Railroad case, 208,
   212–213
Western Union, 235–239, 262–265
would-be corporate raiders vs.,
   277–282
Gould, Jay, careers before Wall Street
  Burhans store, 37–38, 40–41
  Leupp and Lee partnership. *see*
   Leupp, Charles M.
  as orator, 38–39
  Shakersville Road Corporation, 33
  survey teacher at Roxbury Academy,
   38, 40
  surveying, 24–27, 31–35
  writing *History of Delaware County*,
   34, 41–42
  Zaddock Pratt partnership. *see* Pratt
   & Gould
Gould, Jay, Erie Railroad
  A&S war, 155–161
  abusing law as board member,
   118–125
  adding ferryboats, 155
  British suit against, 188–189,
   192–196, 203–207
  brokerage firms, 209–212
  case against, 211–213
  coup within board, 204–206
  Drew manipulates stock in, 208
  ferryboat business, 155
  fights against Vanderbilt, 127–131,
   150–151, 185
  framing British and Wall Street
   shareholders, 140–147
  framing British shareholders,
   187–188, 192–196
  framing Erie Bill, 132–137
  Gould's fortune after ouster from,
   207

Gould's lucrative side deals, 185–186

Grand Opera House offices, 152–154

lucrative side deals, 185–186

Morosini and. *see* Morosini, Giovanni Pertinax

politics within, 186, 194

problems of, 187, 192

settles all claims against him, 212–213

Gould, Jay, personal qualities

as "smartest man in America", 151

ambition, 14, 31, 91

antisocial, 189–191, 250

attitude toward press, 127–128, 217–218

awareness of the shortness of life, 39

benevolence through anonymity, 281–282

collecting antique classic works, 154

devotion to family, 84–87, 190–191, 248–249, 251–258

disdain of alcohol, 27–28

economy of action, 90–91

editorials after death, 296

enemies of, 91

even temperedness of, 14

exhaustion of, 248, 275

financial abilities of, 14

friends of, 91

on honesty, 22–23

inscrutability, 260

James Fisk compared to, 113, 153–154, 190–191

love of children, 84

love of flowers, 2, 154, 189, 252–253, 285–286

mentoring relationships, 265–266, 281

as orator, 38–39

physical appearance, 12, 153, 212, 247

poor health of, 34–35, 90, 275, 284–286, 293–296

problem-solving skills, 18–19, 33, 153

public view of, 245

relationship to Abram, 231

religious beliefs, 27–28, 39

reputation after death, 1–6

reputation as villain, 178–183, 218–219

romantic arts, 40

seriousness, 127

as socially uncouth youth, 80

tenacity, 21

Gould, Jay Fred (nephew), 231, 254

Gould, Jay II (second grandchild)

birth of, 287

inheritance from Gould, 298

as tennis champion, 309

WW I service of, 302

Gould, John Burr (father)

alcoholism in later life of, 27, 32

on birth of George, 85

birth, marriage and children of, 10–12

failing health of, 32–33

funeral of, 92–93

political beliefs of, 15–17

Roxbury tin business and, 23–24

tragic life of, 13–15

Gould, Kingdon (first grandchild)

birth of, 283

happy life of, 309

WW I enlistment of, 302

Gould, Kingdon, Jr., 310–311

Gould, Marjorie, 310

Gould, Mary, 311

Gould, Mary (More), mother, 11–12, 14–15

Gould, Mary (Polly), sister

death of, 37

engagement of, 23

on Gould's failing health at eighteen, 34–35

illness of, 30

Gould, Mary Ann (Corbin), 15

Gould, Maugham Carter, 310

Gould, Nancy (sister), 15
Gould, Sarah (sister), 255
  friendship with Ellie, 93
  on Gould refusing father's tin
    business, 24
  on Gould's feelings about his father,
    74
  Gould's health at wedding of, 34
  inheritance from Gould, 298
  leather manufacturing business of
    husband, 45–46
  memories of Gould's childhood,
    15–16
  memories of mother, 14
  as schoolteacher, 23
Gould, Sarah Cantine (Shrady),
    daughter-in-law, 295, 301
Gould, Sophia (Kegler), 231
Gould, Viola Kathrine (Clemmons),
    305–306
Gould, Vivien, 309–310
Goulding, John, 111
The Goulds (Hoyt), 81
Gouldsboro Manufacturing Company,
    70
Gouldsboro tannery, 53–58. *see also*
    Leupp, Charles M.
Gouldsboro War, 72–73
Gouldsboro, naming of, 51
Grand Opera House
  overview of, 152–154
  purchasing with Erie money, 187
  The Twelve Temptations extravaganza,
    189
Grant, Julia, 163, 171, 173
Grant, President Ulysses S.
  discussion with Boutwell, 174
  Gould cultivating, 79, 163–164
  Gould's gold speculations and,
    166–170
Gray, Amos, 39
Greeley, Carlos S., 240–241
Greeley, Horace, 170, 217
Green, Norvin, 264
greenhouse, 252–253

Grimm, Suzi, 48
Guggenheim, Daniel, 306

Hall, George, 204
Hamilton, Alexander, 76
Hardenbergh land grant, 16
Harlem Railroad, 100
Harley, Nancy, 11
Harriman, Oliver, 306
Harriman, W.H., 299
Harrington, George, 236–237
Harris, Clara, 89
Harris, Hamilton, 33, 89–90, 132–134
Harris, Ira, 89
Harrod, Fanny, 107, 112, 200
Hart, William T., 87, 89
Hayes, Nehemiah, 9
Heath, Robert A., 188
Heath, William, 119, 175–176
Herter Brothers, 254
Hilton, John, 204
History of Delaware County (Munsell), 9
*History of Delaware County and the
    Border Wars of New York* (Gould)
  on Calico Indian down-renters,
    16–17
  fire destroys manuscript, 41
  on migration of ancestors, 9–10
  the writing of, 34
Hodgskin, James B., 169
Hopkins, A. L., 270, 290
Horsley-Beresford, Arthur George
    Marcus Douglas de la Poer,
    309–310
Horsley-Beresford, John Graham Hope
    de la Poer, 309–310
Horsley-Beresford, Marcus Hugh de la
    Poer, 309–310
Horsley-Beresford, Vivien (Gould),
    309–310
Hough, Reverend Asahel
  Anna's marriage to, 31
  Gould's help to, 85
  Gould's reunion with, 74
Howard Association, 281

Hudson River Association, 101
Hudson River Railroad, 100
Hughes, Elizabeth, 84
Huntington, Collis P.
    Central Pacific line and, 220
    compromise with Gould, 260–261
    dealings with Gould, 226–227

ICRA (Interstate Commerce Railway
    Association), 289–290
Ingersoll, Julia (Pratt), 6, 58
Ingersoll, Robert G., 264
Ingraham, Daniel P., 121
Inman, Israel, 9
International Jazz Festival, 309
Interstate Commerce Act of 1887,
    288–290
Interstate Commerce Railway
    Association (ICRA), 289–290
Iowa pool, 241

Jaffray, Edward, 294
James Fisk, Jr. ferryboat, 155
Jay Cooke and Company, 224
Jay Gould ferryboat, 155
Jekyll Island, 301
Jerome, Leonard, 56
Jordan, Eben D., 108–112, 115–116
Jordan, Marsh & Company, 108–110
Juan-les-Pins, 308–309
judges, Supreme Court, 119–120

Kansas & Texas (Katy) Line, 259–260
Kansas City Line, 243
Kansas Pacific Railroad, 236
    amalgamating rival lines, 244
    American Union agreements with,
        262
    Gould achieves control of, 240–243
    Villard's investment in, 241
Katy (Kansas & Texas) Line, 259–260
Keene, James R., 180
Kegler, Sophia, 231
Keith & Barton Ranch, 230–231

Kelly, Helen, 308
Kelso, John, 198
Key, Philip Barton, 194
Kimber, Arthur, 170
Kingdon, Edith. *see* Gould, Edith
    (Kingdon), daughter-in-law
Kirkside Park, 304
Klein, Maury, 182–183, 186
Knights of Labor, 280–281

La Caze, Florence, 308–309
La Force, Elizabeth, 307
La Force, Jean Comte de Caumont,
    307
Lake Shore & Michigan Southern
    Line
    UP Railroad and, 222–223
    Vanderbilt purchases, 178
    William H. Vanderbilt heads, 233
Lane, Frederick
    coup within Erie board and,
        204–205
    on Erie executive committee, 137,
        141
    Gould's bear trap and, 144–145
Lawlor, Frank, 131
leather tanning business
    with Leupp and Lee. *see* Leupp,
        Charles M.
    Northrop-Palen speculation, 45–46
    Pratt & Gould partnership. *see* Pratt
        & Gould
    Tunkhannock tannery, 86
Lee, David W.
    background of, 61
    Gouldsboro War and, 73–74
    Leupp and, 60
    Leupp's estate and, 69–73
    Leupp's mental state, 62, 64–65
    Leupp's suicide, 65–67
    partnership with Gould, 62–65
Legal Tender Act, 164
Leupp, Charles M.
    background of, 61–62
    estate settlement of, 69–74

Gould's first dealings with, 57
mental state of, 62–64
newspapers demonize Gould about,
    180
partnership with Gould, 60, 62–65
suicide of, 65–67
Leupp, Laura, 65–66
Lincoln, Abraham, 86, 89–90
Lockwood & Company, 178
Lockwood, Legrand, 178
Lombard Street, 141–142
Lord and Burnham, 252
Love Letters, 311
Loveland, William A.H., 240
Lynch, Tommy, 205–206, 213
Lyndhurst, 251–254, 285–286,
    287–288, 307–308

MacCracken, Henry Mitchell, 5
MacIntosh, Charles, 144–145
Mangold, Ferdinand, 252, 287–288,
    304
Manhattan Elevated
  creation of, 268
  George Gould loses, 299
  Gould ruins Cyrus Field's play to
      control, 278–279
  Gould's plan to purchase, 269–273
Manhattan's Swamp, 55
Mansfield, Helen Josephine "Josie"
  after death of James Fisk, 199
  appearances at Grand Opera House,
      153
  on death of James Fisk, 198
  Edward Stokes affair and, 191–192,
      194–196
  as mistress of James Fisk, 131–132,
      141
Margaretville Hospital, 304
Marrin, Joseph J., 216–217
Marsh, Nathaniel, 96
Martin, Henry, 95
Masterson, Hugh, 128–129
McComb, Henry, 222
McHenry, James

Gould's confrontation with, 192–196
Gould's move to corner gold and,
    165
manipulating Erie stock for
    A&GW, 207
organizing coup within Erie board,
    204–207
McLaury, John William, 38–39, 43
McQuade, James, 160
Merritt, George, 251
Metropolitan Elevated
  Gould's bear campaigns, 269–272
  growth of, 267–268
  Manhattan Elevated and, 268–269
Metropolitan Opera House, 250–251
Mexican-American War, 56
Michigan Central Line, 239
Miller, Daniel S., Jr., 140, 192
Miller, Helen Day. *see* Gould, Helen
    Day "Ellie" (Miller), wife
Mills, Darius Ogden, 254
Mills, Ogden, 1
Miniegerode, Meade, 152
Missouri Pacific
  1884 depression and, 278
  Abram Gould with, 278
  expanding web of, 259
  George Gould loses, 299
  Gould acquires, 243–245
  strike at, 280–281
money market, 142
Moore, Lucy. *see* Fisk, Lucy (Moore)
More family (mother's kin), 5–6, 11–12
More, Alexander Taylor (grandfather)
  alcoholism of, 27
  marriage of, 11
  mousetrap invention of, 29–30,
      180–181
More, Betty Taylor, 11
More, Iram (cousin)
  mousetrap incident, 29–30
  relationship with Gould, 26–27
  surveying with Gould, 32
More, John, 11
More, Mary (mother), 11–12, 14–15

More, Nancy (Harley), 11
Moresville, 11
Morgan, J. P., 160
Morosini, Giovanni Pertinax
  elopement of daughter, 282
  Gould, Smith & Martin account
    books and, 213
  on Gould's anonymous charitable
    giving, 219
  Gould's bear trap and, 144–145
  Gould's relationship with, 139–141,
    249, 286, 290–291
  Washington Connor & Company
    employment, 277
Morris, Clara, 107
Morton, Levi P., 203–204, 235
Mount Vernon Ladies Association, 282
Munn, John P., 284–285, 294–295
Myers, Gustavus, 179–183

Narragansett Steamship Company,
  151, 163
National Banking Act, 164
National Trust for Historic
  Preservation, 307–308
New Jersey Southern Railroad, 225
New York Central, 100, 128–129, 233
New York Commercial Advertiser, 212
New York Elevated
  Gould gains influence on, 270
  Gould's bear campaigns against,
    269–272
  growth of, 267–268
  Manhattan Elevated and, 268–269
New York General Railroad Act of
  1850, 82–83
New York Herald
  on Black Friday, 180–181
  on Erie's enormous safe, 152
  on federal gold policy, 172
  on Gould's burial, 5
  on Gould's death, 2
  on mousetrap incident, 29–30
  on questionable Erie manipulation,
    121, 146

  on Western Union consolidation,
    263
New York Loan and Improvement
  Company, 267–268
New York State Agricultural Society,
  34, 41
New York Stock Exchange. *see also*
  Wall Street
  "Gold Room", 164
  evolution of, 76
  financial panic of 1873–1875 and,
    224–225
New York Sun, 222
New York Times
  on Black Friday, 175, 180
  on genius of Gould, 260
  on gold conspiracy, 170
  on Gould and Fisk evening score
    with Vanderbilt, 151
  on Gould's burial, 5
  on Gould's death, 2
  on Marrin attack against Gould, 217
New York Tribune
  on 1860 Wall Street, 75
  on Black Friday, 180
  on gold conspiracy, 170
  on Marrin attack against Gould, 217
  on Western Union consolidation,
    263
New York University (NYU), 303,
  308–309
New York World
  Gould condemns railroad strikers,
    233
  Gould purchases, 217–218, 259
  Gould sells, 275
  on Gould's death, 2–3, 4
  on Gould's grief at death of Ellie, 4
  on Gould's love of railroads, 246
  on Manhattan Elevated, 269
Ninth Regiment, N.Y. Militia,
  188–189, 191, 198–199
Norcross, Henry, 293
Northern Pacific Railroad,
  224

Northrop, Alice (niece)
on Cyrus Field, 278–279
on Gould helping her family, 255–256
on Gould not being afraid to die, 295
on Gould's attitude toward press, 217–218
on Gould's burial, 5
on Gould's personal qualities, 247–248
marriage of, 304
on Russell Sage's cheapness, 215
on threats to family's safety, 253–254
Northrop, George W. (brother-in-law)
Jay's health at wedding of, 34
leather manufacturing business of, 45–46
suicide of, 255–256
Northrop, Howard Gould (nephew), 37
Northrop, Ida (niece), 255
Northrop, Reid (nephew), 255, 291
Northrop, Sarah, 255–256
Norvell, Caleb, 172, 174–175
NYU (New York University), 303, 308–309

Occidental & Oriental Steamship Company, 226–227
Oliver, James
at death of Gould's sister, 37
on Gould as student, 22
visits from Gould, 42–43
Oregon and California Railroad, 241
Oregon Steamship Company, 241
organized labor strikes, 279–281
Orton, William, 236–237
Osborne, Anna (grandmother), 9, 10
Osgood, Charles S., 130
Osheowitz, Michael, 302–303
Otis, H. N., 204

Pacific Mail, 208–210, 225–226
Pacific Railroad Act, 220

Pacific Steamship Company, 102
Palais Mediterranee, 308
Palen, Anna, 304
Palen, Caroline, 255
Palen, Dr. Gilbert J., 304
Palen, Dr. Gilbert M., 304
Palen, Edward, 45–46
Palen, Gilbert
leather manufacturing business, 45–46, 86
marriage of, 74
relationship with Gould, 254
Palen, Walter Gould, 255
Panic of 1857, 56–57, 59–60
Patchin, Joseph, 9
Patenotre, Yvonne, 307
Patterson, James W., 221
Paulding, William, 251
Peckham, Judge Rufus, 157–158
Pennsylvania Railroad, 98, 238
Perkins, Charles E., 289
Pierrepont, Judge Edward, 136
Pike's Opera House, 151–152
Plymouth Rock, 237
Porter, Horace, 168, 267
Pourtales, Count Joseph, 307
Pratt & Gould, 49–60
bought by Gould, 58–60
business problems, 53–58
Panic of 1857, 56–57
partnership formed, 49–51
Pratt, Abigail (Watson), 48
Pratt, Beda (Dickerman), 48
Pratt, Esther (Dickerman), 48
Pratt, George Watson, 48, 53, 55–56
Pratt, H.D.V., 159
Pratt, Julia. *see* Ingersoll, Julia (Pratt)
Pratt, Mary (Watson), 48
Pratt, Suzi (Grimm), 48
Pratt, Zaddock
great fortune of, 46–48
memoirs of, 58
newspapers demonize Gould about, 180
owed money upon Gould's death, 6

partnership with Gould. *see* Pratt &
   Gould
powerful ego of, 48
tragic personal life of, 48
Providence steamship, 163
Pruyn, Robert H., 157–158
Pulitzer, Joseph, 3, 275
Pullman, George M., 267

R&W (Rutland & Washington
   Railroad), 82–83, 86–87
Railroad Times, 183
railroads
   1887 Interstate Commerce Act,
      288–290
   Albany & Susquehanna (A&S),
      155–156
   American Refrigerator Transit, 291
   Atlantic & Great Western
      (A&GW), 97–98, 115, 192–193,
      207
   Baltimore and Ohio (B&O), 239
   Boston, Hartford and Erie (BH&E),
      98–99, 115–116, 136
   Central Branch, 243
   Central Pacific, 226–227, 244
   Chicago & Northwestern, 210–212
   Delaware & Lackawanna, 50
   Denver Pacific, 242, 244
   elevated. *see* Manhattan Elevated;
      Metropolitan Elevated; New York
      Elevated
   Erie. *see* Erie Railroad
   Harlem, 100
   Hudson River, 100
   Kansas & Texas (Katy), 259–260
   Kansas City, 243
   Kansas Pacific Railroad. *see* Kansas
      Pacific Railroad
   Lake Shore & Michigan Southern,
      178, 222–223, 233
   Missouri Pacific. *see* Missouri Pacific
   New Jersey Southern, 225
   New York Central, 100, 128–129,
      233
   Northern Pacific, 224
   Oregon and California, 241
   Pacific Railroad Act, 220
   Pennsylvania, 98, 238
   profiteers in the Panic of 1857,
      56–57
   Rutland & Washington (R&W),
      82–83, 86–87
   Texas & Pacfic, 259, 280
   Troy, Salem & Rutland, 87, 89–90
   UP. *see* UP (Union Pacific) Railroad
   Wabash, 243
Ramsdell, Homer, 204
Ramsey, Joseph H., 155–157, 159
Raphael, Henry L., 188
Rapid Transit Commission, 267
Rathbone, Major Henry R., 89
Reeder, Andrew H., 72, 79
Reformed Church of Roxbury, 303
Reid, Whitelaw, 4, 217
Reiff, Josiah, 236–238
Republican Party, 79, 186
Rogers, Hiram, 177
Roosevelt, Cornelius Van Schaack, 79
Roosevelt, Theodore, 270
Rose's Brook, 9
Roxbury
   Gould family members return to live
      near, 304–305
   Gould's ancestors settle in, 10
   Gould's career at Roxbury Academy,
      38, 40
   Gould's childhood in, 7–8
   Gould's last trip with grandchildren
      to, 286–287
   Nellie gifts town of, 303–304
   response to Gould's death, 5–6
Russell Sage Foundation, 216
Ryan, Love B., 106

Sage, Olivia (Slocum), 215–216
Sage, Russell, 215–228
   background of, 215
   cheapness of, 215–216
   Gould's relationship with, 216, 249

Manhattan Elevated securities, 269
  near murder of, 293
  price war with Gould's railroad, 226
Saratoga, 286
Schell, Richard, 121, 222–223
Scott, Tom, 222, 238, 259
Seligman, Jesse, 3–4
Seligman, Joseph, 176, 249
Selover, A. A., 253
Shakersville Road Corporation, 33
Sharp, John, 294
Shattemuc Canoe Club, 301
Shearman, Thomas G.
  A&S Railroad war, 157
  death of James Fisk, 197–198
  Erie board vs. Vanderbilt, 121,
    150–151
Shepard, Finley J., 305
Shrady, Sarah Cantine (daughter-in-
    law), 295, 301
Sickles, Daniel E., 193–194, 204–206
Simons, M.R., 204
Sinclair, George, 300–301
Sinclair, Guinevere, 300–301
Sinclair, Jane, 300–301
Sinclair, Sir Edward, 300
Sisson, Charles, 204
Slocum, Olivia, 215–216
Smith, Gould & Martin trading firm,
    95, 169, 211–213
Smith, Henry N.
  Albany & Susquehanna Railroad
    and, 159
  failed partnership with Gould, 208
  Gould trading gold through, 169
  Gould's move to stealth bear,
    173–174
  Northwestern Railroad and,
    210–212
  Pacific Mail and, 210
  of Smith, Gould & Martin, 95
Snow, Alice. *see* Northrop, Alice (niece)
Snow, Charles Henry, 304, 309
Snow, Helen Gould, 304
Snow, Henry Nicholas, 304

"special stinkpot", 195–196
Speyers, Albert, 176
Squires, David, 9–10
Squires, George, 9
SS *Central America*, 56
Stanford, Leland, 220
Stanton, Edwin M., 194
Stead, W.T., 219
Stedman, Edmund Clarence, 122
Stokes, Edward S. (Ned)
  affair with Fisk's lover, 191–192
  comparing Marrin attack with, 217
  contest with Fisk, 195
  killing of James Fisk, 196–198
  trial and sentencing of, 199
Stone Jug schoolhouse, 17
The Story of Helen Gould (Northrop),
    304
The Story of the Western Railroads
    (Reigel), 245
Strong, George Templeton, 120
Stroudsburg, 59
Supreme Court, 119–120
Sutherland, Judge, 144, 149–150
Swamp, Manhattan's, 55
Sweeny, Peter B., 130–131

Talcott, Hannah, 8
Talleyrand-Perigord, Duc Hellie de,
    307
tanning. *see* leather tanning business
"Taps", 167
Taylor, Moses, 56
Taylor's Hotel, 127
telegraph business
  1884 competitors to Gould's, 278
  Gould builds American Union, 262
  Western Union. *see* Western Union
Tenth National Bank, 168, 176
Terry, Margaret, 283
Texas & Pacfic, 280
  Gould purchases, 259
theodolite, 26
Thompson, Henry, 204
Thoreau, Henry David, 46

"Thugs of Erie", 149
Thurman Act, 231
Tilden, Samuel J., 267
Tillson, Oliver J., 26
Tripler, Thomas H., 197
Troy, Salem & Rutland Railroad, 87, 89–90
tuberculosis, 284, 293–296
Tunkhannock tannery, 86
Tweed, Boss
    conviction and death of, 209
    death of James Fisk, 197–198
    dining hangout of, 152
    elected to Erie board, 140
    political defeat of, 194
    protecting Erie from British shareholders, 188
    representing Vanderbilt, 133
The Twelve Temptations, 189

U.S. Treasury
    Black Friday testimony and, 181–182
    Butterfield as assistant treasurer, 167
    gold conspiracy and, 170
    Gould's wish to manipulate gold, 165
    greenback price of gold after Civil War, 164
Union Pacific. *see* UP (Union Pacific) Railroad
unionism, labor strikes, 279–281
United States Express Company, 185
United States Hotel, 286
UP (Union Pacific) Railroad, 219–227
    Gould loses control 1884–1890, 277–278
    Gould saves fate of, 225
    Gould seizes control, 219–220, 222–224, 291–293
    Gould tames Pacific Mail, 225–227
    history of, 220–221
UP (Union Pacific) Railroad, Gould's management of, 229–246

acquiring more railroad properties in West, 240–243
amalgamating rival lines, 244–245
building up business along UP track, 233–234
combined assets of, 259
focus on business fundamentals, 231–234
independent lines and, 243–244
newspapers demonization of, 245
overview of, 229
public view of, 245
telegraph business, 235–239, 261–265
testimony on Capitol Hill, 280
touring UP line regularly, 229–231

Van Amberg's Circus, 107
Van Amburgh, Peter
    Gould farm business, 23–24
    Gould tin business, 35, 37
    marriage of, 40
    on Pratt's Kingston speech, 49
    visits from Gould, 43, 287–288
Van Valkenburg, John W., 157–160
Vanderbilt, "Commodore" Cornelius, 120
    background and career of, 99–102
    Civil War profits of, 56
    comparing Drew with, 100
    Erie Bill and, 132–135
    Erie executives vs., 118–124, 127–129, 135–137
    Erie shares and, 99, 115–118
    Erie vs. New York Central rate war, 185
    Gould and Fisk even score with, 150–151
    on Gould's personal appearance, 212
    Lake Shore & Michigan Southern Line purchase, 178
    Union Pacific control of, 222
Vanderbilt, William H.
    Gould allies himself with, 233
    overseeing family interests, 239

surrenders Western Union to Gould,
        263
Vanderbilt, William K., 250–251
Villa Marianna, 302
Villard, Henry, 1, 240–243

Wabash Line, 243
Wainswright, Carroll Livingston, 310
Wainswright, Edith (Gould), 310
Wainswright, Stuvyesant II, 310
Wall Street. *see also* Gould, Jay, career
        on Wall Street
    Civil War and, 76–77
    evolution of New York Stock
        Exchange, 75–76
    late nineteenth century, 75
    profiteers in the Panic of 1857,
        56–57
Wall Street: A History (Geisst), 58, 66
Wandle, Richard, 196
Ward, Attorney General, 270
Wardell, Thomas, 232
Warshow, Robert I., 59
Washington Connor & Company, 277,
        291
Watson, Abigail, 48
Watson, Mary, 48
Watson, Peter H., 207, 208, 212–213
Weed, Thurlow, 219
West Settlement, 10, 11
Westbrook, Theodore R., 270–271

Western Union
    1884 competitors, 278
    George Gould loses, 299
    Gould consolidates American Union
        with, 262–265
    Gould merges A&P with, 235–239
    organized labor strike at, 279–280
wet-spent tanbark process, 53–54, 57
White, Justin, 204
White, Stanford, 303
Willard Hotel, 108–109
Willard, Edward K., 175
Williams, Ben, 84
Willis, Nathaniel Parker, 61
Wilson, D. M., 82–83
Wilson, Henry, 221
Wilson, Price & Company, Leather
        Merchants, 70–71, 73
wireless business. *see* telegraph business
Wood, Annie, 131
Woodlawn Cemetery, 4–5, 284
Woodward, W. S., 170
Work, Frank
    compensation owed to, 135
    on Erie Board, 99
    efforts to takeover Erie, 116–118
    failure of Vanderbilt's injunctions,
        118–119
    suspended from Erie board, 121–122
World War I, 302
Wyoming Coal and Mining Company,
        232